CISCO

Cisco Networking Simplified

Second Edition

Jim Doherty

Neil Anderson

Paul Della Maggiora

Illustrations by Nathan Clement

Cisco Press

800 East 96th Street

Indianapolis, IN 46240 USA

Cisco Networking Simplified, Second Edition

Jim Doherty, Neil Anderson, Paul Della Maggiora

Copyright© 2008 Cisco Systems, Inc.

Published by:
Cisco Press
800 East 96th Street
Indianapolis, IN 46240 USA

Printed in the United States of America

Third Printing January 2009

Library of Congress Cataloging-in-Publication Data:

Doherty, Jim.
  Cisco networking simplified / Jim Doherty, Neil Anderson, Paul Della Maggiora. -- 2nd ed.
    p. cm.
  ISBN 978-1-58720-199-8 (pbk.)
  1. Computer networks. I. Anderson, Neil. II. Della Maggiora, Paul L.
III. Title.
  TK5105.8.C57D44 2007
  004.6—dc22
                              2007046376

ISBN-13: 978-1-58720-199-8

ISBN-10: 1-58720-199-2

Warning and Disclaimer

This book is designed to provide information about Cisco networking. Every effort has been made to make this book as complete and accurate as possible, but no warranty or fitness is implied.

The information is provided on an "as is" basis. The authors, Cisco Press, and Cisco Systems, Inc. shall have neither liability nor responsibility to any person or entity with respect to any loss or damages arising from the information contained in this book or from the use of the discs or programs that may accompany it.

The opinions expressed in this book belong to the authors and are not necessarily those of Cisco Systems, Inc.Third

Publisher

Paul Boger

Associate Publisher

Dave Dusthimer

Cisco Representative

Anthony Wolfenden

Cisco Press Program Manager

Jeff Brady

Executive Editor

Karen Gettman

Managing Editor

Patrick Kanouse

Development Editor

Sheri Cain

Senior Project Editor

Tonya Simpson

Copy Editor

Gayle Johnson

Technical Editors

Bradley Mitchell, Matthew Stein

Editorial Assistant

Vanessa Evans

Cover Designer

Louisa Adair

Interior Design and Composition

Mark Shirar

Proofreader

Paula Lowell

Indexer

Heather McNeil

CISCO

Americas Headquarters
Cisco Systems, Inc.
170 West Tasman Drive
San Jose, CA 95134-1706
USA
www.cisco.com
Tel: 408 526-4000
800 553-NETS (6387)
Fax: 408 527-0883

Asia Pacific Headquarters
Cisco Systems, Inc.
168 Robinson Road
#28-01 Capital Tower
Singapore 068912
www.cisco.com
Tel: +65 6317 7777
Fax: +65 6317 7799

Europe Headquarters
Cisco Systems International BV
Haarlerbergpark
Haarlerbergweg 13-19
1101 CH Amsterdam
The Netherlands
www-europe.cisco.com
Tel: +31 0 800 020 0791
Fax: +31 0 20 357 1100

Cisco has more than 200 offices worldwide. Addresses, phone numbers, and fax numbers are listed on the Cisco Website at www.cisco.com/go/offices.

Trademark Acknowledgments

All terms mentioned in this book that are known to be trademarks or service marks have been appropriately capitalized. Cisco Press or Cisco Systems, Inc., cannot attest to the accuracy of this information. Use of a term in this book should not be regarded as affecting the validity of any trademark or service mark.

Feedback Information

At Cisco Press, our goal is to create in-depth technical books of the highest quality and value. Each book is crafted with care and precision, undergoing rigorous development that involves the unique expertise of members from the professional technical community.

Readers' feedback is a natural continuation of this process. If you have any comments regarding how we could improve the quality of this book, or otherwise alter it to better suit your needs, you can contact us through e-mail at feedback@ciscopress.com. Please make sure to include the book title and ISBN in your message.

We greatly appreciate your assistance.

Corporate and Government Sales

The publisher offers excellent discounts on this book when ordered in quantity for bulk purchases or special sales, which may include electronic versions and/or custom covers and content particular to your business, training goals, marketing focus, and branding interests. For more information, please contact:

U.S. Corporate and Government Sales
1-800-382-3419
corpsales@pearsontechgroup.com

For sales outside the United States, please contact:

International Sales
international@pearsoned.com

About the Technical Reviewers

Bradley Mitchell is a freelance writer covering technology topics, specializing in computer networking. Online, he has produced the About.com Wireless/Networking site since 2000. He also is a senior engineer at Intel Corporation. Over the past 14 years at Intel he has served in various capacities for research and development of software and network systems. He obtained a master's degree in computer science from the University of Illinois and a bachelor's degree from MIT.

Matthew Stein is a marketing manager for Enterprise Solutions Marketing (ESM) at Cisco. In his role, he defines and develops network service solutions for the enterprise market, which spans multiple networking technologies and drives business growth, performance, and IT efficiencies. He previously worked in the Wireless Business Unit of Cisco, where he was responsible for leading the development and marketing integration of Enterprise networking solutions for the Cisco Aironet Wireless product line. Before joining Cisco in May 2000, Stein served as a database design system engineer for GE Lighting. He also was a system engineer for the Center for Brain Imaging at the Medical College of Wisconsin. He received his bachelor of science degree in electrical engineering from Case Western Reserve University.

Dedications

This book is dedicated to Bradley Mitchell.

Bradley was introduced to us by our publisher as a technical reviewer when we wrote our first book together back in 2004 (*Home Networking Simplified*).

We were so happy with his effort, his insightful comments, and his technical expertise that we asked him to be a reviewer on the next book. And on the one after that. And so on and so on until we look back and realize that over five titles, the entire set of the *Networking Simplified* series, Bradley has been a critical part of our writing team, and our books are better for it.

This is not to say that our other reviewers along the way have not been great. They have. But Bradley catches errors that no one else catches (writers, reviewers, publishing team). He is constantly making sure that we have our audience in mind and advises us to rewrite sections when have gone off the deep end. And when we refer to a 128-digit number (and then feel compelled to give an example of one), Bradley actually counts the digits, lets us know that we left off two 0s at the beginning, and then reminds us that you probably don't care about seeing the actual number anyway.

It's nearly impossible to attain perfection in a book like this, but Bradley gets us much, much closer than we would have otherwise. This book, and all our books, are better than they would have been, because Bradley took the time to help us make them better.

We've never had a chance to meet him in person. When we do, we'll shake his hand and buy him a beer (or maybe five—one for each book). In the meantime, we hope this is enough.

Acknowledgments

Jim and Neil would like to thank the following people:

Our families, whom we lied to after the last book, when we said we would not do this again, and who put up with our working late nights and weekends. This time, we mean it.

Our publisher and the fine team at Cisco Press and Pearson Education. We would especially like to thank our editor, Sheri Cain, who bravely agreed to join us on another project; our production manager, Patrick Kanouse; Chris Cleveland; Karen Gettman; Tonya Simpson; Jennifer Gallant; Gayle Johnson; and the rest of the Cisco Press team working behind the scenes.

As always, we want to thank our illustrator, Nathan Clement at Stickman Studios (http://www.stickman-studio.com/), who never fails to deliver a great product.

A special thanks to our technical reviewers, Bradley Mitchell and Matthew Stein, who worked hard on our readers' behalf to keep us honest and accurate.

We would also like to thank the following people at Cisco who helped with content and questions: Tim Szigeti, Brian Cox, Ron Maxam, John Strika, Mike Herbert, Jason Frazier, Max Ardica, Stephenie Chastain, Joel King, May Konfong, Damon Li, Martin Pueblas, Chris O'Brien, and Roland Dobbins.

This Book Is Safari Enabled

The Safari® Enabled icon on the cover of your favorite technology book means the book is available through Safari Bookshelf. When you buy this book, you get free access to the online edition for 45 days.

Safari Bookshelf is an electronic reference library that lets you easily search thousands of technical books, find code samples, download chapters, and access technical information whenever and wherever you need it.

To gain 45-day Safari Enabled access to this book:

- Go to http://www.ciscopress.com/safarienabled.
- Complete the brief registration form.
- Enter the coupon code ZLF2-MMFG-PY15-LFGX-STWJ.

If you have difficulty registering on Safari Bookshelf or accessing the online edition, please e-mail customer-service@safaribooksonline.com.

Contents

Introduction

Welcome, and thank you for taking a look at this book! Unlike the vast array of networking books written by geeks for geeks, this book was written for you and for anyone who wants to understand the computer networking phenomenon that has taken the world by storm. (In other words, it's by geeks for nongeeks.) We understand that the vast majority of people working in this industry are not networking experts and that it is difficult to understand complex technical and business issues before knowing the answers to such questions as "How does the web work?," "What is a router?," and "What is an IP address?"

Whether you are a home computer user who has just purchased a broadband Internet connection or a company executive who wants to understand what your IT staff is talking about, this book is for you.

If you've decided that you want to make a career change, or if you are in school pursuing a Cisco certification, we believe that this book will serve both as a good primer, introducing the concepts of networking in clear and simple terms, and as a useful reference book as you grow in your career.

What's New in This Edition?

Five years ago, when Paul Della Maggiora and Jim Doherty wrote the first edition, we were trying to fill a gap in the market with a book that explained a broad selection of networking technologies and concepts for the beginner or nontechnical person. Upon sharing our early work, we realized we might be on to something. More talks with college interns, Cisco Academy students, and nontechnical executives at Cisco customers indicated demand for a show-me-what-it-is type of book. This book provides at-a-glance text and illustrations that explain a particular concept or technology in plain and simple language. The material illustrates how these concepts relate to our everyday lives.

We are pleased with the reception the book has received since it was first published. We have received a great deal of positive feedback both from our intended audience and, much to our surprise, from very technical people as well. In fact, the book has had enough interest that we were approached to write a second edition to cover all the new technologies that have come about in the last five years. After all was said and done, about half of this book ended up being new.

Among the biggest additions to this version are the topics covering security, communication tools, and wireless technologies. Security has become one of the biggest areas of investment for networking as companies attempt to protect their network and data from ever-increasing threats and attacks. Communication tools have also changed quite a bit in five years, as both voice and video tools have become more integrated and more sophisticated. Finally, wireless is everywhere now, and users expect all the networking tools on the wired network to be on the wireless network as well.

Another change in this book is that Neil Anderson has joined the writing team. Neil is the coauthor of four other *Networking Simplified* books that we have written since the original release of *Cisco Networking Simplified*. Neil is a great addition to the team and brings a wealth of expertise and insight to this edition.

So How Do I Use This Thing?

The book is divided into nine theme-based parts, each with several chapters covering a network concept or technology. Each chapter contains some or all of the following: a part summary, topic at-a-glance pages, and whiteboard illustrations of relevant concepts. The part summary provides a quick and easy introduction to the topic, so you should generally read it first. Useful for future reference are the topic at-a-glance pages, which illustrate core concepts. And the whiteboard illustrations demonstrate important concepts simply and graphically.

The flow of this book is a bit different from the first time around. In this edition, we took a building-block approach:

- Part I: Networking Fundamentals
- Part II: Networking Infrastructure
- Part III: Network Design
- Part IV: Network Availability
- Part V: Securing the Network
- Part VI: Data Center and Application Networking
- Part VII: Unified Communications
- Part VIII: Mobility
- Part IX: Virtualized Networks

We believe that this approach helps you get from the basics to the more advanced topics more easily. This approach also makes it easier to jump directly into a single topic of interest and understand the big picture.

The illustrations and descriptions of the topics serve to answer the primary questions "What is it?", "Why should I care?", and "What problems need to be solved?". We use "big animal" pictures to explain many of the concepts and avoid the temptation to dive into nitty-gritty details. If you are reading this book, you need to know, for example, what a router does, but not how to actually program one.

The second time around, we had as much fun as the first time through writing and illustrating this book. We also had the benefit of experience and are hopeful that we put it to good use. We hope you find this book both useful and entertaining. If it ends up being your primary reference for networking, so much the better.

Part I

Networking Fundamentals

Before we begin talking about specific networking technologies and applications, it's worth taking a few pages to go over some networking fundamentals. Networks exist for the sole purpose of sharing information between people or machines. However, to share information, rules must be followed to ensure that the myriad combinations of devices, transports, hardware, and software can communicate smoothly.

In "How Computers Communicate," we cover the most basic aspects of computer networking, starting with the OSI model. This communication model is the basis for all other topics discussed in this book, so it's a great place to start.

In "TCP/IP and IP Addressing," we explore how two of the most popular protocols in use today work. TCP/IP is the communication protocol that drives the Internet as well as most corporate traffic. We then go a bit deeper into the Internet Protocol with a discussion of IP addressing, the concept that allows shared information to reach its intended destination. We end the chapter with an overview of IPv6. The addressing scheme discussed here (known as IPv4) has been in service for years. However, there has been some concern in recent years that Internet has grown beyond the current IP addressing scheme's ability to serve an ever-growing demand. Changing addressing schemes this far into networking's history provides some interesting challenges, which we will also explore.

"Internet Applications" provides a look at two of the most common applications—e-mail and web browsing. This chapter provides some background on how these applications came about and provides a summary of how they work. This should be helpful, because you probably use these applications every day.

How Computers Communicate

The OSI Model

At some point, everyone involved with networking comes across a reference to the Open Systems Interconnection (OSI) seven-layer model. Because this model provides the architectural framework for all of network and computing communication, it's a good place to start. Even if you don't ever plan on setting up your own network, being familiar with this model is essential to understanding how it all works.

The OSI seven-layer model describes the functions for computers to communicate with each other. The International Organization for Standardization (ISO) published this model in 1984 to describe a layered approach for providing network services using a reference set of protocols called OSI. The basis of the definition is that each of the seven layers has a particular function it must perform, and each layer needs to know how to communicate with only the layers immediately above and below it.

The advantages of the OSI approach may not be readily apparent. But this simple concept of having layers understand only those adjacent to themselves allows communications systems to be easily adapted and modified as technologies evolve. For example, as new technologies are introduced in a lower layer, such as Layer 1, upper layers do not necessarily need to be changed. Instead, the adaptations at Layer 2 allow the layers above to use the new technologies transparently. Imagine if all web browsers and e-mail programs had to be replaced every time a new wireless network standard were introduced.

When the OSI networking model was defined, there was little standardization among network equipment manufacturers. Customers generally had to standardize on a particular vendor's often proprietary hardware and software to have devices communicate with each other. As a result of the ISO's and other standardization efforts, networking customers can mix and match hardware when running open-standards protocols, such as Internet Protocol (IP).

Open Versus Proprietary Systems

Although the open-source model is well-known today, when the OSI model was being developed, there was an ongoing struggle to balance technical openness with competitive advantage. At that time, each individual network equipment vendor saw it as an advantage to develop technologies that other companies could not copy or interact with. Proprietary systems let a vendor claim competitive advantage as well as collect fees from other vendors it might choose to share the technology with.

However, proprietary systems can complicate the network administrator's job by locking him or her into one vendor, reducing competitiveness and allowing the vendor to charge higher prices. If the vendor goes out of business or abandons the technology, no one is left to support or enhance the technology.

The alternative is an open-systems approach in which standards bodies, such as the Institute of Electrical and Electronic Engineers (IEEE) or ISO, define technologies. Ethernet, Transmission Control Protocol/Internet Protocol (TCP/IP), and Spanning Tree Protocol (STP) are examples of technologies that became standards. Today it is almost impossible to gain market traction with a product that does not at least allow an open interface for other vendors to work with. Any network-equipment vendor can implement an open standard.

Seven Layers

The following list outlines the seven layers of the OSI model from the bottom up:

- **Layer 1, physical:** The physical layer is responsible for converting a frame (the output from Layer 2) into electrical signals to be transmitted over the network. The actual physical network can be copper wiring, optical fiber, wireless radio signals, or any other medium that can carry signals. (We often joke about running networks over barbed wire. It's just a joke, but it actually can be done.) This layer also provides a method for the receiving device to validate that the data was not corrupted during transmission.

- **Layer 2, data link:** The data link layer is responsible for establishing the most elemental form of communication session between two different devices so that they may exchange Layer 3 protocols. For computer networks, the data link layer adds a header, which identifies the particular Layer 3 protocol used and the source and destination hardware addresses (also known as Media Access Control [MAC] addresses). At this point, the packet (the Layer 3 output) is successfully processed into a Layer 2 Frame and is ready to go onto the network. Ethernet switching and bridging operate at this level.

- **Layer 3, network:** The network layer is where the majority of communications protocols do their work, relying on Layers 2 and 1 to send and receive messages to other computers or network devices. The network layer adds another header to the front of the packet, which identifies the unique source and destination IP addresses of the sender and receiver. The process of routing IP packets occurs at this level.

- **Layer 4, transport:** The transport layer is responsible for taking the chunk of data from the application and preparing it for shipment onto the network. Prepping data for transport involves chopping the chunk into smaller pieces and adding a header that identifies the sending and receiving application (otherwise known as port numbers). For example, Hypertext Transfer Protocol (HTTP) web traffic uses port 80, and FTP traffic uses port 21. Each piece of data and its associated headers is called a packet.

- **Layer 5, session:** The session layer manages connections between hosts. If the application on one host needs to talk to the application on another, the session layer sets up the connection and ensures that resources are available to facilitate the connection. Networking folks tend to refer to Layers 5 to 7 collectively as the application layers.

- **Layer 6, presentation:** The presentation layer provides formatting services for the application layer. For example, file encryption happens at this layer, as does format conversion.

- **Layer 7, application:** The application layer provides networking services to a user or application. For example, when an e-mail is sent, the application layer begins the process of taking the data from the e-mail program and preparing it to be put onto a network, progressing through Layers 6 through 1.

The combination of the seven layers is often called a stack. A transmitting workstation traverses the stack from Layer 7 through Layer 1, converting the application data into network signals. The receiving workstation traverses the stack in the opposite direction: from Layer 1 to Layer 7. It converts the received transmission back into a chunk of data for the running application.

When the OSI model was created, there was an industry initiative that tried to implement a universal set of OSI network protocols, but it was not adopted. Most popular protocols today generally use design principles that are similar to and compatible with the OSI model, but they deviate from it in some areas for various technical reasons. That said, the OSI model is still considered the basis of all network communication.

At-a-Glance: OSI Model

Why Should I Care About the OSI Model?

The Open Systems Interconnection (OSI) model is a conceptual framework that defines network functions and schemes. The framework simplifies complex network interactions by breaking them into simple modular elements. This open-standards approach allows many independent developers to work on separate network functions, which can then be combined in a "plug-and-play" manner.

The OSI model serves as a guideline for creating and implementing network standards, devices, and internetworking schemes. Advantages of using the OSI model include the following:

- It breaks interrelated aspects of network operation into less-complex elements.

- It enables companies and individual engineers to specialize design and development efforts on modular functions.

- It provides standard interfaces for plug-and-play compatibility and multivendor integration.

- It abstracts different layers of the network from each other to provide easier adoption of new technologies within a layer.

OSI Layers and Definitions

The OSI layers are defined as follows:

Layer 1: Physical

Layer 2: Data link

Layer 3: Network

Layer 4: Transport

Layer 5: Session

Layer 6: Presentation

Layer 7: Application

The four lower layers (called the data flow layers) define connection protocols and methods for exchanging data.

The three upper layers (called the application layers) define how the applications within the end stations communicate with each other and with users.

Several mnemonics have been developed to help you memorize the layers and their order. Here's one:

Please Do Not Throw Sausage Pizza Away

What Problems Need to Be Solved?

An OSI layer can communicate only with the layers immediately above and below it on the stack, and with its peer layer on another device. A process must be used so that information (including data and stack instructions) can be passed down the stack, across the network, and back up the stack on the peer device.

At-a-Glance: OSI Model

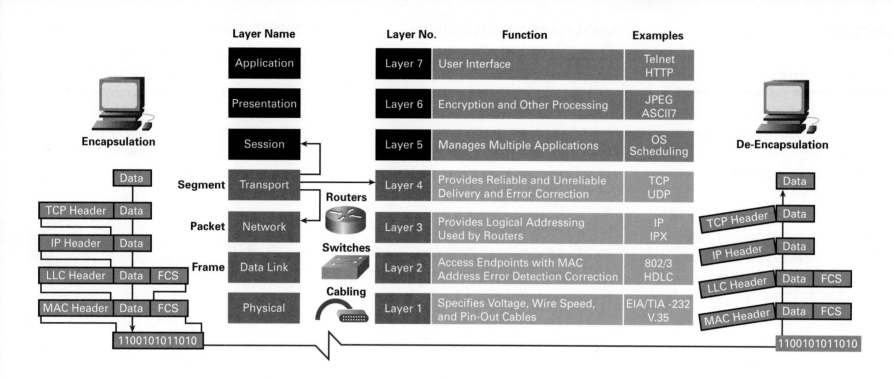

Communicating Between Layers

Each layer of the OSI model uses its own protocol to communicate with its peer layer in the destination device. The OSI model specifies how each layer communicates with the layers above and below it, allowing vendors to focus on specific layers that will work with any other vendor's adjacent layers.

Information is exchanged between layers using protocol data units (PDU). PDUs include control information (in the form of headers and trailers) and user data. PDUs include different types of information as they go up or down the layers (called "the stack"). To clarify where the PDU is on the stack, it is given a distinct name at each of the lower levels.

In other words, a PDU that is a segment (Layer 4) includes all the application layer's information. A packet (Layer 3) includes network layer control information in addition to the data and control information contained at the transport layer. Similarly, a frame (Layer 2) is a PDU that includes data link layer control information in addition to the upper layer control information and data. Finally, PDUs at the physical layer (Layer 1) are called bits.

At-a-Glance: OSI Model

Encapsulation

The process of passing data down the stack using PDUs is called data encapsulation. Encapsulation works as follows: When a layer receives a PDU from the layer above it, it encapsulates the PDU with a header and trailer and then passes the PDU down to the next layer. The control information that is added to the PDU is read by the peer layer on the remote device. Think of this as like putting a letter in an envelope, which has the destination address on it. The envelope is then put in a mailbag with a zip code on it. The bag is then placed in large box with a city name on it. The box is then put on a plane for transport to the city.

De-encapsulation

De-encapsulation, the opposite of encapsulation, is the process of passing information up the stack. When a layer receives a PDU from the layer below, it does the following:

1. It reads the control information provided by the peer source device.

2. The layer strips the control information (header) from the frame.

3. It processes the data (usually passing it up the stack).

Each subsequent layer performs this same de-encapsulation process. To continue the preceding example, when the plane arrives, the box of mail is removed from the plane. The mailbags are taken out of the boxes and are sent to the correct post office. The letters are removed from the mailbags and are delivered to the correct address. The intended recipient opens the envelope and reads the letter.

Extra Layers?

Discussions among technical purists can often lead to philosophical or budgetary debates that can quickly derail otherwise-productive meetings. These discussions are often referred to as Layer 8 (political) and Layer 9 (financial) debates. Although these layers are not really part of the OSI model, they are usually the underlying cause of heated technology arguments.

Another common joke among networking professionals is the type of networking problem referred to as a "Layer 8 issue." Because the network, computers, and applications stop at Layer 7, Layer 8 sometimes represents the end user actually using the system. So if you hear your IT person snicker to his colleagues that your IT trouble ticket is closed and it was a "Layer 8 issue," the IT person is referring to you.

Internet Infrastructure: How It All Connects

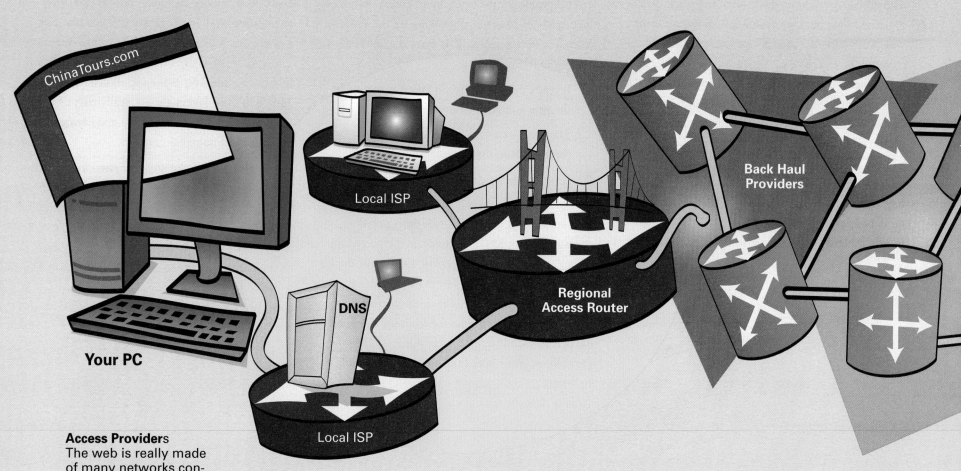

ChinaTours.com

Your PC

Local ISP

DNS

Local ISP

Regional
Access Router

**Back Haul
Providers**

Access Providers
The web is really made
of many networks con-
nected in a hierarchy. Local Internet
service providers (ISPs) typically give
residential and small business access
to the Internet. Regional providers
typically connect several local ISPs to
each other and to back haul providers
that connect with other regional
providers.

Domain Name Server (DNS)
This server maps domain names to
their IP addresses. One of the reasons
that the Internet has taken off in use and
popularity is because www.cisco.com
is much easier to remember than
25.156.10.4.

Internet Infrastructure: How It All Connects

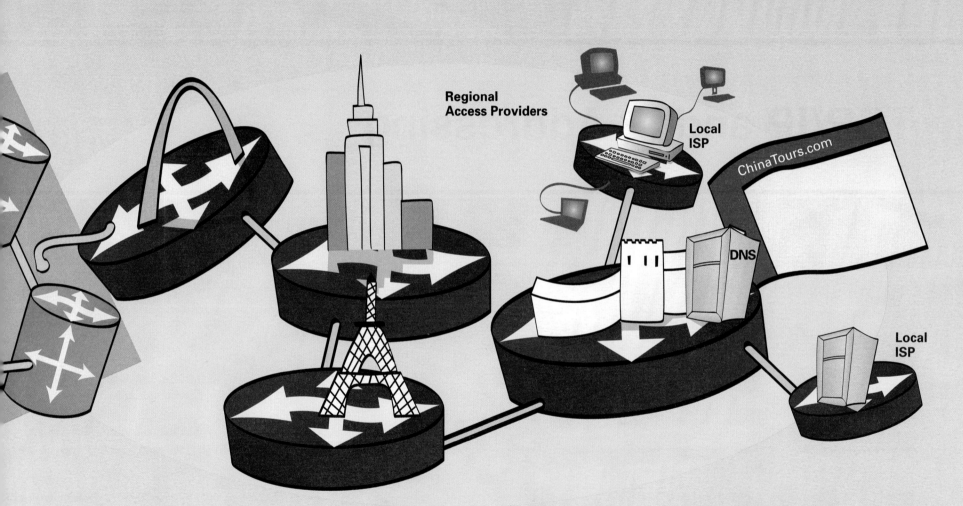

Regional Access Providers

Local ISP

ChinaTours.com

DNS

Local ISP

Web Servers
All web pages are stored on computers called web servers. Thousands of these servers can be dedicated servers for companies, hosting servers that house many personal pages, or even single computers housing individual pages.

Back Haul Providers
A few back haul providers comprise the high-speed backbone of the Internet. Only a handful of these providers are capable of handling the massive amounts of Internet traffic that continues to grow. Many parts of the back haul providers overlap with each other, which improves both the speed and reliability of the network.

TCP/IP and IP Addressing

Computers Speaking the Same Language

The Internet protocols comprise the most popular, nonproprietary data-networking protocol suite in the world. The Internet protocols are communication protocols used by electronic devices to talk to each other. Initially, computers were the primary clients of IP protocols, but other types of electronic devices can connect to IP networks, including printers, cellular phones, and MP3 players. Today, even common devices such as vending machines, dishwashers, and cars are being connected to IP networks.

The two best-known Internet protocols are Transmission Control Protocol (TCP) and Internet Protocol (IP). The Defense Advanced Research Projects Agency (DARPA) developed the Internet protocols in the mid-1970s. DARPA funded Stanford University and Bolt, Beranek, and Newman (BBN) to develop a set of protocols that would allow different types of computers at various research locations to communicate over a common packet-switched network. The result of this research produced the Internet protocol suite, which was later distributed for free with the Berkeley Software Distribution (BSD) UNIX operating system.

From there, IP became the primary networking protocol, serving as the basis for the World Wide Web (WWW) and the Internet in general. Internet protocols are discussed and adopted in the public domain. Technical bulletins called Requests for Comments (RFC) documents proposed protocols and practices. These documents are reviewed, edited, published, and analyzed, and then are accepted by the Internet community (this process takes years).

The Internet protocol suite also comprises application-based protocols, including definitions for the following:

- Electronic mail (Simple Mail Transfer Protocol [SMTP])

- Terminal emulation (Telnet)

- File transfer (File Transfer Protocol [FTP])

- HTTP

IP is considered a Layer 3 protocol according to the OSI model, and TCP is a Layer 4 protocol.

What Is an Address?

For computers to send and receive information to each other, they must have some form of addressing so that each end device on the network knows what information to read and what information to ignore. This capability is important both for the computers that ultimately use the information and for the devices that deliver information to end stations, such as switches and routers. Every computer on a network has two addresses:

- **MAC address:** A manufacturer-allocated ID number (such as a global serial number) that is permanent and unique to every network device on Earth. MAC addresses are analogous to a social security number or other national identification number. You have only one, it stays the same wherever you go, and no two people (devices) have the same number. MAC address are formatted using six pairs of hexadecimal numbers, such as 01-23-45-67-89-AB.

  Hexadecimal or "hex" is a base 16 numbering scheme that uses the numbers 0 through 9 and the letters A through F to count from 0 to 15. This might seem odd, but it provides an easy translation from binary (which uses only 1s and 0s), which is the language of all computers.

- **IP address:** This address is what matters most to basic networking. Unlike a MAC address, the IP address of any device is temporary and can be changed. It is often assigned by the network itself and is analogous to your street address. It only needs to be unique within a network. Someone else's network might use the same IP address, much like another town might have the same street (for example, 101 Main Street). Every device on an IP network is given an IP address, which looks like this: 192.168.1.100.

The format of this address is called dotted-decimal notation. The period separators are pronounced "dot," as in one ninety two dot one sixty eight dot...." Because of some rules with binary, the largest number in each section is 255.

In addition to breaking up the number, the dots that appear in IP addresses allow us to break the address into parts that represent networks and hosts. In this case, the "network" portion refers to a company, university, government agency, or your private network. The hosts would be the addresses of all the computers on the individual network. If you think of the network portion of the address as a street, the hosts would be all the houses on that street. If you could see the IP addresses of everyone who is on the same network segment as you, you would notice that the network portion of the address is the same for all computers, and the host portion changes from computer to computer. An example will probably help. Think of an IP address as being like your home address for the post office: state.city.street.house-number.

Each number in the IP address provides a more and more specific location so that the Internet can find your computer among millions of other computers. The Internet is not organized geographically like the postal system, though. The components of the address (intentionally oversimplified) are major-network.minor-network.local-network.device.

Dynamically Allocated IP Addresses

A network administrator is responsible for assigning which devices receive which IP addresses in a corporate network. The admin assigns an IP address to a device in one of two ways: by configuring the device with a specific address or by letting the device automatically learn its address from the network. Dynamic Host Configuration Protocol (DHCP) is the protocol used for automatic IP address assignment. Dynamic addressing saves considerable administrative effort and conserves IP addressing space. It can be difficult to manually administer IP addresses for every computer and device on a network. Most networks use DHCP to automatically assign an available IP address to a device when it connects to the network. Generally, devices that don't move around receive fixed addresses, known as static addressing. For example, servers, routers, and switches usually receive static IP addresses. The rest use dynamic addressing. For home networks you do not need a network administrator to set up your address; instead, a home broadband router allocates IP addresses via DHCP.

Domain Names and Relationship to IP Addresses

Because IP addresses are difficult to remember in their dotted-decimal notation, a naming convention called domain names was established that's more natural for people to use. Domain names such as www.cisco.com are registered and associated with a particular public IP address. The Domain Name System (DNS) maps a readable name to an IP address. For example, when you enter http://www.cisco.com into a browser, the PC uses the DNS protocol to contact a DNS name server. The name server translates the name http://www.cisco.com into the actual IP address for that host.

Matching Domain Names to IP Addresses

Coulda Been
To order, just visit our website at 216.43.96.26!

Actually Is
Matching Domain Names to IP Addresses

1 You actually type an alias when you input a URL.

www.cisco.com

?

cisco.com=172.13...
coke.com=273.12...
nfl.com=432.56...
ibm.com=347.52...
nbc.com=137.86...
fritos.com=753.21...
wendys.com=691.47...

Internet

How many websites do you have memorized? How many do you think you could memorize with only IP addresses available?

http:// www.cisco.com

3 Finally, the browser connects to the correct IP address.

Welcome to Cisco Systems!

2
DNS Server
Instead of going to the site, the browser must match the URL to the IP address. It does this at a domain name server. There are many of these all over, and they must be synched up.

At-a-Glance: TCP/IP

Why Should I Care About TCP/IP?

TCP/IP is the best-known and most popular protocol suite used today. Its ease of use and widespread adoption are some of the best reasons for the Internet explosion that is taking place.

Encompassed within the TCP/IP protocol is the capability to offer reliable, connection-based packet transfer (sometimes called synchronous) as well as less reliable, connectionless transfers (also called asynchronous).

What Problems Need to Be Solved?

TCP is a connection-oriented, reliable protocol that breaks messages into segments and reassembles them at the destination station (it also resends packets not received at the destination). TCP also provides virtual circuits between applications.

A connection-oriented protocol establishes and maintains a connection during a transmission. The protocol must establish the connection before sending data. As soon as the data transfer is complete, the session is torn down.

User Datagram Protocol (UDP) is an alternative protocol to TCP that also operates at Layer 4. UDP is considered an "unreliable," connectionless protocol. Although "unreliable" may have a negative connotation, in cases where real-time information is being exchanged (such as a voice conversation), taking the time to set up a connection and resend dropped packets can do more harm than good.

Endpoints in TCP/IP are identified by IP addresses. IP addressing is covered in the next At-a-Glance.

TCP/IP Datagrams

TCP/IP information is sent via datagrams. A single message may be broken into a series of datagrams that must be reassembled at their destination. Three layers are associated with the TCP/IP protocol stack:

- **Application layer:** This layer specifies protocols for e-mail, file transfer, remote login, and other applications. Network management is also supported.

- **Transport layer:** This layer allows multiple upper-layer applications to use the same data stream. TCP and UDP protocols provide flow control and reliability.

- **Network layer:** Several protocols operate at the network layer, including IP, ICMP, ARP, and RARP.

IP provides connectionless, best-effort routing of datagrams.

TCP/IP hosts use Internet Control Message Protocol (ICMP) to carry error and control messages with IP datagrams. For example, a process called ping allows one station to discover a host on another network.

Address Resolution Protocol (ARP) allows communication on a multiaccess medium such as Ethernet by mapping known IP addresses to MAC addresses.

Reverse Address Resolution Protocol (RARP) is used to map a known MAC address to an IP address.

How TCP Connections Are Established

End stations exchange control bits called SYN (for synchronize) and Initial Sequence Numbers (ISN) to synchronize during connection establishment. TCP/IP uses what is known as a three-way handshake to establish connections.

To synchronize the connection, each side sends its own initial sequence number and expects to receive a confirmation in an acknowledgment (ACK) from the other side. The following figure shows an example.

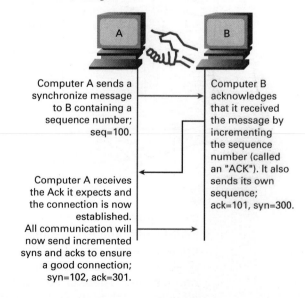

Computer A sends a synchronize message to B containing a sequence number; seq=100.

Computer B acknowledges that it received the message by incrementing the sequence number (called an "ACK"). It also sends its own sequence; ack=101, syn=300.

Computer A receives the Ack it expects and the connection is now established. All communication will now send incremented syns and acks to ensure a good connection; syn=102, ack=301.

At-a-Glance: TCP/IP

TCP Windowing

One way to structure a communications protocol is to have the receiver acknowledge every packet received from a sender. Although this is the most reliable method, it can add unnecessary overhead, especially on fairly reliable connection media. Windowing is a compromise that reduces overhead by acknowledging packets only after a specified number have been received.

The window size from one end station informs the other side of the connection how much it can accept at one time. With a window size of 1, each segment must be acknowledged before another segment is sent. This is the least efficient use of bandwidth. A window size of 7 means that an acknowledgment needs to be sent after the receipt of seven segments; this allows better utilization of bandwidth. A windowing example is shown in the figure.

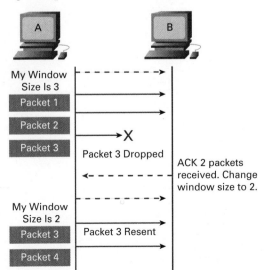

UDP

UDP is a connectionless, unreliable Layer 4 protocol. Unreliable in this sense means that the protocol does not ensure that every packet will reach its destination. UDP is used for applications that provide their own error recovery process or when retransmission does not make sense. UDP is simple and efficient, trading reliability for speed.

Why not resend? It may not be obvious why you would not resend dropped packets if you had the option to do so. However, real-time applications such as voice and video could be disrupted by receiving old packets out of order. For example, suppose a packet containing a portion of speech is received 2 seconds later than the rest of the conversation. Playing the sound out into the earpiece probably will sound like poor audio quality to the user, because the user is listening further into the conversation. In these cases, the application usually can conceal the dropped packets from the end user so long as they account for a small percentage of the total.

Port Numbers

TCP and UDP can send data from several upper-layer applications on the same datagram. Port numbers (also called socket numbers) are used to keep track of different conversations crossing the network at any given time. Some of the more well-known port numbers are controlled by the Internet

Assigned Numbers Authority (IANA). For example, Telnet is always defined by port 23. Applications that do not use well-known port numbers have numbers randomly assigned from a specific range.

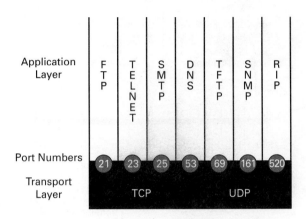

The use of port numbers is what allows you to watch streaming video on your computer while checking e-mails and downloading documents from a web page all at the same time. All three may use TCP/IP, but use of a port number allows the applications to distinguish which are video and which are e-mail packets.

At-a-Glance: TCP/IP

History of TCP/IP

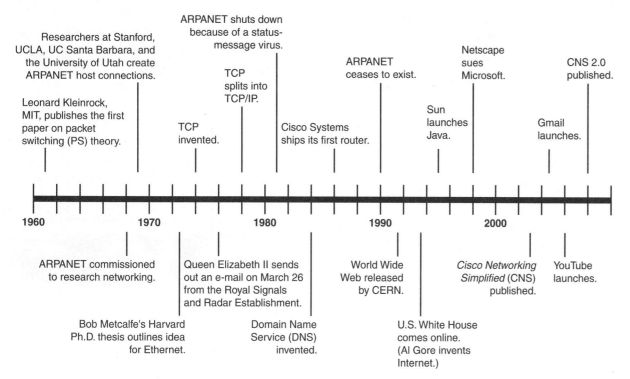

Researchers at Stanford, UCLA, UC Santa Barbara, and the University of Utah create ARPANET host connections.

ARPANET shuts down because of a status-message virus.

TCP splits into TCP/IP.

Netscape sues Microsoft.

ARPANET ceases to exist.

CNS 2.0 published.

Leonard Kleinrock, MIT, publishes the first paper on packet switching (PS) theory.

TCP invented.

Cisco Systems ships its first router.

Sun launches Java.

Gmail launches.

1960   1970   1980   1990   2000

ARPANET commissioned to research networking.

Queen Elizabeth II sends out an e-mail on March 26 from the Royal Signals and Radar Establishment.

World Wide Web released by CERN.

Cisco Networking Simplified (CNS) published.

YouTube launches.

Bob Metcalfe's Harvard Ph.D. thesis outlines idea for Ethernet.

Domain Name Service (DNS) invented.

U.S. White House comes online. (Al Gore invents Internet.)

At-a-Glance: IP Addressing

Why Should I Care About IP Addressing?

Behind every website, Universal Resource Locator (URL), and computer or other device connected to the Internet is a number that uniquely identifies that device. This unique identifier is called an IP address. These addresses are the key components of the routing schemes used over the Internet. For example, if you are downloading a data sheet from www.cisco.com to your computer, the header of the packets comprising the document includes both the host address (in this case, the IP address of Cisco's public server) and the destination address (your PC).

What Problems Need to Be Solved?

Each IP address is a 32-bit number, which means that there are about 4.3 trillion address combinations. These addresses must be allocated in a way that balances the need for administrative and routing efficiency with the need to retain as many usable addresses as possible.

Dotted decimal: The most common notation for describing an IP address is dotted decimal. Dotted decimal breaks a 32-bit binary number into four 8-bit numbers (represented in decimal form), which is called an *octet*. Each octet is separated by a period, which aids in the organizational scheme to be discussed. For example, the binary address 00001010100000001011001000101110 can be represented in dotted decimal as 10.128.178.46.

Logical Versus Physical

MAC addresses are considered physical addresses because they are assigned to pieces of hardware by the manufacturer and cannot be reassigned.

IP addresses are assigned by a network administrator and have meaning only in a TCP/IP network. These addresses are used solely for routing purposes and can be reassigned.

Host and network: Rather than assigning numbers at random to various endpoints (which would be extremely difficult to manage), every company and organization listed on the Internet is given a block of public address numbers to use. This is accomplished by using a two-part addressing scheme that identifies a network and host. This two-part scheme allows the following:

- All the endpoints within a network share the same network number.
- The remaining bits identify each host within that network.

128	10	173	46
10000000	00001010	10110010	00101110
Network		Host	

In the figure, the first two octets (128.10) identify a company with an Internet presence (it's the address of the router that accesses the Internet). All computers and servers within the company's network share the same network address. The next two octets identify a specific endpoint (computer, server, printer, and so on). In this example the company has 65,536 addresses it can assign (16 bits, or 2^{16}). Therefore, all devices in this network would have an address between 128.10.0.1 and 128.10.255.255.

Address Classes

When the IP address scheme was developed, only the first octet was used to identify the network portion of the address. At the time it was assumed that 254 networks would be more than enough to cover the research groups and universities using this protocol. As usage grew, however, it became clear that more network designations would be needed (each with fewer hosts). This issue led to the development of address classes.

Addresses are segmented into five classes (A through E). Classes A, B, and C are the most common. Class A has 8 network bits and 24 host bits. Class B has 16 network bits and 16 host bits, and Class C has 24 network bits and 8 host bits. This scheme was based on the assumption that there would be many more small networks (each with fewer endpoints) than large networks in the world. Class D is used for multicast, and Class E is reserved for research. The following table breaks down the three main classes. Note that the Class A address starting with 127 is reserved.

At-a-Glance: IP Addressing

Classes	First Octet Range	Network Bits	Possible Networks	Host Bits	No. of Hosts per Network
A	1–126	8	126	24	16,777,216
B	128–191	16	16,384	16	65,536
C	192–223	24	2,097,152	8	256

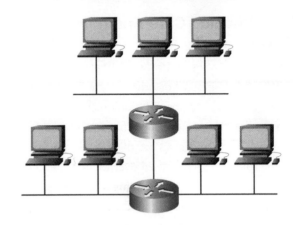

The total number of available hosts on a network can be derived by using the formula 2^n-2, where n is the number of host bits. The -2 accounts for an octet with all 0s, which is reserved for network identification, and all 1s, which is reserved for sending a broadcast message to all hosts.

Subnetting

Subnetting is a method of segmenting hosts within a network and providing additional structure. Without subnets, an organization operates as a flat network. These flat topologies result in short routing tables, but as the network grows, the use of bandwidth becomes inefficient.

In the figure, a Class B network is flat, with a single broadcast and collision domain. Collision domains are explained in more detail in the Ethernet chapter. For now, just think of them as a small network segment with a handful of devices. Adding Layer 2 switches to the network creates more collision domains but does not control broadcasts.

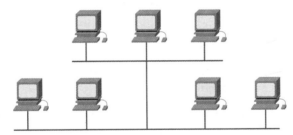

In the next figure, the same network has been subdivided into several segments or subnets. This is accomplished by using the third octet (part of the host address space for a Class B network) to segment the network. Note that the outside world sees this network the same as in the previous figure.

Subnetting is a bit complex at first pass. Think of it like a street address. For a house, the street address may provide the needed addressability to reach all the house's occupants. Now consider an apartment building. The street address only gets you to the right building. You need to know in which apartment the occupant you are seeking resides. In this crude example, the apartment number acts a bit like a subnet.

Subnet Masks

Routers use a subnet mask to determine which parts of the IP address correspond to the network, the subnet, and the host. The mask is a 32-bit number in the same format as the IP address. The mask is a string of consecutive 1s starting from the most-significant bits, representing the network ID, followed by a string of consecutive 0s, representing the host ID portion of the address bits.

At-a-Glance: IP Addressing

Each address class has a default subnet mask (A = /8, B = /16, C = /24). The default subnet masks only the network portion of the address, the effect of which is no subnetting. With each bit of subnetting beyond the default, you can create 2^n-2 subnets. The preceding example has 254 subnets, each with 254 hosts. This counts the address ending with .0, but not the address ending in .255.

Continuing with the preceding analogy, the subnet mask tells the network devices how many apartments are in the building.

Identifying Subnet Addresses

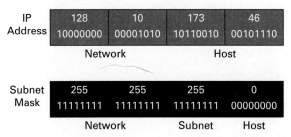

This subnet mask can also be written as "/24", where 24 represents the number of 1s in the subnet mask.

Given an IP address and subnet mask, you can identify the subnet address, broadcast address, and first and last usable addresses within a subnet as follows:

1. Write down the 32-bit address and the subnet mask below that (174.24.4.176/26 is shown in the following figure).

2. Draw a vertical line just after the last 1 bit in the subnet mask.

3. Copy the portion of the IP address to the left of the line. Place all 1s for the remaining free spaces to the right. This is the broadcast address for the subnet.

4. The first and last address can also be found by placing ...0001 and ...1110, respectively, in the remaining free spaces.

5. Copy the portion of the IP address to the left of the line. Place all 0s for the remaining free spaces to the right. This is the subnet number.

174.24.4.176	10101110001100000000100 10110000	Host
255.255.255.192	11111111111111111111111 11000000	Mask
174.24.4.128	10101110001100000000100 10000000	Subnet
174.24.4.191	10101110001100000000100 10111111	Broadcast

At-a-Glance: IPv6

Why Should I Care About IPv6?

The addressing scheme used for the TCP/IP protocols is IP version 4 (IPv4). This scheme uses a 32-bit binary number to identify networks and end stations. The 32-bit scheme yields about 4 billion addresses, but because of the dotted-decimal system (which breaks the number into four sections of 8 bits each) and other considerations, there are really only about 250 million usable addresses. When the scheme was originally developed in the 1980s, no one ever thought that running out of addresses would be a possibility. However, the explosion of the Internet, along with the increased number of Internet-capable devices, such as cell phones and PDAs (which need an IP address), has made running out of IPv4 addresses a serious concern. The chart shows the trend of address space, starting in 1980. It shows the address space running out sometime before 2010.

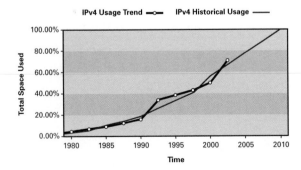

What Problems Need to Be Solved?

Network Address Translation (NAT) and Port Address Translation (PAT) were developed as solutions to the diminishing availability of IP addresses. NAT and PAT, as implemented today in many network routers, allow a company or user to share a single or a few assigned public IP addresses among many private addresses (which are not bound by an address authority).

Although these schemes preserve address space and provide anonymity, the benefits come at the cost of individuality. This eliminates the very reason for networking (and the Internet): allowing peer-to-peer collaboration through shared applications.

IP version 6 (IPv6) provides an answer to the problem of running out of address space. It also allows for the restoration of a true end-to-end model in which hosts can connect to each other unobstructed and with greater flexibility. Some of the key elements of IPv6 include allowing each host to have a unique global IP address, the ability to maintain connectivity even when in motion and roaming, and the ability to natively secure host communications.

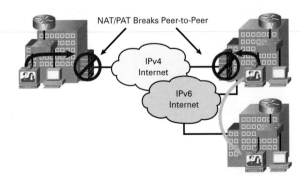

IPv6 Addresses

The 128-bit address used in IPv6 allows for a greater number of addresses and subnets (enough space for 10^{15} endpoints—340,282,366,920,938, 463,463,374,607,431,768,211,456 total!).

IPv6 was designed to give every user on Earth multiple global addresses that can be used for a wide variety of devices, including cell phones, PDAs, IP-enabled vehicles, consumer electronics, and many more. In addition to providing more address space, IPv6 has the following advantages over IPv4:

• Easier address management and delegation

• Easy address autoconfiguration

• Embedded IPsec (short for IP Security—encrypted IP)

• Optimized routing

• Duplicate Address Detection (DAD)

IPv6 Notation

The first figure demonstrates the notation and shortcuts for IPv6 addresses.

An IPv6 address uses the first 64 bits in the address for the network ID and the second 64 bits for the host ID. The network ID is separated into *prefix* chunks. The next figure shows the address hierarchy.

At-a-Glance: IPv6

128 bits are expressed as 8
fields of 16 bits in Hex notation:

2031:0000:130F:0000:0000:09C0:876A:130B

As a shorthand, leading zeros
in each field are optional:

2031:0:130F:0:0:9C0:876A:130B

Also, successive fields of 0
can be represented as ::

2031:0:130F::9C0:876A:130B

The :: shorthand can be used
only once per address:

2031::130F::9C0:876A:130B

2031:0:130F::9C0:876A:130B

2031::130F::9C0:876A:130B

The IPv4 address 192.168.30.1 is
0:0:0:0:0:0:192.168.30.1 in IPv6
but can be written as ::192.168.30.1.

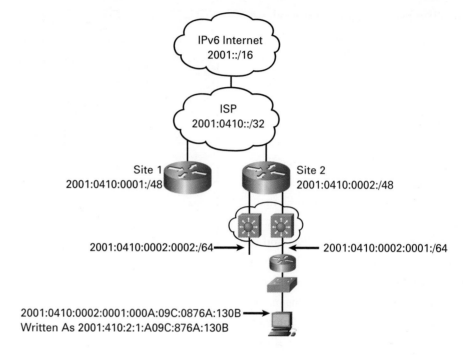

IPv6 Internet
2001::/16

ISP
2001:0410::/32

Site 1
2001:0410:0001:/48

Site 2
2001:0410:0002:/48

2001:0410:0002:0002:/64 →   ← 2001:0410:0002:0001:/64

2001:0410:0002:0001:000A:09C:0876A:130B →
Written As 2001:410:2:1:A09C:876A:130B

IPv6 Autoconfiguration

IPv4 deployments use one of two methods to assign IP addresses to a host: static assignment (which is management-intensive) or DHCP/BOOTP, which automatically assigns IP addresses to hosts upon booting onto the network.

IPv6 provides a feature called *stateless autoconfiguration*, which is similar to DHCP. Unlike DHCP, however, stateless autoconfiguration does not require the use of a special DHCP application or server when providing addresses to simple network devices that do not support DHCP (such as robotic arms used in manufacturing).

Using DHCP, any router interface that has an IPv6 address assigned to it becomes the "provider" of IP

addresses on the network to which it is attached. Safeguards are built into IPv6 that prevent duplicate addresses. This feature is called Duplicate Address Detection. With the IPv4 protocol, nothing prevents two hosts from joining the network with identical IP addresses. The operating system or application may be able to detect the problem, but often unpredictable results occur.

IPv6 Security

IPv6 has embedded support for IPsec (a common protocol for encryption). Currently the host operating system (OS) can configure an IPsec tunnel

between the host and any other host that has IPv6 support. With IPv4 the vast majority of IPsec deployments are network-based and unknown to host devices. With IPv6 IPsec, the host could create an encrypted data connection between itself and another device on the network. This means that network administrators do not need to set up the encryption, because hosts can do it themselves on demand.

IPv6 Mobility

IPv6 supports a greater array of features for the mobile user, whether the mobile device is a cell phone, PDA, laptop computer, or moving vehicle.

At-a-Glance: IPv6

Mobile IPv6 (MIPv6) supports a more streamlined approach to routing packets to and from the mobile device. It also supports IPsec between the mobile device and other network devices and hosts.

IPv6 Transition

There have been many predictions over the years about IPv6 migration, but the fact is that the IPv4 workarounds that have been developed in the meantime have been pretty good. It could be that despite being a superior solution to the address scarcity issue, IPv6 may never displace IPv4 and its work-arounds. To underscore this point, look back at the chart at the beginning of this section. Here we are in 2007, with only limited deployments of IPv6, and with many more devices on the Internet than anticipated back in the late 1990s, but IPv4 keeps chugging along.

Several factors may finally cause the transition—first as IPv6 "islands" connected with IPv4 networks, and then finally into end-to-end IPv6 networks. These factors include the U.S. federal government mandating that its networks must be IPv6-capable by a certain date, Microsoft adopting IPv6 into Windows starting with Vista, and Japan adopting IPv6 as its country network addressing standard.

At a minimum, it is important for network administrators and companies to understand IPv6 and its potential impacts so that they are prepared if and when the transition occurs.

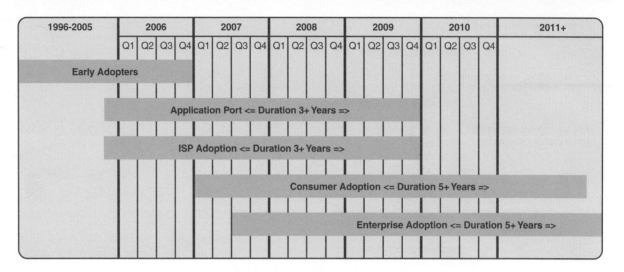

E-Europe, E-Japan, North America IPv6 Task Force,...

NAT and PAT

**Comparative Features of NAT
(Network Address Translation)**

Static NAT
- All Addresses Preassigned
- Address Assignments Do Not Change
- 1 Inside = 1 Outside
- Good for Security

Dynamic NAT
- Assigns Outside Address from Pool to Inside Address
- Address Assignments Only Last for a Single Communication Session
- Good for Security
- Preserves Address Space But Can Run Out of Outside Addresses

**Comparative Features of PAT
(Port Address Translation)**

- A Form of Dynamic NAT
- Uses One Outside Address For Many Inside Addresses (Call Overloading)
- Many Inside = 1 Outside
- Port Numbers (Usually Very High) Assigned on a Per-Session Basis
- Fools Packet Instead of Address
- Increases Address Space

NAT Table

Inside Addresses	Outside Addresses
10.0.0.1	172.1.5.1
10.0.0.2	172.1.5.2
10.0.0.3	172.1.5.3
etc.	etc.

PAT Table

Inside Addresses	Outside Addresses
10.0.0.1:1256	17.1.5.1:1256
10.0.0.2:1567	17.1.5.1:1567
10.0.0.3:1683	17.1.5.1:1683
etc.	etc.

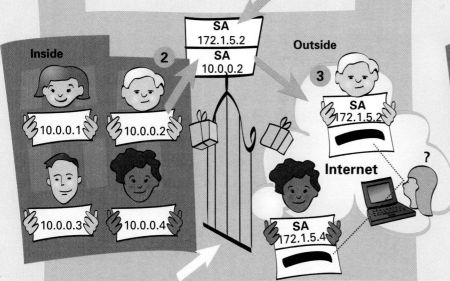

The router gateway maps the inside address to the outside address.

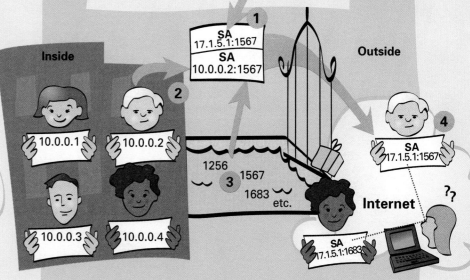

Internet Applications

The Internet and Its Applications

What makes the Internet useful and interesting to the average person is not the network, but rather the applications that operate on the network. The two most common Internet applications in use today are e-mail and web browsers.

E-Mail

E-mail is one of the most common network applications in use today. Although it might seem relatively new, e-mail was invented in the early 1970s. Back then, of course, there was no Internet as we know it today, so having e-mail was a bit like owning a car before there was a highway system.

Today, e-mail is so widespread that ISPs just assume that you want an e-mail address and automatically assign you one (or even several) when you begin your service agreement.

E-Mail Tools

There are two basic ways to create, send, and receive e-mails: with an e-mail client and with a web-based e-mail tool:

- **E-mail clients** that are installed on individual machines are in wide use today. The most popular are Microsoft Outlook/Outlook Express. E-mail clients allow for the creation, distribution, retrieval, and storage of e-mails (as well as some other useful features). These types of clients were originally designed so that e-mails to and from an account could be accessed from a single machine.

  E-mail clients physically move the e-mail from the e-mail server to your PC's hard drive. After the e-mail is downloaded, it no longer exists in the e-mail provider's network. The e-mail exists in your e-mail client program (on the PC's hard drive) until you delete it.

- **Web-based e-mail tools,** such as Google Mail, allow users to access their e-mail from any machine connected to the Internet. Users log in to the website with their registered name and password. Then they are given access to a web-based e-mail client that has all the basic abilities of e-mail clients, such as the ability to create, send, and receive e-mails. Many have more advanced features, such as the ability to send and receive file attachments and create and use address books.

Web-based e-mail tools differ from e-mail clients in that the e-mail is not downloaded to your PC's hard drive. It exists only on the e-mail provider's network until you delete it. Some people use a combination of web-based e-mail and e-mail clients. For example, you may use the web-based e-mail tool to access your e-mail when you are away from home and not using your home PC. When you are at home, you could then use your e-mail client.

What's Up with the @ Sign?

All e-mail addresses are made up of two parts: a recipient part and a domain name. An @ symbol separates the two parts to denote that a recipient is unique within a domain name. The domain name is usually the name of your ISP (or your company if you have e-mail there), and, like a website, an e-mail domain has an associated IP address. This allows (actually, requires) the use of a DNS server to translate the domain name portion of an e-mail address to the IP address of the server where the e-mail account resides.

The recipient part is the chosen identifier that you are known by within the e-mail domain. There are a lot of possibilities for choosing the recipient. Here are a few popular styles:

Firstname.Lastname	John.Brown
FirstinitialLastname	JBrown
Nickname	DowntownJohnnyBrown
Personalized license plate	L8RG8R
Other obscure reference	GrassyKnoll63

When picking an e-mail address, remember that sometimes you'll have to verbally tell someone your e-mail address, so "X3UT67B" is inadvisable.

Sending E-Mails

E-mails are distributed using a (OSI Layer 7) protocol called Simple Mail Transfer Protocol (SMTP). SMTP normally operates on powerful computers dedicated to e-mail distribution, called SMTP servers. When you create and send an e-mail, your e-mail client sends the file to the SMTP server. The server pulls out the addresses from the message. (You can send e-mails to multiple recipients.) For each domain name, the SMTP server must send a message to a DNS to get the IP address of each recipient's e-mail server. If the recipient is on the same server as you (that is, if you send an e-mail to someone with the same domain name), this step is unnecessary.

After your SMTP server knows the IP address of the recipient's server, your SMTP server transfers the e-mail message to the recipient's SMTP server. If there are multiple recipients in different e-mail domains, a separate copy of the e-mail is transferred to each recipient's SMTP server. According to the name of the protocol, this is all pretty simple.

Receiving E-Mails

E-mail is often received via a different server than the one that sends e-mail. The type of server depends on which type of e-mail tool you use. For those using an e-mail client, your e-mail is probably delivered to you via the most common method, Post Office Protocol 3 (POP3) server. (We have no idea what happened to the first two.) The POP3 server receives all its e-mails from SMTP servers and sorts them into file spaces dedicated to each user (much the same way mail is put into post office boxes at a local post office—thus the name).

When you open your e-mail client, it contacts the POP3 server to request all the new e-mails. The e-mails are then transferred to your PC, and in most cases the e-mails are erased from the POP3 server.

Another common method (or protocol) for mail retrieval is an Internet Mail Access Protocol (IMAP) server. This is the protocol normally used by web-based e-mail clients, and corporate e-mail systems such as Microsoft Exchange. The IMAP server receives and sorts e-mail in much the same way as a POP3 server. Unlike POP3, however, IMAP does not transfer the e-mails to the machine of the account holder; instead, it keeps e-mail on the server. This allows users to connect to use their e-mail account from multiple machines. IMAP also allows for *server-side filtering*, a method of presorting e-mail based on rules before it even gets to your PC. It's kind of like having a friendly postal worker who sorts all your bills to the top and magazines to the bottom.

Two main issues with IMAP servers are storage space and working offline. Most Internet e-mail services put a limit on the amount of storage each subscriber gets (some charge extra for additional storage space). In addition, these services often limit the file size of attachments (such as photos). The other issue is the ability to work *offline* or when not connected to the Internet. One solution is called *caching*, which temporarily places the subscriber's e-mail information on whatever PC he or she wants to work offline with. When the user reconnects, any e-mails created while offline are sent, and any new incoming e-mails can be viewed.

Web Browsing

Browsing web pages on the Internet is another common network application. Browsers run on a computer and allow a viewer to see website content. Website content resides on a server, a powerful computer with a lot of disk space and lots of computing cycles. The protocol that allows browsers and servers to communicate is HTTP.

What Are HTTP and HTML, and What Do They Do?

You might have noticed that many Internet sites include the letters *HTTP* in the site address that appears in the address line of your web browser. HTTP (another OSI Layer 7 protocol) defines the rules for transferring information, files, and multimedia on web pages. Hypertext Markup Language (HTML) is the language used within HTTP. HTML is actually a fairly simple, easy-to-learn computer language that embeds symbols into a text file to specify visual or functional characteristics such as font size, page boundaries, and application usages (such as launching an e-mail tool when a user clicks certain links).

When the developer of an HTTP file (or web page) wants to allow for a jump to a different place on the page, or even a jump to a new page, he or she simply places the appropriate symbols into the file. People viewing the page just see the link, which is most commonly specified with blue, underlined text. The ease of jumping from site to site (called *web surfing*) is one of the reasons for the proliferation of websites on, and growth of, the Internet.

Several free and commercial tools allow you to create a web page using HTML without having to know all the rules.

One of the issues with HTML is that it is fairly limited as far as what it can do given that it works only on text and still pictures. To achieve some of the really cool moving graphics and web page features, other tools such as Flash, XML, JavaScript, or other scripting languages are needed.

E-Mail

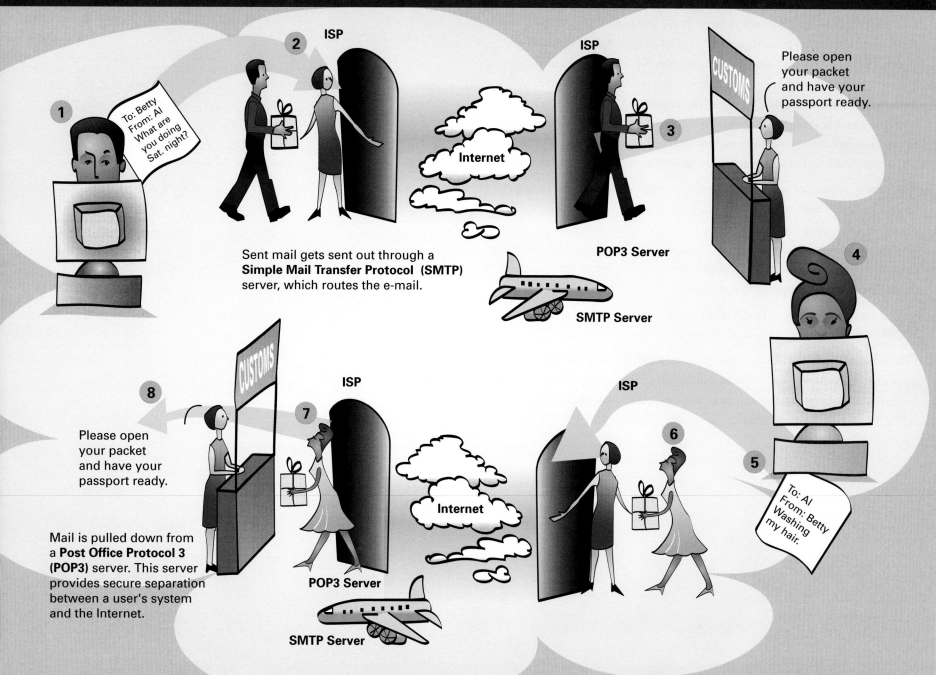

Peer-to-Peer Sharing

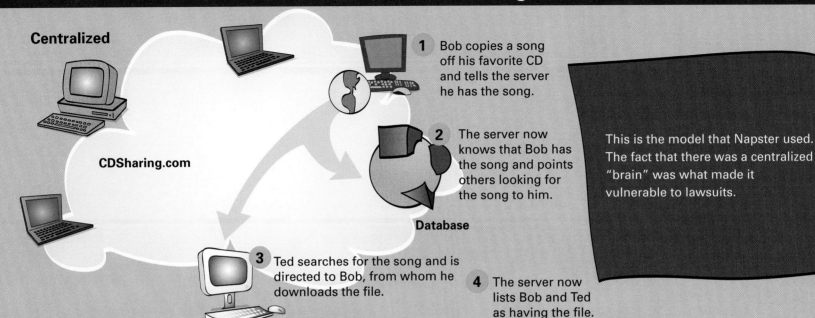

Centralized

CDSharing.com

1 Bob copies a song off his favorite CD and tells the server he has the song.

2 The server now knows that Bob has the song and points others looking for the song to him.

Database

3 Ted searches for the song and is directed to Bob, from whom he downloads the file.

4 The server now lists Bob and Ted as having the file.

This is the model that Napster used. The fact that there was a centralized "brain" was what made it vulnerable to lawsuits.

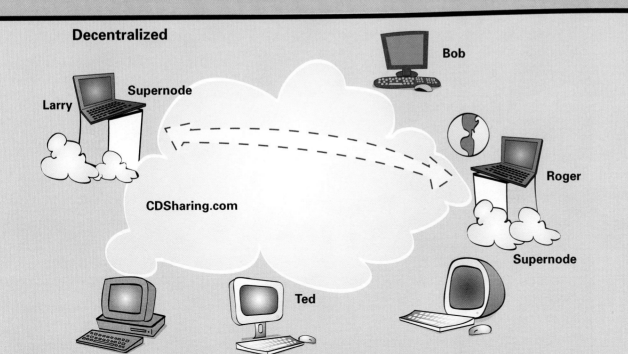

Decentralized

Larry

Supernode

Bob

CDSharing.com

Roger

Supernode

Ted

In a decentralized model, several hundred supernodes take the place of a centralized "brain." A supernode is a user who volunteers to keep the user database information on his or her computer.

Supernode users come on- and offline all the time so each one acts as the "brain" for a very small percentage of the overall system time (which makes it very difficult to sue anyone).

Part II

Networking Infrastructure

With the fundamentals of networking under our belt, we can now take a closer look at the infrastructure that makes up the networks we all use. This section focuses on the switches and routers that make up networks, along with the protocols that drive them.

We start this section with a discussion of the Ethernet protocol, which defines the rules and processes by which computers in a local area communicate. Long before the Internet was in use, computers communicated locally using the Ethernet protocol, and it is still widely used.

We then move on to local-area network (LAN) switching, an extension of the Ethernet protocol required when there are more computers in a local segment than can communicate efficiently. Switching is one of the core technologies in networking.

One of the necessities in networking is link redundancy, something that makes it more likely that data reaches its intended target. Sometimes, however, link redundancy can create loops in the network, which causes an explosion of administrative traffic that can take down a network in a matter of minutes. Spanning Tree is one of the mechanisms that keeps these "broadcast storms" from wiping out your local network, so we look at how this important protocol works.

We end this section with routing, which provides the basis for network communication over long distances. The advent of routing allowed the growth of the Internet and corporate networking as we know it today. This section explores how routing works and how routers communicate.

Ethernet

History of Ethernet

Robert Metcalfe developed Ethernet at the famous Xerox Palo Alto Research Center (PARC) in 1972. The folks at Xerox PARC had developed a personal workstation with a graphical user interface. They needed a technology to network these workstations with their newly developed laser printers. (Remember, the first PC, the MITS altair, was not introduced to the public until 1975.)

Metcalfe originally called this network the Alto Aloha Network. He changed the name to Ethernet in 1973 to make it clear that any type of device could connect to his network. He chose the name "ether" because the network carried bits to every workstation in the same manner that scientists once thought waves were propagated through space by the "luminiferous ether."

Metcalfe's first external publication concerning Ethernet was available to the public in 1976. Metcalfe left Xerox, and in 1979 he got Digital Equipment Corporation (DEC), Intel, and Xerox to agree on a common Ethernet standard called DIX. In 1982, the Institute of Electrical and Electronic Engineers (IEEE) adopted a standard based on Metcalfe's Ethernet.

Ethernet took off in academic networks and some corporate networks. It was cheap, and public domain protocols such as Internet Protocol (IP) ran natively on it. However, another company (IBM) wanted the world to adopt its protocol instead, called Token Ring. Before switching was introduced, Ethernet was more difficult to troubleshoot than Token Ring. Although Ethernet was less expensive to implement, larger corporations chose Token Ring because of their relationship with IBM and the ability to more easily troubleshoot problems.

Early Ethernet used media such as coaxial cable, and a network could literally be a single long, continuous segment of coax cable tied into many computers. (This cable was known as Thinnet or Thicknet, depending on the thickness of the coax used.) When someone accidentally kicked the cable under his or her desk, this often produced a slight break in the network. A break meant that no one on the network could communicate, not just the poor schmuck who kicked the cable. Debugging usually entailed crawling under desks and following the cable until the break was found.

In contrast, Token Ring had more sophisticated tools (than crawling on your knees) for finding the breaks. It was usually pretty obvious where the token stopped being passed and, voilà, you had your culprit.

The battle for the LAN continued for more than ten years, until eventually Ethernet became the predominant technology. Arguably, it was the widespread adoption of Ethernet switching that drove the final nail in Token Ring's coffin. Other LAN technologies, such as AppleTalk and Novell IPX, have been and continue to be introduced, but Ethernet prevails as the predominant technology for local high-speed connectivity.

Thankfully, we have left behind early media such as coax for more sophisticated technologies.

What Is Ethernet?

Ethernet describes a system that links the computers in a building or within a local area. It consists of hardware (a network interface card), software, and cabling used to connect the computers. All computers on an Ethernet are attached to a shared data link, as opposed to traditional point-to-point networks, in which a single device connects to another single device.

Because all computers share the same data link on an Ethernet network, the network needs a protocol to handle contention if multiple computers want to transmit data at the same time, because only one can talk at a time without causing interference. Metcalfe's invention introduced the carrier sense multiple access collision detect (CSMA/CD) protocol. CSMA/CD defines how a computer should listen to the network before transmitting. If the network is quiet, the computer can transmit its data. However, a problem arises if more than one computer listens, hears silence, and transmits at the same time: The data collides. The collision-detect part of CSMA/CD defines a method in which transmitting computers back off when collisions occur and randomly attempt to restart transmission. Ethernet originally operated at 3 Mbps, but today it operates at speeds ranging from 10 Mbps (that's 10 million bits per second) to 10 Gbps (that's 10 billion bits per second).

Evolution of Ethernet

When Metcalfe originally developed Ethernet, computers were connected to a single copper cable. The physical limitations of a piece of copper cable carrying electrical signals restricted how far computers could be from each other on an Ethernet. Repeaters helped alleviate the distance limitations. *Repeaters* are small devices that regenerate an electrical signal at the original signal strength. This process allows an Ethernet to extend across an office floor that might exceed the Ethernet distance limitations.

The addition or removal of a device on the Ethernet cable disrupts the network for all other connected devices. A device called an Ethernet *hub* solves this problem. First, each port on a hub is actually a repeater. Second, hubs let computers insert or remove themselves nondisruptively from the network. Finally, hubs simplify Ethernet troubleshooting and administration. As networks grow larger, companies need to fit more and more computers onto an Ethernet. As the number of computers increases, the number of collisions on the network increases. As collisions increase, useful network traffic decreases (administrative traffic actually increases because of all the error messages getting passed around). Networks come to a grinding halt when too many collisions occur.

Ethernet *bridges* resolve this problem by physically breaking an Ethernet into two or more segments. This arrangement means that devices communicating on one side of the bridge do not collide with devices communicating on the other side of the bridge. Bridges also learn which devices are on each side and only transfer traffic to the network containing the destination device. A two-port bridge also doubles the bandwidth previously available, because each port is a separate Ethernet.

Ethernet bridges evolved to solve the problem of connecting Ethernet networks to Token Ring networks. This process of translating a packet from one LAN technology to another is called *translational bridging*.

As Ethernet networks continue to grow in a corporation, they become more complex, connecting hundreds and thousands of devices. Ethernet switches allow network administrators to dynamically break their networks into multiple Ethernet segments.

Initially, switches operated as multiport Ethernet bridges. But eventually, as the cost per port decreased significantly, Ethernet switches replaced hubs, in which each connected device receives its own dedicated Ethernet bandwidth. With switches, collisions are no longer an issue, because connections between computer and switch can be point-to-point, and the Ethernet can both send and receive traffic at the same time. This ability to send and receive simultaneously is called *full duplex*, as opposed to traditional Ethernet, which operated at *half duplex*. Half duplex means that a device can receive or transmit traffic on the network, but not at the same time. If both happen at the same time, a collision occurs.

This is different from subnetting in a couple of distinct ways. First, Ethernet is a Layer 2 protocol, and subnetting has to do with IP addressing (which is a Layer 3 function). Second, IP addressing is a logical segmentation scheme, and switching is a physical separation, because each end station has a dedicated physical port on the switch.

At-a-Glance: Ethernet

Why Should I Care About Ethernet?

Ethernet was developed in 1972 as a way to connect newly invented computers to newly invented laser printers. It was recognized even at that time as a remarkable technology breakthrough. However, very few people would have wagered that the ability to connect computers and devices would change human communication on the same scale as the invention of the telephone and change business on the scale of the Industrial Revolution. Several competing protocols have emerged since 1972, but Ethernet remains the dominant standard for connecting computers into local-area networks (LAN). For many years Ethernet was dominant in home networks as well. Ethernet has been mostly replaced by wireless technologies in the home networking market. Wireless or Wi-Fi is covered in Part VIII, "Mobility."

What Problems Need to Be Solved?

Ethernet is a shared resource in which end stations (computers, servers, and so on) all have access to the transmission medium at the same time. The result is that only one device can send information at a time. Given this limitation, two viable solutions exist:

- **Use a sharing mechanism:** If all end stations are forced to share a common wire, rules must exist to ensure that each end station waits its turn before transmitting. In the event of simultaneous transmissions, rules must exist for retransmitting.

- **Divide the shared segments, and insulate them:** Another solution to the limitations of shared resources is to use devices that reduce the number of end stations sharing a resource at any given time.

Ethernet Collisions

In a traditional LAN, several users would all share the same port on a network device and would compete for resources (bandwidth). The main limitation of such a setup is that only one device can transmit at a time. Segments that share resources in this manner are called collision domains, because if two or more devices transmit at the same time, the information "collides," and both end points must resend their information (at different times). Typically the devices both wait a random amount of time before attempting to retransmit.

This method works well for a small number of users on a segment, each having relatively low bandwidth requirements. As the number of users increases, the efficiency of collision domains decreases sharply, to the point where overhead traffic (management and control) clogs the network.

Smaller Segments

Segments can be divided to reduce the number of users and increase the bandwidth available to each user in the segment. Each new segment created results in a new collision domain. Traffic from one segment or collision domain does not interfere with other segments, thereby increasing the available bandwidth of each segment. In the following figure, each segment has greater bandwidth, but all segments are still on a common backbone and must share the available bandwidth. This approach works best when care is taken to make sure that the largest users of bandwidth are placed in separate segments.

There are a few basic methods for segmenting an Ethernet LAN into more collision domains:

- Use bridges to split collision domains.

- Use switches to provide dedicated domains to each host.

- Use routers to route traffic between domains (and to not route traffic that does not matter to the other domain).

This sheet discusses segmenting using bridges and routers (switching is covered in the next chapter).

Single Segment, Multiple Collision Domains

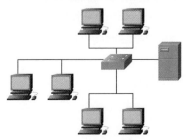

Multiple Segments, Multiple Collision Domains

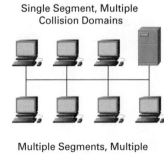

At-a-Glance: Ethernet

Increasing Bandwidth

In addition to creating additional segments to increase available bandwidth, you can use a faster medium such as optical fiber or Gigabit Ethernet. Although these technologies are faster, they are still shared media, so collision domains will still exist and will eventually experience the same problems as slower media.

Ethernet Segments

A segment is the simplest form of network, in which all devices are directly connected. In this type of arrangement, if any of the computers gets disconnected, or if one is added, the segment is disabled.

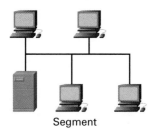

Segment

Hubs

Hubs enable you to add and remove computers without disabling the network, but they do not create additional collision domains.

Repeaters

Repeaters simply extend the transmission distance of an Ethernet segment.

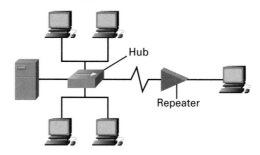

Bridges

Bridges are simple Layer 2 devices that create new segments, resulting in fewer collisions. Bridges must learn the addresses of the computers on each segment to avoid forwarding traffic to the wrong port. Unlike hubs, which are usually used for networks with a small number of end stations (4 to 8), bridges can handle much larger networks with dozens of end stations.

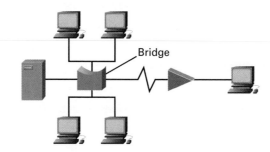

Switched Ethernet

A LAN switch can be thought of as a high-speed, multiport bridge with a brain. Switches don't just allow each end station to have a dedicated port (meaning that no collisions occur). They also allow end stations to transmit and receive at the same time (using full duplex), greatly increasing the LAN's efficiency.

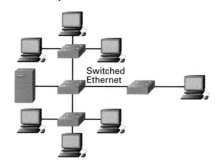

LAN Routers

LAN-based routers greatly extend the speed, distance, and intelligence of Ethernet LANs. Routers also allow traffic to be sent along multiple paths.

Routers, however, require a common protocol between the router and end stations.

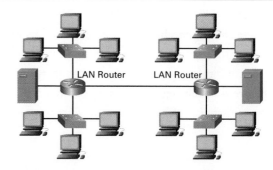

At-a-Glance: Ethernet

What They Gave Away

In the 1970s Xerox Corporation assembled a group of talented researchers to investigate new technologies. The new group was located in the newly opened Palo Alto Research Center (PARC), well away from the corporate headquarters in Connecticut.

In addition to developing Ethernet, the brilliant folks at the PARC invented the technology for what eventually became the personal computer (PC), the graphical user interface (GUI), laser printing, and very-large-scale integration (VLSI).

Inexplicably, Xerox Corporation failed to recognize the brilliance (and commercial viability) of many of these homegrown innovations and let them walk out the door.

To give you an idea of what this cost Xerox in terms of opportunity, the worldwide budget for Ethernet equipment was more than $7 billion in 2006 and was expected to grow to more than $10 billion by 2009. Just imagine if a single company owned the assets of Apple, Intel, Cisco, HP, and Microsoft. There almost was such a company. Its name is Xerox.

Reducing Collisions on Ethernet

When End Stations Share a Single Switch

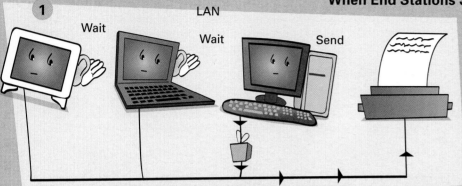

1 LAN — Wait · Wait · Send

Before sending data, end stations "listen" for other traffic. If they hear none, it's OK to send.

2 Send · Send · Wait

Sometimes, two or more end stations will hear nothing and send data simultaneously.

3 Shrapnel

This causes the data frames to collide, destroying all the frames (which must be resent).

4

After the collision, each end station starts a random timer that must expire before it can try to resend the data.

The Switch Port Option

Switch ports have become relatively inexpensive, so now each end station gets a dedicated port. The result: no more collisions.

LAN Switching

Fast Computers Need Faster Networks

The PC emerged as the most common desktop computer in the 1980s. LANs emerged as a way to network PCs in a common location. Networking technologies such as Token Ring and Ethernet allowed users to share resources such as printers and exchange files with each other. As originally defined, Ethernet and Token Ring provided network access to multiple devices on the same network segment or ring. These LAN technologies have inherent limitations as to how many devices can connect to a single segment, as well as the physical distance between computers. Desktop computers got faster, the number of computers grew, operating systems began *multitasking* (allowing multiple tasks to operate at the same time), and applications became more network-centric. All these advancements resulted in congestion on LANs.

To address these issues, two device types emerged: repeaters and bridges. *Repeaters* are simple Open Systems Interconnection (OSI) Layer 1 devices that allow networks to extend beyond their defined physical distances (which were limited to about 150 feet without the use of a repeater).

Bridges are OSI Layer 2 devices that physically split a segment into two and reduce the amount of traffic on either side of the bridge. This setup allows more devices to connect to the LAN and reduces congestion. LAN switches emerged as a natural extension of bridging, revolutionizing the concept of local-area networking.

Switching Basics: It's a Bridge

Network devices have one primary purpose: to pass network traffic from one segment to another. (There are exceptions, of course, such as network analyzers, which inspect traffic as it goes by.) With devices that independently make forwarding decisions, traffic can travel from its source to the destination. The higher up the OSI model a device operates, the deeper it looks into a packet to make a forwarding decision. Railroad-switching stations provide a similar example. The switches enable a train to enter the appropriate tracks (path) that take it to its final destination. If the switches are set wrong, a train can end up traveling to the wrong destination or traveling in a circle.

Switching technology emerged as the replacement for bridging. Switches provide all the features of traditional bridging and more. Compared to bridges, switches provide superior throughput performance, higher port density, and lower per-port cost.

The different types of bridging include the following:

- Transparent bridging primarily occurs in Ethernet networks.
- Source-route bridging occurs in Token Ring networks.
- Translational bridging occurs between different media. For example, a translational bridge might connect a Token Ring network to an Ethernet network.

Bridging and switching occur at the data link layer (Layer 2 in the OSI model), which means that bridges control data flow, provide transmission error handling, and enable access to physical media. Basic bridging is not complicated: A bridge or switch analyzes an incoming frame, determines where to forward the frame based on the packet's header information (which contains information on the source and destination addresses), and forwards the frame toward its destination. With transparent bridging, forwarding decisions happen one hop (or network segment) at a time. With source-route bridging, the frame contains a predetermined path to the destination.

Bridges and switches divide networks into smaller, self-contained units. Because only a portion of the traffic is forwarded, bridging reduces the overall traffic that devices see on each connected network. The bridge acts as a kind of firewall in that it prevents frame-level errors from propagating from one segment to another. Bridges also accommodate communication among more devices than are supported on a single segment or ring.

Bridges and switches essentially extend the effective length of a LAN, permitting more workstations to communicate with each other within a single broadcast domain. The primary difference between switches and bridges is that bridges segment a LAN into a few smaller segments. Switches, through their increased port density and speed, permit segmentation on a much larger scale. Modern-day switches used in corporate networks have hundreds of ports per chassis (unlike the four-port box connected to your cable modem).

Additionally, modern-day switches interconnect LAN segments operating at different speeds.

Switching describes technologies that are an extension of traditional bridges. Switches connect two or more LAN segments and make forwarding decisions about whether to transmit packets from one segment to another. When a frame arrives, the switch inspects the destination and source Media Access Control (MAC) addresses in the packet. (This is an example of *store-and-forward switching*.) The switch places an entry in a table indicating that the source MAC address is located off the switch interface on which the packet arrived. The bridge then consults the same table for an entry for the destination MAC address. If it has an entry for the destination MAC address, and the entry indicates that the MAC address is located on a different port from which the packet was received, the switch forwards the frame to the specified port.

If the switch table indicates that the destination MAC address is located on the same interface on which the frame was just received, the bridge does not forward the frame. Why send it back onto the network segment from which it came? This decision is where a switch reduces network congestion. Finally, if the destination MAC address is not in the switch's table, this indicates that the switch has not yet seen a frame destined for this MAC address. In this case, the switch then forwards the frames out all other ports (called *flooding*) except the one on which the packet was received.

At their core, switches are multiport bridges. However, switches have radically matured into intelligent devices, replacing both bridges and hubs. Switches not only reduce traffic through the use of bridge tables, but also offer new functionality that supports high-speed connections, virtual LANs, and even traditional routing.

Switching Ethernets

As switch Ethernet ports became less expensive, switches replaced hubs in the wiring closet. Initially, when switches were introduced, network administrators plugged hubs (containing multiple hosts) into switch ports. But eventually, it became cost-effective to plug the hosts directly into a switch port. This arrangement gives each host its own dedicated Ethernet and removes the possibility of collisions. Because a dedicated switch connection has only two devices (the switch and the host), you can configure an Ethernet switch port as *full duplex*. This means that a device can receive incoming traffic and transmit traffic simultaneously. End stations have considerably more bandwidth when they use switches. Ethernet can run at multiple speeds: 10 Mbps, 100 Mbps, 1 Gbps, and 10 Gbps. Therefore, switches can provide connectivity at these speeds. However, network applications and the web create considerably more network traffic, reintroducing new congestion problems. Switches can use quality of service (QoS) and other mechanisms to help solve the congestion issue.

Switches Take Over the World

As switches established themselves in networks, vendors added increasing functionality. Modern switches can perform forwarding decisions based on Layer 3 routing, as well as on Layer 4 and above. Even though switches can perform the functions of other higher-layer devices such as routers and content switches, you still must separate these functionalities to avoid single points of failure. Switches are the workhorse of networks, providing functionality across almost all layers of the OSI model reliably and quickly. Switches can also provide power to devices such as IP-based phones using the same Ethernet connection. Again, this applies to very large switches serving corporate networks rather than the switches in a small office or home.

At-a-Glance: Switching

Why Should I Care About Switching?

Advances in switching technology combined with a decrease in switch prices have made computer networks a common and increasingly important aspect of business today.

What Problems Need to Be Solved?

- **MAC address learning:** Switches must learn about the network to make intelligent decisions. Because of the size and changing nature of networks, switches have learned how to discover network addresses and keep track of network changes. Switches do this by finding the address information contained in the frames flowing through the network, and they maintain private tables with that information.

- **Forwarding and filtering:** Switches must decide what to do with traffic. These decisions are based on the switch's knowledge of the network.

- **Segmenting end stations:** Switches must also have mechanisms for segregating users into logical groupings (virtual LANs [VLAN] or broadcast domains) to allow efficient provisioning of service.

Broadcast and Collision Domains

From time to time, a device on the network will want to communicate with all other "local" devices at the same time. Typically, this occurs when a device wants to query the network for an IP address, when a device is newly added to a network, or when a change occurs in the network.

A group of devices that receive all broadcast messages from members of that group is called a broadcast domain. Network broadcast domains typically are segmented with Layer 3 devices (routers).

Think of a broadcast domain as like standing in your yard and yelling as loudly as you can. The neighbors who hear you are within your broadcast domain.

Forwarding and Filtering

From a network efficiency standpoint, it is easy to see that it is much better for the network when the switch knows all the addresses on every port. However, it is not always practical to enter this information manually. As the network grows and changes are made, it becomes almost impossible to keep up.

Legacy Switches

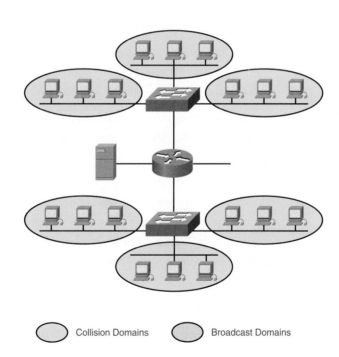

Modern Switches

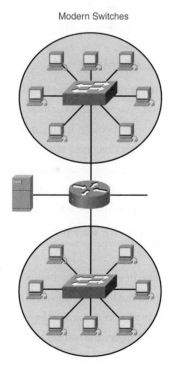

Collision Domains   Broadcast Domains

At-a-Glance: Switching

A switch always does something when it receives traffic. The preference is to send the traffic out a specific port (called filtering), but this works only when the location of the intended destination is known. When the destination address is unknown, the switch forwards the traffic out every port, except the one on which the traffic was received. This process is called flooding. Think of this as a guy calling every number in the phone book because he lost a woman's number from the night before.

Address Learning

A switch must learn the addresses of the devices attached to it. First it inspects the source address of all the traffic sent through it. Then it associates the port the traffic was received on with the MAC address listed. The following example illustrates this concept. The MAC addresses are not in the correct format and are shown for clarity only:

• **Time 0:** The switch shown has an empty MAC address table.

• **Time 1:** The device attached to port 2 sends a message intended for the device on port 0. This kicks off two actions within the switch. First, the switch now knows the address associated with the device on port 2, so it enters the information into its table. Second, because it does not have an association for the device the traffic is intended for (the computer on port 0), the switch floods the message out all ports except the one on which it was received.

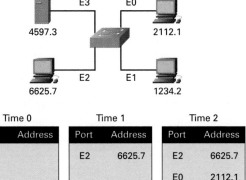

• **Time 2:** The device on port 0 replies to the message. The switch associates the source address of the message with port 0.

Any future communications involving either of these end stations will not require these steps, because the switch now knows which ports they are associated with.

This process happens all the time in every switch. For most switches, when a table entry has reached a certain "age" and has not been referenced in a while, it can be removed. This process is called *aging out*.

Frame Transmission Modes

Switches typically are Layer 2 devices (some switches now perform Layer 3 and higher functions). According to the OSI model, the data unit processed by a switch is called a frame. Switches must balance speed and accuracy (no errors) when processing frames, because typically they are measured on both attributes.

The three primary frame switching modes are as follows:

• **Cut-through:** Also known as fast-forward. The switch checks only the destination address and immediately begins forwarding the frame. This can decrease latency but also can transmit frames containing errors.

• **Store-and-forward:** The switch waits to receive the entire frame before forwarding. The entire frame is read, and a cyclic redundancy check (CRC) is performed. If the CRC is bad, the frame is discarded. Although this method increases latency (processing time), it also tends to minimize errors.

• **Fragment-free (modified cut-through):** The switch reads the first 64 bytes before forwarding the frame. 64 bytes is the minimum number of bytes necessary to detect and filter out collision frames.

At-a-Glance: Switching

Virtual LANs (VLAN)

VLANs provide the means to logically group several end stations with common sets of requirements. VLANs are independent of physical locations, meaning that two end stations connected to different switches on different floors can belong to the same VLAN. Typically the logical grouping follows workgroup functions such as engineering or finance, but this can be customized.

With VLANS it is much easier to assign access rules and provision services to groups of users regardless of their physical location. For example, using VLANs you can give all members of a project team access to project files by virtue of their VLAN membership. This ability also makes it easier to add or delete users without rerunning cables or changing network addresses.

VLANs also create their own broadcast domains without the addition of Layer 3 devices.

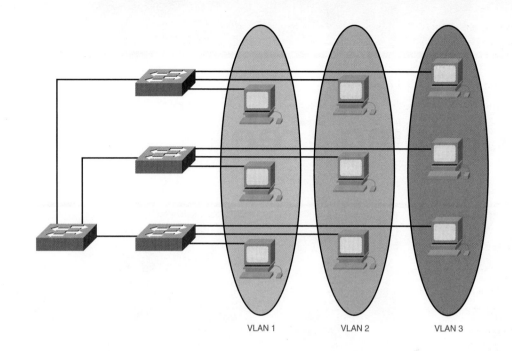

VLAN 1   VLAN 2   VLAN 3

Spanning Tree

Network Loops

With increased reliance on the network, many companies wanted redundancy built into their switched networks. In the event of a failure, alternative paths could still be used to switch and forward packets. One drawback of this approach is that network loops can occur. Loops form when redundant connections between switches form a circular path. This leads to a condition in which the same packets can travel endlessly around the same path in a circle.

Loops can be deadly, bringing whole networks to a halt, especially when IP services such as multicast and broadcast are enabled. Because of this possibility, it is always a good practice to break up Layer 2 networks with Layer 3 routers.

Sometimes, the Earth Is Flat

As with most networking technologies, there has sometimes been a pendulum effect in the popularity of Layer 2 bridged (flat) networks versus Layer 3 routed networks. Cisco's initial business convinced customers to insert routing devices to break up their predominantly flat, bridged networks to more efficiently transmit traffic and reduce the number of users affected when broadcast storms and loops occurred.

However, in the mid-1990s, LAN switches became wildly popular for replacing bridges and hubs. The "flat Earth" craze went so far as to swing the pendulum back, with competitive sayings such as "Switch if you can; route if you must." Again, network administrators relearned the consequences of building massive Layer 2 networks: One loop in the network could kill an entire network.

Today, the role of switching and bridging is more clearly defined. Experience has shown that networks are more resilient and recover from failures more quickly when they use Layer 3 redundancy instead of Layer 2 (spanning tree).

Preventing Network Loops

Spanning Tree Protocol (STP) is a Layer 2 protocol designed to run on bridges and switches. The main purpose of spanning tree is to prevent loops from forming in a switched network. The de facto implementation of STP is based on the Institute of Electrical and Electronic Engineers (IEEE) 802.1d standard.

With redundant Layer 2 links, only one path is active at a time. When that path goes down, another path becomes active.

New Internet standards improve the efficiency of STP:

- **802.1w Rapid Spanning Tree Protocol (RSTP):** By default, traditional 802.1d STP treated every port the same concerning the time it took to transition into an active state. It took switch ports anywhere from 30 to 180 seconds to transition into a forwarding state, which was an eternity in computer time. 802.1w defines shortcuts based on what is connected to the switch port; they allow quicker transition times.

- **802.1s Multiple Spanning Tree (MST):** Switches that implement VLANs traditionally needed to run one spanning-tree process per VLAN. Networks with hundreds of VLANs required each switch to have enough spanning-tree instances running to match one instance per VLAN. This setup is CPU-intensive on the switches and complicates recovery after a network event. 802.1s MST reduces the overall number of spanning-tree instances by mapping multiple VLANs with similar topologies to a single spanning-tree instance. MST improves traffic load balancing and network recovery time.

Spanning-Tree Fundamentals

As previously mentioned, STP dynamically prevents loops in Layer 2 switched networks. STP defines a tree that spans all switches in a LAN by forcing certain redundant paths in the network into a blocked state. If a link that previously forwarded traffic becomes unavailable, STP dynamically reconfigures the network to redirect traffic flow by activating the appropriate standby path. Switches dynamically determine the state of the spanning tree by exchanging information with others using bridge protocol data units (BPDU). These packets contain information on each switch's view of the network. The absence of a regularly scheduled BPDU from a neighbor switch indicates that that switch has disappeared.

The first order of business with spanning tree is for all the switches in the spanning tree to elect a root. The root serves as the focal point for the rest of the switched network. After the root is elected (or designated by a network administrator), each switch's proximity to the root determines all forwarding and blocking decisions. Switches dynamically determine the root through the exchange of BPDUs containing root IDs. When determining the winner, smaller is better. If the root ID on Switch A is lower than that of Switch B, Switch A becomes the root. Traditionally, each VLAN on a switch had to have its own root, which could add considerable overhead to switches with a lot of VLANs. 802.1s MST resolved this issue. After a root is elected, switches implement the following rules for traditional 802.1d STP:

- All ports on the root switch must be in a forwarding state.

- After a switch determines that it is not the root, it must identify the port that is closest to the root (called the root port) and put it in a forwarding state.

- When multiple nonroot switches occupy a common segment, they must determine which switch has the shortest path to the root (called the designated port) and put it in a forwarding state.

- All other ports connected to another switch or bridge must be in a blocking state. This arrangement is how STP prevents loops.

When a port first becomes active (for example, when a switch boots up), 802.1d STP requires that the port not forward traffic until the switch has had time to determine the state of the rest of the spanning tree. Specifically, a port must transition through the following three states:

- **Listening:** The port is blocked. However, the switch transmits and receives BPDUs to determine the state of the spanning tree. This state lasts 15 seconds by default.

- **Learning:** The port remains blocked and continues receiving and transmitting BPDUs. However, it also receives traffic and begins building a bridge table based on the source MAC addresses of the traffic it receives. This state lasts 15 seconds by default.

- **Forwarding:** If the switch determines that a port does not need to be blocked, it may begin forwarding traffic.

This process ensures that loops do not form when there is a topology change. However, if a failure occurs, all switches must go through the three states in the list. It takes at least 30 seconds for each switch to begin forwarding again. As far as network availability, this delay is generally too long for a recovery to occur.

Both proprietary and public-domain methods reduce the transition from blocking to forwarding. 802.1s, as mentioned earlier, enables specific types of switch ports to transition instantaneously, or nearly so. Basically, these shortcuts require careful planning. If a switch port is configured to expect a PC connected to it, and another switch is connected to the port instead, catastrophic temporary loops can form. Spanning tree is an elegant solution for networks to automatically adjust to topology changes.

At-a-Glance: Spanning Tree

Why Should I Care About Spanning Tree?

Designing a redundant network is one of the key methods of keeping your network available at all times. Unfortunately, this can cause loops in a Layer 2 network, which often results in serious problems, including a complete network shutdown.

STP prevents looping traffic in a redundantly switched/bridged network by allowing traffic through only a single path to other parts of the network. Any redundant paths are shut off until they are needed (typically when the primary link goes down).

What Problems Need to Be Solved?

To maintain the benefits of a redundant network while simultaneously preventing the problems associated with loops, the network must perform the following functions:

1. Recognize that a loop exists.

2. Designate one of the redundant links as primary and the other(s) as backup.

3. Switch traffic only through the primary link.

4. Check the health of both links at regular intervals.

5. In the event of a primary link failure, switch traffic to (one of) the backup link(s).

Problems with Loops

Although redundancy can prevent a single point of failure from causing the entire switched network to fail, it can also cause problems such as broadcast storms, multiple copies of frames, and MAC address table instability.

Broadcast Storms

A broadcast storm refers to the infinite flooding of frames. Broadcast storms can quickly shut down a network.

An example of a broadcast storm is shown here.

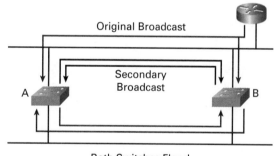

Both Switches Flood
the Broadcast

1. A broadcast frame is sent by another segment and is received by the top ports of switches A and B.

2. Both switches check the destination and flood the frame out to the bottom segment.

3. Both switches receive the frames on the bottom ports and flood copies to the top segment.

4. The switches have no way of knowing that the same frame is being sent repeatedly.

In a large switched network, multiple loops can exist. In networks such as this, the number of broadcast frames generated can grow exponentially in a matter of seconds. When this happens, the network becomes overwhelmed and ceases to function.

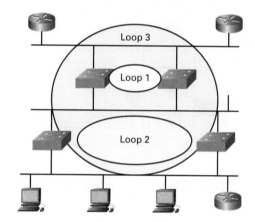

Multiple Copies of the Same Frame

Many protocols cannot correctly handle duplicate transmissions. In particular, protocols that use sequence numbering, such as TCP/IP, assume that the sequence has reached its maximum value and has begun to recycle the sequence. Other protocols process the duplicate frame with unpredictable results.

MAC Address Table Instability

A switch's MAC database becomes unstable if it receives the same frame on different ports. This can happen because of a transmission error, a hacking attempt (hackers try to spoof switches by pretending to be a valid workstation), or when loops exist.

At-a-Glance: Spanning Tree

In the figure, Host Q sends a frame to Router Y. Both switches also receive the frame on Port 0 and associate that port with Host Q. If the router's address is unknown, both switches flood the frame out port 1. The switches now receive the frame on port 1 and incorrectly associate host Q's MAC address with that port. This process repeats indefinitely.

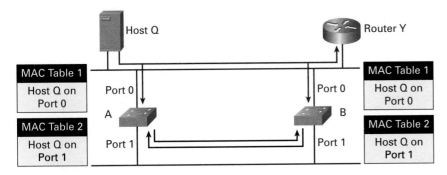

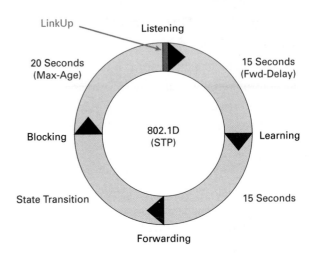

How Spanning Tree Works

Port Roles

Spanning tree works by assigning roles to switches and ports to ensure only one path through the switched network at any one time. The roles assigned are root bridge, root port, designated port, and nondesignated port. There is only one root bridge in any loop and only one designated port in any one segment. On the root bridge, all ports are designated.

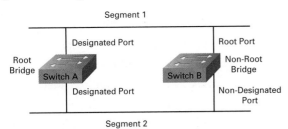

Port States

When a link goes down, spanning tree activates a previously blocked, redundant link. To avoid temporary loops while the network recalculates paths, the selection of the root bridge is based on either an assigned number or a random number such as a MAC address, which is arbitrary. Switches avoid sending traffic until the network converges on the new information. At any given time, all switch ports are in one of the four states shown in blue.

Every port must go through this sequence before it can be set to the forwarding (traffic-passing) state. This process can take up to 50 seconds (a very long period in switch time). The figure shows the time required for each step in turning on new paths. In situations in which it is critical to have instantaneous failovers, tools are available that allow the switch port to immediately go from the blocking state to the forwarding state.

On the root bridge, all ports are set to the forwarding state. For the nonroot bridge, only the root port is set to the forwarding state.

Assessing the Health of Links

Switches running spanning tree exchange information with a BPDU, sent at regular intervals. This message is basically an "I'm alive" message informing the switches that the active path is still operational.

At-a-Glance: Spanning Tree

Recalculating Paths

When a link fails, the network topology must change. Connectivity is reestablished by placing key blocked ports in the forwarding state. For example, if the BPDU is not received after a timer expires, spanning tree begins recalculating the network. In the figure, Switch B is now the root bridge.

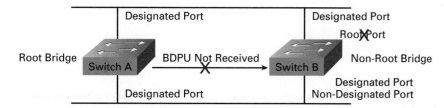

Looking again at the diagram in the "Port States" section, spanning tree can take up to 50 seconds to converge. However, emerging real-time applications such as voice and video cannot tolerate such a delay. RSTP is the answer to this problem, because it is not a timer-based protocol, and it can converge much faster than 802.1d (STP).

RSTP significantly speeds up the recalculation process after a topology change occurs in the network. RSTP works by designating an alternative port and a backup port. These ports are allowed to immediately enter the forwarding state rather than passively waiting for the network to converge. Edge port and link type are new variables defined in RSTP. It is important to know that, if you use RSTP, situations could occur in which loops temporarily exist in networks (it takes only seconds for things to get out of control). It's all about making trade-offs.

Reflections on Spanning Tree

I think that I shall never see a graph more lovely than a tree. A tree whose crucial property is loop-free connectivity. A tree that must be sure to span so packets can reach every LAN. First, the root must be selected; by ID, it is elected. Least-cost paths from root are traced; in the tree these paths are placed. A mesh is made by folks like me, then bridges find a spanning tree.

—Radia Perlman, the inventor of spanning tree

Routing

Routers

Whereas switches and bridges operate at OSI Layer 2 (the data link layer), *routers* primarily operate at OSI Layer 3 (the network layer). Like bridging, the primary act of routing involves moving packets across a network from a source to a destination. The difference involves the information that is used to make the forwarding decisions. Routers make decisions based on network layer protocols such as Internet Protocol (IP) and Novell NetWare Internetwork Packet Exchange (IPX).

Routing gained popularity in the mid- to late 1980s as a result of internetworks growing beyond the capability of bridges. Before this popularity, networks were relatively small and isolated, and bridges could handle the jobs of forwarding and segmentation. However, as networks grew, routers facilitated larger scaling and more intelligent growth across wider physical distances. Although routers are more expensive and complex than bridges, routing is the core of the Internet today.

Routers Talk Among Themselves to Find Routes

Routing involves two processes: determining optimal routing paths through a network, and forwarding packets along those paths. Routing algorithms make the optimal path determination. As they determine routes, tables on the router store the information. Routers communicate with each other and maintain their routing tables through the exchange of messages over the network. Routing updates are one particular type of message. A *routing update* contains all or part of another router's routing table and allows each router to build a detailed picture of the overall network topology.

Routing algorithms fill routing tables with various types of information. The primary piece of information relevant to routing is the *next hop*. Next-hop associations tell a router that it can reach a particular destination by sending a packet to a particular router representing the next hop on the way to its final destination.

The process of exchanging information between routers is done using a routing protocol. Put simply, a routing protocol is a series of messages that routers use to exchange information about whether particular links are up or down, and about other next-hop routers in the network. Three of the most common routing protocols in use today are Open Shortest Path First (OSPF), Enhanced Interior Gateway Routing Protocol (EIGRP), and Border Gateway Protocol (BGP).

Routers Route Packets

When a router receives a packet, it attempts to associate the destination network address in the packet to an appropriate next hop in its routing table. In addition to next-hop associations, routers store other pertinent information in routing tables. For multiple paths to a destination, a routing table might contain information that allows the router to determine the desirability of one path over another.

After a router determines an optimal path for a packet, it must forward the packet toward the destination. The process of a router moving a packet from its received port to the outgoing destination port is called *switching*. Although the process of switching a packet on a router is similar to that of a Layer 2 switch, the decision criteria and the actual handling of the packet are different. When a computer determines that it must send a packet to another host, it specifies in the packet how to reach the destination network. If the destination is unknown, the router typically drops the packet. If the destination is known, the router changes the destination physical address in the packet to contain that of the next hop. The router then transmits the packet out the destination interface.

The next hop can be either the final destination or another router. Each router in the process performs the same operation. As the packet moves through the network, each router modifies the physical address stored in the packet but leaves the network address untouched (because it determines the final destination).

Routers Bridge and Switches Route

In an ideal world, everything does what it is defined to do. This is not the case with network devices. Routers can provide bridging functionality, and switches are quickly becoming the high-density port, high-speed router of the campus. Network devices, including switches and routers, make forwarding decisions on OSI layers higher than the network layer. For example, routers can provide firewall functionality in which the router inspects Layer 4 packet information, and switches such as content switches can perform forwarding decisions based on Layer 5 through 7 packet information (such as the URL in an HTTP packet).

At-a-Glance: Routing

Why Should I Care About Routing?

Routing is one of the fundamental aspects of networking. Routers can learn possible routes (rather than having to have the route manually configured and constantly updated). This is one of the primary reasons that ARPANET, which originally connected seven sites, was able to scale exponentially into the modern Internet in only a few years. Many routers today have address tables with more than 100,000 entries, and they are updated constantly.

What Problems Need to Be Solved?

Routed networks are often large and complex, and it would be prohibitively difficult to manage and update network information on all routers all the time. To account for this, several algorithms have been developed. These algorithms allow the routers to learn about the network and then make decisions based on that information.

To learn paths (or routes) through a network and then decide where to send packets, a router must know the following information:

- **Destination address:** This is typically the IP address of the data's (packet) destination.

- **Source address:** The router also needs to know where the information came from (typically an IP address).

- **Possible routes:** These are likely routes that can get information from the present location or source to some other location (the destination or closest known point).

- **Best route:** Routers also must know the best ("best" can mean many things) path to the intended destination.

- **Status of routes:** Routers also keep track of the current state of routes to ensure timely delivery of information.

What Exactly Does "Best" Mean?

Routers often make decisions about the best possible path to get information from a source to a destination. "Best" is loosely defined; it depends on what the network values. These measurements of value are called metrics. The network administrator determines which metrics the network values. Here are several metrics:

- **Hop count:** How many times a packet goes through a router.

- **Delay:** The amount of time required to reach the destination.

- **Reliability:** The bit error rate of each network link.

- **Maximum Transmission Unit (MTU):** The maximum message length (or packet size) allowed on the path.

- **Cost:** An arbitrary value based on a network administrator-determined value. Usually some combination of other metrics.

Static Versus Dynamic

Routers must learn about the network around them to determine where to send packets. This information can be either manually entered (static routes) or learned from other routers in the network (dynamic routes):

- **Static routes:** When a network administrator manually enters information about a route, it is considered a static route. This information can be changed only by a network administrator (in other words, the router doesn't learn about network events). Static routes allow for tight control of packets but become difficult to maintain and are prone to human error. However, static routes may be used to work around a temporary problem or for performance enhancement.

- **Dynamic routes:** Routers on a network can learn about possible routes and current route status from other routers in the network. Routes learned in this way are called dynamic routes. Unlike static routes, any changes in the network are learned without administrative intervention and are automatically propagated throughout the network.

Flat Versus Hierarchical

With flat networks, all routers must keep track of all other routers on the network. As networks grow, the amount of information contained in the routing tables becomes larger and larger.

At-a-Glance: Routing

Although this method is simple, it can result in poor network performance as the number of routing updates grows exponentially with each new router.

Hierarchical networks segment routers into logical groupings. This simplifies routing tables and greatly reduces overheard traffic.

Intradomain Versus Interdomain

Intradomain and interdomain routing can be easily understood in the context of large-scale hierarchical networks. In this regard, think of each segment as its own autonomous network. Within each autonomous network, intradomain routing protocols (also called Interior Gateway Protocols [IGP]) are used to exchange routing information and forward packets. Interdomain routing protocols (also called Exterior Gateway Protocols [EGP]) are used between autonomous networks. This distinction is made because there are different performance requirements for internal and external networks.

Distance Vector Versus Link-State

The two main classes of routing are distance vector routing and link-state routing.

With distance vector routing, also called "routing by rumor," routers share their routing table information with each other. Each router provides and receives updates from its direct neighbor. In the figure, Router B shares information with Routers A and C. Router C shares routing information with Routers B and D. A distance vector describes the direction (port) and the distance (number of hops or other metric) to some other router. When a router receives information from another router, it increments whatever metric is being used. This process is called distance accumulation. Routers using this method know the distance between any two points in the network, but they do not know the exact topology of an internetwork.

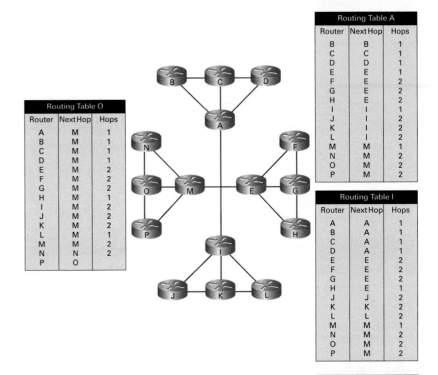

Routing Table A

Router	Next Hop	Hops
B	B	1
C	C	1
D	D	1
E	E	1
F	E	2
G	E	2
H	E	2
I	I	1
J	I	2
K	I	2
L	I	2
M	M	1
N	M	2
O	M	2
P	M	2

Routing Table O

Router	Next Hop	Hops
A	M	1
B	M	1
C	M	1
D	M	1
E	M	2
F	M	2
G	M	2
H	M	1
I	M	2
J	M	2
K	M	2
L	M	1
M	M	2
N	N	
P	O	

Routing Table I

Router	Next Hop	Hops
A	A	1
B	A	1
C	A	1
D	A	1
E	E	2
F	E	2
G	E	2
H	E	1
J	J	2
K	K	2
L	L	1
M	M	2
N	M	2
O	M	2
P	M	2

Routing Table A1

Router	Next	Hops
A2	A2	1
A3	A3	1
A4	A4	1
Any B	B1	1
Any C	B2	1
Any D	B3	1

Routing Table D3

Router	Next	Hops
D1	D1	1
D2	D2	1
D4	D4	1
All Others	D1	1

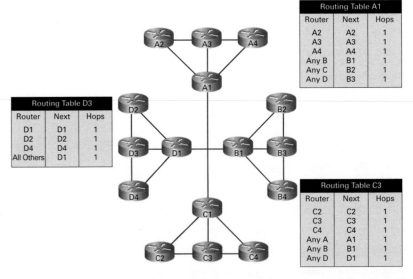

Routing Table C3

Router	Next	Hops
C2	C2	1
C3	C3	1
C4	C4	1
Any A	A1	1
Any B	B1	1
Any D	D1	1

At-a-Glance: Routing

How Information Is Discovered with Distance Vectors

Network discovery is the process of learning about nondirectly connected routers. During network discovery, routers accumulate metrics and learn the best paths to various destinations in the network. In the figure, each directly connected network has a distance of 0. Router A learns about other networks based on information it receives from Router B. Routers increment the distance metric for any route learned by an adjacent router. In other words, Router A increments by 1 any distance information it learns about other routers from Router B.

As more time goes by, the router learns more about the network and can process packets more efficiently.

Link-State Routing

With link-state routing (also known as shortest path first [SPF]), each router maintains a database of topology information for the entire network.

Link-state routing provides better scaling than distance-vector routing, because it sends updates only when there is a change in the network, and then it sends only information specific to the change that occurred. Distance vector uses regular updates and sends the whole routing table every time. Link-state routing also uses a hierarchical model, limiting the scope of route changes that occur.

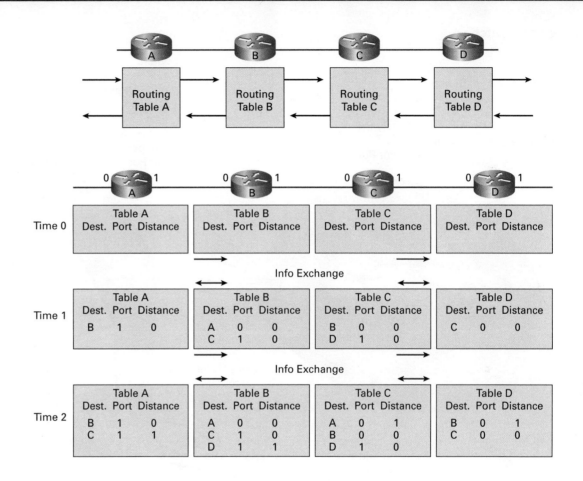

Routing and Switching

Routers and Switches

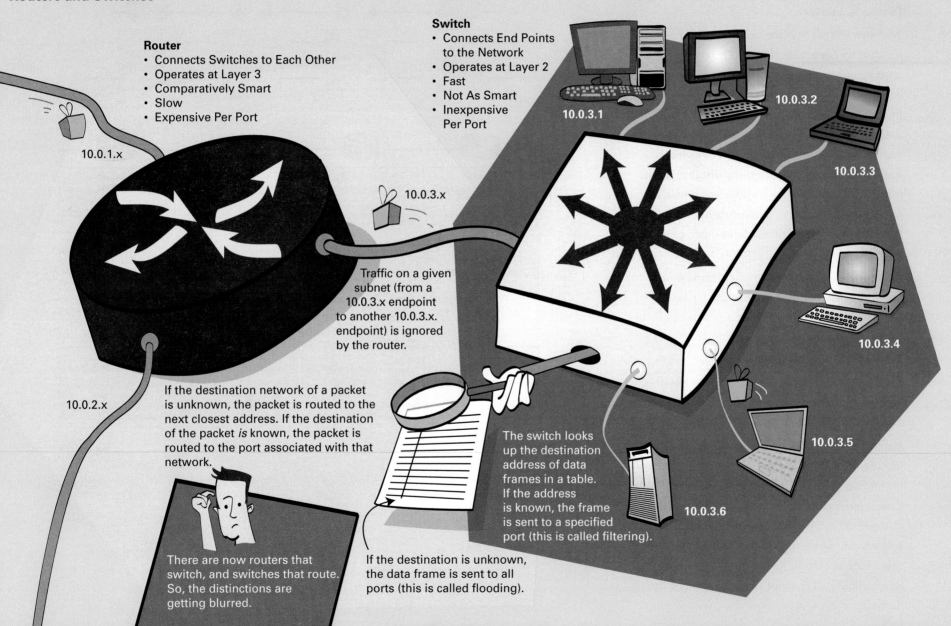

Router
- Connects Switches to Each Other
- Operates at Layer 3
- Comparatively Smart
- Slow
- Expensive Per Port

Switch
- Connects End Points to the Network
- Operates at Layer 2
- Fast
- Not As Smart
- Inexpensive Per Port

10.0.1.x

10.0.3.x

10.0.2.x

10.0.3.1

10.0.3.2

10.0.3.3

10.0.3.4

10.0.3.5

10.0.3.6

Traffic on a given subnet (from a 10.0.3.x endpoint to another 10.0.3.x. endpoint) is ignored by the router.

If the destination network of a packet is unknown, the packet is routed to the next closest address. If the destination of the packet *is* known, the packet is routed to the port associated with that network.

The switch looks up the destination address of data frames in a table. If the address is known, the frame is sent to a specified port (this is called filtering).

There are now routers that switch, and switches that route. So, the distinctions are getting blurred.

If the destination is unknown, the data frame is sent to all ports (this is called flooding).

Routing and Switching

Connectivity

Router
- Connects Switches to Each Other
- Connects Buildings

Switch
- Connects Devices Together Quickly
- Connects End Points to the Network

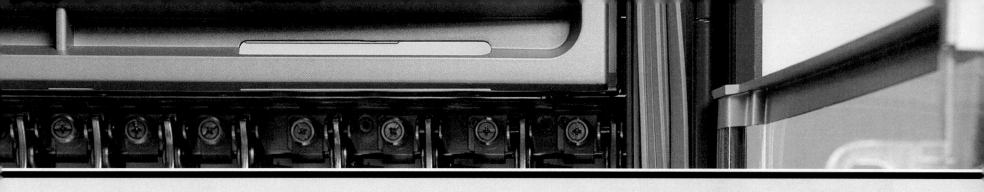

Part III

Network Design

Parts I and II looked at how computers communicate, with the OSI model as well as switching and routing protocols. The good news is that pretty much anything you put on a network is covered by these principles, so all a designer has to do is apply them. The bad news is that the networks can get big—make that very big, as in tens of thousands of routers and switches connecting hundreds of thousands of devices.

To ensure that the network can continue to operate on a massive scale, some good design practices must be put into place. Part III covers some of these principles, which almost always apply to enterprise-scale networks.

The first thing we need to design is the main campus or headquarters network. "Campus Networks and Hierarchical Design" shows you how a local network is constructed for a large company.

As soon as the main campus network is up and running, a company will likely want to communicate with other smaller sites using wide-area networks (WAN). "WAN Network Design" covers a number of WAN technologies, including Frame Relay, Asynchronous Transfer Mode (ATM), and MPLS.

We also explore broadband technologies. With the advent of high-speed Internet, many enterprise employees can telecommute without losing access to their enterprise applications. This section shows how ISDN, cable, and DSL work. Wireless is also a consideration here, but we'll save the wireless discussion for later in this book.

We close the WAN discussion with the section "Optical Technologies." Optical technologies use light signals rather than electrical impulses, which creates a different set of challenges to overcome. Optical is becoming increasingly popular because of its incredible bandwidth, so it's worth looking at (no pun intended).

Finally, you want the data you send over the WAN to go somewhere, and that somewhere is often a branch office. At one time branch offices were often handled with nothing more than a router supported by a local "IT guy." Today, branch offices are often as complicated as headquarters networks, with some interesting challenges as far as data and application access.

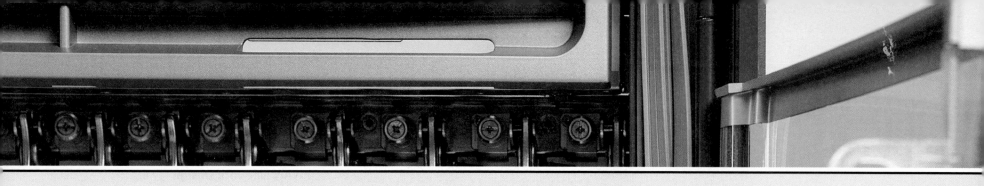

Campus Networks and Hierarchical Design

Building Networks for Ease of Use

Campus, as it applies to networking, typically describes the routers, switches, network appliances, and servers that make up the networking infrastructure for a set of buildings located in close proximity. A campus can be the manufacturing site of a large corporation, the headquarters for a bank, or a college campus.

A design goal for campus networks is to separate buildings, floors, workgroups, and server farms into smaller Layer 3 groups to prevent network faults from affecting large populations of users. Layer 3 routers provide natural boundaries against debilitating network problems such as broadcast storms and loops. Over time, the hierarchical approach to network design has proven the most effective. The three primary layers of a hierarchical campus are as follows:

- **Core (sometimes called the backbone):** The core is the central thoroughfare for corporate traffic. All other parts of the network eventually feed into the core. You should design the core to switch packets as quickly as possible. This level should not include operations that might slow the switching of the packet: The distribution layer should handle any packet manipulation or filtering that needs to occur.

- **Distribution:** The distribution layer provides policy-based connectivity and boundaries between the access layers and the core. For example, a building of 20 floors might have a distribution network that connects each floor with the core. It is at this layer that packets should be filtered or manipulated. Therefore, as soon as packets are "prepped," the core simply needs to switch them quickly to the destination distribution location.

- **Access:** The access layer provides user access to the network. It is at this point that users are permitted (or denied) access into the corporate network. Typically, each person sitting at a desk has a cable that runs to a wiring closet and connects to a switch; hence, this level is where the user accesses the network.

If these layers are a little hard to follow, think of them as you would a national mail system. Access is like your local post office, where everyone first "connects" to send their letters. Distribution is like a regional mail center that receives mail from lots of neighborhood post offices, sorting and prepping them to move on in the mail system. Some local mail may be routed within the region, back to local post offices in the next town. Others may need to go cross-country to other regional mail centers. The core is like the backbone shipping network between postal regions. It carries mail from state to state in large shipping containers, such as trucks and planes. It must be fast, efficient, and able to handle large capacity.

The distribution and core layers of the network provide vital services by aggregating groups of users and services. Therefore, if a distribution or core device dies, this can affect large communities of users. For this reason, reducing the chance of failure in these layers reduces and possibly prevents unnecessary and unplanned outages. Redundant network paths, redundant hardware, and fault-tolerant-related network protocols (such as Hot Standby Router Protocol [HSRP]) all help a network recover quickly (and hopefully transparently to the users) after a failure.

Companies prefer to reduce the number of routed protocols traversing the core layer. In the early 1990s, before the massive popularity of TCP/IP and the Internet, backbones carried the predominant protocols of the day: Novell, DECnet, AppleTalk, NetBIOS, and Banyan VINES. Having so many protocols complicated design issues. As TCP/IP became the de facto networking protocol, companies worked to eliminate the non-IP traffic from the core.

At-a-Glance: Hierarchical Campus Design

Why Should I Care About Campus Design?

Campus networks represent an enormous investment for businesses. When correctly designed, a campus network can enhance business efficiency and lower operational cost. Additionally, a properly designed network can position a business for future growth.

A modular or hierarchal network is made from building blocks that are easier to replicate, redesign, and grow. Each time a module is added or removed, there shouldn't be a need to redesign the whole network. Distinct blocks can be put into and out of service without impacting other blocks or the network core. This greatly enhances troubleshooting, isolating problems, and network management.

The hierarchy consists of three functional divisions (or layers): the core, distribution, and access layers:

- The access layer provides the first level of access to the network. Layer 2 switching, security, and quality of service (QoS) happen at this layer.

- The distribution layer aggregates wiring closets and provides policy enforcement. When Layer 3 protocols are used at this layer, benefits such as load balancing, fast convergence, and scalability are realized. This layer also provides default gateway redundancy to end stations.

- The core is the backbone of the network. This layer is designed to be fast-converging, highly reliable, and stable. Also designed with Layer 3 protocols, the core provides load balancing, fast convergence, and scalability.

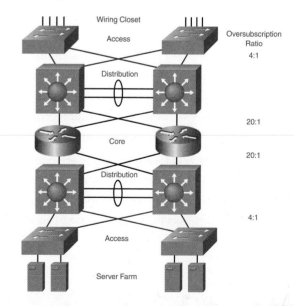

At-a-Glance: Hierarchical Campus Design

Campus Design Best Practices

High Availability

High availability refers to the network's ability to recover from different types of failures. High availability should be designed in at many layers. With a sound design, network stability is easily achieved, troubleshooting is made easier, and human error is reduced.

- **Layer 1:** Redundant links and hardware provide alternative physical paths through the network.
- **Layers 2 and 3:** Protocols such as spanning tree, HSRP, and others provide alternative path awareness and fast convergence.
- **Application availability:** The application server and client processes must support failover for maximum availability.

Oversubscription

Oversubscription occurs when there are more traffic-generating endpoints than the network can accommodate at a single time. Most networks are built with some amount of oversubscription. For example, the Public Switched Telephone Network (PSTN) is not designed for everyone to make a call at the same time. It is assumed that only a certain percentage of people need to make calls at one time. (Mother's Day in the U.S. is by far the single busiest day for the PSTN.)

In the preceding figure, the network has 20:1 oversubscription from access to distribution and 4:1 oversubscription from distribution to core. QoS should be used to ensure that real-time traffic such as voice and video, or critical data such as SAP traffic, is not dropped or delayed.

Redundancy

Redundancy is a key part of designing a highly available network. However, although some redundancy is good, too much can actually be bad for a network. Issues with convergence (the network's ability to recover from a bad link) can result. Too much redundancy can also make troubleshooting and management difficult.

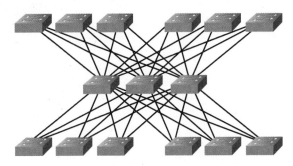

This figure shows an example of redundancy gone wrong.

Campus Size Design Considerations

Size really does matter. Some general rules of thumb are listed for various campus sizes.

Small Campus

The figure shows the recommended design for a campus with fewer than 200 edge ports. This design collapses the core and distribution into one layer, which limits scaling to a few access switches.

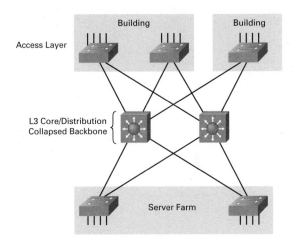

At-a-Glance: Hierarchical Campus Design

Medium Campus

This design is recommended for campuses with 200 to 1000 ports. A separate distribution layer allows for future growth. A redundant core ensures high availability and allows equal-cost paths.

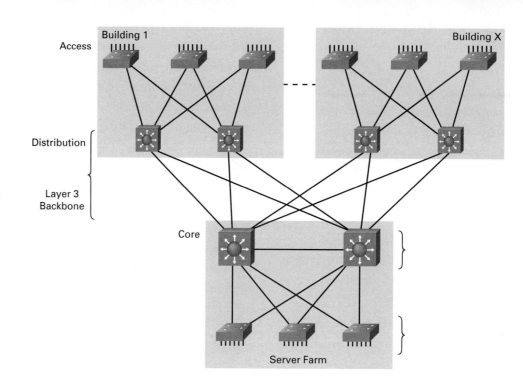

At-a-Glance: Hierarchical Campus Design

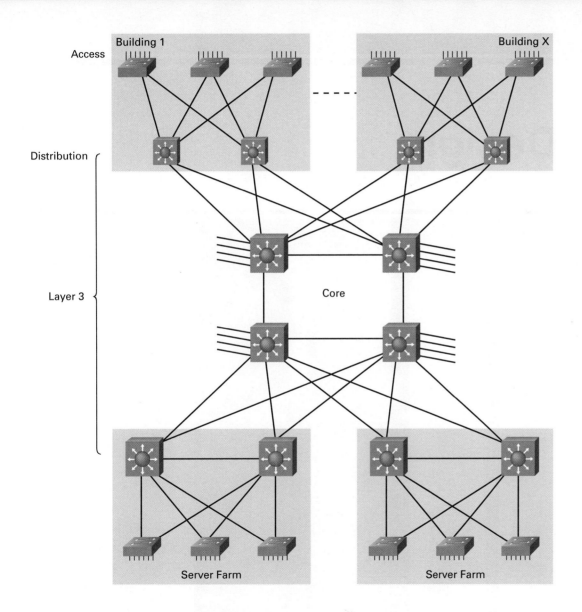

Large Campus

This is a very high-performance design for campuses with more than 1000 ports or for those seeking cutting-edge design. A feature-rich core aggregates many distribution switches.

Additional buildings and server farms can be easily added anytime.

Campus Services

Services such as QoS, IP Multicast, and security must also be carefully considered in any campus design strategy. These topics are covered in depth elsewhere in this book.

WAN Network Design

Moving Traffic Across the Street and the World

How does a company connect the network in its New York office to the network in its Los Angeles office? It doesn't make sense to run a private cable across the U.S. Instead, the company subscribes to wide-area services. A *wide-area network (WAN)* is a network that covers a broad geographic area and often uses transmission facilities provided by service providers. WAN functionality occurs at Layers 1 to 3 in the Open Systems Interconnection (OSI) reference model.

The bicoastal company just mentioned would contact its service provider to purchase WAN connectivity between the offices. WAN services are leased from service providers that charge either a monthly flat fee or fees based on the amount of data transmitted. The more bandwidth required for a WAN circuit, the greater the usage charges are. Service providers can use a single national network to provide WAN services for many different corporate customers. In this way it is not necessary for each company to physically connect every office to every other office. Imagine the cross-country cables involved in connecting just one large company, let alone thousands.

WAN Services

Three types of transport are used with WANs:

- **Point-to-point:** Also known as leased line, a point-to-point connection is a pre-established link from one site, across a service provider's network, to a remote site. The carrier establishes the point-to-point link for the customer's private use.

- **Circuit switching:** A service provider establishes a dedicated physical circuit into a carrier network for two or more connections. Unlike point-to-point, which has exactly two sites connected to a single connection, multiple sites privately connect into a carrier's switched network to communicate with each other. Circuit switching operates like a normal telephone call. ISDN is an example of circuit-switched WAN technology.

- **Packet switching:** This type of transport is similar to circuit switching in that multiple sites privately connect into a carrier-switched network.

However, packet switching involves the statistical multiplexing of packets across shared circuits. Frame Relay, Multiprotocol Label Switching (MPLS), broadband DSL and cable, and Metro Ethernet are all examples of packet switching.

Some WAN technologies, such as Frame Relay and Asynchronous Transfer Mode (ATM), use *virtual circuits* to ensure reliable communication between two network devices. The two types of virtual circuits are *switched virtual circuits (SVC)* and *permanent virtual circuits (PVC)*. An SVC is dynamically established on demand and is torn down when transmission is complete. A connection uses SVCs when data transmission between devices is sporadic. A PVC is a permanently established logical circuit and is useful for connections between two devices in which data transfer is constant.

WAN dialup services are available as alternative backup technologies for traditional WAN services. As the name implies, dialup services use plain old telephone service (POTS) and are inexpensive (but relatively slow) alternatives when the main WAN service goes down. Cisco routers offer two popular types of dialup services: *dial-on-demand routing (DDR)* and *dial backup*. DDR can be triggered automatically when the primary connection goes down or when a traffic threshold is reached. Dial backup initiates a dial connection to another router after it determines that the primary WAN service is unavailable. The dial connection remains active until the WAN service returns.

Integrated Services Digital Network

Integrated Services Digital Network (ISDN) is a set of technologies developed to carry voice, video, and data across telephone networks. ISDN operates at Layers 1 to 3 in the OSI reference model. ISDN was the first broadband service deployed in the home. It operated at two to four times the speed of the modem technologies of the day and provided "always-on" connectivity compared to modem dialup. For many years ISDN received a lot of hype that it never quite lived up to. Eventually it was dealt a death blow as far as home use with the advent of DSL and high-speed cable services. However, it is still in use in some businesses, so it's worth a quick look here.

Frame Relay

Frame Relay is a packet-switched WAN service that operates at the physical and logical layers of the OSI reference model. Frame Relay was originally designed to operate over ISDN but today operates over a variety of network interfaces. Typical communication speeds for Frame Relay are between 56 kbps and 2 Mbps (although lower and higher speeds are supported). Frame Relay provides connection-oriented services using virtual circuits. A Frame Relay virtual circuit is a logical connection between two data terminal equipment (DTE) devices across a Frame Relay packet-switched network. A data-link connection identifier (DLCI) uniquely identifies each virtual circuit. You can multiplex multiple virtual circuits on a single physical circuit.

Frame Relay switched networks provide simple congestion-notification mechanisms. Frame Relay switching equipment can mark a Frame Relay packet with front-end congestion notification (FECN) or back-end congestion notification (BECN). The equipment marks the packets with a FECN or BECN if congestion occurs during the transmission of the packet. The DTE equipment at the other end of a circuit notices whether a packet has experienced congestion and notifies a higher layer that congestion has occurred. Additionally, the equipment can mark a packet as discard eligible (DE) to indicate that it is less important, which means that it can be dropped if congestion occurs.

ATM

ATM is a standard for cell-based relay that carries voice, video, and data in small, fixed-size cells. ATM networks are connection-oriented networks that combine the benefits of circuit switching (guaranteed capacity and constant transmission delay) with those of packet switching (flexibility and efficiency for intermittent traffic). ATM transmits at speeds from a few Mbps to many Gbps.

High-speed ATM circuits typically require optic-fiber cables to transmit such high speeds. Speeds of these circuits are characterized as "Optical Carrier" class and are represented as OC-*number*. The number represents the multiple of the base OC-1 standard circuit, which can carry 51.84 Mbps. Common circuit speeds are OC-3 (155.52 Mbps), OC-12 (622.08 Mbps), and OC-192 (9953.28 Mbps, or roughly 10 Gbps).

Traditional circuit-based networks use time-division multiplexing (TDM), in which users are assigned a predetermined time slot; no other device can transmit during this time slot. If a station has a lot of data to send, it can transmit only during its time slot, even if the other time slots are empty. Conversely, if the station has nothing to transmit, the time slot is sent empty and is wasted. This arrangement is called *synchronous transmission*.

ATM is asynchronous, meaning that time slots are available on demand. This allows for a more efficient use of available bandwidth. ATM uses single-sized cells (as opposed to the variable-sized frames in Frame Relay), which have 53 bytes. Computers usually define things in powers of 2 or 8. The 53-byte cell size represents a compromise between the phone-standards folks and the data-standards folks.

ATM networks have two devices: ATM switches and ATM endpoints. ATM switches accept cells from an endpoint or another switch, evaluate the cell header, and quickly forward the cell out another interface toward the destination. An ATM endpoint contains an ATM network interface adapter and is responsible for converting digital data into cells and back again. Examples of ATM endpoints include workstations, LAN switches, routers, and video coder-decoders (codecs).

ATM networks can mark traffic after it is converted from its original data format to require different types of handling. Some traffic, such as voice and video, must be transferred through the network at regular intervals with little variation in delay. Otherwise, the destination receives low-quality voice or video transmission. Data traffic is less sensitive to network delays and can be handled differently.

To ensure the appropriate delivery for each of these traffic types, ATM devices employ QoS mechanisms that involve reserving bandwidth, shaping traffic to meet the reserved bandwidth, and policing traffic that exceeds the reservation.

MPLS

MPLS is a highly efficient WAN service that companies are quickly adopting either as a replacement for legacy Frame Relay and ATM WANs or as a second high-speed WAN service. MPLS is discussed in more depth in a later section.

Broadband

Increasingly, companies are leveraging cable, DSL, and other types of broadband Internet services to deploy WAN services. They offer low-cost, high-bandwidth connectivity that is often suitable for small branch office locations, such as retail stores, small insurance office branches, and gas stations and convenience stores. Broadband services are discussed in more depth in a later section.

Virtual Private Networks (VPN)

A VPN is a secured connection between two devices over a shared, unsecured network. VPNs have been used for some time for mobile devices such as laptops to connect to their corporate headquarters over the Internet. This is typically called a remote-access VPN. Encryption provides security so that no one else on the Internet can eavesdrop on the data being sent back and forth. Increasingly, companies are taking advantage of VPNs to also connect branch offices to headquarters locations over the Internet, called a site-to-site VPN. Site-to-site VPNs can be a very cost-effective way to connect relatively small locations to corporate headquarters over Internet services, such as broadband cable and DSL. VPNs are also used to some degree to authenticate users to local access points in a wireless environment. VPNs are addressed in a bit more depth in a later section.

WAN Devices

Numerous types of devices are associated with WAN service delivery. The first is a WAN switch. Usually located in a carrier's network, a WAN switch is a multiport internetworking device whose job is moving traffic from source to destination. Routers at the customer sites attach to the edges of the carrier's switched network (for Frame Relay and ATM). WAN switches operate at Layer 2, the data link layer, of the OSI model.

For many packet-switched services, often a WAN router is used at both the access location, often called the Customer Premises Equipment (CPE), and the nearest connectivity location of the WAN service provider, often called the Point of Presence (PoP). Modern packet-switched services, such as MPLS, broadband, and the Internet, rely on very large, very high-speed routers to route traffic across the service provider network between PoPs. These routers form the backbone of the modern Internet and global WAN connectivity services and are sometimes called core routers. Routers sitting at the edges of the network, providing WAN access to businesses, are often called edge routers.

At-a-Glance: Frame Relay

Why Should I Care About Frame Relay?

Frame Relay is one of the predominant WAN transport methods for connecting remote sites because of its relative cost and reliability. It is on the decline as IP-based networks expand their reach. Still, whenever two or more locations must have data connectivity, Frame Relay is an option.

Frame Relay offers known performance and manageability and is the most common mode of private network connectivity.

What Problems Need to Be Solved?

Frame Relay is a connection-oriented Layer 2 protocol that allows several data connections (virtual circuits) to be multiplexed onto a single physical link. Error correction and flow control are often performed by the higher-layer protocols, so the primary consideration for Frame Relay is establishing connections between customer equipment.

A connection identifier is used to map packets to outbound ports on the service provider's switch. When the switch receives a frame, a lookup table is used to map the frame to the correct outbound port. The entire path to the destination is determined before the frame is sent.

Frame Relay only specifies the connection between a router and a service provider's local access switching equipment. The data transmission within the service provider's Frame Relay cloud is not specified.

Frame Relay Equipment

Two general categories of Frame Relay equipment are data terminal equipment (DTE) and data communications equipment (DCE).

DTE is the terminating equipment used by companies or organizations using Frame Relay connections. DTE is typically located on the customer premises. DTE can be owned by the customer or rented by the Frame Relay provider. Examples of DTE devices are terminals, PCs, routers, and bridges.

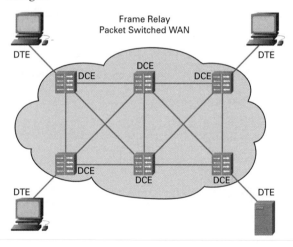

Frame Relay Packet Switched WAN

DCEs are carrier-owned internetworking devices. DCEs provide clocking and switching services in a network.

The connection between a DTE device and a DCE device consists of a physical layer component and a link layer component. The physical component defines the mechanical, electrical, functional, and procedural specifications for the connection between the devices. One of the most commonly used physical layer interface specifications is the recommended standard EIA/TIA-232 specification. The link layer component defines the protocol that establishes the connection between the DTE device, such as a router, and the DCE device, such as a switch.

Virtual Circuits

Frame Relay connections are established using logical connections called virtual circuits. Virtual circuits can pass through several DCE devices throughout the Frame Relay Packet-Switched Network (PSN). Several virtual circuits can be multiplexed into a single physical circuit for transmission across the network. The two types of virtual circuits are switched virtual circuits (SVC) and permanent virtual circuits (PVC).

Switched Virtual Circuit (SVC)

An SVC is a temporary connection used for sporadic data transfer between DTE devices across the Frame Relay network.

SVC sessions have four distinct operational states: Call Setup, Data Transfer, Idle, and Call Termination.

If the connection is Idle for some predetermined amount of time, the connection is terminated. After termination, a new call must be established for data to flow again.

At-a-Glance: Frame Relay

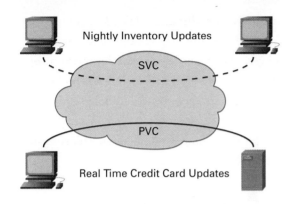

Nightly Inventory Updates

SVC

PVC

Real Time Credit Card Updates

Permanent Virtual Circuit (PVC)

A PVC is an established connection that remains up at all times. PVCs should be used when frequent and consistent data transfer occurs between DTE devices.

With PVCs, no call setups or termination procedures are required. The operational states are Data Transfer and Idle.

PVCs are almost always chosen over SVC because of the management overhead requirements of SVC and the limited advantages over PVCs.

Local Management Interface (LMI)

LMI is a signaling standard used to manage a connection between a router and a Frame Relay switch. LMIs track and manage keepalive mechanisms, multicast messages, and status.

Data Link Connection Identifier

Frame Relay virtual circuits are identified by data-link connection identifiers (DLCI). DLCI values

typically are assigned by the Frame Relay service provider.

Frame Relay DLCIs are of local significance only. In other words, the DLCI values are unique only at the endpoints, not over WANs. Therefore, two DTE devices connected by a virtual circuit might use a different DLCI value to refer to the same connection.

In addition, two DTEs can be connected on the same virtual circuit but still have different DLCIs. The following figure shows how a single virtual circuit might be assigned a different DLCI value on each end of the connection.

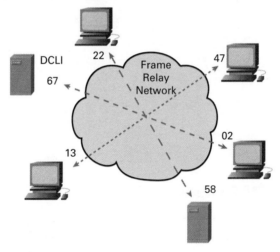

DCLI 22   47

67   Frame
            Relay
            Network

13   02

            58

Congestion Notification

Frame Relay reduces network overhead by implementing simple congestion notification mechanisms.

Frame Relay uses two methods of congestion notification: Forward Explicit Congestion Notification (FECN) and Backward Explicit Congestion Notification (BECN).

FECN sends a message to the destination device when a Frame Relay switch senses congestion in the network. A DTE device receiving this message can relay this information to a higher-layer protocol for processing. In turn, the protocol can initiate flow control or simply ignore the message.

BECN sends a message to the source router when a Frame Relay switch senses congestion in the network. A BECN message requests a reduced data transmission rate. BECN messages are also relayed to the higher-layer protocols, which can initiate some form of flow control, or traffic shaping. In some cases, the higher-layer protocols ignore BECN messages.

Performance

Frame Relay is often used for connections up to 1.5 Mbps. Because of the wide expansion of IP availability, Frame Relay typically is installed to connect remote sites to the network.

At-a-Glance: Asynchronous Transfer Mode (ATM)

Why Should I Care About ATM?

Asynchronous Transfer Mode (ATM) is one of the primary Layer 2 WAN transport protocols. Originally developed as high-speed public WAN transport for voice, video, and data, ATM was later modified by the ATM Forum to include transport over private networks. Although LAN implementations of ATM have never been popular (because of the explosion of Ethernet's popularity), use of ATM on WANs is widespread. This application, however, is also being challenged by Ethernet-based WANs.

What Problems Need to Be Solved?

ATM faces the same problems as the other Layer 2 transport protocols—namely, the establishment of connections and the format of the information.

ATM was developed before the availability of QoS and traffic engineering. When it was developed, it was one of the only protocols that could provide differentiated service for customers or traffic types.

ATM Devices

ATM networks are made up of ATM switches and ATM endpoints. ATM switches are responsible for moving cells through the ATM network. ATM endpoints (including workstations, routers, data service units (DSU), LAN switches, and video codecs, all require an ATM interface adapter to access the ATM network.

ATM Network Interfaces

ATM networks are composed of ATM switches interconnected by point-to-point ATM links. The links connecting the switches come in two forms. User-network interfaces (UNI) connect ATM endpoints to ATM switches. Network Node Interfaces (NNI) connect ATM switches together.

UNIs and NNIs can be further classified by the type of network the switch resides in (public or private). The figure shows examples of several interfaces.

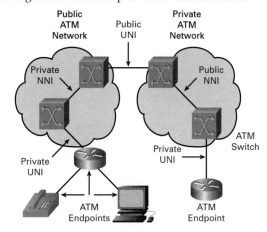

ATM Features

ATM implements two features that make it both useful and interesting (well, interesting in a network geek kind of way). The two concepts are asynchronous transmission and fixed cell size.

Asynchronous Transmission

The Asynchronous part of ATM refers to the protocol's ability to use a more efficient version of

time-division multiplexing (TDM). Multiplexing is a method of combining multiple data streams onto a single physical or logical connection. Time division means that each data stream has an assigned slot in a repeating sequence. Although this is much more efficient than giving each data stream its own physical connection, there are still some inefficiencies, as shown here.

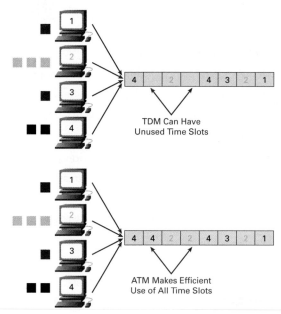

With standard TDM, each end station essentially owns a time slot, preventing any other end station from using it, even when it is idle. With asynchronous TDM, each end station is assigned a primary time slot, with which it has priority over other end stations. However, when an unused slot exists, any station can use it in addition to its assigned slot.

At-a-Glance: Asynchronous Transfer Mode (ATM)

Fixed Cell Size

ATM delivers information in fixed-size units called cells. Every ATM cell, regardless of the type of information (voice, video, data), is exactly 53 bytes with 48 bytes of information and 5 bytes of header (overhead) information. This is different from other protocols that can increase the cell size and actually increase the header or overhead traffic on a network. There are two distinct advantages in using fixed cell sizes that outweigh the cost of the additional overhead.

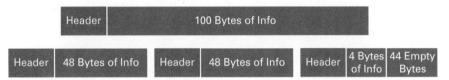

The main advantage of fixed cell sizes is that the serialization delay or the delay of processing cells is deterministic (regular and predictable), which aids in network management. This feature also makes ATM well suited for voice and video traffic, which is time-sensitive. With fixed-length cells, there is no danger of a voice cell getting "stuck in traffic" behind a large data cell.

The recent adoption of Voice over IP (VoIP) is beginning to chip away at the advantage of ATM, because voice and video can now run efficiently over IP-based WANs.

ATM Connections

ATM is a connection-based service that uses two primary types of circuits: permanent virtual circuits (PVC) and switched virtual circuits (SVC). ATM also can use a connectionless service, but it is relatively rare, so it is not discussed in detail.

A connection-based service means that a connection must be requested, established, and confirmed before any user information (such as voice, video, or data) is sent.

PVCs typically are used for direct connections between sites. Similar to a leased line, the connection remains open even when idle. PVCs guarantee availability, but they must be manually configured.

SVCs are set up and torn down dynamically. The connection is open only while information is being actively sent. SVCs use a signaling protocol between the ATM endpoint and the ATM switch to establish a dynamic connection. SVCs are more flexible than PVCs but require additional overhead. An SVC is similar to a phone call. Unlike the SVCs used (or not used) in Frame Relay, the use of SVCs in ATM is common.

Virtual Connection

As mentioned, ATM is a connection-based protocol. ATM connections are established using a combination of virtual paths and virtual channels.

An ATM connection is actually composed of a number of virtual channels that can take different physical paths through the network. Virtual channels are then bundled into logical groups called virtual paths. Several virtual paths can also be bundled into a larger logical grouping called a transmission path. All of this is transparent to the user. The figure illustrates this concept.

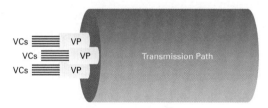

LAN Emulation (LANE)

LAN Emulation is a standard that allows end stations connected via an ATM network to communicate as if they were connected across an Ethernet or Token Ring LAN, but at a much faster speed.

LANE uses LAN emulation clients (LEC) and LAN emulation servers (LES) for forwarding and control, which take the place of those functions performed in a traditional LAN. When used in this manner they are called emulated LANs or ELANs.

LANE requires no modification of the higher-layer protocols and therefore is transparent to the application's use.

Multiprotocol Label Switching (MPLS) Services

MPLS is a Layer 2 WAN backbone technology that delivers WAN and MAN services, traffic engineering capabilities, and a converged network infrastructure that can also be used to aggregate and transport Frame Relay, ATM, and IP traffic. Originally developed by Cisco in the form of tag switching, MPLS was adopted as an Internet standard by the Internet Engineering Task Force (IETF). Service providers are the primary implementers of the technology.

Service providers offer MPLS services as an alternative to their traditional Frame Relay, leased line, and ATM services. With MPLS networks, service providers can offer services similar to traditional WAN technologies at lower costs and provide additional IP-based services previously not available.

At the heart of MPLS is an encapsulation scheme that serves as an alternative to traditional IP routing. When a packet comes into the service provider edge, a router assigns a tag to the packet based on the destination IP network. The tag is a type of shorthand for a traditional IP-based route. After the tag is applied, the router forwards the packet into the MPLS core. The core routers read the label, apply the appropriate services, and forward the packet based on the label. As soon as the packet reaches the destination edge of the service provider network, the MPLS label is removed, and the IP packet is forwarded onto the IP network.

Traffic engineering is a core component for service providers that allows them to deliver services predictably for each of their customers. MPLS traffic engineering expands on the capabilities offered by ATM and Frame Relay. Tagged IP packets are routed through the MPLS core based on the resources required by the packet and available network resources. The MPLS network chooses the shortest path for a traffic flow based on its resource requirements. Resource requirements are determined by the size and priority of a traffic flow. MPLS networks can honor IP QoS by delivering both best-effort delivery as well as time and bandwidth-sensitive guarantees.

One of the MPLS services that service providers offer is virtual private networks. Using MPLS labels, service providers can deliver IP-based services to many customers without the complexity of traditional Frame Relay or ATM circuit management. Customers can use private or public IP addressing without concern about overlapping other customer addressing.

Another advantage of MPLS networks is any-to-any connectivity. Whereas in Frame Relay and ATM networks, connections are point-to-point, MPLS services allow customers to connect into the service and easily reach any other office connected to the service. This removes some of the complexity of traffic engineering that corporate customers would have to do themselves and allows the service provider to offer an important value-added service as a WAN provider.

MPLS VPN services are as secure as Frame Relay in that one customer cannot see the traffic from another customer even though they traverse the same MPLS network. For additional security, customers can place firewalls between their private network and the service providers, as well as encrypt the traffic as it goes into the MPLS network. As long as the packets have standard IP headers, the MPLS network can ship the packet to its destination.

Because MPLS networks look like a private intranet to the connected IP networks, service providers can offer additional IP-based services such as QoS, telephony support within the VPN, and centralized services such as web hosting.

At-a-Glance: MPLS

Why Should I Care About MPLS?

Multiprotocol Label Switching (MPLS) was originally developed to speed up the routing of packets through the WAN network. Since its development, the speed of traditional routing has sped up considerably, but MPLS still has many benefits.

MPLS enables service providers (SP) to offer additional services to its enterprise customers, including VPNs, improved traffic engineering, QoS, Layer 2 tunneling, and multiprotocol support.

MPLS can be deployed like a multiservice-based network, providing an IP-based alternative to Frame Relay, ATM, and leased line. This presents a cost savings to service providers. Rather than building separate networks for IP, Frame Relay, and ATM users, MPLS allows the SP to build a single MPLS network and support them all.

What Problems Need to Be Solved?

In an MPLS network all packets must be differentiated from each other. This is done by labeling each packet. To add a label to a packet, the network must first determine all the normal information that a typical router would. In other words, the first router that a packet encounters must fully analyze the header, from which the label will be made. (Multiple labels may be used, such as when a packet traverses multiple MPLS networks.)

As soon as the packet has a label, the rest of the routers in the network must have a way to act on the information contained in the label.

Equipment and Stuff

The three primary equipment types in MPLS networks are customer premises equipment (CPE), provider edge (PE), and provider routers (P):

- **CPE:** This is equipment on the customer site. All traffic leaving the local site is routed through this point. This is often called customer equipment (CE).

- **PE:** Located at the ingress point of the SP network, this is the equipment that assigns (and removes) labels. The PE can either be routers or high-end switches. This is also referred to as the Edge Label Switch Router (ELSR).

- **P:** Located in the core of the SP network, provider (P) routers forward packets based on their labels. This is also called a Label Switch Router (LSR).

Label information is distributed throughout the network using the Label Distribution Protocol (LDP).

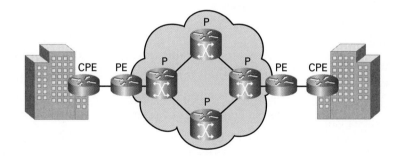

MPLS Labels

The forwarding mechanism in MPLS uses a label to decide where and how to send packets or cells through the network. The label is applied at the ingress to the SP network and is removed at the network egress point. The router responsible for adding the label is the only network router that needs to process the entire packet header. The information contained in the header, along with the preconfigured instructions, is used to generate the label. Labels can be based on IP destinations (this is what traditional routing uses) and other parameters, such as IP sources, QoS, VPN membership, or specific routes for traffic engineering purposes. MPLS is also designed to support forwarding mechanisms from other protocols. MPLS tags are 4 bytes or 32 bits long, which aids the speed at which the rest of the routers can process the forwarding information (IP headers are much longer than that).

At-a-Glance: MPLS

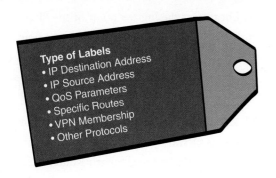

Type of Labels
• IP Destination Address
• IP Source Address
• QoS Parameters
• Specific Routes
• VPN Membership
• Other Protocols

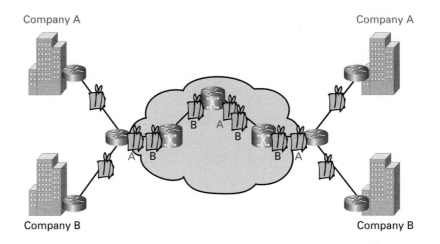

MPLS Security

An additional benefit of MPLS is a small measure of security (as compared to Frame Relay or ATM). As illustrated in the figure, as soon as the packet or cell from a company enters the SP network, the label assigned essentially keeps that packet segregated from all other customers' packets/cells. Because there is no place where one customer can view another customer's packet/cells, there is no danger of having someone outside the SP network snoop for packets. Obviously this would not stop someone bent on illegally accessing a company's information, but it does remove the possibility of someone claiming that he "accidentally" received the information. Unfortunately, the number of incidents of people or groups intentionally stealing or monitoring data has been on the rise over the past several years. Because of this trend, many people no longer consider MPLS to be "inherently secure," as it was once billed.

Many companies opt for encryption using technologies such as IPsec (IP Security) to provide data

security for their traffic traversing MPLS networks (and, in general, any WAN type). This is especially true where companies have offices with connections in developing and emerging countries, where the trust level of in-country providers may be lower than in the U.S. and Europe.

MPLS Architecture

MPLS is divided into two layers or planes, each having a specific function in the network. The layers are the Control plane and the Data plane. The Control plane is responsible for the exchange of routing information (including labels) between adjacent devices. The Data plane handles forwarding operations.

It is important to note that MPLS is no more or less secure than Frame or ATM. Also, there is a common misconception that MPLS is encrypted.

Although it is possible to encrypt MPLS, it is not encrypted by default.

How Does the Router Know Where to Send Stuff?

The routers in an MPLS network forward packets based on labels, but the router must know the relationship between a label and path through the network. This relationship is established and communicated throughout the network using Forwarding Equivalence Classes (FEC). A FEC is a specific path through the network of LSRs and is equal to the destination network, stored in an IP routing table. The LSRs simply look at the label and forward the packet based on the contents of the FEC. This is much simpler, faster, and more flexible than traditional IP routing. Sometimes a packet arrives at a router without a label (if it

At-a-Glance: MPLS

came from a non-MPLS network). When this happens, it is the router's job to add a label so that the packet can be properly forwarded through the MPLS network.

Other MPLS Features

Traffic engineering is the ability to dynamically define routes based on known demand or alternative available routes. Traffic engineering can also be used to optimize network usage.

Intelligent rerouting refers to an MPLS network's ability to reroute based on network congestion. Rather than changing the route on a packet-by-packet basis, MPLS can reroute on a flow-by-flow basis.

MPLS is particularly well suited to support VPNs. With a VPN, the packets from one enterprise are transparent to all other enterprise VPNs. The labels and the FECs effectively segregate VPN traffic from other packets on the MPLS network.

MPLS Layer 2 tunneling, also known as Any Transport over MPLS (AToM), allows an SP to transport Frame Relay and ATM over an MPLS-based network. This increases the range of services that the SP can offer.

MPLS Traffic Separation

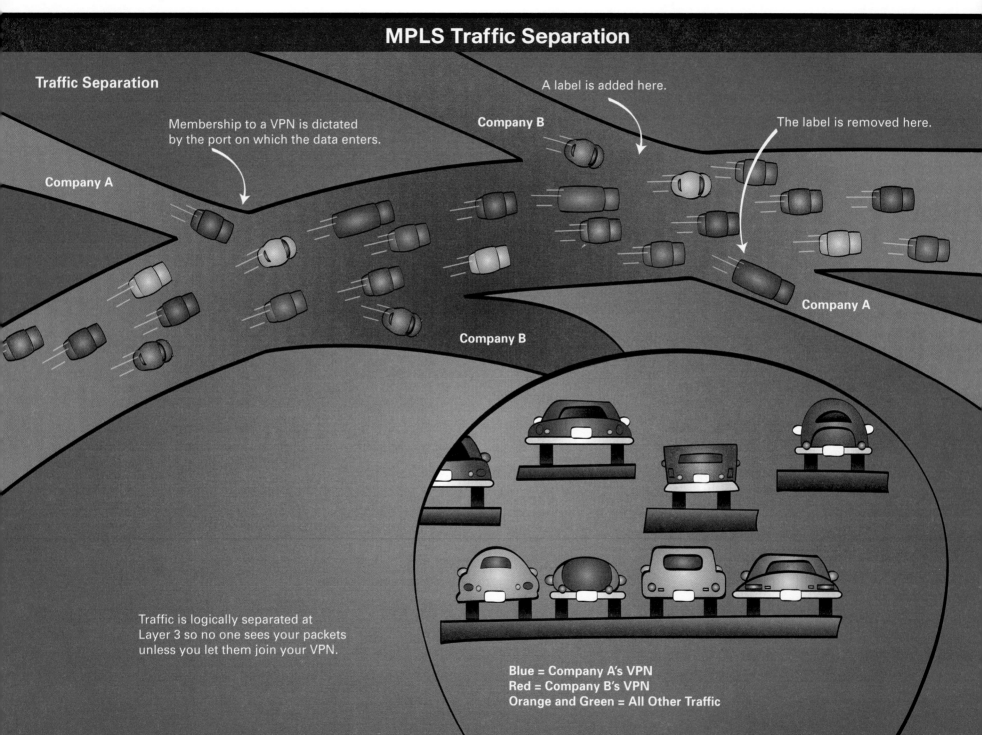

Traffic Separation

Membership to a VPN is dictated by the port on which the data enters.

A label is added here.

The label is removed here.

Company A

Company B

Company A

Company B

Traffic is logically separated at Layer 3 so no one sees your packets unless you let them join your VPN.

Blue = Company A's VPN
Red = Company B's VPN
Orange and Green = All Other Traffic

Broadband Technologies

Always-on Access

Before the late 1990s, people connected remotely to their offices or the Internet using dialup connections. An always-on remote network connection was not possible for a reasonable price. To connect to the corporate network, the user ran a program that dialed a phone number. Unless the user had a second phone line, being online prohibited incoming or outgoing phone calls.

The user entered a user ID and password to gain access to the system. The fastest speed available over phone lines was 56 kbps, which was fine until the web became popular in the 1990s. Downloading large pictures, documents, applications, and audio files took what seemed like forever. Then, along came broadband.

Broadband networking offered a reasonable high-speed alternative to traditional dialup networking. Using existing service connections to houses (such as phone wiring, cable TV coaxial cable, or even satellite), service providers offered Internet services at many times the speed of dialup. Downloading large files became palatable with broadband. Broadband technologies allow service providers to offer always-on connectivity similar to what people use in a corporate network. Computers on the broadband network always have access to the network; there is no intermediate dialup step. Sit down, load the browser, and off you go.

High-speed Internet access to homes offers new levels of productivity and entertainment not possible before the commercialization of the Internet and the web. Aside from apparent uses such as online shopping and video streaming, corporations can accommodate road warriors and work-from-home folks in a way not previously possible. Using encryption technologies, an employee with a laptop computer can securely access her corporate network from any Internet access point in the world. Additionally, employees can attach IP phones, allowing them to work on their computers and make calls from their office-phone extensions as if they were sitting at their desks.

Broadband Technology Evolution

Integrated Services Digital Network (ISDN) was the first commercially viable broadband option available. Using existing phone lines, home users commonly subscribed to a Basic Rate Interface (BRI), which had a throughput maximum of 128 kbps. ISDN had some significant adoption in Europe, but in the U.S., ISDN was eclipsed by more cost-effective broadband technologies before it had a chance to become commonplace. Cable modem and digital subscriber line (DSL) services became the premier broadband technologies. Although other broadband technologies existed, the primary determination of a technology's viability was access to "last mile" wiring to houses. Anything that required new wiring probably wouldn't make it. Other technologies that take advantage of other media exist, such as satellite television dishes, but they did not become widely adopted.

For those requiring even higher throughput, some providers now offer fiber links to homes as a premier service. This is already popular throughout major cities in Asia and is being installed in several cities in the U.S. as well.

Cable Modem

Cable modems provide high-speed data communication using existing cable television coaxial cabling. Current implementations of cable-modem technologies offer speeds as fast as Ethernet (greater than 10 Mbps). This means that a file that takes 2 minutes to transfer over ISDN takes 2 seconds over a cable modem. Cable modem can provide higher speeds than traditional leased lines, with lower cost and easier installation. Because a cable-modem connection is permanently established, it cannot dial multiple locations directly. As a result, cable-modem access must be to the Internet. This restriction means that employees can connect to their company's network only if the company provides access through the Internet. Usually, this is done through a secure VPN connection.

DSL

Like cable modems, DSL provides high-speed Internet access for reasonable cost using existing cabling to houses and businesses. DSL carves off a portion of the telephone line to use for data transmission without interfering with existing phone service. Because of the multiple flavors of DSL services, DSL is generically referred to as xDSL. The two popular forms of xDSL service currently available are Asymmetric DSL (ADSL) and Symmetric DSL (SDSL). ADSL provides faster download speeds because traffic toward the user is given more bandwidth than traffic from the user. SDSL assigns equal bandwidth in both directions. ADSL is most often used for residential service, and SDSL is most often used in commercial settings, because of their different usage models.

Which One Is Better?

Both DSL and cable modems provide high-speed Internet access at a relatively low cost. Both provide always-on connectivity. Both have technical advantages and disadvantages. Either technology makes a good to-the-home or small-office solution for Internet connectivity. Because both technologies are always on, a firewall must protect the local network from Internet-based attacks. Some practical issues affect how widespread the technologies become. Virtually all businesses and homes have telephone lines, which means that DSL is possible, but fewer homes and businesses have cable TV connections. In general, neither is "better," and both types of service offer very high-speed connectivity for relatively low cost.

In some cases, though, there may not be a choice if you live in an area not serviced by cable, for example. When both services exist, the quality and price may be the tipping point between the two services. A great deal of information on setting up cable and DSL networks can be found in *Home Networking Simplified* (Cisco Press, 2006).

At-a-Glance: ISDN

Why Should I Care About ISDN?

Today, data traffic dominates voice traffic, and there is a move toward transporting voice over data networks. Before the technology explosion of the late 1990s, however, voice networks were much more prevalent than data networks, and engineers focused on sending data over voice networks. Integrated Services Digital Network (ISDN) is a collection of standards that define how to integrate a data architecture into the Public Switched Telephone Network (PSTN). ISDN standards define both the hardware and call setup schemes.

In addition to data communications, ISDN provides other benefits:

- Multiple traffic feeds. Voice, video, telex, and packet-switched data are all available over ISDN.

- Fast call setup. ISDN uses out-of-band (D, or delta channel) signaling for call setup. ISDN calls can often be set up and completed in less than 1 second.

- The ability to combine data channels for increased bandwidth. With multiple channels, one form of ISDN is capable of 128 kbps, whereas leased lines usually provide only 56 kbps in North America.

- The ability to purchase digital services directly from the local phone company, without the expense and hassle of purchasing a dedicated leased line.

Although the benefits of ISDN have largely been eclipsed by standard routers and cable Internet access, it is still used in areas where cable is unavailable or as a dial backup in case of private WAN failure. ISDN also has useful applications within the public telephone system (increased performance of call setup) that largely go unnoticed by end users.

What Problems Need to Be Solved?

ISDN is incompatible with many other protocols and requires special equipment to operate.

ISDN also must run over multiple wires and must have mechanisms for breaking up and reassembling signals.

ISDN and Internet Access

ISDN has been around for many years. Although the business applications were well used, ISDN struggled for many years to fulfill its original promise to home users. Often referred to pejoratively as "It Still Does Nothing," it was for year a solution in search of a problem. All of that changed with the advent of the Internet and the ever-increasing need for bandwidth from every house on the block.

ISDN solves two of the major issues with the rising need for broadband connectivity:

- It's already there. ISDN runs over standard phone lines, which means that nearly every household is a potential ISDN customer.

- It's relatively fast. ISDN offers more than twice the available bandwidth over the same phone lines not running ISDN. A single ISDN line supports 128 kbps bandwidth, but multiple lines can also be aggregated using a multiplexer, resulting in speeds of 256 kbps or sometimes even 384 Kbps.

ISDN Standard Access Methods

ISDN has two types of interfaces: Basic Rate Interface (BRI) and Primary Rate Interface (PRI). Both types are broken into bearer channels (B), which carry data, and delta channels, which carry signal and call control information. The D channel can also be used for low-rate packet data (such as alarms).

- BRI has two B channels (64 kbps each) and one delta D channel (16 kbps). BRI is sometimes written as 2B+D.

BRI (2B+D)
2 Bearer (B) Channels
64 kbps Each Used for Data

Bandwidth = 128 kbps

1 Data (D) Channel
16 kbps Used for Signaling

- In North America and Japan, PRI has 23 B channels and one D channel (all channels are 64 kbps). In Europe, PRI has 30 B channels and one D channel. PRI is sometimes written as 23B+D.

At-a-Glance: ISDN

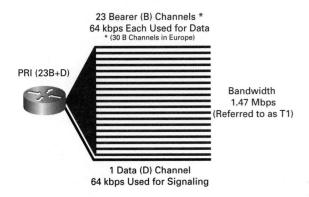

Making an ISDN Call

Before any data or voice traffic is sent over the B channels, a connection must be made using the D channel. The D channel initiates the call by establishing a path between switches and passing information about the source and called numbers. When the destination receives the setup information, it uses the D channel to signal the ISDN switch that is available. After this connection is completed, the B channels can begin exchanging data and voice.

ISDN Device Types and Reference Points

ISDN specifies both the equipment and the connection points between equipment to ensure compatibility with the PSTN and among ISDN vendors.

- **TE1:** Terminal endpoint 1. TE1s are devices that have a native ISDN interface.

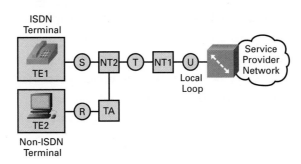

- **NT2:** Network termination 2. An NT2 aggregates and switches all ISDN lines at the customer service site using a customer switching device.

- **NT1:** Network termination 1. NT1s convert signals into a form used by the ISDN line. An NT1 plugs into a standard phone jack.

- **TE2:** Terminal endpoint 2. A TE2 is a non-ISDN terminal. TEs require a terminal adapter.

- **TA:** Terminal adapter. A TA performs protocol conversion from non-ISDN (such as EIA/TIA-232, V.35, and other signals) into ISDN signals.

- **R:** A connection point between a non-ISDN-compatible device and a terminal adapter.

- **S:** The connection point into the customer switching device (NT2). Enables calls between customer equipment.

- **T:** The outbound connection from the NT2 to the ISDN network. This reference point is electrically identical to the S interface.

- **U:** The connection point between NT1 and the ISDN network.

Service Provider Identifiers (SPID)

SPIDs are assigned by your service provider to identify your switch at the central office. A company's SPID is linked to the services that have been ordered from the phone company. When a connection to the central office is made, the SPID tells the switch which services the company is entitled to.

A separate SPID can be configured for each channel of the BRI. SPID requirements are dependent on both the software revision and the switch type. SPIDs are required only in the U.S.

At-a-Glance: Broadband

Why Should I Care About Broadband?

The availability of high-speed Internet or business-class access from the home has dramatically changed the way people work, seek entertainment, and connect to the rest of the world.

Whether working from home with a high-speed IP telephony–enabled connection, downloading movies on-line, or sending pictures to friends and family, broadband has made the promise of true multi-media capable home connections a reality.

What Problems Need to Be Solved?

The key to broadband access to the home was finding a way to offer the service at a price that would be acceptable to the majority of users while still being profitable for the service providers. With the decreasing cost of high-speed routers and switches, the major cost component of the service was connecting local high-speed aggregation points with the homes in the area. This part of the network has been defined as "the last mile." The whole business case boiled down to this: The only way to make broadband access profitable was to already have the last-mile infrastructure in place, and the only businesses that had that were the local phone company and the local cable TV provider.

Both industries then figured out innovative ways to solve the technical issues of making broadband work.

The Need for Speed

The availability of high-speed Internet connections begs the question "Why does anyone need high-speed connections in the first place?"

With the availability of all forms of multimedia in demand on the Internet, the following graph may offer some perspective. As a point of reference, a high-quality digital recording of a song is about 9 Mb.

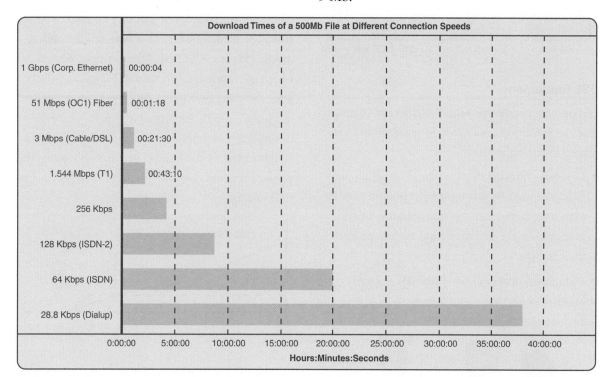

Digital Subscriber Line (DSL)

DSL uses the existing phone wires connected to virtually every home in most countries. The twisted-pair wires that provide phone service are ideal, because the available frequency ranges on the wires far exceed those required to carry a voice conversation. Human speech occupies frequencies of roughly 4000 hertz (4 kHz) or less. The copper wires that provide phone service can carry in the range of 1 to 2 million hertz (1 to 2 MHz). DSL provides more downstream data (from the Internet to you) than upstream data (from you

At-a-Glance: Broadband

to the Internet) based on user profiles, but this can be changed for businesses or those running web servers.

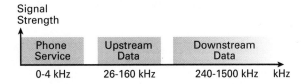

Signal Strength

Phone Service	Upstream Data	Downstream Data
0-4 kHz	26-160 kHz	240-1500 kHz

kHz

DSL Equipment

DSL requires some specialized equipment to ensure that the voice and data are kept separate and are routed to the right place.

• **Low-pass filters (LPF)** are placed on all phone jacks not used by a computer to prevent interference from high-frequency data signals. DSL modems are the interface from the phone line to the computer.

• **DSL access multiplexers (DSLAM)** aggregate hundreds of signals from homes and are the access point to the Internet.

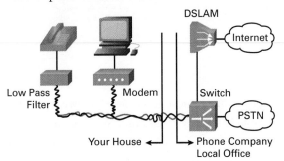

Limitations and Advantages

DSL signals are distance-sensitive, which means that the available throughput decreases the farther your house is from the service provider. The maximum distance is about 18,000 feet. DSL signals cannot be amplified, nor can they be converted from one medium to another between the DSL modem and the DSLAM. (For example, optical-fiber extensions are not possible.) Typically the DSL company performs a line test to ensure that the service can be supported at a particular residence. The good news for DSL is that throughput is unaffected by the number of users so long as the phone company continues to add DSLAMs to support new users.

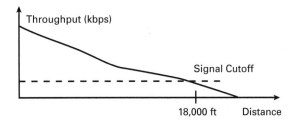

Cable

Cable uses the same basic principle as DSL in that the bandwidth needed to accomplish the primary function is only a fraction of the available bandwidth on the wire or, in this case, cable. Cable is a slightly different concept in how it divides the available frequencies.

The cable spectrum is already divided up into several hundred 6-MHz blocks to account for the various cable channels. Your cable-ready TV simply tunes its receiver to the frequency that corresponds to the channel you have chosen. To add Internet capabilities, each user is assigned one or more blocks for downstream data (each 6-MHz block is good for about 30 Mbps of data). For the upstream piece, the lower end of the spectrum is divided into 2-MHz blocks, because most people download more information than they upload. Each subscriber is assigned one or more 2-MHz blocks.

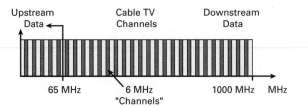

At-a-Glance: Broadband

Cable Equipment

Adding cable Internet service requires only a cable modem to home users, because cable-ready televisions provide their own filtering. Therefore, interference between data and TV signals is not an issue. At the cable company a Cable Modem Termination System (CMTS) is required to aggregate upstream and downstream.

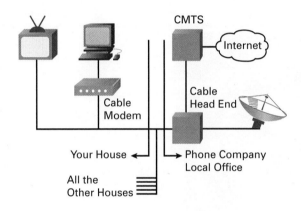

Limitations and Advantages

A CMTS has a fixed number of slots (1000), meaning that there is a limit on how many subscribers can access the service with a particular CMTS. With relatively few subscribers, each user enjoys greater throughput than when the number of subscribers reaches its maximum, and each user is assigned a single pair of "channels." Cable is not distance-sensitive, though, and the signal can be amplified if needed. There is also an issue with cable not being available to all homes. You usually can take a phone line for granted at a home, but that is not the case with cable.

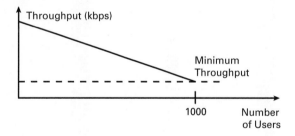

Virtual Private Networks

Secure Networking Over the Internet

Traditional WAN networking involved dedicated circuits running Frame Relay or leased lines. Although prices have recently decreased, the cost of these private circuits continues to be relatively high.

In addition to dedicated WAN connections, corporations had to maintain large banks of dialup modems (or outsource the dial-in to a vendor) so that workers could remotely access the corporate network with modems. In both cases, the goal was to extend the corporate network to remote locations and individuals. With the widespread implementation of the Internet, IP connectivity is accessible from people's houses as well as public locations, such as airports and coffee shops. Service providers find it more cost-effective to offer IP-based WAN services as opposed to dedicated circuits. Corporations must provide extensive Internet services to their employees, partners, and customers to remain competitive. Given the confluence of IP public and corporate networks, extending the corporate network to places other than the main campus is more economical and practical.

Virtual private networks (VPN) allow corporations to replace their dedicated private networks (such as Frame Relay, ATM, and leased line) with "virtually" private networks. This means that their data traverses public IP networks but is secure because of authentication and encryption. Because of the Internet and service provider IP networks, networks of equivalent bandwidth end up being cheaper than dedicated services. With the availability of Internet connectivity, VPNs allow users to access their corporate networks securely from homes, hotels, businesses, and other public locations. VPNs also provide the ability to work from home, creating telecommuters. For example, call-center employees can answer phones from home, using IP phones and contact center applications such as Cisco IP Contact Center.

With the convergence of voice, video, and data, VPNs add value not previously available with dialup and WAN services. IP connectivity to the corporation eliminates the need for separate fax, data, phone, and video lines. However, because using a VPN involves heavy data crunching to encrypt traffic, and data typically traverses the public Internet, unpredictable delay and jitter can affect voice and video quality.

The term *VPN* actually defines two different concepts for virtual networks. To corporations, a VPN typically means that encrypted traffic (using IPsec) is tunneled through public IP networks. To service providers, VPN typically describes a tag-switching-based IP service, which does not involve encryption. This discussion focuses on IPsec-based VPNs.

The four types of VPN connectivity are as follows:

- **Site-to-site:** Connects remote corporate locations to the corporate network. The remote site typically has multiple users sharing access to the corporate network.

- **Remote access:** Individual users gain access to the corporate network either over dialup or broadband network. Also called teleworker.

- **Extranet:** Similar to site-to-site, except that the VPN connects separate companies.

- **Wireless authentication:** VPN technology can also be used to secure wireless users in a corporate environment.

Security concerns increase, because both companies must protect their networks from each other. Because they traverse public IP networks, VPNs introduce security considerations that were not as important with private dial-in or WAN topologies. In general, providing security means encrypting corporate-bound traffic using secure authentication. For site-to-site VPNs, providing security typically means adding security measures such as firewalls, intrusion detection, and NAT/PAT. IPsec provides a way to manage encryption between multiple hosts using secure communications. Encrypting devices (such as routers or end-station PCs) inspect traffic ready to be transmitted. A set of rules on the device determines whether a particular packet must be encrypted. For example, a packet destined for the Internet can be left unencrypted, but a packet destined for the corporate network must be encrypted.

If a packet is to be encrypted, the device scrambles the contents, rendering them unreadable. Different encryption algorithms determine how difficult an encrypted packet is to crack. An encryption scheme that is more difficult for an intruder to decode requires more computing cycles than one that is less difficult. VPNs are point-to-point, meaning that every connection has only two endpoints. A single device (such as a WAN aggregation router) can have multiple remote sites, and users terminate their connections on the one box, but there is still one connection (or tunnel) per pair.

For each encrypted tunnel, the two endpoints must first authenticate each other and ensure that the other end is who it claims to be. In encryption terms, this means that each endpoint must establish a security association (SA) with the other. Essentially, this involves the trusted exchange of information between the two hosts that allows each to verify the identity of the other. This process is called *Internet Key Exchange (IKE)*. After both sides determine that the other side is who it claims and that they can trust each other, they can send encrypted data across the VPN.

At-a-Glance: VPNs

Why Should I Care About VPNs?

A virtual private network (VPN) is a set of solutions and technologies designed to make secure (encrypted) site-to-site and remote-access connections over public networks. These connections provide low-cost alternatives to dedicated private WANs and allow telecommuters to connect to the corporate network via cable, DSL, or dialup.

VPN connections can be set up quickly over existing infrastructures and provide an excellent alternative to dedicated private networks such as Frame Relay and ATM.

Benefits of VPN include the following:

- **Cost savings:** VPNs use cost-effective public IP networks to connect remote-office users to the main corporate site, eliminating expensive dedicated WAN links.

- **Security:** VPNs provide a high level of security using advanced encryption and authentication protocols.

- **Scalability:** VPNs can be easily set up over the existing Internet infrastructure, allowing corporations to add large amounts of capacity without adding significant infrastructure.

- **Compatibility with broadband technology:** VPNs allow mobile workers, telecommuters, and day extenders to take advantage of high-speed broadband connectivity such as DSL and cable for corporate connectivity.

- **Ease of access:** Network access can be provided from anywhere in the world by local Internet access points of presence (POP).

VPNs offer almost the same level of information security as traditional private networks and can be simpler to set up, less expensive to operate, and easier to administer.

What Problems Need to Be Solved?

The two primary technical issues in setting up VPNs are

- **Tunneling:** Tunneling is the process of encapsulating the protocol header and trailer of one network protocol into the protocol header and trailer of another. Before the packet is sent across the network, it is encapsulated with new header information that allows an intermediary network to recognize and deliver it. When the transmission ends, the tunneling header is stripped off, and the original packet is delivered to the destination.

- **Encryption:** Although tunneling allows data to be carried across a third-party network, it does not protect the data from unauthorized inspection or viewing. To ensure that tunneled transmissions are not intercepted, traffic over a VPN is typically encrypted. It is important to realize, however, that encrypted data can still be intercepted, and attempts can be made to decrypt captured data.

Deployment Modes

Site-to-site VPNs link company headquarters, remote locations, branch offices, and e-business partners to an internal network over one shared infrastructure. Site-to-site VPNs can be intranets or extranets. It is not uncommon for extranets to traverse multiple service providers.

Remote-access VPNs allow corporate users and mobile workers to access a corporate intranet securely by using their cable, DSL, or the local numbers of an ISP to dial in and connect to the network. Leveraging local ISP dialup infrastructures enables companies to reduce communications expenses and increase productivity due to the robust technology that supports the Internet and other public networks.

VPN Architecture

Several methods (both Layer 2 and Layer 3) and technologies are available for those who want to establish a VPN. VPNs can be established and managed on the customer premises or over the network by the service provider. It is also possible to combine several of these methods to meet a specific need.

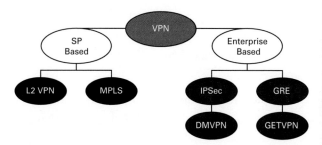

Generic Routing Encapsulation (GRE)

Generic Routing Encapsulation (GRE) is a workaround method for routing over an IP network packets that are otherwise unroutable. You can also use GRE to route multicast packets over incompatible networks. GRE can route non-IP protocols (such as AppleTalk, Internetwork Packet Exchange, or IPX) over IP networks. The next figure illustrates the concept of encapsulating a packet. When the GRE packet reaches the destination network, the GRE header and trailer are stripped off, and the original protocol works as usual.

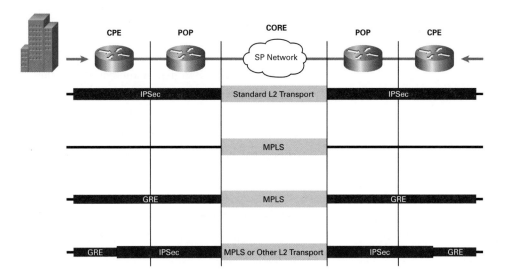

- **IPsec tunnels over a service provider network:** This setup is a trusted, virtual, point-to-point connection.

- **MPLS VPN:** When they enter the service-provider network, packets are assigned labels, and they are routed according to forwarding instructions.

- **Simple GRE over an L2 transport:** You can use this setup to transport AppleTalk over an IP net-

work. A company that needs to send AppleTalk over a secure link can implement this setup using a service provider and MPLS or another method.

This scenario could be implemented by a company needing to transport AppleTalk over a secure link.

By itself, GRE provides no data security; it simply provides a way to "tunnel" IP and non-IP packets across an IP network.

IPsec

IPsec is an Internet standard for the establishment and management of data privacy between network entities over unprotected networks such as the Internet.

IPsec security services are provided at the network layer, allowing simple and effective encryption of IP traffic. Before IPsec, data had to be encrypted on an application basis, or hardware encryptors had to be added to the network. None of this was standardized at the time, so companies tended to use proprietary solutions, limiting the sharing of secure information to trusted partners, customers, and resellers.

With IPsec networks, tunnels essentially serve as point-to-point "virtual circuits" through a service provider's network.

As a side note, IPsec is built in to the IPv6 standard to ensure standardization of data security in future networks.

VPN Architecture

Several methods (both Layer 2 and Layer 3) and technologies are available to establish a VPN. You can establish and manage VPNs on the customer site or over the network with a service provider.

Dynamic Multipoint VPNs (DMVPN)

Site-to-site VPNs that use IPsec for encryption typically were set up in advance and in a point-to-point topology. Each tunnel must be configured

At-a-Glance: VPNs

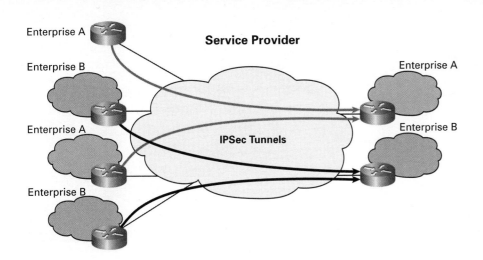

between a branch office and a headquarters site. A WAN headend aggregating many thousands of branch office connections could literally have tens of thousands of configuration commands required to deploy a WAN service. DMVPNs simplify the deployment.

There are two types of DMVPN topologies:

- **Hub-and-spoke DMVPN** connects many branch offices (spokes) to a central location (hub). DMVPN simplifies the configuration by enabling a single multipoint tunnel to be configured on the hub. Then new branches joining the VPN can simply establish new connections to the hub (after being properly authenticated) without requiring extensive reconfiguration of the hub. Traffic in a hub-and-spoke DMVPN still flows from a spoke to the hub and back to other spokes, as required.

- **Spoke-to-spoke DMVPN** allows branch offices (spokes) to dynamically establish on-demand connections to other branch offices (spokes), whenever traffic is needed between the two locations, without requiring all traffic go through the hub connections.

DMVPNs offer several distinct advantages over traditional IPsec VPNs, including easier configuration and "touchless" deployment of new branch offices, as well as the potential for partially or fully meshed WAN services for customers who have heavy requirements for branch-to-branch traffic.

MPLS

MPLS uses a method of forwarding packets that is based on labels. The labels may correspond to IP destination networks, as in traditional IP forwarding, but they can also represent other parameters, source addresses, QoS, or other protocols.

MPLS implements label swapping between different modules within the network. The two main components in an MPLS network are the control plane and the data plane. The control plane takes care of routing exchanges and the exchange of labels between adjacent devices. The data plane forwards packets based on labels and is independent of routing or label exchange protocols.

MPLS is designed for use on virtually any medium and Layer 2 encapsulation. For frame-based encapsulations, MPLS inserts a 32-bit label between the Layer 2 and Layer 3 headers ("frame-mode" MPLS).

MPLS allows service providers to offer enterprises services similar to those found in Frame Relay or ATM networks, with the conveniences of an IP network. With MPLS networks, VPNs operate as logical "ships in the night" across a common routed backbone. The VPN appears as a "private" routed WAN to the enterprise.

Establishing a VPN Connection

Abe needs to work remotely with the corporate network. How can he do it securely?

1 **Establishing Identity**

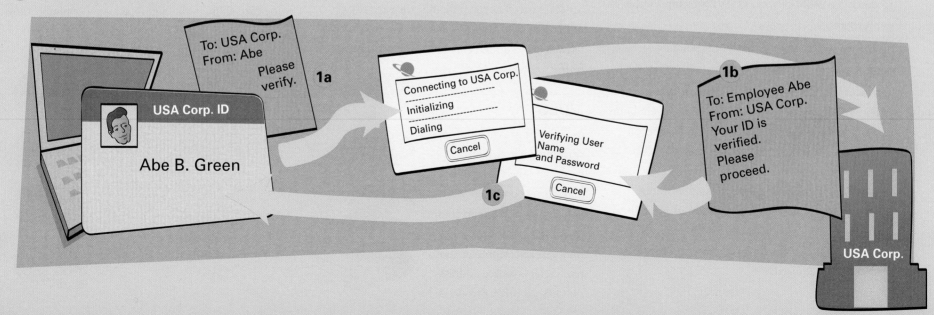

To: USA Corp.
From: Abe
Please verify.

1a

USA Corp. ID

Abe B. Green

Connecting to USA Corp.
Initializing
Dialing
Cancel

Verifying User Name and Password
Cancel

1c

1b

To: Employee Abe
From: USA Corp.
Your ID is verified.
Please proceed.

Establishing a VPN Connection

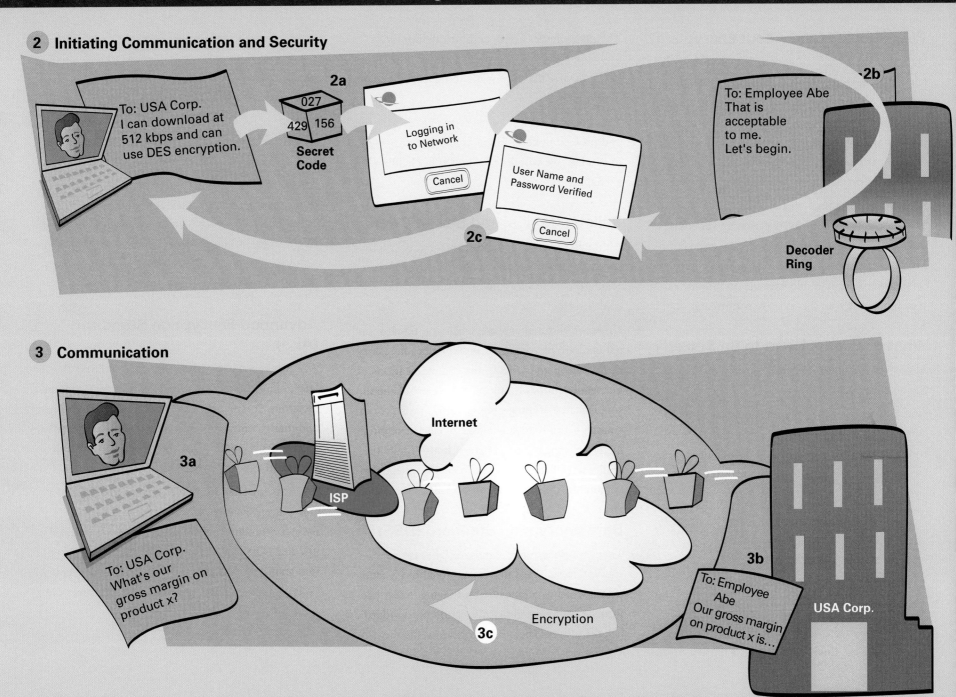

2 Initiating Communication and Security

To: USA Corp. I can download at 512 kbps and can use DES encryption.

2a

027 429 156

Secret Code

Logging in to Network

Cancel

User Name and Password Verified

Cancel

2c

To: Employee Abe That is acceptable to me. Let's begin.

2b

Decoder Ring

3 Communication

3a

To: USA Corp. What's our gross margin on product x?

ISP

Internet

3b

To: Employee Abe Our gross margin on product x is…

USA Corp.

Encryption

3c

At-a-Glance: Encryption

Why Should I Care About Encryption?

Data that travels across unsecured networks is vulnerable to anyone who wants to read, alter, or forge information. Using easily obtained tools such as protocol analyzers, just about anybody can read packets and gain access to classified information. Hostile parties can tamper with packets, hinder delivery, or prevent network communications.

Encryption provides a means to scramble and protect information as it travels across an otherwise unsecured network. Different levels of encryption can keep anyone who has access to packets from being able to decipher the message or, in some cases, even figure out who the message is from and to.

What Problems Need to Be Solved?

Almost all methods of encryption rely one two basic items: codes and keys.

First, a mathematical code must be developed so that only those possessing the right keys to the equation can properly code and decode messages. Extremely complicated mathematical functions are used to encrypt and decrypt data.

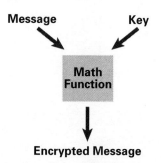

The mathematics are so complex that without knowing both the encryption code and the right key, it is virtually impossible to figure out the original message.

The second key piece of encryption is distributing and protecting keys. There are a number of ways to do this. We will discuss the Diffie-Hellman key exchange in this sheet.

Bullets, Bombs, and Secret Codes

Although this might sound surprising, encryption codes and cryptography methods fall under the same export laws as guns, ammunition, and explosives!

However, this makes sense when you think about national security issues. It is sometimes necessary to eavesdrop and wiretap the communications of unfriendly entities. Limiting the export of the most sophisticated cryptography methods protects our country's ability to stay ahead of eavesdropping methods being used against us. It also limits the ability of unfriendly parties to encrypt their own communications. So we can eavesdrop if required.

Data Encryption Standard (DES)

The Data Encryption Standard (DES) is one encryption standard that uses a fixed block algorithm, which is a fancy way of saying that it performs a complicated math function on standard lengths of bits. The DES algorithm splits the

blocks in two, encrypting one half using a key value and a complicated algorithm. The two halves are rejoined and then resplit. The process is repeated number of times until the output is secure.

Triple Data Encryption Standard (3DES)

Triple (3DES) DES encryption encrypts messages using three separate passes of the DES algorithm. 3DES provides a very high degree of message security, but depending on processor speeds, it can take up to three times more processor power than standard DES to encrypt a data block.

Advanced Encryption Standard (AES)

The Advanced Encryption Standard (AES) is the latest algorithm adopted for securing data communications. It is widely used by the U.S. government and many companies. It is quickly becoming the de facto encryption algorithm everywhere it is not subject to export restrictions.

AES was invented by two Belgians, Joan Daemen and Vincent Rijmen. It was submitted for an industry standard proposal and was standardized in 2002. AES is also the fundamental data encryption standard used by the Wi-Fi Protected Access 2 (WPA2) method to secure wireless networks.

At-a-Glance: Encryption

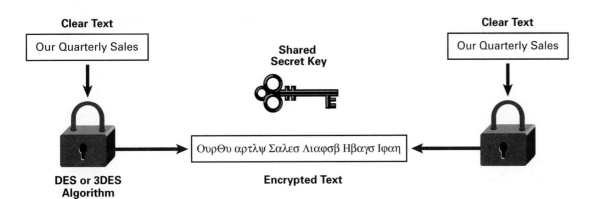

Clear Text

Our Quarterly Sales

Shared Secret Key

Clear Text

Our Quarterly Sales

ΟυρΘυ αρτλψ Σαλεσ Λιαφσβ Ηβαγσ Ιφαη

DES or 3DES Algorithm

Encrypted Text

Using Keys to Encrypt Stuff

The process of encrypting and decrypting data is made possible through the use of keys. Without the correct key, third parties are unable to unscramble a coded message (however, any code can eventually be cracked given enough computing power and time). Some encryption methods use the concept of a public key/private key pair to encode/decode messages. A public key is mathematically derived from the private key using a mathematical method called *factoring*. A detailed explanation of factoring is beyond the scope of this section, but the important thing about factoring is that it makes it nearly impossible to figure out a private key by looking at the public key.

The result of an encryption is called a *hash*. Using a private or session key, messages can be encoded. Public keys are used to ensure that the message is authentic and unchanged, and the private key is used to decode the message.

Diffie-Hellman Key Exchange

Understanding how encryption uses keys is only half the battle. You must also have a secure way of negotiating and passing keys without a third party obtaining them, even when the keys are exchanged over insecure links. The Diffie-Hellman key exchange protocol was designed for just this purpose. The exchange is secure because keys are never transmitted in clear text, so they are exceptionally difficult to figure out. Key interception is prevented using two known prime numbers that have a special mathematical relationship to one another, making it possible for two parties to agree on a shared secret key. But it is impossible for eavesdroppers to determine what this secret key is (even if they know the shared primes). Here is a

very basic example of how this works. (Remember in math class when you asked, "When will I ever use this?" Well, here you go!)

N = prime number

G = a root of N

User 1 creates a very large random number A

User 2 creates a very large random number B

User 1 sends A to User 2

User 2 sends B to User 1

A = GA * (crazy math function using N)

B = GB * (crazy math function using N)

Both parties can now figure out the key (K) as

K = ([A]) B * (crazy math function using N)

K = ([B]) A * (crazy math function using N)

At-a-Glance: Encryption

Application Layer Encryption	**Network Layer Encryption**	**Data Link Layer Encryption**

◄—— Encrypted ——►

Data

Data

Data

◄— Encrypted —►

◄—— Encrypted ——►

L3/4	Data

L3/4	Data

L3/4	Data

◄— Encrypted —►

◄—— Encrypted ——►

◄—— Encrypted ——►

L2	L3/4	Data

L2	L3/4	Data

L2	L3/4	Data

Where You Encrypt Matters

Encryption can be implemented at one of three OSI layers: the application, data link, or network layer. Each layer has advantages and disadvantages.

For application layer encryption, each application must be upgraded to support encryption, and all hosts that communicate with the applications must speak the same encryption language. This can often mean replacing all hosts in a network, but it does not necessarily require any network upgrades, because traffic is unaffected.

Network layer encryption can be done anywhere in the network (at the ingress and egress, for example) and does not require all hosts to be upgraded. It also leaves pertinent Layer 3 and 4 information in the clear for use in routing. Network layer encryption has a good balance of security and cost.

Data link layer encryption is very secure, because everything (including IP addresses) is encrypted. The downside is that each router must decrypt the traffic at every link and then re-encrypt it as soon as the correct path is determined. This is very slow, and every router must be upgraded.

Client Authentication

1 Jill wants to buy something on eAuction with her credit card.

eAuction
Nj2Yc3
Login

Prove to me you are eAuction.

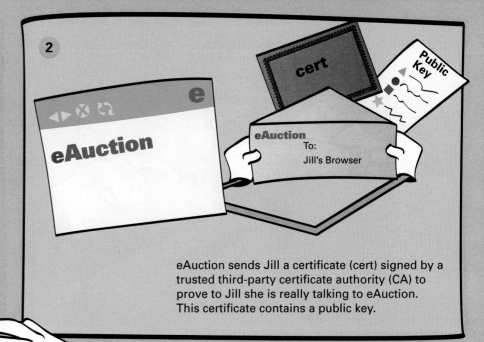

2 eAuction sends Jill a certificate (cert) signed by a trusted third-party certificate authority (CA) to prove to Jill she is really talking to eAuction. This certificate contains a public key.

eAuction

cert

Public Key

eAuction
To:
Jill's Browser

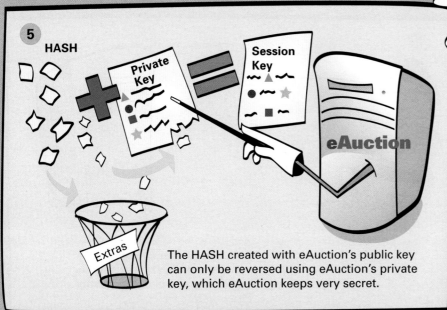

5 HASH

Private Key + = Session Key

eAuction

Extras

The HASH created with eAuction's public key can only be reversed using eAuction's private key, which eAuction keeps very secret.

6 Even if the original certificate was forged (which is possible), without access to the private key, Jill's information cannot be read.

Hacker's Bedroom

Hacker Only Gets Garbage:
((97mdpejr\\\,,,/#
$3~||*&[||

Sniffer Software

Rats.

Client Authentication

3 Question: But how can Jill share the session key with eAuction without everyone else seeing it, too?

Now that Jill has verified that she is talking to eAuction, she will need to generate a session key that will be used to encrypt the information sent back and forth between her and eAuction.

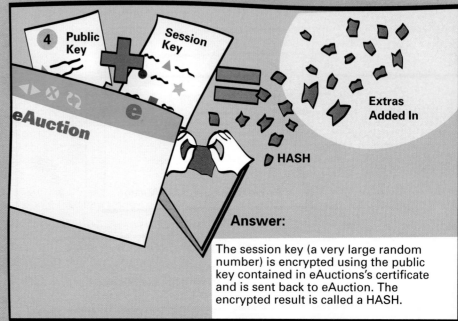

4 Public Key

Session Key

Extras Added In

HASH

Answer:

The session key (a very large random number) is encrypted using the public key contained in eAuctions's certificate and is sent back to eAuction. The encrypted result is called a HASH.

7

Now both Jill and eAuction know the session key that encrypts all their communication for the length of their communication.

8

Now that eAuction trusts Jill and Jill trusts eAuction, she can now securely purchase a slightly used *Martini Party Starter Kit*.

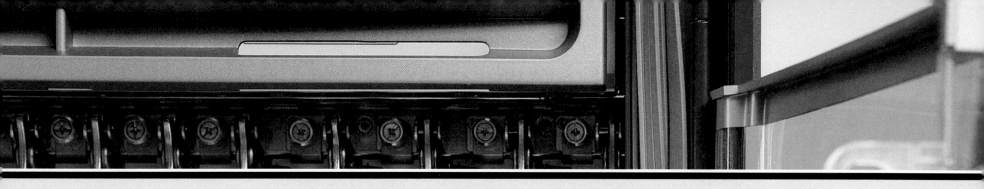

Optical Technologies

LANs, WANs—and Now MANs

The explosive growth of the Internet and Internet Protocol (IP) applications such as voice, video, and storage area networks (SAN) has boosted bandwidth demands for corporations. With LAN network speeds ranging from 10 Mbps to 10 Gbps, and QoS playing an important role in the delivery of this data, there must be an alternative to traditional WAN and LAN services for connecting metropolitan-area networks (MAN). Network connections that traditionally carried T1 and T3 speeds of data now require fiber channel, Enterprise System Connection (ESCON), Gigabit Ethernet, and 10 Gigabit Ethernet to satisfy demand. The increased demand coupled with the advances in optical technology have dramatically increased capacity and reduced cost, making it attractive for service providers to offer fiber-based network services for the metro market.

Fiber-based metropolitan networks address business needs in three areas:

- **Data networking and migration:** Optical networking technologies offer many data speeds and connections that support a variety of networking technologies, such as IP, synchronous optical network (SONET), ATM, and TDM. Networks can consolidate multiple wavelengths of traffic onto a single fiber to provide multiservice transport and facilitate the migration from traditional electrical networking technologies to a common optical transport.

- **Disaster recovery and business continuance:** Having a backup data center with backup storage is a primary consideration for most large businesses today. Metro optical networks provide fast, campus-to-campus transport with redundancy. Real-time disaster-recovery solutions, such as synchronous mirroring, guarantee that mission-critical data is securely and remotely mirrored to avoid any data loss in the event of a disaster.

- **Storage consolidation:** Network attached storage (NAS), when integrated with SAN applications, provides IP-based storage consolidation and file sharing. You can use multiple file storage access methods (such as Network File System [NFS] and CIFS) against the same storage farm to share unique data with multiple users and applications. Metro optical networks facilitate not only the implementation of storage, but also the extension of storage beyond a single data center.

- **Residential fiber:** As fiber becomes more cost-effective, it has begun to penetrate the home market, particularly in Japan and Korea. Don't be surprised if you see it being offered in your neighborhood soon.

SONET, DWDM, and DPT

Three primary optical technologies are employed today:

- Synchronous Optical NET (SONET)
- Dense wavelength division multiplexing (DWDM)
- Dynamic packet transport (DPT)

All three convert electrical signals into light and vice versa. Fiber-Optic Transmission Systems (FOTS) do the conversion. Fiber-optic signals are not susceptible to electrical interference. The signals can transmit over long distances and send more information than traditional electrical transports. The combination of these benefits provides lower costs than traditional data electrical transport mechanisms. Service providers have offered SONET services for some time. Benefits of SONET networks include high-speed network services that meet voice-transport requirements as well as survivability and availability needs. SONET network speeds currently range from 51.84 Mbps (OC-1) to 9953.28 Mbps (OC-192).

You can connect SONET nodes in the following ways:

- **Point-to-point**
- **Linear:** Each device connects to the devices before and after it, with up to 16 devices total.
- **Unidirectional path-switched ring (UPSR):** All traffic is homed to a central location.
- **Two-fiber bidirectional line-switched ring (2F BLSR):** Traffic is local to each set of neighbors, and bandwidth is reusable.
- **Four-fiber bidirectional line-switched ring (4F BLSR):** The same as 2F BLSR, except with multiple rings for diversity.

DWDM is based on the premise that optical signals of differing wavelengths do not interfere with each other. Wavelength division multiplexing (WDM) differs from time-division multiplexing technologies (such as SONET) in the following ways:

- TDM employs a single wavelength across a fiber. Data is divided into channels so that multiple channels can travel across a single fiber.

- WDM employs multiple wavelengths (lambdas) per fiber, which allows multiple channels per fiber (up to 160). Each lambda can include multiple TDM channels.

DWDM offers scalability over traditional TDM technologies. Because data can travel considerably farther across DWDM than traditional TDM (120 km versus 40 km), you need fewer repeaters. DWDM also allows for higher capacity across long-haul fibers as well as quick provisioning in metro networks. Metro DWDM needs to be cheap and simple to install and manage. It must also be independent of bit rate and protocol as a transport and provide 16 to 32 channels per fiber. DWDM nodes attach to each other in a ring pattern using optical add-drop multiplexers, which add and drop traffic at each remote site, and all traffic is homed to a central site.

DPT uses SONET/SDH framing and employs intelligent protection switching in the event of fiber facility or node failure or signal degradation. DPT uses a bidirectional, counterrotating ring structure for metro applications and a star structure with a central switching device for service PoP backbones. DPT facilitates the bridging of dark fiber, WDM, and SONET networks. On a campus-ring application, DPT interconnects buildings, data centers, and WAN services. It allows the extension of real-time applications as well as multisite distributed VPNs. DPT metro loop rings allow the delivery of voice, video, and Internet connectivity to businesses and high-rise residential buildings.

At-a-Glance: Metro Optical

Why Should I Care About Metro Optical?

Companies, universities, and government organizations often have several campuses in proximity to one another. In addition to the very high bandwidth requirements for application sharing and communication between campuses, there is also a need to support applications such as

- Business resilience (disaster recovery)
- Storage consolidation (centralized data)
- Distributed workplace (resources throughout the network)

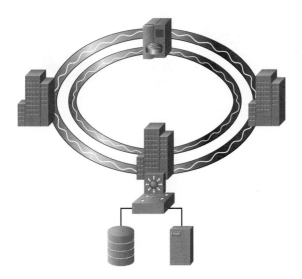

Fiber-optic networks can carry large amounts of multiple types of services simultaneously. They can also provide connectivity between LANs, access to WANs, and consolidation of SAN/NAS applications.

What Problems Need to Be Solved?

Optical networking uses pulses of light to transmit data over fiber-optic cables. These pulses of light are subject to degradation as they travel down the fiber, but in general the deterioration is less than that of copper, so fiber-optic signals can travel much farther.

Metro fiber-optic networks have a range 20 to 250 km. They can be deployed as point-to-point, ring, and mesh topologies. The four main protocols are Optical Ethernet, CWDM, DWDM, and SONET.

Fiber Basics

The two types of optical fiber are multimode and single-mode. With multimode fiber, light propagates in the form of multiple wavelengths, each taking a slightly different path. Multimode fiber is used primarily in systems with short transmission distances (less than 2 km). Single-mode fiber has only one mode in which light can propagate. Single-mode fiber is usually used for long-distance and high-bandwidth applications.

Multimode Fiber

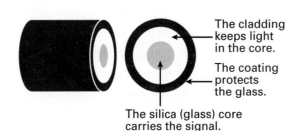

The cladding keeps light in the core.

The coating protects the glass.

The silica (glass) core carries the signal.

Key Design Criteria

As they travel down fibers, optical signals are subject to deterioration in the form of attenuation, dispersion and nonlinearities, chromatic distortion, and polarization mode distortion. These factors limit the distance and bandwidth of optical signals.

Attenuation is a loss of power over distance. In some cases amplifiers may be used to boost power.

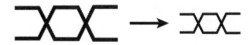

Dispersion and nonlinearities can erode signal clarity. This is a function of distance and speed.

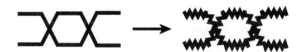

Chromatic distortion causes a spreading of the signal over distance. This can cause signals to interfere with each other.

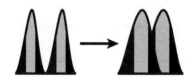

At-a-Glance: Metro Optical

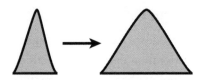

Polarization or mode distortion is another phenomenon. At 10-Gb rates and higher, signals tend to broaden as they travel down the fiber, causing intersignal interference.

Multiplexing

Multiplexing is the process of combining multiple signals over a single wire, fiber, or link. With time-division multiplexing (TDM), lower-speed signals are brought in, assigned time slots, and placed into a higher-speed serial output. On the receiving end, the signals are reconstructed.

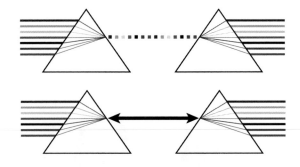

One of the properties of light is that light waves of different wavelengths do not interfere with one another within a medium. Because of this property, each individual wavelength of light can represent a different channel of information. By combining

light pulses of different wavelengths, many channels can be transmitted across a single fiber simultaneously. This is called Wavelength Division Multiplexing (WDM). WDM is a variation of Frequency Division Multiplexing (FDM).

Optical Ethernet

Gigabit Ethernet is the simplest and cheapest (least expensive) form of optical transport. Optical Ethernet uses a device called a Gigabit Interface Converter (GBIC), which plugs into a switch port and converts an Ethernet stream to an optical signal. Ethernet can leverage the growing service provider Metro Ethernet infrastructure or dark fiber.

CWDM

Coarse Wavelength Division Multiplexing (CWDM) uses wavelength-specific pairs of GBICs to combine up to eight optical signals onto a single fiber.

Each switch pair is fitted with one or more pairs of GBICs. Each GBIC pair is tuned to a specific frequency that allows the switch to add (mux) or pluck out (demux) a single beam of light (data stream).

CWDM can be deployed as ring or point-to-point. One major drawback of CWDM is that it cannot be amplified, which makes this solution distance-limited. The rule-of-thumb maximum distance is 80 km for point-to-point or a ring circumference of 30 km.

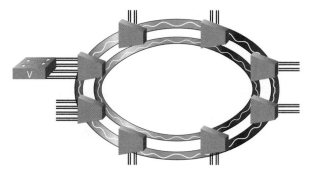

At-a-Glance: Metro Optical

DWDM

Dense Wavelength Division Multiplexing (DWDM) uses the same multiplexing scheme as CWDM. DWDM signals, however, are spaced much more closely together, allowing DWDM systems to multiplex up to 32 signals on a single fiber.

DWDM signals can be amplified, making the system ideal for backup data centers or larger (more geographically dispersed) campuses. With amplification, DWDM signals can be transmitted up to 250 km.

SONET

Synchronous Optical Network (SONET) is a Layer 1 technology that supports the high transmission rates (155 Mbps to 10 Gbps) needed in metro applications.

SONET serves as a backbone transport for other technologies such as Ethernet and ATM. It is commonly used by service providers for transport (metro and long-haul). SONET also has extensive OAMP (Operation, Administrative, Maintenance, and Provisioning) capabilities, allowing precise fault detection and rapid (50 ms) failover.

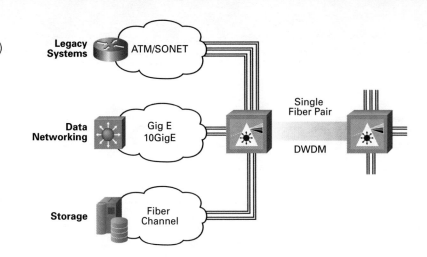

Branch Office Network Designs

Highly centralized companies typically have large centralized networks at one or a few locations. This allows you to locate your network staff centrally and focus on the service level of one or a couple campus networks.

This was the typical network of the past, with one or a few rather large headquarters locations. If branch offices were required, they typically were connected to the headquarters location. They provided minimal services, usually just a nightly synchronization or upload of the day's transactions, so that the mother ship could track the progress of sales, inventory, and other important data. Many companies just had dialup connections, used to upload "batch" data overnight and download new information from headquarters needed for the next day's business.

Loss of connection with the headquarters site often meant that the branch office was essentially unable to perform day-to-day business transactions until the connection was restored. This often meant huge productivity drains for companies with somewhat unreliable connections, and it often resulted in branch employees feeling like second-class citizens.

Distributed Workforce

Increasingly, companies are taking advantage of distributed workforces, with nearly half or even the majority of employees working at locations other than a headquarters site. With such a significant number of the company's resources located remotely, network designs needed to change.

It is no longer acceptable to provide minimal services to branch offices. They must have the same level of services as a headquarters site. After all, why have half your workforce be much less productive than those at the headquarters?

Branch office networks therefore must be able to provide the same level of networking services as a headquarters network (also called a campus). Not only must the services be reliable, but they also must be more extensive. Instead of nightly uploads, branch employees need real-time access to the same applications and databases of information that headquarters employees have. They also need access to the same phone services, access to the Internet, wireless, videoconferencing, e-learning, and many others.

The network design had to evolve to be able to support essentially every headquarters network service and application for all branch employees, seamlessly, as if the branch employees were working at the same location as the headquarters employees.

Distributed Office Challenges

The norm today for most companies is to have one or a few large headquarters sites, several fairly large regional offices, and a significant number of branch offices. The number of branch offices often depends on the business model or industry segment the company is in. For example, a retail store chain may have two headquarters locations (often one is for geographic redundancy in case of a catastrophic event) and several hundred or thousand stores (which are essentially branch offices). Similarly, banks typically have two or three central headquarters sites where their data centers are located, and they may have hundreds or thousands of bank branches. Energy companies may have tens of thousands of branch locations, such as gas stations.

Distributed offices and workforces mean distributed networks, interconnected to foster the best communications and network services across the whole company between employees, no matter where they are working. This presents challenges, such as how to connect hundreds or thousands of branch office networks in a scalable way, how to provide reliable network services at sometimes far-flung locations, and how to scale the IT department to manage all this.

At-a-Glance: Branch Office Design

Why Should I Care About Branch Office Design?

Branch offices now typically contain 40 percent or more of a company's employees, especially since the advent of globalization, in which major branches are operated in local markets throughout the world. These branch office employees need to be as productive as those at headquarters. Therefore, they need access to the same applications and level of network services.

Adding branches to the network and providing the employees with network services in an ad hoc manner can easily result in a jigsaw puzzle that increases both the cost and complexity of the network. This patchwork approach can also create security holes that attackers can exploit. This is especially true with overseas branches, where extra measures must often be taken to ensure that security and services meet the needs of the remote branch.

Because of this, branch networks should be carefully architected with the full suite of network services in mind from the start.

What Problems Need to Be Solved?

Several factors must be taken into consideration for branch networks:

- Branch offices must have a reliable connection to the headquarters site(s) and to other branches.

- Branch employees must have access to the same level of services and applications as HQ employees.

- The network may need to connect hundreds or thousands of locations without opening hundreds or thousands of security holes.

- A balance must be struck between having centralized applications for manageability and having distributed applications for fast access and survivability.

- Branch networks must be cost-effective, efficiently using bandwidth and other resources.

Architecting a Branch Network

Many network services need to be considered when planning a branch office:

- WAN services

- LAN services

- Network fundamental services such as DHCP and QoS

- Security services such as firewall and intrusion prevention

- Identity services such as 802.1x and access control

- Mobility services such as wireless LAN access

- Unified Communications services such as telephony, conferencing, and collaboration

- Application networking services such as file services and access to applications

- Network virtualization

In addition, each of these services must efficiently mesh into a broader company-wide subsystem. For example, branch security services must work in concert with security services at headquarters and other branch offices to thwart security breaches company-wide. Also, if the controlling central site goes away, the branch network must be able to provide some subset service level for each of these network services.

Scaling the Branch

As branches grow in size or criticality, they demand different design approaches:

- Relatively small branches may have a single WAN connection to the headquarters site. They typically collapse as many services as possible into a single networking product, such as an Integrated Services Router (ISR).

- Medium or critical branches may have multiple WAN connections to one or more headquarters or regional sites. These sites often distribute services across two ISRs in a redundant configuration.

- Large or very critical branches may have multiple WAN connections to one or more headquarters or regional sites. Large branches usually distribute services across two ISRs in a redundant configuration. They may offload critical services such as security and Unified Communications to dedicated devices.

At-a-Glance: Branch Office Design

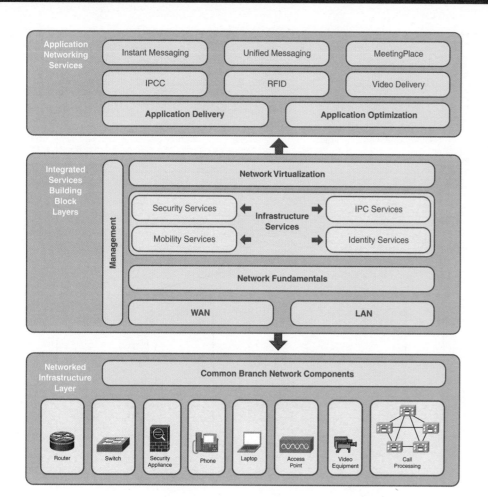

Application Networking Services
- Instant Messaging
- Unified Messaging
- MeetingPlace
- IPCC
- RFID
- Video Delivery
- **Application Delivery**
- **Application Optimization**

Integrated Services Building Block Layers
- Management
- Network Virtualization
- Security Services ← Infrastructure Services → IPC Services
- Mobility Services ← → Identity Services
- Network Fundamentals
- WAN
- LAN

Networked Infrastructure Layer
Common Branch Network Components
- Router
- Switch
- Security Appliance
- Phone
- Laptop
- Access Point
- Video Equipment
- Call Processing

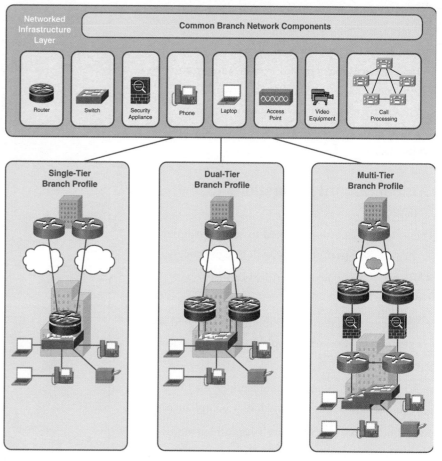

Networked Infrastructure Layer
Common Branch Network Components
- Router
- Switch
- Security Appliance
- Phone
- Laptop
- Access Point
- Video Equipment
- Call Processing

- Single-Tier Branch Profile
- Dual-Tier Branch Profile
- Multi-Tier Branch Profile

Critical Design Questions to Answer

Before the branch is architected, the following questions must be answered:

- What level of high availability or survivability is required?

- How many employees are located at the branch office?

- What types of network and communications services are needed?

- What is the future growth potential for the location?

Branch Security

Extending corporate networking and communications services to many locations creates many new security threat entry points. Therefore, the "hardening" of the branch network through infrastructure protection mechanisms is critical. Many companies

At-a-Glance: Branch Office Design

that maintain a good security posture at their headquarters leave themselves vulnerable at branch offices. Branch networks need the same level of security services and protection as headquarters campus networks. Ideally, branch networks and campus networks should work in concert to exchange information about security threats and intrusions.

Critical Security Questions to Answer

The following questions related to security should be answered as part of the branch design process:

- What are the company's critical security policies?

- What new potential vulnerabilities are created by extending all corporate applications and services to many locations?

- What types of secure communications may be required for industry or regulatory compliance?

- Are local laws being followed regarding employee privacy in international locations?

- What is the security management strategy?

Branch Communication

Unified Communications capability must also be integrated into a company's branch networks to ensure maximum productivity and efficiency. Services such as call control and routing, gateways to the PSTN, and conferencing circuits (to name

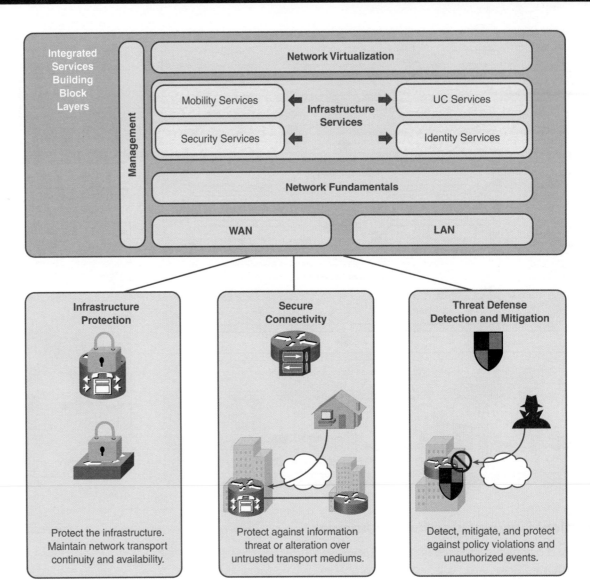

Infrastructure Protection

Protect the infrastructure. Maintain network transport continuity and availability.

Secure Connectivity

Protect against information threat or alteration over untrusted transport mediums.

Threat Defense Detection and Mitigation

Detect, mitigate, and protect against policy violations and unauthorized events.

At-a-Glance: Branch Office Design

but a few) may be provided by dedicated devices or via ISR. Unified Communication services factor heavily into branch office network design in terms of required high availability, bandwidth, and survivability/failover. ISRs can provide Unified Communications services such as Survivable Remote-Site Telephony (SRST), which can take over call control and routing services from the central site in the event of an outage.

Critical Communication Questions to Answer

- What types of Unified Communications services are needed now and in the future?
- Will the Unified Communications architecture be heavily centralized or distributed?
- Which Unified Communications services will be provided locally?

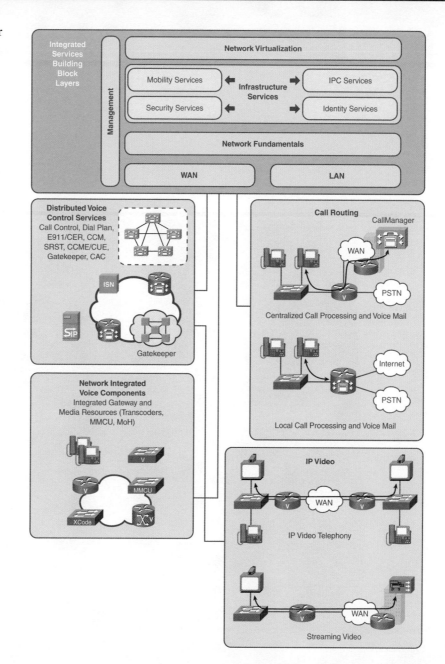

Part IV

Network Availability

One of the most important aspects of networking is keeping the network running—at all times, under any circumstances, even during times of excessive use or stress. Actually, *especially* during times of excessive use or stress. Why? Because a downed network can mean millions of dollars per minute in lost revenue. Consider a large retailer with 3000 stores that processes hundreds of credit card transactions per minute. If it cannot accept credit card purchases, it delays or loses sales.

The first section explores the importance and best practices of network availability and resilience, starting with high availability. It's always best to avoid a disaster rather than recover from one, and high availability refers to the design principles aimed at keeping the network up. "Control Plane Protection" and "QoS Resiliency" look at using existing networking technologies to help network administrators keep the network running. Control plane protection looks at keeping the "brains" and "heart" of the network working when the data side is compromised. QoS resiliency is the practice of using a prioritization scheme (originally developed for maintaining voice over IP quality) to dump traffic that appears to be an attack on the network to keep the "real" data flowing.

Sometimes it is not possible to avoid network outages despite good designs and proper planning. "Disaster Recovery" looks at how companies can best prepare to get the network up and the data restored in the event of an unavoidable outage, or possibly loss of a site.

The final topic is network management. Some large companies have an entire staff of IT professionals dedicated to managing the network to ensure that it operates efficiently. This section provides a view into what it takes to run a network.

High Availability

Designing networks for high availability

- Prevents financial loss

- Prevents productivity loss

- Reduces reactive support costs

- Improves customer satisfaction and loyalty

Network availability (often called "high availability") is the design and measurement of a network in terms of accessibility of network services. The network must be *available* for people to access the services on it. High availability simply refers to the desire to have the network available all the time, or as close to all the time as possible. *Network uptime* is the term used to describe the availability of the network.

As networks have migrated from mainframe-based client/server models to hybrid distributed networks (both client/server and peer-to-peer), measuring availability has become more complex. In addition to routers and switches, devices such as ATMs, credit-card readers at point of sale, web services, and automated check-in at airports must be available at all times. If they are down, business cannot be conducted, and revenue is affected.

Businesses measure their network downtime in terms of average cost per hour.

For example, if a portion of a credit card transaction network goes down such that businesses are unable to process sales transactions (meaning that customers will use different cards or cash), the credit card company may end up losing millions of dollars per hour.

Terms that are common when discussing availability are *24/7/365* and *five nines*. 24/7/365 refers to having the network up 24 hours a day, 7 days a week, 365 days a year (366 on leap years). This is a reflection of several trends:

- Businesses are international in nature. So while people in the U.S. sleep, their coworkers in Australia and Japan are conducting business and need access to network resources.

- Web presence allows companies to have their shop "open" 24 hours a day.

- Home users now expect and rely on continuous connectivity for TV, phone service, basic Internet, and home business.

Five nines refers to the measurement of availability in terms of a percentage: 99.999 percent. This implies that the "network" is available 99.999 percent of the time (and unavailable for 0.001 percent of the time). This type of measurement, borrowed from the world of the Public Switched Telephone Network (PSTN), made sense in the mainframe world (in which the measurement became used), in which a set of hosts were measured. However, today's networks are distributed and made up of hundreds or thousands of devices, so it is sometimes difficult to determine. For example, if part of the network is down, was the outage sufficient enough to classify as downtime? If so, which parts?

High availability seems like a no-brainer: Of course we want networks available all the time, so why is it such an interesting topic? The answer is that any network can be made available even 100 percent of the time, but the costs to do so would be enormous. So often, high availability ends up being a compromise of desire for uptime balanced with costs.

In terms of availability, the following table shows how the measurement translates into downtime per year:

Availability	Nines	Downtime Per Year
99.000 Percent	Two Nines	3 Days, 15 Hours, 36 Minutes
99.900 Percent	Three Nines	8 Hours, 46 Minutes
99.990 Percent	Four Nines	53 Minutes
99.9990 Percent	Five Nines	5 Minutes

This indicates that five-nines availability means that the network is unavailable for a total of 5 minutes per year. (This is only unplanned downtime. Removing a router for maintenance or replacement doesn't count.) Yeesh! So how do you design a network such that devices are always working?

First, what contributes to the network's unavailability?

- **Security holes:** Attacks on networks, even when security is not entirely breached, can cause outages or serious degradation of service levels.

- **Human error:** People sometimes pull on the wrong cable or mistype when setting up a routing table.

- **Failed devices:** Sometimes electronics just break.

- **Bugs:** Network software is pretty complicated. Even extensive testing may not cover all scenarios.

- **Power outages:** Unexpected power outages can take out critical network resources.

- **Service provider outage:** The service provider is prone to all the same issues on its network.

- **Natural disasters:** Disasters such as Hurricane Katrina can wipe out power and accessibility to an entire region. Even smaller events such as ice storms, tornadoes, and thunderstorms can cause a problem.

- **Backhoe:** In the ongoing battle of backhoes versus buried cables, backhoes are up about 5,345,910 to 0.

- **Acts of war or terror:** The more critical networks become, the bigger their value as a target.

- **Upgrades or hardware replacement:** Sometimes, you cannot replace a piece of equipment without turning it off.

Notice that most of these examples are not planned and thus generally are outside the control of the network administrator. It is also worth noting that human error tends to be the leading cause of network outages. It is the design of the network that allows (or prohibits) the network to be available during these planned and unplanned network outages.

The following design practices increase network availability:

Concept	Example
Hardware redundancy	Redundant hardware, processors, and cooling fans. Devices acting in parallel. The ability to "hot swap" devices or components without interrupting network operation (sometimes called an in-service upgrade).
Software availability features	Includes features such as HSRP, nonstop forwarding, spanning tree, fast route processor switchover, and nondisruptive upgrades.
Network/server redundancy	Redundant data centers mirror each other. If one data center (with its servers, databases, and networking gear) were to become unavailable, the network would automatically reroute to a redundant data center with minimal data loss.
Link/carrier availability	Multihoming servers, multiple link connections between switches and routers, subscriptions to several different service providers.
Clean implementation/ cable management	Human error being what it is, steps can be taken to minimize the chances of human error. Implementing a network cleanly (such as labeling cables, tying down cables, using simple network designs, using up-to-date network diagrams, and so on) helps prevent human error.
Backup power/ temperature management	Using backup power on primary network and server equipment ensures that when the power goes out, you have an alternative power source to keep the most critical devices operational.
Network monitoring	Monitoring the network, servers, and devices allows network administrators to detect problems or outages quickly, which contributes to minimizing network downtime.
Reduction of network complexity	Selecting a simple, logical, repetitive network design over a complex one simplifies the ability to troubleshoot and grow the network. It also reduces the chances of human error.
Change control management	Change control management is the process of introducing changes to the network in a controlled and monitored way. This includes testing changes before moving them to the production network, researching software upgrades for known bugs, having a backout plan in case the change causes a failure or doesn't take effect correctly, and making one change at a time. An expert or two should also review the proposed changes.

Concept	Example
Training	Nothing is more important than having a properly trained staff. This reduces human error significantly by eliminating mistakes made from ignorance.
Backup/automatic recovery	You cannot prevent failures from happening eventually. You can, however, put systems in place that keep users from noticing them.
Security posture and policies	Make sure that the network is adequately protected from security threats, both from outside and inside. Have measures in place to alert and quickly isolate security threat sources.

Reaching consistent uptime is unlikely to happen if any of the following exist:

- Single points of failure (edge card, edge router, single trunk)
- Outage required for hardware and software upgrades
- Long recovery time for reboot or switchover
- Untested hardware spares available on site
- Long repair times because of a lack of troubleshooting guides
- Inappropriate environmental conditions
- High probability of redundancy failure (failure is not detected and redundancy is not implemented)
- High probability of double failures
- Long convergence time for rerouting traffic around a failed trunk or router in the core

Because outages do occur, the goal of network administrators should be to reduce the outage time as much as possible.

At-a-Glance: High Availability

Why Should I Care About High Availability?

A highly available network means that the network and the applications that are used on it are both operational and accessible at all times. As more and more businesses use networking to conduct their day-to-day business, networking becomes a critical aspect of business. To put this in perspective, you only need to look at the cost of a network outage. The following numbers reflect the average cost of *one hour* of downtime for various types of businesses:

Manufacturing	$201,000
Retail	$79,000
Healthcare	$107,000
Transportation and logistics	$107,000
Financial	$188,000

Source: Infonetics, "The Costs of Enterprise Downtime," 2005

Designing a network for high availability

• Prevents financial loss

• Prevents productivity loss

• Reduces reactive support costs

• Improves customer satisfaction and loyalty

What Affects Network Availability?

The three most common causes of network failures are operational (human) errors, network equipment (hardware) failures, and software failures:

• Operational errors are usually the result of poor change-management processes or the lack of training and documentation.

• Network equipment failures include hardware failures, power outages, overheating, and the dreaded backhoe.

• Software failures can be caused by software crashes, unsuccessful switchovers, or latent code failures.

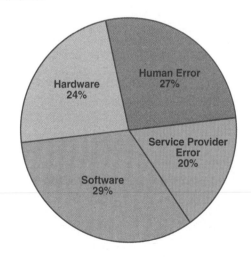

Source: Infonetics, "The Costs of Enterprise Downtime," 2005

How Is Availability Measured?

The two most common methods for measuring availability are "number of nines" and defects per million (DPM). Number of nines refers to the measurement of availability in terms of a percentage. For example, five nines implies that the network is available 99.999 percent of the time (and is unavailable for .001 percent of the time). Although this measurement is still very common, it is really a holdover from the PSTN and mainframe worlds, where only the availability of large centralized hosts was measured. Modern networks are distributed and are made up of hundreds and thousands of devices. In this case, defects per million is a more realistic measurement. DPM is the number of defects per one million hours of operation.

Availability	DPM	Downtime Per Year
99.000 Percent	10,000	3 Days, 15 Hours, 36 Minutes
99.900 Percent	1000	8 Hours, 46 Minutes
99.990 Percent	100	53 Minutes
99.9990 Percent	10	5 Minutes

At-a-Glance: High Availability

Best Practices

Hardware redundancy means redundant hardware, processors, power supplies, and links. The network should be designed such that there are no single points of failure for critical hardware (such as core switches). Hardware availability should also allow you to hot-swap cards or other devices without interrupting the device's operation (an in-service upgrade).

Reducing Network Complexity

Although some redundancy is good (and necessary), overdoing it can cause more problems than it solves. Selecting a simple, logical, and repetitive network design over a complex one simplifies troubleshooting and growing the network. There is a trade-off between expenses and risk. A good design maintains the proper balance between the two extremes.

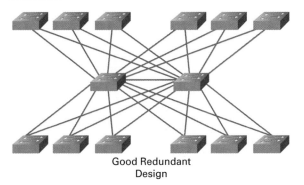
Good Redundant
Design

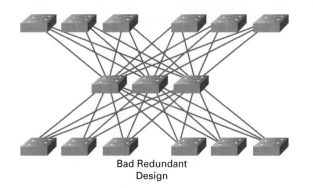
Bad Redundant
Design

The extra core switch adds much
complexity with little additional benefit.

Software Availability

Software availability refers to both reliability-based protocols such as Spanning Tree Protocol and Hot Standby Router Protocol (HSRP) as well as reliable code and nondisruptive upgrades.

Spanning tree, HSRP, and other protocols instruct the network or its components how to behave in the event of a failure. Failure in this case could be a power outage, a hardware failure, a disconnected cable, or any number of things. These protocols provide rules to reroute packets and reconfigure paths. Convergence is the process of applying these rules to the resolution of any such network errors. A converged network is one that, from a user standpoint, has recovered from a failure and can now process instructions and/or requests.

Link/Carrier Availability

Another component in building highly available networks is understanding your service provider's plans and policies for network availability. Service provider issues are the fourth largest source of network downtime for companies.

For business-critical applications it may be worthwhile to purchase a secondary service from another service provider. This second link can sometimes be used for load sharing.

Clean Implementation/Cable Management

This best practice may seem like a waste of time when you first implement a network, but disorganized cabling and poor implementation can increase the probability of, and hinder the timely resolution of, network disasters.

Network Monitoring

Monitoring the network servers and devices allows network administrators to detect problems or outages quickly, which contributes to minimizing network downtime. The goal is to detect problems before they affect the network's ability to pass traffic. Network management software typically is used to monitor the network.

At-a-Glance: High Availability

Network/Server Redundancy

Redundant data centers mirror each other such that if one data center (with its servers, databases, and networking gear) were to become unavailable, the network would automatically reroute to a redundant data center with minimal data loss. Dual data centers can also provide load sharing when both are available.

Training

Nothing is more important than having a properly trained staff. Up-to-date, comprehensive training can significantly reduce failures. Human error will always exist, but you can limit that exposure through documentation, good design practices, and training. Human error can be forgiven, but ignorance cannot. Train your staff on security, monitoring tools, disaster recovery procedures, and new technologies. Never stop training.

Change Control Management

Always expect the worst when first installing upgrades—it will save you time and trouble in the long run. Introduce all changes to the network in a controlled way. This includes testing changes before moving them onto the production network, researching software upgrades for known bugs, and having a backout plan in case the change causes a failure or doesn't take correctly.

Software should be thoroughly tested and used in a real (quarantined) or simulated real environment before being put on the network. Avoid "bleeding-edge" or inadequately tested code. Procedures should also be put in place for the introduction of new or updated code. Shutting down the network, loading new code, and hoping it all works when turned back on is usually a bad idea. New code should be introduced first on segmented, noncritical parts of the network. Plan for the worst case when loading new code.

Security Posture and Policies

Security is an entire practice of its own that we will not cover here. But it is important to point out that security is a critical aspect of network reliability and availability. An attack on a company's network, creating downtime and productivity losses, can be just as devastating to a company as industrial espionage and losing trade secrets.

Continually evaluate the assets on the network to be protected. Incorporate strong security measures to protect not only company assets (such as data information servers), but also the network itself.

Control Plane

When Good Networks Go Bad

One of the most basic and critical functions of the network is to provide a way for network administrators to provision and maintain the network devices themselves. Functions that need to be performed include establishing new connections, updating the network topology, monitoring network throughput and performance, and enforcing security and service policies. All this (and more) is performed by the control plane in a network device. The control plane is responsible for providing an interface to the network administrator, receiving commands, acting on them, and providing response.

When networks are functioning optimally, the control plane may be used only for monitoring to make sure that the network continues to function. When something goes wrong, the control plane functions are critical. They enable the network administrator to understand what is happening, take corrective actions, and monitor the effect of the changes. If the control plane is compromised and unable to respond, the network device (and network) can get into a "locked up" state. In this state, no network changes are possible, no monitoring is available, and there is no visibility into the operational state.

The control plane is sometimes called the out-of-band network, meaning that it is outside the band of the network services themselves (for example, forwarding packets). This is sometimes a hard concept for people new to networking to grasp. Think of it like the controls of your car. The car engine runs and turns the tires, carrying you down the street. Applying the brakes slows down, applying the gas speeds up, and turning the wheel changes direction. Imagine if you were to lose these important control plane functions in your car. No matter how hard you steer or push the pedals, the car doesn't respond.

More important, perhaps, suppose the data plane (the functions that receive and forward packets) is also experiencing difficulty. Lack of a functioning control plane means that the network can quickly go into an unavailable state, without possibility of quick recovery without more drastic actions (such as a complete reboot). What would cause either the data plane or control plane to "seize up" and be inaccessible? Sometimes network faults occur where either a software bug or configuration error is introduced. Other times a network may be under attack from malicious individuals who are consciously attempting to thwart normal network functions to cause problems or take over control of network devices.

One of the main challenges with network devices (at least legacy ones) is when the same processor inside the device is responsible for servicing both the data and control planes. In such an architecture, when the data plane becomes overwhelmed, so can the control plane. This is a frustrating condition for network administrators. Even if they know the actions to take to correct the network, they are unable to get a response from the network device to do so.

Control Plane Protection

Control Plane Protection (sometimes called Control Plane Policing or CoPP) involves taking explicit measures to ensure that no matter what occurs with the data plane, the control plane continues to function and be responsive. Possible control plane protection methods include the following:

- Preserving CPU "bandwidth" as a high priority for control plane services
- Safeguards on the data plane to prevent CPU overruns
- Separate CPU processors for the data plane and control plane

Control Plane Protection is a critical element of network availability. It ensures that the network can operate normally even under adverse conditions and that the network administrator can always quickly access the network device and take corrective actions.

At-a-Glance: Control Plane Protection

Why Should I Care About Control Plane Protection?

The network is said to have two planes: a control plane and a data plane. The data plane simply refers to the information that is being transported. The control plane refers to the directions or instructions on what the network is supposed to do with the data. Under normal network operating conditions, the control plane is used to manage a network device such as a switch or router.

Typical control plane functions include checking the status of links, monitoring traffic flows, and making configuration changes to the network device. It is critical to maintain control plane functions, especially when the network has a problem or is not performing as expected. If control plane functions are lost or compromised, it may not be possible for a network administrator to control operation of the network. Data will be lost, misdirected, or unable to reach its intended destination. Control Plane Protection guards against this type of problem.

What Problems Need to Be Solved?

If a network device is overwhelmed by sustained high volumes of traffic, CPU utilization becomes too high, causing resource shortages such as low memory or loss of control plane functionality. Some network devices, especially those sharing a single CPU to service both traffic forwarding and control plane functions, can be compromised, leading to an unresponsive device.

Enabling the network administrator to monitor network devices and make necessary configuration changes is critical to detection and the possible mitigation of attacks.

Severe compromises of the control plane could also result in the inability of routing protocols to properly function, resulting in loss of traffic forwarding and network functions.

How Does Control Plane Protection Work?

Denial of service (DoS) and distributed denial of service (DDoS) attacks typically try to overwhelm a device with traffic to the point of instability. Control Plane Policing (CoPP) uses QoS traffic policies to restrict the amount of traffic destined for network devices (see "At-a-Glance: QoS Resiliency").

This type of traffic throttling ensures that critical control plane traffic, such as routing protocols, configuration changes, and network monitoring, can occur normally, even when a system is forwarding a high amount of traffic in the data plane.

As shown in the figure, several stages of CoPP may be used, first in hardware at a linecard level, as well as a final control mechanism on ingress to the main CPU (most likely done in software).

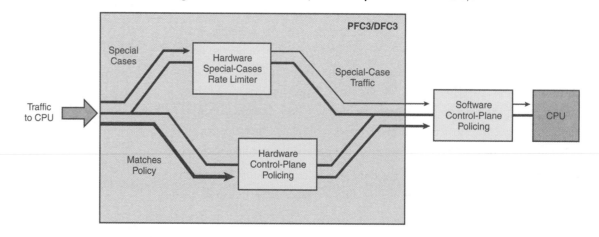

Control Plane Policing

CoPP implementations are dependent on the product type and device architecture.

For some switches, forwarding can occur without involving the main device CPU, shown in the figure as linecard to linecard. Traffic limiting can be enforced to ensure that control traffic needing to be serviced by

At-a-Glance: Control Plane Protection

the main CPU is appropriate, by enforcing a number of queues into the main CPU. No one class of requests (such as traffic) can overwhelm the other classes, such as control commands.

Dedicated CPUs

In cases where more robust network availability is essential, more sophisticated network devices may use an architecture that provides more guarantees of availability.

For example, in some cases it may be advisable or even necessary to use dedicated CPUs for control plane activity. As shown in the figure, separate processors handle data plane and control plane requests. In this way, the control plane processor should always be available to process requests, even if the data plane processor is overwhelmed.

Why not always use dedicated processors? The answer is simply cost and complexity. In smaller network devices, it may be cost-prohibitive to add processors, and this also may add too much complexity to the device. High availability is usually a trade-off between cost/complexity and the need for uptime.

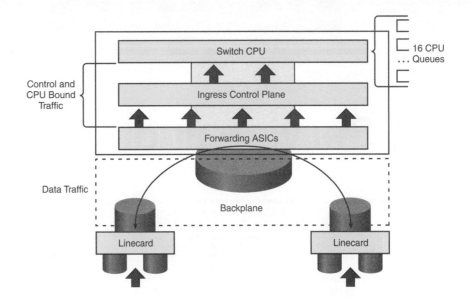

Quality of Service and Network Availability

Quality of Service as Network Protection?

Quality of Service (QoS) is commonly used in networks to provide prioritization of critical network traffic or traffic with special requirements. For example, in a converged network with data and other types of traffic such as voice over IP (VoIP) and video over IP (see Part VII, "Unified Communications"), QoS is used to manage the special requirements of voice and video communications, providing low delay (typically less than 250 milliseconds end-to-end), low jitter (typically less than 10 or 20 milliseconds), and low packet loss (typically less than 0.5 percent of packets). Exceeding these values can cause poor-quality VoIP calls and frustrate users.

QoS also has a role to play in highly available networks. Often when one or more devices (such as laptops) on the network have been compromised with malicious software, such as a virus or worm, they can be used as a launching point for attacks on other parts of the network, such as network devices or application servers. If such an attack comes from outside the network, such as from the Internet, or from a single laptop on the network, it can often be easily recognized and halted, if not prevented. However, when attacks originate from several or many devices, and those same devices appear to be sending legitimate traffic over the network, they can be very difficult to locate and halt.

Scavenger QoS

Scavenger QoS operates on the principle that if we know a typical application's behavior on a device and on the network, we can build safeguards into the network to recognize and stop an application if it is not behaving normally. For example, if we know that a particular port on the network has an IP-enabled telephone connected to it, and we know that device normally transmits less than, say, 150 kbps of RTP traffic packets, and suddenly we see more than 4 Mbps of RTP traffic from that port, an anomaly exists. This might indicate a malfunctioning or compromised device. Worse yet is that this traffic typically is marked extremely high priority in the network to preserve voice quality.

Scavenger QoS works by defining limits on ports that if a configured traffic limit is exceeded, the packets exceeding the limits are remarked to a much lower priority that essentially tells the network it is okay to transmit these packets whenever it has the time. If the network is under severe congestion (meaning that it is getting overwhelmed with traffic), it might be okay to "starve" the traffic marked as Scavenger class, meaning that it gets delayed to the point where it is dropped.

Scavenger QoS is almost "anti-QoS" in the sense that when used in this way QoS has the opposite effect of QoS for voice-quality applications (discussed later in this book). In short, QoS typically identifies critical traffic types (such as voice traffic) and *raises* these packets' priority on the network. Scavenger QoS identifies certain types of traffic and then *lowers* these packets' priority on the network. This difference is key.

Building such safeguards into the network is another step in keeping a highly available network functioning, even when devices malfunction severely. Or a security threat may be in progress, attempting to compromise either the network's availability or integrity.

At-a-Glance: QoS for Network Resiliency

Why Should I Care About QoS for Network Resiliency?

As companies rely more and more on the network for business applications, including voice, video, and data, the requirements for network stability have gone up as well. Under normal operations, a properly designed network can handle the traffic required by all network users. But what about those times when the traffic usage goes beyond what the network can handle?

When a network experiences traffic spikes due to legitimate or illegitimate traffic, congestion in the network can degrade critical and delay-sensitive traffic such as VoIP and other mission-critical applications. Highly available networks must incorporate protections so that mission-critical applications continue to function, even when unexpected events occur. QoS resiliency is one such protection method.

QoS Basics

Quality of service is commonly used to prioritize delay-sensitive applications such as VoIP and mission-critical data (see Part VII).

However, the same method that allows QoS to distinguish between high-priority and normal traffic can also be used to distinguish between normal traffic and traffic of an unknown type or origin. It can also be used in conjunction with policing mechanisms to limit the amount of legitimate traffic.

Traffic exceeding defined thresholds can be marked as Scavenger class traffic by QoS. This new type of traffic can then be aggressively dropped when the network experiences congestion.

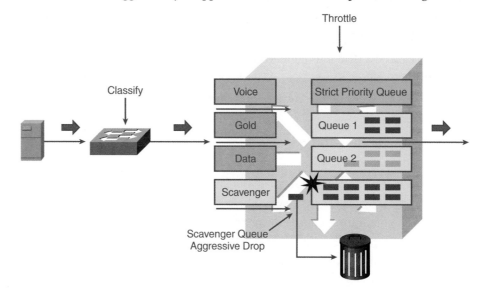

QoS: Protecting the Good, Dumping the Bad

To see how this works, let's use an example of a self-replicating worm or virus that clogs the network with traffic. QoS will have already marked voice and video traffic as high priority, so they get a fixed percentage of bandwidth whenever they are present. QoS can also now mark data from certain applications, such as an Enterprise Resource Planning (ERP) or Customer Relationship Management (CRM) system, as a second class of traffic, which is also allocated bandwidth.

Other types of traffic may be considered "data" traffic and be assigned to a third class.

A final class of traffic is the Scavenger class. If bandwidth is available, the traffic gets through, but never at the expense of the stuff we need to run the business. This ensures that the network remains available to the important types of traffic.

What Is "Normal"?

Scavenger traffic can be defined as abnormal traffic, which means that you need to understand what is normal. The best way to go about this is to analyze and understand traffic flows on the network at

At-a-Glance: QoS for Network Resiliency

different times over a period of days or weeks. After the norms have been established (a baseline) for traffic from certain sources, applications, or even ports, limits can then be set such that a very large increase in e-mail traffic can be assumed to be caused by a virus or other attack. Even noncritical traffic such as point-to-point file sharing can have limits set. Traffic (mission-critical or otherwise) that exceeds the preset limits gets remarked to the lower Scavenger class of service.

If the network is congested, the Scavenger class is aggressively dropped. Sources or hosts generating normal traffic flow levels remain at their normal status and are given their expected levels of service by the network. This has the effect of protecting the network from abnormal amounts of traffic, even when it appears as the right types of traffic on the network.

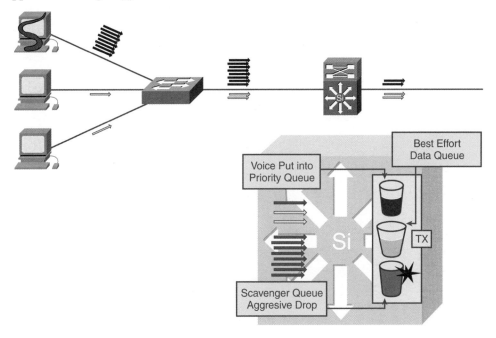

Don't Go It Alone

QoS Scavenger class alone does not solve the entire problem of protecting against traffic spikes, because the edge network devices still must deal with large traffic volumes coming from outside the network.

Tools such as CoPP must also be used to guard against network-wide impacts of worm, DoS, and DDoS attacks.

Defining Scavenger Traffic/ Normal Traffic

During "normal" traffic conditions, the network operates within its designed capacity. During these periods, QoS is used for Priority Queuing to ensure low latency and jitter for VoIP.

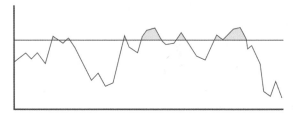

Scavenger traffic is serviced with very low packet loss during these periods.

First-Order Traffic Anomalies

All end systems generate traffic spikes. However, sustained traffic loads beyond what has been determined as "normal" from any given source device must be considered suspect and marked as Scavenger. Spikes that do not last longer than a predetermined period are considered first-order traffic anomalies, and no direct action is taken.

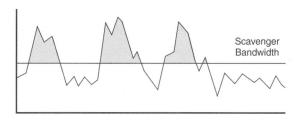

At-a-Glance: QoS for Network Resiliency

Second-Order Traffic Anomaly

Traffic spikes are pretty common in networking. Because networks typically are oversubscribed (as described in Part III, "Network Design"), seeing spikes that exceed bandwidth thresholds is expected and can even be tolerated. However, when the spikes turn into plateaus (meaning that the thresholds are exceeded for a sustained period), the network could be under attack. These sustained periods of very high usage are called second-order traffic anomalies. They are the reason that scavenger QoS exists.

During times of "abnormal" traffic (during a worm attack, for example) traffic marked as Scavenger is aggressively dropped. Priority queuing ensures low latency and jitter for VoIP.

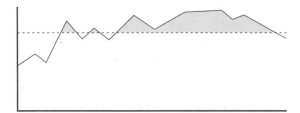

Switches, ports, or applications that are not generating abnormal traffic volumes continue to receive normal network service levels.

Disaster Recovery

What Happens When the Network Stops Working

Disaster recovery (DR) is the planning process for how you restore network and computer services or continue operating in the event of a natural or human disaster. The process includes identifying the hardware and software required to run business-critical applications and the associated processes that provide a smooth transition from the event. A DR plan assesses the loss of time and loss of data that are acceptable to the business. Within those limits, DR moves processing to an alternative location after a catastrophic event. The alternative location must have all the components of the production site already in place before the disaster. The move to an alternative location requires an understanding of five key components:

- **Equipment:** What equipment is affected? Which servers, disks, and networks?
- **Data:** Which databases and data are affected?
- **People:** Who is responsible for recovery?
- **Location:** Where does the recovery take place?
- **Network:** How do we switch the network to the recovery location?

Statistically, fire is the leading cause of disaster. Examples of other possible disasters include storms, floods, earthquakes, chemical accidents, nuclear accidents, wars, terrorist attacks, cold winter weather, extreme heat, and airplane crashes (loss of key staff). The planning process includes all the different locations and determines the political stability of the critical business locations. For each possible disaster that could affect a site, the disaster team assesses the impact on the business in advance. The team addresses the following questions:

- How much of the organization's resources (including data, equipment, and staff) could be lost? What are the replacement costs?
- What efforts would be required to rebuild?
- How long would it take to recover?
- What would be the impact on the overall organization?
- What customers would be affected? What would be the impact on them?
- How much would the disaster affect the share price and market confidence?

DR Planning

After outlining possible threats, the DR team ranks the services and systems according to three categories: mission-critical, important, and not so important. The ranking determines the depth of planning, funding, and resiliency. A DR team takes the following steps:

STEP 1   Form a planning group.

STEP 2   Perform risk assessments and audits.

STEP 3   Establish priorities for the network and applications.

STEP 4   Develop recovery strategies.

STEP 5   Prepare an up-to-date inventory and documentation of the plan.

STEP 6   Develop verification criteria and procedures.

STEP 7   Implement the plan.

STEP 8   Perform periodic drills to ensure that staff remains ready.

The team identifies recovery action for the applications staff, system administrators, database administrators, and network staff.

Resiliency and Backup Services

Business resiliency is the ability to recover from any network failure or issue, whether it is related to disaster, link failures, hardware, design, or network services. A highly available network (built for resiliency) is the bedrock of effective and timely disaster recovery. Consider the following areas of the network for resiliency:

- Network links
  — Carrier diversity
  — Local loop diversity
  — Facilities resiliency
  — Building wiring resiliency

- Hardware resiliency
  — Power, security, and disaster
  — Redundant hardware and onsite spare equipment
  — Mean time to repair (MTTR)
  — Network path availability

- Network design
  — Highly available campus designs
  — Redundant data center designs
  — Survivable WAN and branch office designs

- Network services resiliency
  — Domain Name System (DNS) resiliency
  — Dynamic Host Configuration Protocol (DHCP) resiliency
  — Other services resiliency

Preparedness Testing

The final step of any DR is testing processes and systems. Just as firefighters practice fighting different types of fires to hone their skills and reactions, the DR team should plan mock disasters to ensure that systems, network services, and data all transition as expected and that all the people involved understand their parts in the transition.

At-a-Glance: Disaster Recovery: Business Continuance

Why Should I Care About Disaster Recovery?

System outages can be devastating to a business. Regardless of the cause, any outage can cost a company hundreds of thousands or even millions of dollars per hour of system downtime.

Disaster recovery is the planning and implementation of systems and practices to ensure that when disasters do occur, the core business functions continue to operate.

Many people prefer to use the term "business continuance" rather than "disaster recovery," because the term implies that disaster (business stoppage) can be avoided with proper planning and implementation.

What Are Typical Causes of Disasters?

Disaster can come in all shapes and sizes. For the sake of simplicity we have organized "typical" causes of business disruptions into a few broad categories.

Natural Disasters

- Earthquake
- Flood
- Hurricane/typhoon or tornado
- Blizzard or ice storm
- Forest fire
- Biological pandemic

Unintentional Man-Made Disasters

- Backhoe
- Fire
- Illness (loss of staff)
- Power outage

Intentional Man-Made Disasters

- Act of war
- Terrorism
- Hacking
- Work stoppage

What Problems Need to Be Solved?

A disaster recovery plan has four phases: assessment, planning, testing, and implementation/recovery. For each risk assessed, a plan must put into place. Although disruptions can come in many forms, we will concentrate on network services and critical applications and data.

Also keep in mind that availability and business continuity come with a price tag. It's worth doing an assessment to get to a sweet spot where the cost benefits and risks are in the proper balance.

Disruption	Solution
Phone Service Interrupted	Multichannel Communications Strategy
Network Services Disrupted	Distributed, Redundant Network Design
Mission-Critical Applications Down	Business Continuance Plan (Standby Data Center Backup)
Can't Get to the Office	Secure Remote Access and Flexible Communications (Mobility, Telecommuting)
Productivity Constrained	Innovative IP Applications

At-a-Glance: Disaster Recovery: Business Continuance

Before a Disaster Occurs

Risk Assessment

The first step in a business continuance plan is to assess the business criticality and downtime impact of each business application. The risk assessment should consider how a temporary or extended loss of each application and function impacts the business, with regards to the following:

- Financial losses (lost revenue)
- Operation disruption
- Customer satisfaction and retention
- Lost productivity
- Brand dilution
- Legal liability
- Stock price
- Credit rating

For each system, application, or function deemed critical, a backup/recovery plan must be implemented.

Planning for a Disaster

After the critical systems, data, and applications have been identified and assessed, a plan must be developed. A business continuance plan has two primary components: designing the network for high availability, and backing up critical systems in geographically separated buildings.

Networks designed for high availability are resilient to disruptions such as faulty hardware, disconnected or broken cables ("backhoe failures"), and power outages.

When more severe disasters (such as a building fire or earthquake) strike, however, entire data centers and application server farms can be wiped out. The only way to recover gracefully from such an event is to have a completely backed-up secondary data center, as shown in the figure.

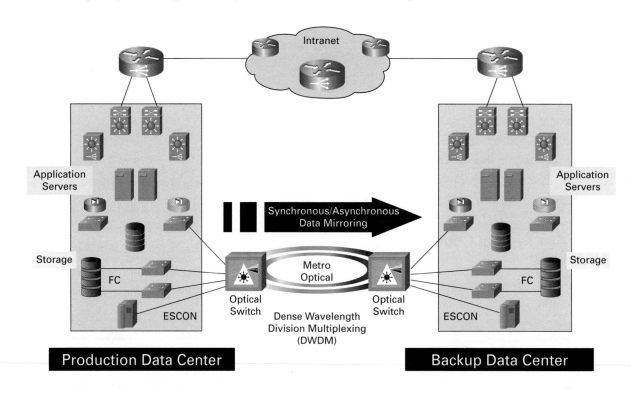

When planning for disasters, remember that there should be considerations beyond the network. For example, what if the phone lines and cellular systems go down also? What if flooding or fire makes local transportation difficult or impossible? Widespread disasters (such as Hurricane Katrina) can impact all infrastructure and basic services for entire regions. The big disasters don't confine themselves to the network. Neither should your planning.

At-a-Glance: Disaster Recovery: Business Continuance

Backing Up Systems

There are a number of ways to back up data centers and application farms. Some companies back up systems each night after the close of business. In this case, the worst-case data loss is a single day.

Another backup scheme is called synchronous data mirroring. It allows companies to perform real-time backups with no lag, ensuring that virtually no data is lost in the event of a natural or man-made disaster. An added benefit of synchronous data mirroring is that both systems can be online at the same time, providing load and application sharing, which can increase overall productivity. The main challenge with synchronous data mirroring is the potential significant slowing of application performance. To achieve synchronous remote mirroring without affecting application performance, high-speed, low-latency connections, such as Dense Wavelength Division Multiplexing (DWDM) over optical fiber, are preferred.

Such architectures for synchronous mirrored data centers that are both active are sometimes called an "active-active" model. For large companies, they are a necessity. For smaller companies this might be cost-prohibitive, so other methods of backup are necessary.

Preparedness Testing

One of the best ways to ensure either a smooth recovery from, or the complete avoidance of, a disaster is to provide staff with real-world training simulations. Allowing IT staff to practice different disaster scenarios will greatly improve their ability to cope with actual disasters.

Such "mock" disasters are common for training in healthcare, emergency response, and law enforcement agencies. They are just as effective for training corporate network staff.

After a Disaster Occurs

Recovery to Normal Operations

Practice and planning are put to the test if disaster strikes. To avoid confusion, or worse (such as causing more damage), a checklist should be developed as part of the planning effort and should be followed when the time comes. The checklist will vary from business to business and situation to situation, but most will closely resemble the following example:

1. Make sure that your people are safe. Are all personnel accounted for? Consider sending home noncritical personnel to avoid confusion.

2. Check to make sure the backup systems are online.

3. Assess the likelihood of additional or secondary disasters. An earthquake, for example, could spark fires or burst gas or water mains.

4. Monitor the network to ensure business continuation.

Restoring Primary Systems

Depending on the severity of damage to, and the duration of downtime for, primary systems, the restoration of these systems may also disrupt business.

Backing up data stored on the backup systems and restoring the primary systems must be taken into account.

Disaster Recovery

Normal Operation

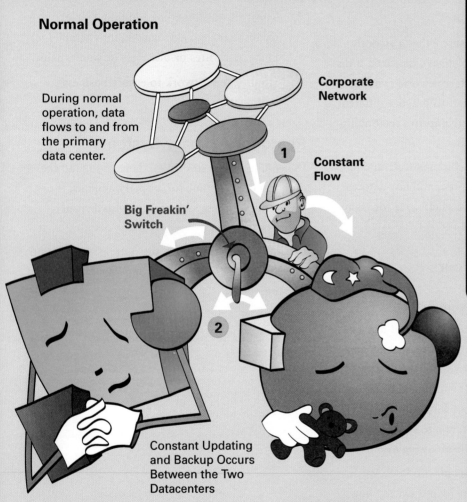

During normal operation, data flows to and from the primary data center.

Corporate Network

1 **Constant Flow**

Big Freakin' Switch

2

Constant Updating and Backup Occurs Between the Two Datacenters

Data Center 1
- Credit Card Numbers
- Bank Transactions
- Expense Database

Data Center 2
It can be idle during normal operation or help balance the workload. Data is backed up at regular intervals or constantly if performing load balancing.

Disaster Recovery

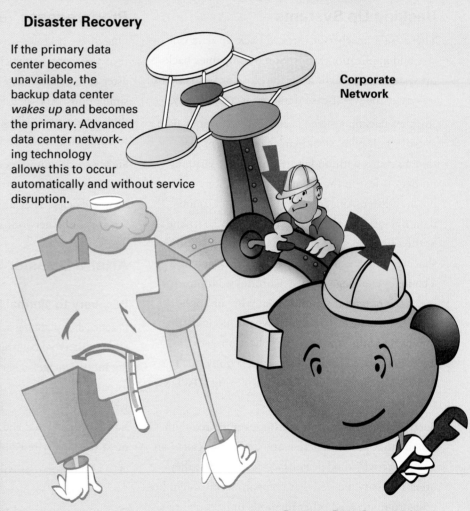

If the primary data center becomes unavailable, the backup data center *wakes up* and becomes the primary. Advanced data center network- ing technology allows this to occur automatically and without service disruption.

Corporate Network

Because Data Center 2 has been constantly backed up, little or no data is lost in the event of fire, flood, mouse attack, or other disaster.

Network Management

Keeping the Network Alive from Afar

Network management is the process of documenting, monitoring, troubleshooting, and configuring network devices. Network management gives visibility to the networking staff. The routers and switches in a network have the same components as a regular PC. There are a CPU (or two), memory, storage, and network interfaces. The primary difference from a PC is that network equipment is highly optimized to perform certain functions, such as passing packets quickly. The nature of today's networks is that network equipment is distributed everywhere. Remote branches, data centers, locations around the world—all these places on the network have routers, switches, servers, and other networking gear.

Network administrators are responsible for the health and well-being of a company's network. Their goal generally is to provide uninterrupted network services. If a network outage or fault occurs, they want to know about it as soon as possible and isolate the problem quickly. When a problem occurs in the network, it can bring business to a grinding halt.

The network administrators must find, isolate, and fix the fault as quickly as possible to restore business operations. The longer the fault persists, depending on the number of people and processes affected, the greater the monetary losses the company might experience. For example, a manufacturing line might stop operating. Or a stock-trading firm might stop trading. A hospital might lose the ability to track patients. A theme park might be unable to collect tickets.

When a network fault occurs, a network administrator needs to gain visibility to the network, taking into close consideration any changes that might have occurred recently, to determine the source of the problem. Aside from dealing with faults, network management facilitates the orderly upgrade or maintenance of network devices. Remember, a company might have network devices installed all over the world, so it is impractical for a network administrator to physically travel to all the various locations to upgrade code.

Several process models can be adopted to form the basis of a network management process framework, including FCAPS and ITIL.

FCAPS stands for Fault, Configuration, Accounting, Performance, and Security. FCAPS represents the thinking about network operations going back to the 1980s. In short, the areas of network operations and management under FCAPS are broken down into these areas:

- **Fault:** Finding and correcting network problems.

- **Configuration:** Monitoring and controlling network devices and configuration.

- **Accounting:** Ensuring that devices are distributed appropriately and providing the ability to account (and bill) for usage.

- **Performance:** Measuring the throughput in the network and looking for potential bottlenecks. This area is especially important when determining capacity for applications and users.

- **Security:** Protecting the network from inadvertent mistakes and intentional sabotage.

Another more recent network management process framework is the Information Technology Infrastructure Library (ITIL). ITIL takes a more service-oriented viewpoint, focusing on the end services provided by the network, instead of the network itself. The key operational areas of ITIL are as follows:

- **Service strategy** identifies the IT services that could be developed as strategic assets for use by internal or external customers of a business.

- **Service design** develops a service strategy into an IT service design that addresses aspects of the proposed service, including availability, capacity, continuity, and security.

- **Service transition** focuses on implementing and creating a production service, including change management, release management, configuration management, and service knowledge management.

- **Service operation** focuses on the operations aspects to maintain services at defined service levels, including problem management and incident management.

- **Continual service improvement** is the ability to continually improve the quality and service levels of the services the IT department delivers.

FCAPS and ITIL have similarities. ITIL takes a broader perspective, looking at the total lifecycle of network services. ITIL also takes a viewpoint of the services the network is providing rather than the network itself.

Whether you employ FCAPS, ITIL, or another methodology to ensure network availability, management, and operations, it's important that you adopt and use a methodology that meets the company's goals.

The elements that make up an effective network-management strategy are documentation, network-management protocols, and troubleshooting tools.

Network Documentation: A Must-Have

A relatively simple yet often overlooked process of network management is documenting how all the network devices connect to each other. Network documentation becomes indispensable during network problems.

Documentation takes many forms:

- Logical network diagrams show how all the devices are connected.
- Cabling charts document where cable runs in a building. These charts are vital when you want to figure out where the other end of a cable terminates. (Is it an office or another floor?)
- A database correlates IP addresses and other network information with individual users and locations.
- Where more than a couple of people are responsible for a network, you need change-control documentation. Change control is the process of documenting any changes to the network *before* you make them so that a group can review the changes and ensure that one set of changes doesn't overwrite another.
- You can reference logs from network devices when you want to determine the source of a problem.

Cisco devices send *console messages* and Simple Network Management Protocol (SNMP) traps (discussed next) to a remote server for this purpose. By studying the log of messages, a network administrator might be able to determine the source of a problem.

Network-Management Protocols

Many tools and protocols help you effectively manage network devices. These tools and protocols help you configure, back up, monitor, and measure network devices. Network-management software makes efficient use of public domain protocols to discover and manage networks. The first protocol is simply the Transmission Control Protocol/Internet Protocol (TCP/IP) ping tool. Network-management software, in its simplest form, uses ping as a heartbeat monitor. Ping sends a single request to a device, and the device is expected to send back a single response when it receives the request. Thus, if your system does not receive a response for a period of time (remember, packets might drop in the network occasionally, so ping needs to retry three or more times), you can assume that the device is unreachable for some reason.

An unreachable device indicates that somewhere between the network-management workstation and the destination device, packets couldn't pass. Commercial network-management software indicates this fault by coloring a graphical representation of a device red on a map of the network. (Green indicates that everything is okay.) Whereas ping provides a heartbeat, SNMP lets you get and set information between a network-management station and a managed device such as a router or switch.

SNMP is a simple protocol that is similar to a database-retrieval program. The managed device maintains a database of information such as the health of its components (CPU, network interface, buffers) and throughput (how many packets are passing through an interface). Using SNMP, a network administrator can send a new configuration file to a device, upgrade its software, check its health, and measure how many packets are flowing through the device. You can store virtually anything about the device in the database in such a way that a network-management workstation can learn about or configure any aspect of the network device. SNMP also provides *traps*. Rather than a command-and-response, like other SNMP commands, traps are unsolicited responses. Managed devices, such as a router, send a trap when something needs attention. For example, if an interface goes down, a router sends a trap, notifying the network-management workstation. The workstation then indicates that there is a fault on the device. Depending on the vendor, you might use other protocols to manage a device.

Troubleshooting Tools

The final component of network management is troubleshooting tools. These tools help the network administrator isolate and correct a network problem when it occurs.

These tools include cable testers, packet analyzers, and regular computers used to query information on location. Cable testers and other physical-level devices let you determine whether a cable has a physical problem. For example, a cable might be too long and out of spec, or a device nearby might be causing interference and disrupting the flow of traffic. Packet analyzers allow a network administrator to monitor traffic on part of the network. The analyzer not only captures the traffic, but also decodes the contents of each packet into human-readable form. These tools are indispensable when you want to determine the source of a problem or an application's behavior.

Because packet analyzers capture all traffic, a hacker can use the tool not only to observe data as it flows through the network, but also to introduce lethal and disruptive traffic into the network. The final tool is a regular laptop computer. A network administrator can install network-management, packet-analyzer, and database software and carry all the software tools he needs to troubleshoot and correct a problem on location.

At-a-Glance: Network Management

Why Should I Care About Network Management?

If you use a computer attached to a network at work, school, or elsewhere, chances are that the network manager knows about you and the types of programs you use. You are being watched!

Although user supervision is a part of network management (and the part most users tend to worry about), there is much more to it than that.

As networks get more complex and more intelligent, it becomes necessary to put tools in place to help manage the network and ensure that it is operating efficiently and effectively.

What Problems Need to Be Solved?

An ideal network management system is everywhere, all the time. With increased network intelligence and the addition of smart end devices, it is possible to have every point in the network accounted for and part of the overall management reporting system. This can make the task of active network management very difficult.

To handle network management, tasks are usually assigned to one of the five FCAPS categories—fault, configuration, accounting, performance, and security. Each category has its own methods, strategies, and protocols:

- Fault detection and correction. A good network management scheme will quickly find and isolate problems.

- Configuration. As the network grows, manual configuration of devices becomes prohibitively difficult. Configuration also includes monitoring functions.

- Accounting tracks usage, distribution, and billing. In many cases billing is used to justify departmental budgets.

- Performance measures are used to ensure that the network is operating efficiently. If any bottlenecks are found, the network manager can open alternative paths.

- Security measures protect the network. Most people assume that hackers are the biggest threat, but many attacks come from inside the network edge.

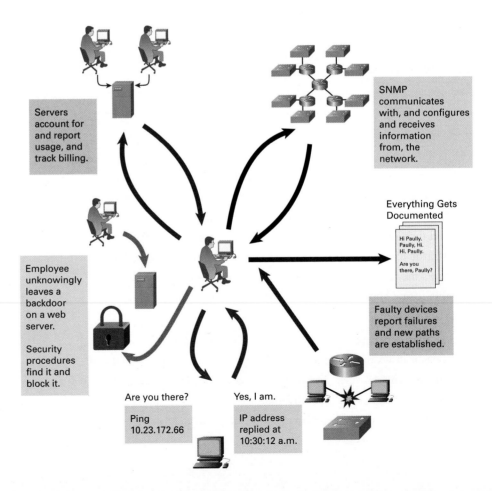

Servers account for and report usage, and track billing.

SNMP communicates with, and configures and receives information from, the network.

Everything Gets Documented

Hi Paully. Paully, Hi. Hi, Paully.
Are you there, Paully?

Employee unknowingly leaves a backdoor on a web server.

Security procedures find it and block it.

Faulty devices report failures and new paths are established.

Are you there?

Ping 10.23.172.66

Yes, I am.

IP address replied at 10:30:12 a.m.

At-a-Glance: Network Management

Nightmare of Mobility

Keeping track of thousands of devices was hard enough for network managers when everything basically stayed put. The huge surge in wireless networking has added hundreds or thousands more mobile devices, including laptops and PDAs, making network managers' jobs harder. Some strategies for keeping track of mobile devices are in covered in Part VIII, "Mobility."

Network Management

Network Management Functions

Monitor

The network manager configures the network and monitors its real-time performance and security.

Network Manager

Performance

L.A. Router
- 3 Packets Lost
- 1587 Packets Sent
- Total Time: 3:11

Security

IDS Reports
- Possible Spoofing
- Attempt on NY Router
- Shut Down
- Monitor

Advantages of Network Management

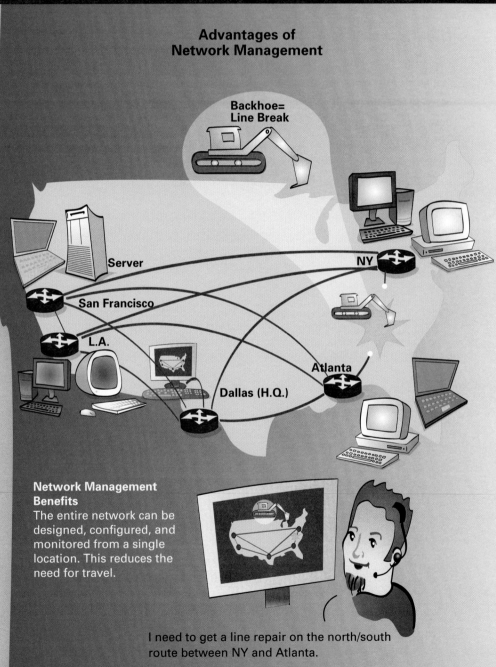

Backhoe= Line Break

Server

San Francisco

L.A.

Dallas (H.Q.)

Atlanta

NY

Network Management Benefits
The entire network can be designed, configured, and monitored from a single location. This reduces the need for travel.

I need to get a line repair on the north/south route between NY and Atlanta.

Part V

Securing the Network

The sad truth is that almost as soon as there were networks, there was a need to secure them. In fact, the need for security is so great that network security has become a multibillion-dollar-per-year industry.

This part begins with a primer on securing the network. Next we cover hacking and one of the earliest strategies to mitigate hacker threats: firewalls.

It would be great if firewalls addressed all our security concerns, but the aggressive nature and sophistication of some network attacks require more sophisticated protection methods. The next topic covered is intrusion detection, which helps network administrators deal with attacks that have penetrated the network perimeter. We follow this with another mitigation method for insider attacks: port-based security.

We conclude the "insider" view of security with identity-based networking and Network Admission Control. Identity-based networking is a method for making people prove they are who they say they are before giving them access to the network. Network Admission Control is a method for preventing network access until the device proves it has the proper security posture.

Sometimes it is important to ensure that your inside employees are conforming to company rules about website access or file-sharing systems and downloads. The section "URL Filtering: Eliminating Unwanted Web Page Access" looks at how this is accomplished. Finally, as a last defense, some companies will want to inspect every packet that comes into the network just to be sure that they are free from malicious software. "Deep Packet Inspection: Controlling Unwanted Applications" looks at how this is accomplished. We also take a brief look at encryption, which protects data as it travels across the network. Another tool in the security arsenal is telemetry, which is an advanced method of monitoring network activity to look for anomalies that might indicate an active network attack.

Finally, we do not want to overlook one of the original methods of security—locking the doors. Part V concludes with a look at physical security, focusing on integrating some traditional technologies such as video surveillance with networking technologies.

Network Security

A company's network is like any other corporate asset: It is valuable, and it affects the company's success and revenue. More than ever, the corporate computer network, and the data on it, is the most valuable asset of many companies. Therefore, it must be protected. Generally, middle- to large-size companies appoint a chief security officer, whose job is to develop and enforce corporate security policies.

Security threats present themselves in many forms:

- A hacker breaking into the network to steal confidential information or destroy corporate data

- A natural disaster such as a fire, tornado, or earthquake destroying computer and network equipment

- A disgruntled employee intentionally trying to modify, steal, or destroy corporate information and devices

- A computer virus or worm

- An act of war or terrorism

Common security threats introduced by people include the following:

- Network packet sniffers

- IP spoofing

- Password attacks

- Distribution of sensitive internal information to external sources

- Man-in-the-middle attacks

Internet security is also a big concern given the exposure of corporate data resources to the publicly accessible Internet. Traditionally, you could achieve security by physically separating corporate networks from public networks. However, with corporate web servers and databases—and the desire to provide access to corporate resources to employees over the Internet, or at overseas locations—companies must be especially diligent at protecting their networks.

Another recent area of security concern is wireless networking. Traditional networking occurred over physical wires or fibers. However, most companies have installed wireless networking in their buildings so that employees can link to the corporate network from conference rooms and other shared locations from their laptop computers. Additionally, service providers now offer public wireless Internet services.

The following sections describe the different categories of network security.

Identity

Identity is the identification of network users, hosts, applications, services, and resources. Examples of technologies that enable identification include 802.1x, Remote Authentication Dial-In User Service (RADIUS), Kerberos, one-time passwords, digital certificates, smart cards, biometrics, and directory services.

Perimeter Security

Perimeter security controls access to critical network applications, data, and services so that only legitimate users and information can access these assets. Examples include access lists on routers and switches, firewalls, virus scanners, and content filters. Perimeter security is particularly important where a business network connects to a shared network, such as the Internet.

Data Privacy

The ability to provide secure communication is crucial when you must protect information from eavesdropping. Digital encryption technologies and protocols such as Internet Protocol Security (IPsec), Secure Socket Layer (SSL), and Secure Real-Time Protocol (SRTP) are commonly used to protect data, especially when being transported over a shared or untrusted network, such as a service provider WAN or public Internet. New technologies such as Digital Rights Management and "data watermarking" are also gaining traction. For wireless networks, encryption and privacy protocols including Wired Equivalent Privacy (WEP) and Wi-Fi Protected Access (WPA) provide similar protections (discussed further in Part VIII, "Mobility").

Security Monitoring

Regardless of how security is implemented, it is still necessary to monitor a network and its components to ensure that the network remains secure. Network security monitoring tools and intrusion detection systems (IDS) provide visibility into the network's security status. State-of-the-art security monitoring includes additional systems for anomaly detection and telemetry: intelligently recognizing potential threats within the network and determining their point of origin(s).

Policy Enforcement

Tools and technologies are worthless without well-defined security policies. Effective policies balance the imposition of security measures against the productivity gains realized with little security. Centralized policy-management tools that can analyze, interpret, configure, and monitor the state of security policies help consolidate the successful deployment of rational security policies. Complying with set policies offers another set of challenges. Functions such as URL filtering can help enforce which places on the Internet employees can reach and which are prohibited because they are out of policy.

At-a-Glance: Network Security

Why Should I Care About Network Security?

As a valuable corporate asset, a company's network must be protected. One of the primary concerns of network administrators is the security of their network. Security attacks can range from malicious attacks, to theft of information, to simple misuse of company resources.

Estimates of costs of true hacking/security breaches are difficult to come by because of the many instances in which losses are not reported. In many cases, data theft is never even detected. It is telling, however, that the resale market for stolen identities is more than $1 billion per year—and identity theft is only a fraction of the total picture. Most troubling, perhaps, is the trend of organized crime entering the market, displacing poorly funded and unorganized lone hackers. This new breed is well funded, has highly skilled IT departments of their own, and can execute highly sophisticated attacks that take place over months or even years.

It's interesting that the majority of unauthorized access and resource misuse continue to come from internal sources. These can be either honest mistakes, disgruntled employees, or contractors or employees who are working for outside groups. In addition, attacks from external sources continue to grow as less-sophisticated hackers gain access to information and power tools designed for hacking. This is shown in the figure.

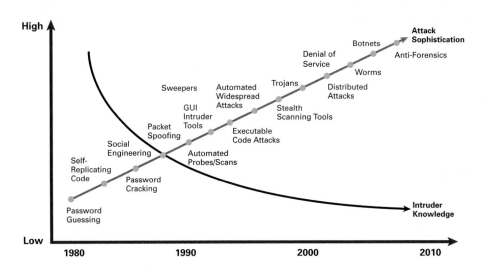

What's more troubling than the increased frequency and sophistication of the attacks is the complacency that many companies show toward updating their security profile. This is especially a concern given the vast increase in mobile devices that access the network from unsecured sources or networks. For companies that ignore this issue, it's probably just a matter of time before a major breach occurs.

What Problems Need to Be Solved?

Security must be an inherent part of every network design based on the principles of protection from the outside (perimeter security) and controlling the inside (internal security). In other words, keep the outsiders out, and keep the insiders honest. You should think of the network as performing dual roles of "gatekeeper" (perimeter) and "hall monitor" (internal).

Balancing Trust Versus Security

Security and trust are opposing concepts. Trust is required for applications to run, but open access can expose a network to attacks or misuse. On the other hand, a very restrictive security policy might limit exposure but also reduce productivity. When security is a primary design consideration, a trust boundary can be determined on a per-user basis, and the proper balance can be struck.

Establishing Identity

The first part of any security design is determining who is on the network. Without some knowledge of who the users are, the network polices would

At-a-Glance: Network Security

need to be generic and would likely be too open, or too restrictive. Identity can include the following:

- User identity based on password, SmartCard, fingerprint, and so on
- Device identity (such as IP Phone) based on IP or MAC address
- Application identity based on IP address or TCP/UDP port number

Identity is tightly linked with authorization. As soon as identity is established, the proper policy for that user, device, or application can be applied, monitored, and enforced.

Perimeter Security

Perimeter security refers to controlling access to critical network applications, data, and services so that only legitimate users and network information can pass through the network. Access typically is controlled with access control lists (ACL) enabled on edge routers and switches, as well as with dedicated firewall appliances. A firewall is a device that permits only authorized traffic to pass (according to a predefined security policy). Other tools, such as virus scanners, content filters, and Intrusion Detection Systems (IDS), also help control traffic.

Data Privacy

Much of the information passing through a network is confidential. Whether it is business-specific (engineering or financial) or personnel (human resources correspondence) information, it must be protected from eavesdropping. Encryption and

data privacy schemes can be implemented at Layer 2 (Layer 2 Tunneling Protocol [L2TP]) or Layer 3 (IPSec [encryption], MPLS [data privacy]). This type of protection is especially important when implementing VPNs.

Security Monitoring

Enabling security measures in a network is not enough. Network administrators must regularly test and monitor the state of security solutions. Using a combination of network vulnerability scanners and intrusion detection systems, the network administrator can monitor and respond to security threats in real time.

In addition to technology monitoring, one of the best security tools continues to be employees who are paying attention. A little training goes a long way.

Policy Enforcement

As networks grow in size and complexity, the requirement for centralized policy management grows as well. Regardless of the existence of sophisticated tools, companies must employ a sound policy with clear guidelines for enforcement. Generally, medium-sized to large companies appoint a chief security officer, whose job is to develop and enforce corporate security policies.

The Top 14 Security Vulnerabilities

The following are the top 14 security vulnerabilities:

1. Inadequate router access control
2. Unsecured and unmonitored remote access points provide easy access to your corporate network
3. Information leakage (through wireless signals, or even social engineering attempts) can provide the attacker with operating system and application information
4. Hosts running unnecessary services
5. Weak, easily guessed, and reused passwords
6. User or test accounts with excessive privileges
7. Misconfigured Internet servers, especially anonymous FTP
8. Misconfigured firewalls
9. Software that is outdated, vulnerable, or left in default configurations
10. Lack of accepted and well-promulgated security policies, procedures, guidelines, and minimum baseline standards
11. Excessive trust relationships, such as Windows Active Directory and UNIX .rhosts and hosts .equiv files, can give hackers unauthorized access to sensitive systems
12. Vulnerabilities inherent in popular peer-to-peer file-sharing programs
13. Inadequate logging, monitoring, and detection capabilities
14. "Promiscuity" of mobile devices such as laptops and PDAs being used in public Wi-Fi environments, guest networks, home networks, and so on and then being reintroduced onto the corporate network

At-a-Glance: Hacking

Why Should I Care About Hacking?

Anyone who accesses a public network should know about hackers and their methods. Failure to understand what they do can leave you and your network exposed.

Thieves and opportunists will always go after an easy target versus a difficult (or well-prepared) one. However, some hackers specifically go after very difficult targets such as government offices or networking companies solely for bragging rights.

What Problems Need to Be Solved?

Hacking really boils down to a few activities:

- **Breaking in:** Breaking into a private network is usually the first part of any hacking scheme (a denial of service [DoS] attack is one notable exception). Most break-ins require a password (which is guessed or stolen), but there are other ways to get in.

- **Breaking stuff:** As soon as they are in a network, many hackers (anarchists in particular) try to break or disable the entire network, or specific parts of it, such as web servers. If data is destroyed, or business disrupted, it can be very expensive for the attacked company.

- **Stealing stuff:** Like most thieves, many hackers are motivated by greed. Plans, schematics, software source code, or intellectual property can be sold to unscrupulous individuals, companies, or government agencies.

- **Leaving a calling card:** Many hackers want to make sure that they get "proper credit" for their work, so they find a way to sign their work or prove that they were in the network. Now that organized crime is moving in and running a business, this is becoming less and less common. The groups making millions from stolen data would rather keep money coming in so that they operate in stealth mode.

Hacks and Attacks

The term "attack" in network-speak refers to any attempt to break into a computer, network, or packet, as well as any attempt to launch a malicious or self-replicating program. There are multiple classifications of attacks, many of which are listed here.

All network attacks can be categorized as active or passive.

Active attacks include injecting malicious files, altering data, or clogging the network. In theory, active attacks can be detected, but passive attacks cannot.

Passive attacks such as eavesdropping do not actually harm the network, but they can be used to obtain information that enables active attacks. People looking for passwords can tirelessly try every combination until they find a working password (brute force). *Man-in-the-middle attacks* occur when a hacker interposes himself between two valid users and eavesdrops for passwords. Passive attacks are difficult to detect.

Remote attacks are conducted by people outside the network (those without a network ID), whereas *local attacks* use an existing account to exploit the system.

Hit-and-run attacks quickly crash systems, whereas *persistent attacks* affect the victims only as long as the attack lasts.

At-a-Glance: Hacking

① Inside Jobs

Most security breaches originate inside the network that is under attack. Inside jobs include such things as password stealing (passwords then can be used or sold), industrial espionage, disgruntled employees looking to harm their employer, or simple misuse.

Many of these security breaches can be thwarted by sound policy enforcement and observant employees who guard their passwords and PCs.

② Rogue Access Points

Rogue access points are unsecured wireless access points that can easily be breached by outsiders. They are often advertised within the local hacker community. Rogue APs are most often connected by well-meaning but ignorant employees in a corporate environment, but the same risk exists on wireless home networks.

③ Back Doors

Administrative shortcuts, configuration errors, easily deciphered passwords, and unsecured remote access can all be exploited for hackers to gain access. With the aid of computerized searchers (bots), if your network has a weakness, it will likely be found.

④ Denial of Service (DoS)

DoS attacks provide a means for bringing down a network without having to gain internal access. DoS attacks work by flooding a network device or application server with bogus traffic (which can be e-mail or IP/ICMP packets).

Distributed DoS (DDoS) is coordinated DoS attacks from multiple sources. DDoS is more difficult to block because it uses multiple, changing source IP addresses that are hard to distinguish from legitimate IP addresses.

With the advent of sophisticated Trojan horse viruses and worms, as well as spyware, home computers are being enlisted by the thousands to become launching points for DDoS attacks, unbeknownst to their owners.

⑤ Anarchists, Crackers, and Kiddies

So who are these people, and why are they attacking your network?

Anarchists just like to break stuff. They usually exploit any target of opportunity.

Crackers are hobbyists or professionals who break passwords and develop Trojan horses or other software (called warez). They either use the software themselves (for bragging rights) or sell it for profit.

Script kiddies are hacker wannabes. They have no real hacker skills, so they buy or download warez, which they launch.

Others include disgruntled employees, terrorists, political operatives, and anyone else who feels slighted, exploited, ripped off, or unloved.

⑥ Viruses and Worms

Viruses and worms are self-replicating programs or code fragments that attach themselves to other programs (viruses) or machines (worms).

Viruses typically stay associated with the local host (one computer), and worms tend to replicate and proliferate through the network.

⑦ Trojan Horses

Trojan horses are the leading cause of all break-ins. Trojan horses are attached to other programs. When downloaded, the hacked software kicks off a virus, password gobbler, or remote-control software that gives the hacker control over the PC, remotely.

At-a-Glance: Hacking

⑧ Botnets

As soon as a computer (or, more likely, many computers) has been compromised via Trojan horse programs, it can be controlled remotely by a hacker. A hacker can then use programs to control this computer to launch attacks, such as DDoS.

The groups of computers under the control of a hacker are called *botnets*. The word comes from robots, meaning computers blindly following commands from their owner, and network, meaning many coordinated computers.

⑨ Sniffing/Spoofing

Sniffing refers to the act of intercepting TCP packets. This can be simple eavesdropping or something more sinister.

Spoofing is the act of sending an illegitimate packet with an expected ACK, which can be guessed, predicted, or obtained by snooping.

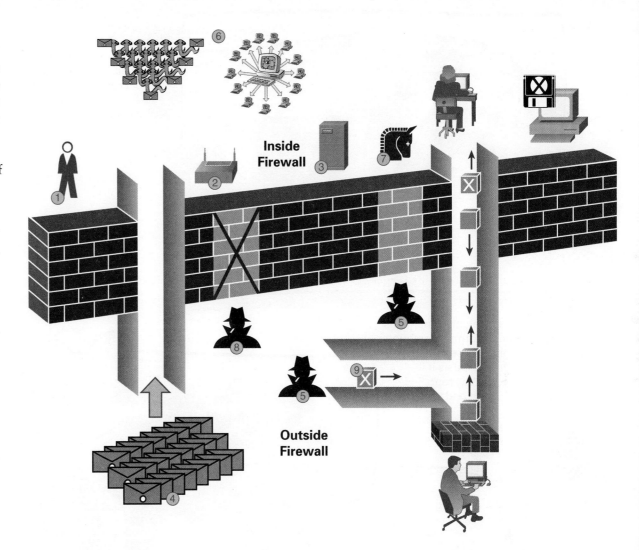

DoS Attacks

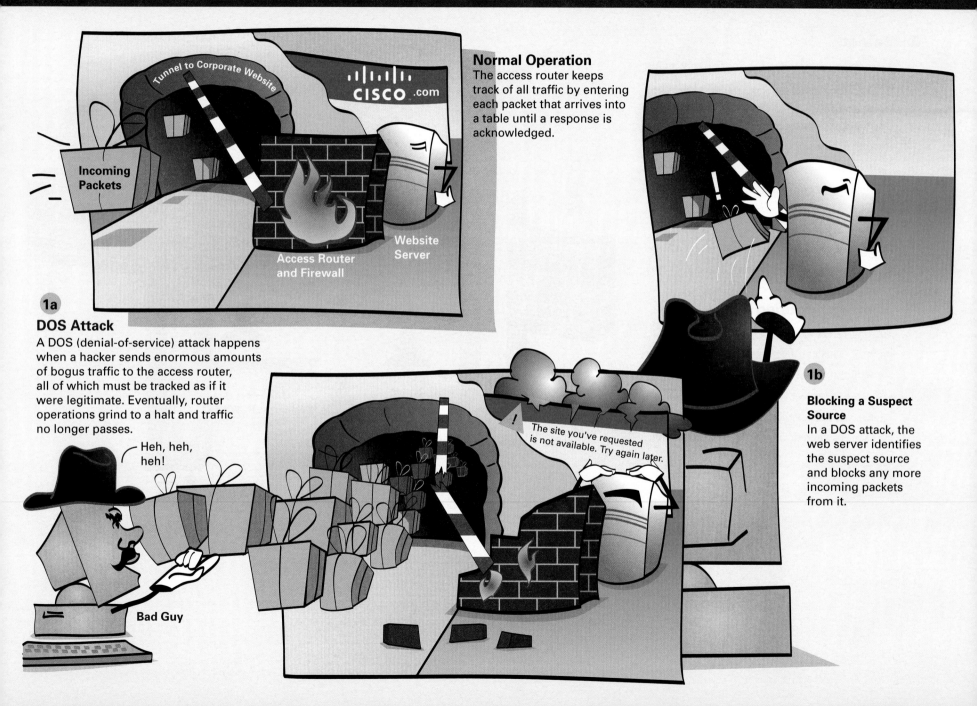

Normal Operation
The access router keeps track of all traffic by entering each packet that arrives into a table until a response is acknowledged.

1a

DOS Attack
A DOS (denial-of-service) attack happens when a hacker sends enormous amounts of bogus traffic to the access router, all of which must be tracked as if it were legitimate. Eventually, router operations grind to a halt and traffic no longer passes.

1b

Blocking a Suspect Source
In a DOS attack, the web server identifies the suspect source and blocks any more incoming packets from it.

DoS Attacks

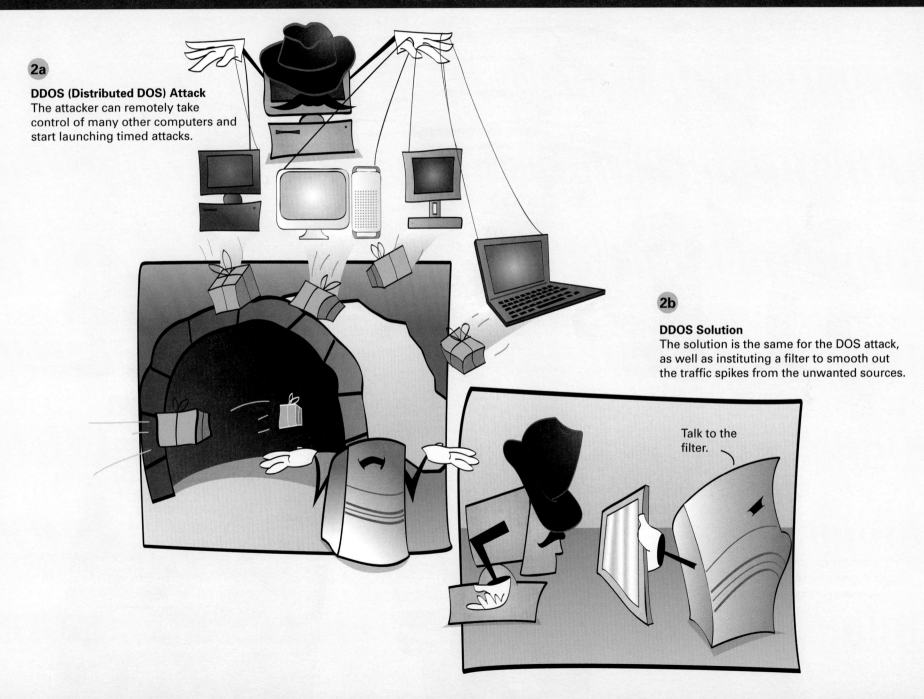

2a

DDOS (Distributed DOS) Attack
The attacker can remotely take control of many other computers and start launching timed attacks.

2b

DDOS Solution
The solution is the same for the DOS attack, as well as instituting a filter to smooth out the traffic spikes from the unwanted sources.

Talk to the filter.

Snooping and Spoofing

Ooh! Jorge will love this one!

Doesn't he have any real work to do?

The hacker now sends his own packet that looks like part of a valid session.

After the hacker penetrates a system, he can easily gain access to information or attack other sites from a "clean" site.

Sniffer Software

Hacker

1 The hacker can gain access to packets by physically accessing a network device such as a router, or by using software tools such as a Trojan horse. A data capture tool (packet sniffer) finds the packets the hacker is interested in.

Prevention
Spoofing and snooping by an external source can be prevented by never allowing an address that is not in your address database to come from outside. Preventing spoofing and snooping by an internal source is typically handled with point-to-point encryption.

Firewalls

Protecting the Perimeter

As more computers connect to public networks, and as their employees connect to work through the Internet, opportunities increase for malicious attacks from hackers and saboteurs. The same applies to internal corporate networks, in that companies must protect their data centers and computing resources from internal and external attacks.

News stories often tell of websites being broken into, computers being erased, corporate data being stolen, and lethal viruses destroying computer systems. With the number of home users taking advantage of broadband "always-on" networks, hackers and data thieves have a whole playground of unsuspecting exposed home networks to tamper with.

Network attacks can occur for a variety of reasons: extortion, fraud, espionage, sabotage, or simple curiosity. The acts themselves can involve a range of activity, including misuse of authorized systems, system break-ins, equipment theft, interception of network traffic, and reconfiguration of computer systems to allow for future access. Because of the nature of global networks, these attacks can (and often do) cross network and national boundaries.

How can home users and corporations protect themselves?

Get Off the Net!

The most secure way to avoid attack is to not connect to a network. Physical security remains an issue, but otherwise going off-net is the most secure method to reduce exposure to security risks.

That's not a practical option.

Instead, there is the concept of perimeter security. Perimeter security traditionally is provided by a firewall. Firewalls sit between an unsafe ("dirty") or WAN side and a safe ("clean") or LAN side.

Sometimes, devices such as web servers or intrusion-monitoring products sit between the WAN and LAN sides. This "limbo" location between the dirty and clean networks is often called the demilitarized zone (DMZ).

For example, a home user could put a firewall between his or her computer and the Internet connection. The side of the firewall that connects to the Internet is the dirty side (meaning that the traffic cannot be trusted), and the side of the firewall that connects to the home network is the clean side (the traffic can be trusted). The firewall inspects packets going in either direction and determines whether the traffic should be allowed to pass through or should be dropped.

The firewall has become the central location to perform perimeter-related activities.

Firewall for Your Protection

Firewalls are designed to combat network-related security threats such as the following:

- **Passive eavesdropping:** Attackers can use packet-capture programs to glean sensitive information or steal username/password combinations.

- **IP address spoofing:** An attacker pretends to be a trusted computer by using an IP address that is within the accepted range of internal IP addresses. This is similar to assumed identity.

- **Port scan:** Servers "listen" for traffic on different ports. For instance, port 80 is where servers listen for web HTTP traffic. Attackers find ways to infiltrate servers through individual server ports.

- **DoS attack:** The attacker attempts to block valid users from accessing servers by creating TCP SYN (or ICMP, or other) packets that exhaust the server and keep it from being able to handle any other valid requests. These types of attacks are also called ping floods.

- **Application layer attack:** These are attacks that exploit the weaknesses of certain applications to obtain illicit access to the hosting server.

Firewalls let you block these and other attacks by inspecting traffic, keeping track of valid sessions, and filtering traffic that looks suspect so that it cannot pass.

Personal Firewalls

Another type of firewall that has become common is the personal firewall. Typically this is a software program on a laptop or computer that acts as a firewall. Its function is slightly different than the firewalls just described. Personal firewalls typically guard a computer or laptop against unauthorized installation of programs, such as a malicious program or spyware installing itself on your computer, commonly without the user's knowledge.

Another function of the personal firewall is to monitor programs on the computer that are trying to access the Internet, enabling the user to allow or deny access program by program. In this way, malicious programs seeking to access the Internet, either to propagate themselves or to report information back to the creator, can be blocked from doing so.

To learn more about this topic, pick up a copy of *Home Network Security Simplified* (Cisco Press, 2006).

At-a-Glance: Firewalls and IDS

Why Should I Care About Firewalls and IDS?

Firewalls and Intrusion Detection Systems (IDS) provide perimeter defense for corporate and personal networks. As hackers have become more sophisticated (and aggressive) in their attacks, so has the technology behind keeping networks safe. Firewalls and IDS were created as a direct response to hackers.

In addition to pure technology advances, a great deal of innovation has occurred concerning how to deploy these systems. This topic is of special importance to companies with websites.

What Problems Need to Be Solved?

The main goal of perimeter security is to keep the bad guys out of the network. The only way to be absolutely sure about perimeter security is to not connect to anything. Most companies rely on the Internet, though, and for some it is a critical aspect of their business. The problem to be solved, then, is how to have an external presence and still be relatively safe against attacks.

The answer is the three-part firewall system, which places external-facing servers in an intermediate zone (DMZ) in the network between two separate firewalls.

What Does a Firewall Do?

Firewalls keep both corporate and personal networks safe from attack by inspecting packets for

known attack profiles and by acting as a proxy between you and the rest of the world.

Profiles (such as virus signatures or rules for packet contents) are usually discovered and maintained by service companies that sell the profile packages for a fee.

The proxy function works by using a third IP address (as opposed to the user's actual source IP address or that of the server) whenever you communicate with the world. That way, no one knows your actual IP address.

Are You a Good Packet or a Bad Packet?

In terms of a firewall system, good packets fall into two categories:

 Good outbound packets are sent by inside users to approved external locations, such as a website.

Good inbound packets originate outside the external firewall. They either correspond to a TCP session originated by an inside user (that is, they can only be response packets) or are accessing publicly available services such as web traffic.

 Bad packets are pretty much everything else (unsolicited packets that are not sent in response to a request from inside). They are discarded for the safety of the network.

Clean Net

The clean net is the interior corporate network. The only "outside" packets permitted on the clean net are those that have been inspected and have the acknowledgment to a TCP packet generated from an inside computer.

Inside Filter

The inside filter performs the functions of both a firewall and intrusion detection system. In addition to blocking attacks such as DoS, it inspects every packet, making sure that no externally initiated TCP sessions reach the clean net, because hackers can gain access by spoofing a session. Any packets of questionable origin get trashed. The inside filter also inspects outbound packets to ensure compliance with corporate policies.

Isolation LAN

The isolation LAN or DMZ acts as a buffer between outside- (web) facing applications and the clean LAN. Servers located in the DMZ are called bastion hosts. Outsiders use them to access public web pages or FTP servers. These servers are protected but are still prone to hackers. Bastion hosts should have as few services as possible and should contain very simple access rules to prevent back doors into the clean LAN.

At-a-Glance: Firewalls and IDS

Outside Filter

The outside filter is a firewall that screens for TCP replies and UDP packets assigned to port numbers associated with whatever bastion hosts are present. This firewall should have only static routes and very clean rules, because complicated processes are prone to errors, and hackers love errors!

The Dirty Net

The Internet is often called "the dirty net" by network and security admins. In the interest of network security, they assume that every packet is sent by a hacker until proven otherwise. The vast majority of users are honest, but this guilty-until-proven-innocent attitude can and does prevent disasters.

Hackers and Their Evil Ways

Hackers use a number of tools and tricks to exploit networks. These include, but are not limited to, DoS attacks, IP address spoofing, viruses, worms, Trojan horses, and e-mail bombs. Many of these attacks are discussed in detail on a separate sheet.

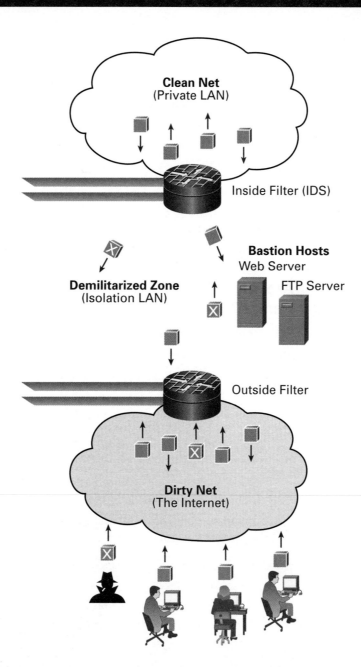

Firewalls and IDS

Outside Traffic

IDS

IDS
The IDS looks deep into every packet for flags that are common to hack attempts or network errors. When a pattern or attack signature is recognized, an alarm is triggered.

1

Firewall Guard

OK

IDS

2

IN

3

Public Corporate Server

O

E-Mail

Web

FTP

The firewall blocks certain types of traffic from entering the corporate network. It is the first line of defense against hackers, but it has its limitations.

Firewall

4

Internal Corporate Network

Nothing gets into the internal corporate network unless it's explicitly requested from inside.

Access and Content Security

Policy   Keep outsiders out. Keep insiders honest.

Full Access

Accountant

Access to Personal Information

Access to Some Project

Blocked

Blocked

Information

Finance Database

Human Resources Database

Full Access

Engineer

Engineering Database

Know Your Enemy

- **Can Get You From Anywhere**
- **Will Look for Easy Targets**
- **Has Lots of Free Time**
  (Does Not Have a Girlfriend)

Whaddya think?
Should I download it?

Yeah. Looks clean.
Send me a copy.

This Download
Is Not a

Virus

Giganto-Gulp

Intrusion Prevention Systems

Intrusion Detection Systems

Firewalls provide a barrier for traffic. However, some traffic may look legitimate and may in fact be legitimate, but it might be carrying devious viruses or attack programs.

Although a firewall is sufficient for home use, corporations tend to have more at risk and choose to invest in extra measures to detect traffic patterns that a firewall can't catch. Intrusion detection provides this ability.

IDSs analyze data in real time to detect, log, and hinder misuse and attacks. Host-based IDSs monitor server operations for any mischievous events. Network-based IDSs monitor network traffic on a specific portion of the network.

Network-based IDSs monitor traffic in real time, looking at a set of packets for known attack signatures. When it detects a particular suspicious data flow, the IDS logs the finding. It then can tell the receiving router to deny the traffic and any future traffic from the source.

Intrusion Prevention Systems

Similar to IDS is the concept of Intrusion Prevention Systems (IPS). Both IDS and IPS require a database of known attack signatures to be programmed into the IDS or IPS network device. However, whereas an IDS typically detects intrusion attempts and logs them or sends alerts to network staff, IPS typically operates "inline" within the network and includes additional measures to halt intrusion attempts in real time.

Although it might seem as though these technologies do the same thing and maybe even replace firewalls, keep in mind that each technology provides an additional layer of security. This approach, called "defense in depth," provides a multilayered approach to security, ensuring that a breach of one system does not put the entire network at risk.

The Problem with False Positives

One of the largest challenges with IDS or IPS is distinguishing real attacks from false positives. These are legitimate traffic that sets off an alarm in an IDS/IPS sensor because some of the traffic pattern matches an attack signature. It's a bit like your neighbor's car alarm going off. If it goes off ten times a week, you start to ignore it, and if the car really gets stolen, no one notices. It is important to tune IDS/IPS implementations to reduce the occurrence of false positives to as close to zero as possible. That way, when a network administrator or information security officer is notified of an intrusion, it is meaningful.

At-a-Glance: Intrusion Detection

Why Should I Care About Intrusion Detection?

Businesses and homes are connected to the Internet using an always-on connection, providing targets for electronic intruders and hackers. Network intrusions and attacks cost businesses money in terms of information theft, productivity losses from compromised services, and remediation costs for compromised hosts. Despite an added focus on network security, intrusions are growing more frequent and more sophisticated. Only automated intrusion detection and prevention solutions can mitigate complex attacks with the speed required or prevent real damage or runaway costs.

What Problems Need to Be Solved?

To be effective, intrusion detection solutions must be active at all entry points to the network, including the following:

- From the Internet
- From branch offices and small offices/home offices
- From inside the company

The system must also provide protection of network assets and services provided by the network, such as servers.

On important aspect of intrusion detection is the ability to operate as a passive detection system, logging potential intrusion events, or as an active prevention system, taking mitigating actions in real time. Intrusion detection must also be able to correlate multiple events over a window of time to detect complex attacks.

Where Can IDS Be Deployed?

Cisco Intrusion Prevention System (CIPS) provides a network-wide approach to intrusion detection and mitigation. IDS/IPS sensors can be deployed as router-based (IOS-IPS), host-based (Cisco Security Agent, CSA), or as appliances in the network. Events from all types of sensors are reported to a central event correlation and management system so that network administrators can monitor intrusion events and take action.

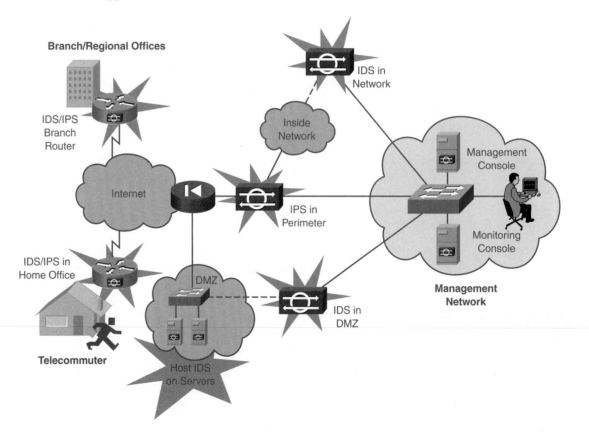

At-a-Glance: Intrusion Detection

Passive Monitoring

An IDS passively monitors packets on the network and logs events. The figure shows the steps involved:

1. Traffic on the network is copied and routed to the IDS Sensor for analysis.

2. If traffic matches an intrusion signature, the signature "fires."

3. IDS Sensor sends an alarm to the management console.

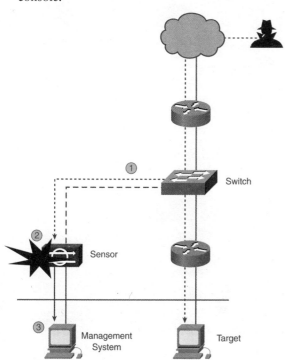

With IDS, packets that are part of the intrusion attempt can still reach the target.

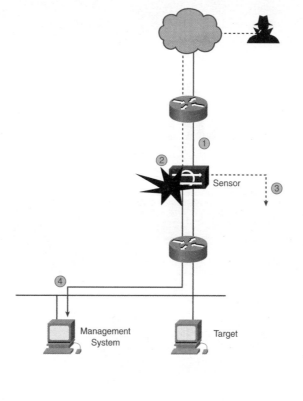

Active Monitoring

An IPS actively monitors packets inline on the network. The figure shows the steps involved:

1. Traffic on the network is not copied but is forwarded through the IPS Sensor for analysis.

2. If traffic matches an intrusion signature, the signature "fires."

3. Traffic that matches the signature is dropped.

4. IPS Sensor also sends an alarm to the management console.

With IPS, packets that are part of the intrusion attempt are prevented from reaching the target.

Sneak Attacks

Sophisticated attacks may involve multiple events (which in this case refers to several packets or sequences of packets) over a period of time. Discrete events can make it difficult to detect an attack. CIPS can correlate multiple events over a time window to recognize a sophisticated attack vector, such as an Internet worm.

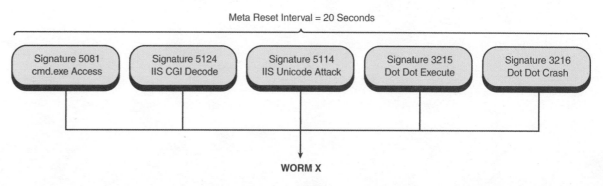

Port-Based Security

Combating Access-Based Attacks

A common entry point for network threats are the wired (and wireless) access ports where devices connect, such as laptops, printers, IP phones, and others. Without appropriate measures, hackers attempting to cause mischief in networks can plug into a port and use it as a launching location to work their way into the rest of the network. Such intrusions may require physical access to the corporate location. Physical security measures such as locked doors, badge readers, video surveillance, and security staff are always a critical line of defense to prevent such attacks.

However, gaining physical access to many corporate locations is not as hard as you might think. A practice known as *tailgating* is one of the most common means to gain entry. Tailgating occurs when an employee of a company swipes her ID badge through a badge reader to unlock an exterior door, and the intruder follows her through the door.

Tailgating can be passive, meaning that the employee may not even notice that the person behind her grabbed the door before it closed. Tailgating also can be active, meaning that the employee out of courtesy actually holds the door open. One very effective tailgating scheme involves the malicious individual approaching the door with an armload of stuff. The employee helpfully opens the door (social engineering makes this possible).

Video surveillance can help prevent such trespassing. But you must train employees to watch for tailgaters. Employees must be willing to challenge individuals who don't display corporate credentials.

Physical access is not necessarily required. A virus, worm, or Trojan horse program can be placed on a laptop that an employee carries inside the business and plugs into the network. A company's wireless connectivity can extend into nearby buildings or parking lots, removing the need for an intruder to enter the company.

Whether a person gains access physically or by using stealth, as soon as he is "inside," he can slip into the nearest empty cubicle or conference room, plug in, and start his attack. A number of measures need to work in concert to totally prevent such maliciousness:

• Port-based security

• Identity-based networking

• Network Admission Control (NAC)

• Wireless network security

The first three topics are discussed in the following sections. Wireless network security is discussed further in Part VIII, "Mobility."

Port-based security involves taking a number of precautions on each wired network access port. Doing so prevents several known types of malicious entry:

• MAC flooding

• Malicious Dynamic Host Configuration Protocol (DHCP) server

• ARP poisoning

• IP address spoofing

Locking down network access ports eliminates one point of entry for hacking and intrusion. Access to the network may still be possible, but several tools commonly used for malicious intrusion into the network are effectively taken out of the hacker's toolbox.

At-a-Glance: Port-Based Security

Why Should I Care About Port-Based Security?

Many networks provide open access to the network via switch ports (the Ethernet connection in the wall has a direct connection to a Layer 2 switch port). Therefore, if you have physical access to a switch port, you have Ethernet access to the network. This is good for productivity, but it creates a security vulnerability.

As soon as access is attained, a user or device can either knowingly or unknowingly (via an infected PC) initiate snooping or a man-in-the-middle attack on the network or other users. Because many security threats originate from inside the company, it is prudent to try to decrease the network's vulnerability to this type of threat.

Controlling access with solutions such as Identity-Based Networking and NAC is an important piece of an overall security policy solution. But these solutions merely keep unauthorized personnel off the network. Users and devices with legitimate access and a clean bill of health are granted access to the network. Nothing prevents them from initiating Layer 2 attacks (this assumes that they have already overcome the NAC defense or have insider access). Port-based security solves this problem.

What Problems Need to Be Solved?

To understand the problem, take a look at the types of attacks that can be launched from an open switch port:

- **MAC flooding:** Flooding an access switch with many bogus MAC addresses can cause a switch to fail, thereby opening a security hole.

- **Malicious DHCP server:** An attacker imitates a legitimate DHCP service (the device that allocates dynamic IP addresses). In doing so, he can intercept DHCP requests and provide bogus responses, which gives him access to other computers.

- **ARP poisoning:** An attacker uses the Address Resolution Protocol (ARP) service (which is used to map IP or network addresses to MAC or hardware addresses) to gain information about legitimate users. This information is used to "fool" the other systems into thinking that they are communicating with a legitimate user or device rather than a hacker.

- **Spoofed IP addresses:** An attacker uses an IP address assigned to another user to gain access to the network, remaining undetected.

Port-based security attempts to prevent all these issues while still giving legitimate users access to reliable Layer 2 services.

Where Port Security Fits

A number of tools are used to ensure the security of internal (Layer 2) networks. Port security is but one of these tools. Other security methods include DHCP snooping, dynamic ARP inspection, and IP Source Guard. These solutions help prevent specific types of Layer 2-based attacks and are part of a comprehensive security strategy.

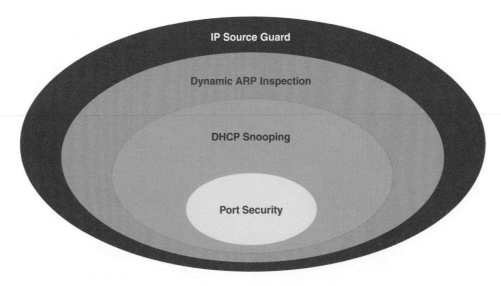

At-a-Glance: Port-Based Security

MAC Flooding

MAC flooding attacks seek to fill up the address tables on a switch. This can cause switch failures that the hacker exploits to gain information and access. This works because switches tend to fail into a state where "sniffing/snooping" becomes much easier for the hacker.

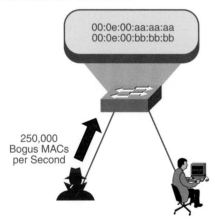

Enabling port security can limit the number of MAC addresses per port to a practical number, such as three. This is an adequate number for most switch ports.

Flooding is halted after the limit is reached, and no additional MAC addresses are accepted.

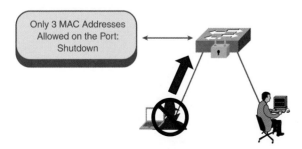

Malicious DHCP Server

Attackers can use malicious DHCP requests and their associated responses to gain control of a legitimate user's device. This can also be used to usurp the legitimate device's access to the network for illegitimate purposes. Hackers can also attempt to flood the legitimate DHCP server with requests for addresses to either overrun the server or exhaust the pool of available addresses, thereby denying service to legitimate users.

If you enable DHCP snooping, DHCP requests per port can be rate-limited to a practical number over a particular time period.

DHCP snooping can also block bogus DHCP responses, ensuring that DHCP responses come from only legitimate DHCP servers.

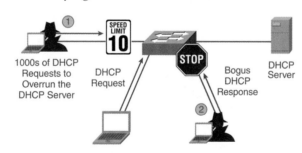

ARP Poisoning/Spoofing

Address Resolution Protocol (ARP) is a tool that allows devices to communicate when they do not have all the information they need about the device that they are trying to communicate with. Attackers can use ARP to learn the MAC and IP

addresses of legitimate users on the network using a technique called "gratuitous ARP." As soon as the hacker has obtained address information, he can use it to conduct man-in-the-middle attacks, sniff passwords, or siphon off data.

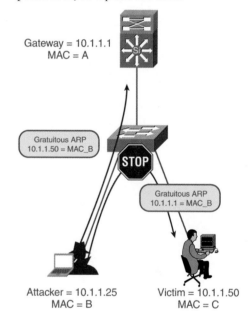

If you enable dynamic ARP inspection, ARP requests can be rate-limited to prevent scanning. Dynamic ARP inspection can also block bogus ARPs and gratuitous ARPs and allow responses to come from only legitimate responders.

Spoofed IP Addresses

Hackers can imitate a legitimate user by obtaining and then using her IP address. As soon as the IP address is obtained, the hacker can fool other

At-a-Glance: Port-Based Security

devices or users into sending him information, or
he can launch another type of attack from a dis-
guised position.

If you enable Source Guard, IP addresses are
tracked to the source port that assigned the
address. Any attempt to use a static IP address or
the IP address from another switch port is blocked,
and access is denied.

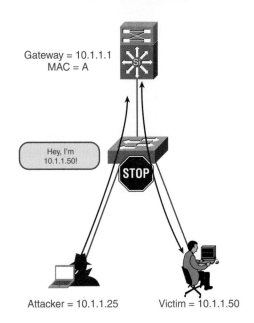

Gateway = 10.1.1.1
MAC = A

Hey, I'm
10.1.1.50!

STOP

Attacker = 10.1.1.25   Victim = 10.1.1.50

Identity-Based Networking

Network Access Conundrum

Legacy networks typically operated under a model of allowing devices to be plugged into the network. As long as they could understand and communicate the basic protocols of OSI Layer 1 (physical layer) and Layer 2 (data link layer), they could get access to the network. The ease of plugging in and getting a "hot" Ethernet connection helped fuel the widespread adoption of networks and speeded the decline of other, more complex methods of connectivity.

Ease of use and security measures are often at odds with each other. The more restrictive network access policies are, often the more difficult it is for network users to jump through the right hoops to be granted access. Such is the quandary for providing network access. Too restrictive means that less-experienced legitimate users may have their network access inadvertently denied. Not restrictive enough means that unauthorized users may easily get on the network, possibly as easily as employees.

Identity-Based Networking

Most modern corporate networks do not provide access to network services to a device or user without first establishing the device's or user's entitlement to those services. Identity-Based Networking Services (IBNS) lets network administrators restrict access to devices that can prove their "identity" to the network.

Identity may involve different types of credentials for different devices. For example, a laptop or computer may require the user to enter his or her corporate user ID and password. Other devices that cannot necessarily respond to a password prompt, such as printers or Network Attached Storage (NAS) devices, may rely on other forms of authentication, such as the device's MAC address or a preloaded digital certificate.

In either case, IBNS operates at the edge of the network on access ports. When a device is plugged into the network, Layers 1 and 2 are established, but before access to the network is permitted, the access switch challenges the device to provide its identity credentials. The credentials provided by the device are passed through the network to authentication servers in the data center and are validated. Validated devices are granted access, and unauthorized devices are prevented from sending traffic to the network.

IBNS dramatically changes the network access model from one of starting with an easily accessible "hot" Ethernet port, requiring only physical access to plug into it, to a model of devices needing to be preauthorized to have even the basic form of network access. Access to a "hot" Ethernet connection is contingent upon the device's proving that it is part of the set of devices that are within the corporate device "family."

802.1x

The network protocol commonly used for IBNS is standardized in the IEEE standard known as 802.1x. 802.1x establishes the communication paths necessary between the device seeking network access and the access switch providing the authentication challenge. All modern OS clients (Windows, Mac, Linux) support 802.1x.

802.1x has also been at the core of corporate wireless network security almost since the inception of wireless networks, providing a critical part of wireless security. Similar to wired, the wireless form of 802.1x requires devices to present credentials to gain access to the wireless network. Unauthenticated devices are refused access.

At-a-Glance: Identity

Why Should I Care About Identity?

The majority of unauthorized access to traditional networks and resource misuse comes from internal sources. Being able to identify users and devices attempting to access the corporate network is the first step of any security solution.

In addition to using identity to solve security concerns and allow network access, validating the identity of users and devices can allow network administrators to provision services and allocate resources to users based on their job functions.

What Problems Need to Be Solved?

A comprehensive network security policy must keep the outsiders out and the insiders honest. Specific goals should include the following:

- Prevent external hackers from having free reign in the network.

- Allow only authorized users into the network.

- Prevent network attacks from within.

- Provide different layers of access for different kinds of users.

To be truly effective, the security policy must do this in a way that does not disrupt business or make authorized access prohibitively difficult.

802.1x Header	EAP Payload

Extensible Authentication Protocol (EAP)

EAP is a flexible protocol (it's actually a framework rather than a protocol, but that is the common usage) used to carry authentication information in any of several formats. The authentication information can include user passwords or predefined security keys.

EAP typically rides on top of another protocol such as 802.1x or RADIUS, which carry the authentication information between the client and the authenticating authority.

What Does Identity Do for Me?

Identity not only prevents unauthorized access, it also lets you know who and where your inside users are. As soon as you know who is on the network, you can apply policies on a per-user basis. This gives a very solid, comprehensive security solution that actually enhances the network's usability rather than reducing it. The following sections show some examples of the advantages of an identity-based security solution.

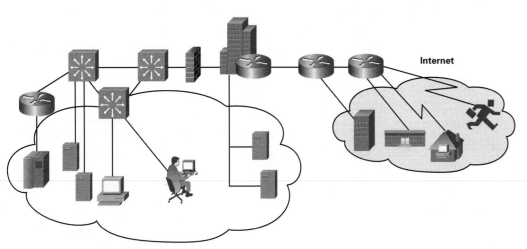

What the Heck Is 802.1x?

802.1x is a set of standards that describe a Layer 2 protocol used to transport higher-level authentication protocols. In English, this means that it is a language used to carry the information payload (such as name and password) between an endpoint (client) and the authenticator (server).

At-a-Glance: Identity

Preventing Unwanted Access

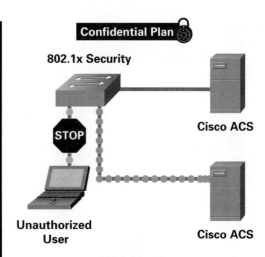

Without Identity
An unauthorized user can connect to the network and download confidential documents.

With Identity
802.1x, used with an access control server (ACS), prevents unauthorized users and outsiders from going where they do not belong.

Limiting Access to Networked Resources

Authorized User

Marketing Employee
(Red VLAN; No Access to HR Server 1)

HR Server 1
Has Confidential HR Info

With Identity
By using 802.1x with extensions, you can specify which networked resources the user can access. For example, only managers have access to HR information.

Without Identity
Access to Human Resources databases and other sensitive material is available to all employees.

At-a-Glance: Identity

User-Based Service Provisioning

Without Identity
Hackers or malicious insiders might try to crash a network by overloading it with requests and traffic.

With Identity
By using 802.1x, the switch can allocate bandwidth and other services on a case-by-case basis. You can deal with an abuse quickly and easily.

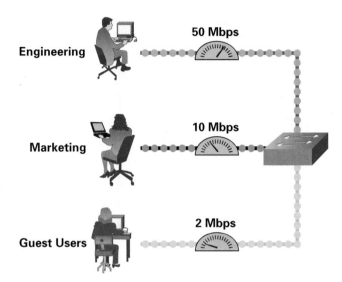

Engineering — 50 Mbps

Marketing — 10 Mbps

Guest Users — 2 Mbps

Working with Authentication Servers

802.1x is only half of the identity story. The information carried by 801.1x must be authenticated by an authentication service. This can be done with name and password validation using a RADIUS or TACACS+ server, or with digital signatures confirmed by a third-party validation technology such as PKI.

RADIUS

Remote Authentication Dial-In User Service (RADIUS) is a protocol used to communicate between a network device and an authentication server or database. RADIUS allows a network device to securely communicate login and authentication information (username/password), as well as arbitrary value pairs using Vendor-Specific Attributes (VSA). RADIUS can also act as a transport for EAP messages. RADIUS refers to the actual server in addition to the protocol.

PKI

Public Key Infrastructure (PKI) is a method of providing identity authentication between two parties via a trusted third party. A PKI certificate is "proof" of identity, signed by the trusted third party. It is the network equivalent of having a valid passport, trusted by the customs agents of all other countries. Just as a passport is signed by the passport office, stating your verified identity and citizenship, a PKI certificate is signed by a certificate authority, stating your verified identity and network associations. Unlike passports, PKI certificates can't be forged.

Hello, **Mr. Customs Agent**.
I have this to validate my identity.

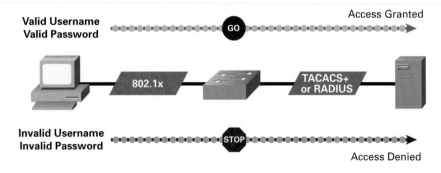

Valid Username
Valid Password — GO — Access Granted

802.1x — TACACS+ or RADIUS

Invalid Username
Invalid Password — STOP — Access Denied

Hello, **authentication server**.
I have this to validate my identity.

Authentication

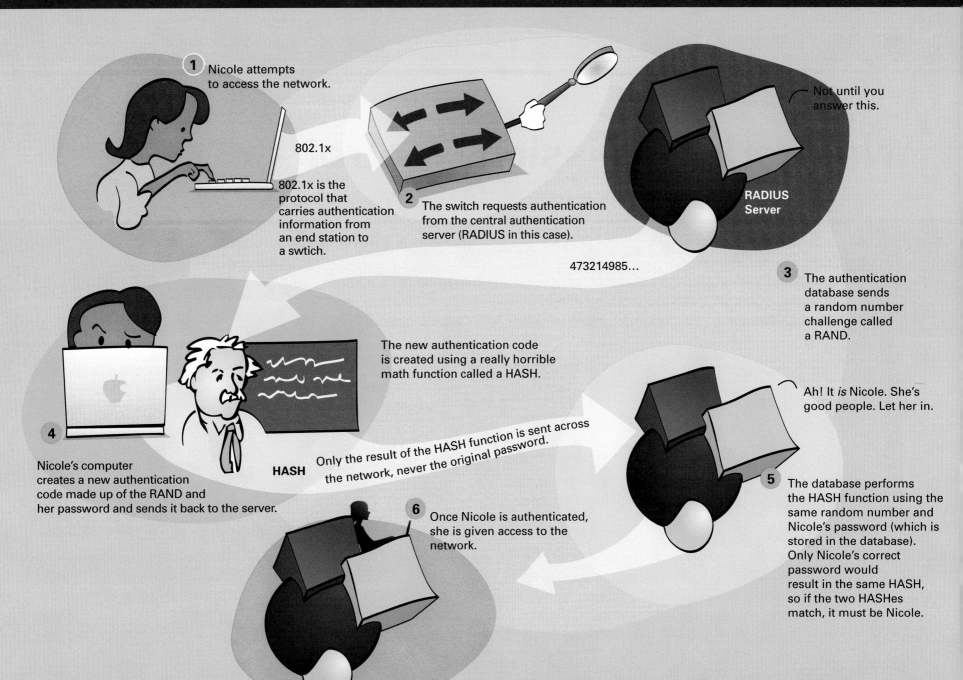

1. Nicole attempts to access the network.

802.1x

802.1x is the protocol that carries authentication information from an end station to a swtich.

2. The switch requests authentication from the central authentication server (RADIUS in this case).

RADIUS Server

Not until you answer this.

473214985…

3. The authentication database sends a random number challenge called a RAND.

The new authentication code is created using a really horrible math function called a HASH.

HASH

Ah! It *is* Nicole. She's good people. Let her in.

4. Nicole's computer creates a new authentication code made up of the RAND and her password and sends it back to the server.

Only the result of the HASH function is sent across the network, never the original password.

5. The database performs the HASH function using the same random number and Nicole's password (which is stored in the database). Only Nicole's correct password would result in the same HASH, so if the two HASHes match, it must be Nicole.

6. Once Nicole is authenticated, she is given access to the network.

Network Admission Control

Combating Virus Outbreaks

Mobility has given corporate employees huge productivity gains. They can access corporate applications from home, while traveling, and via wireless hotspots at coffee shops and airports. Always-on broadband networks have also led to huge strides in productivity. Employees can work from home in the evenings or even during extended periods when they are unable to get to work, such as during an ice storm.

But mobility and flexibility come at a price. Increasingly, corporate computer assets including laptops, PDAs, and handheld computers are used in public environments—home, Wi-Fi hotspots, hotels—which are shared networks. With shared networks also comes the opportunity for more frequent occurrences of computer virus infections. It's a bit like the difference between using a public shower and using the one in your home: You aren't really sure who else has used it and what bacteria might be lurking there.

IBNS takes an important step in ensuring that only authorized devices are allowed to access the network. But what about devices that are authorized but are infected with malicious software, such as viruses, worms, and Trojan horses? Even if a device such as a laptop is being used by a legitimate employee, that says very little about the device's "health." Laptops that are used outside the corporate network and then are brought back into the corporate network present the large threat of introducing malicious software outbreaks inside the company.

Assessing Device "Health"

Plenty of high-quality software applications are available to scan laptops and computers for the presence of malicious software. These include antivirus, anti-spyware, anti-adware, and software inventory programs. Many of these programs require constant updates of their signature databases so that they can always recognize the latest malicious software threats and prevent them from infecting a computer. Whether the signatures are current and whether scans have been scheduled and executed may depend on how long the computer asset has been outside the corporate network, how diligent the user is, and how well the corporate security policies keep up with new threats.

You can do several things to assess a device's health:

- Ensure that the operating system is current and has the latest security patches applied.
- Ensure that end-user applications (such as web browsers) have the latest patches to close known holes or exploits.
- Ensure that any corporate-managed security agents, such as Cisco Security Agent (CSA), are installed, are up to date, and are monitoring the computer asset.
- Ensure that the corporate-managed antivirus program is installed, is current with all updates applied, and has the latest virus signatures.
- Ensure that the antivirus (or other) program has heuristics enabled to detect anomalous behavior that may indicate viruses that are not yet in the signature database.
- Ensure that the corporate-managed anti-spyware/adware program is installed, is current with all updates applied, and has the latest signatures.
- Ensure that the corporate-managed software inventory program is installed and is current with all updates applied.
- Ensure that all the items just listed have recently performed a "scan" of the laptop or other computer asset and that the scan is "clean."

Wow! That's a lot to keep up with. Fortunately, all these security programs have quite a bit of automation to manage retrieving signature updates, performing scans, and so on.

But it's possible that a laptop may have been away from the corporate network for some time and did not have access to the necessary update files. Its also possible that the end user canceled scanning or even disabled the programs. How can we ensure that the laptop is in compliance with the latest security policies and is "clean"?

Network Admission Control

Network Admission Control (NAC) builds on IBNS by providing an additional hurdle that devices must leap before being allowed to access the network. After a laptop passes the identity check (assuming that IBNS is being used), the network provides an additional challenge to the device to assess its health.

Health is determined by the corporate security policy. It typically includes auditing the laptop for proper installation and current operation of mandatory security software programs, such as Cisco Security Agent (CSA), antivirus, anti-spyware/adware, and so on. The device is challenged by the network using a special NAC protocol; it needs to provide its health credentials to the network. The credentials are validated against a policy server. If the device is in compliance, it is allowed to access the network.

If a device is out of compliance, the policy server determines what actions need to be taken. Often a device out of compliance is "quarantined" to a special segment of the network that has access to remediation servers. The latest updates and signatures can be downloaded so that the device can come back into compliance. The device could also be given "guest only" access so that the device has basic Internet connectivity but no access to the internal network.

Some devices, such as printers and other less-intelligent devices, may not be able to participate in a NAC challenge. Such devices may not be susceptible to the same malicious software threats, so they may be exempted. The corporate security policy must specify how these devices are to be handled.

Finally, NAC can be implemented in the network in a couple different ways. The access switches may provide the NAC challenge, similar to how they provide an IBNS challenge. Alternatively, a dedicated set of NAC appliances may provide the challenges further into the network. In either case, NAC can play a critical role in keeping infected devices off the network, where they are likely to infect others.

At-a-Glance: NAC

Why Should I Care About Network Admission Control?

Not too long ago your work computer not only remained at work, it never even moved from your desk. Today, however, your computer probably goes home with you every night, accompanies you on business trips, and maybe even travels with you on vacation. While accompanying you away from work, your computer connects to the corporate network from many different locations from your home, through a Wi-Fi hotspot, from a hotel room, and even from another company's network as a guest user. In addition, many companies allow their employees to access the Internet for personal use.

Although this is great for productivity, this type of mobility also brings many opportunities for employee computers to become infected with viruses, spyware, or other forms of malware.

When infected laptops or other computers are reintroduced into the corporate environment, there is a tremendous opportunity for them to impact other users and devices on the network.

NAC allows network administrators to keep infected computers from gaining network access. This prevents widespread outbreaks, which can cost companies significant productivity losses or cause irretrievable data loss.

What Problems Need to Be Solved?

Several challenges exist with respect to controlling the health of devices on the network:

- **Consistent policy enforcement:** Signatures and revisions for antivirus software and other products must be kept up to date on end-user workstations, especially laptops.

- **Blocking known infections:** Infected end-user devices must be blocked from accessing the network and potentially infecting others.

- **Remediation:** Inoculations must be provided for infected devices to get users back on the network.

In addition to these policy challenges, other complicating factors exist:

- There are many different types of end-user devices, with different operating systems.

- Some devices, such as printers, handheld IP-enabled scanners, and servers, to name just a few, may not be able to respond to challenges regarding their policy health.

- Infected devices need access to some level of network services, isolated from the rest of the network, to install the needed remediation to reinstate their health.

- The cost (time) of a challenge cannot excessively hinder productivity or delay network access in emergency situations.

What Does NAC Do, Exactly?

The presence of a NAC solution adds an additional qualification (beyond login/password or requirement) that must be satisfied before an end-user device is granted access to the network. The device must be compliant with policy (have the updated antivirus signatures) and health (not be currently infected) requirements.

Policy checking can include the following:

- Ensuring that the most recent versions of antivirus software and signatures are installed.

- Ensuring that a virus scan has been performed recently.

- Ensuring that the device is free of viruses, spyware, and other forms of malware.

- Ensuring that other policies as defined by the IT department have been complied with.

A NAC solution has the following components:

- **Subjects:** The devices seeking network access

- **Enforcement points:** The network devices enforcing the IT policies

- **Decision services:** Where "intelligence" about the policies is contained

At-a-Glance: NAC

These components are standard among NAC solutions, but they can be used in different ways.

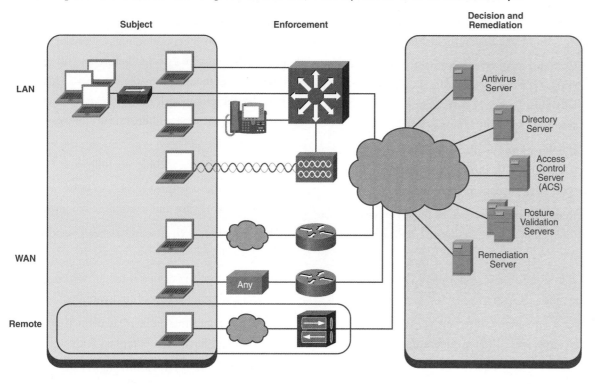

Appliance-Based Cisco Clean Access

In an appliance-based NAC solution, any attempt to access the network is redirected to an appliance called the Clean Access Server (CAS), which performs the NAC challenge. After performing a challenge to and receiving a response from the end-user device, the CAS communicates with the Clean Access Manager (CAM) to check the device's policy.

Typically the challenge-and-response process is very quick and is unnoticeable during the normal network login process. It may take longer if a scan needs to be performed or if the IT department has chosen to enforce a custom policy, such as a check of the file system on the computer for unwanted programs.

If the device is out of policy (also known as "unhealthy"), it is restricted to a quarantine area of the network, where it may be remediated. Access to normal production applications on the network is not allowed.

If a device cannot respond to the NAC challenge (such as a printer), the company security policy must dictate the treatment. It is possible that it may be exempted from the challenge based on its MAC address or other characteristics.

Network-Based Cisco NAC Framework

In a network-based solution, network access attempts are intercepted by an edge-network device, such as a switch or router. In this case the edge device performs the NAC challenge of the end-user device. The device then communicates with the Access Control Server (such as ACS and/or Windows Active Directory) to check the device's policy. If the device is out of policy (also called "unhealthy"), it is restricted to a quarantine area of the network, where it may be remediated. Access to normal production applications on the network is not allowed until the device is in compliance with the NAC policy.

At-a-Glance: NAC

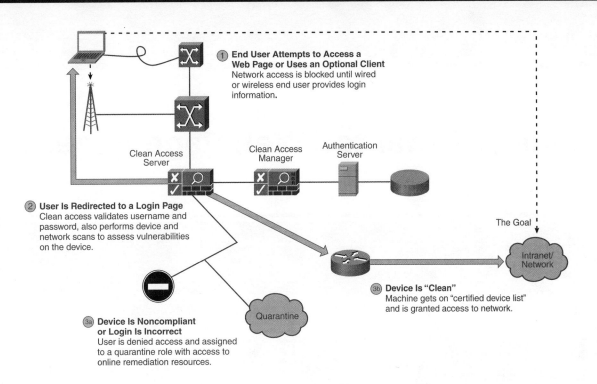

① **End User Attempts to Access a Web Page or Uses an Optional Client**
Network access is blocked until wired or wireless end user provides login information.

② **User Is Redirected to a Login Page**
Clean access validates username and password, also performs device and network scans to assess vulnerabilities on the device.

③a **Device Is Noncompliant or Login Is Incorrect**
User is denied access and assigned to a quarantine role with access to online remediation resources.

③b **Device Is "Clean"**
Machine gets on "certified device list" and is granted access to network.

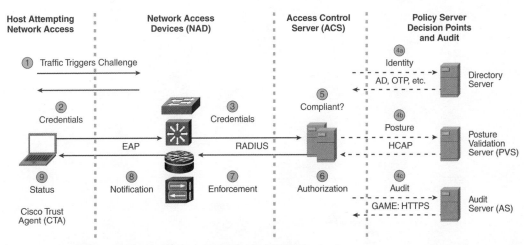

Status: Result of host's interrogation determines access to network: full access, limited access, no access, quarantined access.

URL Filtering: Eliminating Unwanted Web Page Access

Internet Access and Liability Issues

The Internet has provided quite possibly the single largest increase in communications and productivity in modern history. Whether it is keeping up with the latest news, researching a subject, purchasing supplies and components, or blogging with others in a community of interest on a particular topic, the Internet has provided a platform that has revolutionized work, home, and educational environments.

But not everything on the Internet is appropriate for all audiences, at all times, and in all contexts. For example, it is up to each individual whether to access gambling and adult websites from home, but these websites are usually inappropriate for the work environment. Some inappropriate content can even lead to liability issues for corporations. For example, employees viewing pornography at work could expose others to the images, which could lead to harassment lawsuits with serious financial consequences.

Still other websites, such as sports fantasy leagues, social networking sites, and auction sites, may not violate rules of appropriate content, but they can be a drain on employee productivity.

Enforcing Corporate Internet Usage Policies

Enforcing which Internet websites employees may and may not use is a bit tricky. Some websites are pretty obvious, such as online gambling and adult sites. For these sites it is a matter of maintaining a list of restricted websites.

Other sites may not be as clear-cut. For example, it can be argued that online news sites are best viewed at home. However, it can also be argued that the same sites provide valuable business-relevant information, such as on regulatory issues, global economic events, and even important product releases from a competitor. For Internet websites that fall into this "gray area," each company must determine its own definition of "appropriate."

After this has been determined, access to websites that are within corporate policy can be enforced through help from the network using techniques including URL filtering. URL filtering essentially compares a website entered by an employee against a database of restricted websites. If the website is not in the list, access is granted. If it is in the list, typically the employee is given a warning screen that indicates he is trying to access a restricted web page.

These lists can also be time-based in cases where a company doesn't really care what websites the employees visit; it just doesn't want the web traffic to mess up the business traffic during peak work hours.

URL filtering is only as good as the list of restricted websites, which must be continually updated, similar to antivirus signatures. More-sophisticated web filtering techniques can involve scanning the target web page for inappropriate content and making an "on-the-fly" assessment of appropriateness based on the content itself rather than the URL. Content scanning can be fairly effective for text content, but it can lose its effectiveness as the content becomes more rich-media-oriented, such as pictures, video, and flash animations. Rich media is more difficult to scan to determine its appropriateness.

At-a-Glance: URL Filtering

Why Should I Care About URL Filtering?

Internet access has become common in the workplace. In some cases it is critical for businesses, because e-commerce is now the standard mode for business transactions. The Internet is also used as a primary source of information, research, and communication.

Left unchecked, however, employees may knowingly or unknowingly access web content that is inappropriate for the workplace. Employees browsing inappropriate web content damage productivity and also expose a company to potential liability issues. Employees may also visit sites that are high-risk sources of spyware, viruses, Trojan horses, and other malware.

What Problems Need to Be Solved?

The main issue that must be solved is distinguishing between appropriate and inappropriate Internet content. Obvious types of inappropriate sites include

- Sites with adult content, such as pornography
- Online gambling or other gaming sites
- Sites promoting or showing violence or other forms of content that are considered offensive

Other types of sites may be banned for reasons of productivity or policy:

- Entertainment sites, such as sports scores and fantasy sports leagues

- Industry or competitors' job posting sites
- Social networking and entertainment sites, such as MySpace and YouTube
- Subdomains of otherwise-allowed sites. For example, Yahoo! News could be open to access, but the personals forum could be blocked.

Each company must determine its own policies and communicate these policies to its employees. As soon as the policy is set, employees can be prevented from accessing what the company determines to be outside its policies.

Some tailoring of the filtering process by network security staff will likely be needed over time.

How URL Filtering Works

After the list of restricted sites is created, all HTTP requests for content are intercepted by the network and are checked against the policy list. Requests deemed appropriate are allowed, and the web session works without interruption.

Requests for content that are against company policies are blocked and are often redirected to a page stating that the site that was requested was blocked because of inappropriate content. In some cases the company may choose to maintain a log of all blocked requests.

Defining the lists of appropriate and inappropriate content is not trivial given the size and changing nature of the Internet. There are two methods for defining restricted sites.

- **Black/white lists:** A list of URLs manually configured by the network security staff.
- **Third-party server:** Typically a subscription-based service in which a company specializing in inappropriate web content provides a database of URLs.

Using Black/White Lists

If a company chooses to manage its own URL filtering, all the URLs considered out of policy must

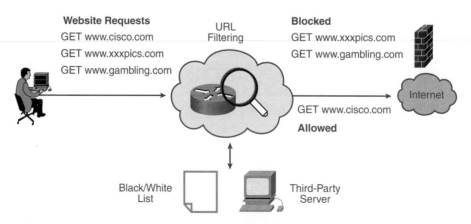

Website Requests
GET www.cisco.com
GET www.xxxpics.com
GET www.gambling.com

URL Filtering

Blocked
GET www.xxxpics.com
GET www.gambling.com

Internet

GET www.cisco.com
Allowed

Black/White List

Third-Party Server

At-a-Glance: URL Filtering

be configured in a black/white list in the network device responsible for intercepting HTTP requests. The pros and cons of this approach are as follows:

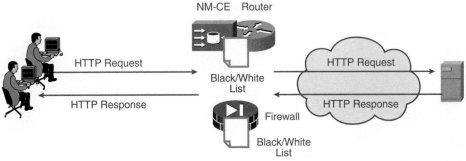

Pros:

• It provides a basic solution if a few specific URLs need to be exempted.

• It allows the company to directly manage the URLs it considers to be out of policy.

• Existing network equipment can be leveraged.

Cons:

• Keeping the URL list up to date can be difficult and time-consuming.

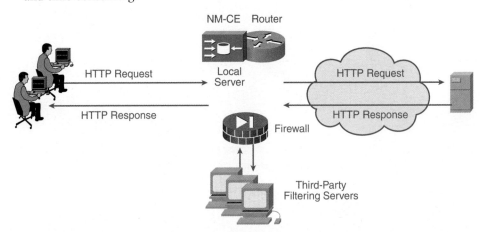

• This approach isn't very scalable for most network security staff.

Using Third-Party Servers

If the company elects to use a third-party server to make filtering decisions, sites considered out of policy are configured in a database on a third-party filtering server.

In this case the network device (such as a firewall or router) responsible for intercepting HTTP requests by employees forwards the request to the third-party server to determine appropriateness.

Servers can be external or run on a local server engine such as the Cisco Content Engine Network Module. The pros and cons of this approach are as follows:

Pros:

• It provides a comprehensive, scalable solution.

• Companies that specialize in appropriate web content manage the URL lists and provide updates.

• Existing network equipment can be leveraged.

• It covers millions of URLs (for the high-end services).

Cons:

• It's a bit less flexible in customizing which URLs a company considers appropriate/inappropriate.

• There is a greater risk of false positives.

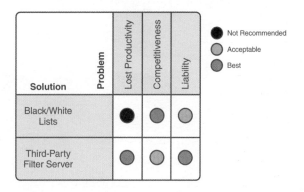

URL Filtering and Firewalls

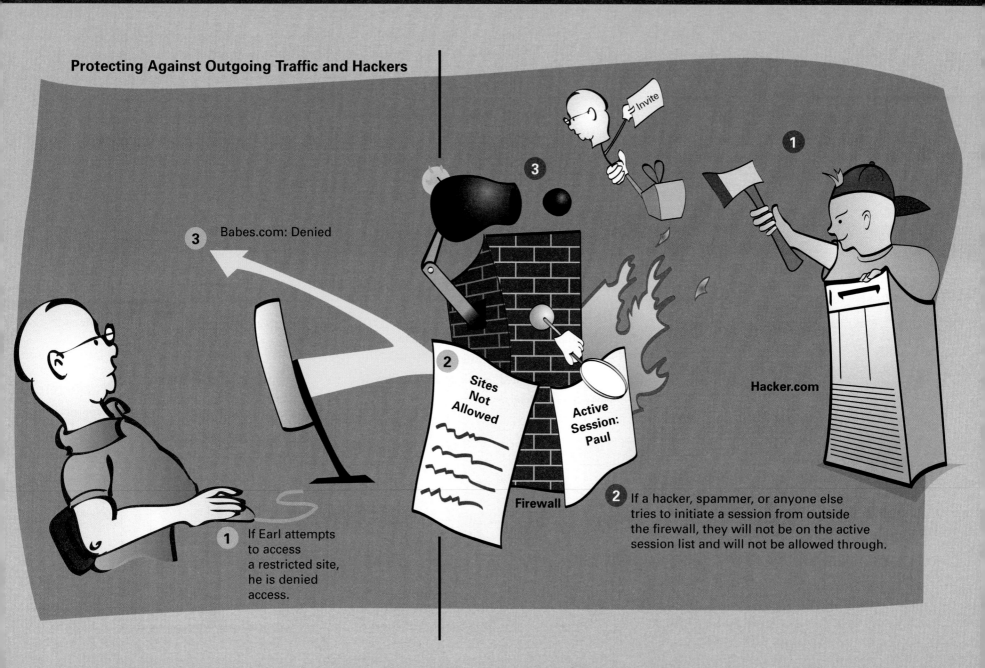

Protecting Against Outgoing Traffic and Hackers

Babes.com: Denied

③

② Sites Not Allowed

Active Session: Paul

Firewall

Hacker.com

① If Earl attempts to access a restricted site, he is denied access.

② If a hacker, spammer, or anyone else tries to initiate a session from outside the firewall, they will not be on the active session list and will not be allowed through.

Deep Packet Inspection: Controlling Unwanted Applications

How Do You Catch a Criminal When Everyone Wears a Mask?

Traditional firewalls can be very effective against network intrusions in which packets are sent from an untrusted network to a trusted one. The IP protocol being used can be checked for appropriateness and to ensure that it is part of a conversation that originated from the trusted side. In this way, security attacks that rely on manipulating certain IP protocols can be halted.

Increasingly, the number of IP protocols used on the network and the Internet is narrowing dramatically. With the popularity of TCP/IP applications, and even more so web-based applications using HTTP, the vast majority of traffic on modern networks ends up being only a couple of IP protocols. In addition, some protocols encapsulate themselves in other IP protocols to avoid problems with firewalls. For example, IPsec may be encapsulated within UDP packets. RTP video streams may be encapsulated within TCP. Finally, when nearly every corporate application becomes a web-based application, HTTP is the predominant protocol.

One of the issues with the huge popularity of protocols such as HTTP and TCP is that we can lose some visibility into what is actually going on with applications on the network. Imagine that all the customers in a bank are wearing masks. The bank gets robbed by people in masks, and the police show up. How are they to figure out who are the criminals and who are the innocent customers?

Deep Packet Inspection

Deep Packet Inspection (DPI) is a technique that allows network security devices such as firewalls to look "deeper" into the IP packet to try to learn its true intent. Instead of relying on fairly standard packet header information (essentially Layers 2 and 3), which again is starting to look the same for every application on the network, DPI can look much further up the OSI stack, into Layers 4 through 7.

With the increased visibility that DPI provides, it is possible for network security devices to understand more about the actual applications being run across the network, what information is being passed, and whether the information is appropriate in the context.

DPI has other potential applications as well. Although we certainly want to halt bad traffic, we also want to accelerate critical traffic. DPI can be one tool used to recognize which applications on the network are vital to the company's business and to give those applications preferential treatment as they are routed through the network.

Finally, a note about encryption. Encryption can be a very effective way to secure communications between two devices, whether it is a laptop encrypting a session across the Internet to the corporate headquarters (such as with IPSec VPN) or securing a voice-over-IP phone call between two IP phones (such as with SRTP).

The downside is that encrypted packets do not lend themselves well to being inspected. Typically network security devices do not have access to the decryption keys required to decode the encrypted packets and to understand what is occurring in the packet conversation. This is an example where one security policy may make it exceptionally difficult to enforce another.

At-a-Glance: Deep Packet Inspection

Why Should I Care About Deep Packet Inspection?

Despite the steady growth in the availability of high-speed network links, companies still find that the bandwidth is constrained. This is due in part to the explosion of increased bandwidth needs of applications such as voice and video, as well as an overall increase in the number of applications in use. This issue is often compounded when employees use applications such as file sharing and peer-to-peer programs that are not critical to the business. Because of these bandwidth constraints, companies must ensure that the bandwidth they have is used efficiently.

Tools such as QoS allow businesses to control which applications receive priority for network resources, but there is still a gap in terms of blocking applications deemed unnecessary for employees to use.

Companies must also guard against the propagation of worms and DoS attacks. Antivirus can help keep malware off employee computers, but the network must be able to recognize and block traffic related to such outbreaks.

Deep packet inspection is a tool that allows companies to look inside a packet to determine whether the packet should be dropped, without causing unbearable delays.

What Problems Need to Be Solved?

Because the whole point of deep packet inspection is to know which packets can be dropped, you first need to determine what you want to get rid of. Typical areas of concern are

- Malicious applications such as worms, viruses, and DoS attacks

- Noncritical applications

  — File-sharing programs designed to share music files between peers

  — Instant messaging

  — Social networking applications, such as MySpace

As soon as the types of threats and applications have been identified, a method must be developed to get rid of all packets that meet the drop criteria, without impacting the packets you want to keep.

Some tailoring of application filtering may be required by network administrators to ensure a good fit with company policies.

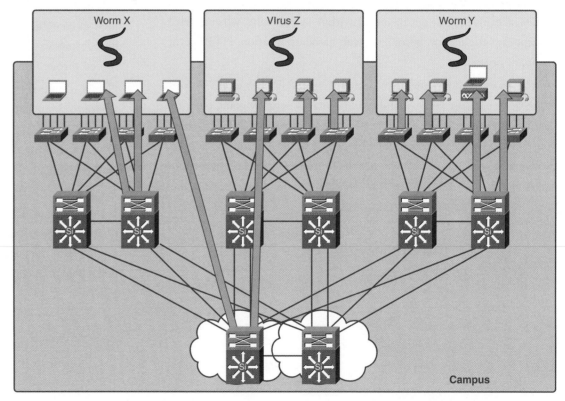

At-a-Glance: Deep Packet Inspection

How Does It Work?

Most network devices have visibility into only the header portion of an IP packet. This limits the amount of information the device can act on. Common network protocols such as TCP/IP and UDP (used by most applications) do not provide enough information in the packet header about the application in use.

For network administrators to have visibility into the applications consuming network resources, some form of deep packet inspection is required.

Traditional packet inspection can determine whether the packet is appropriate within the protocol. For example, TCP/IP can reject invalid packets.

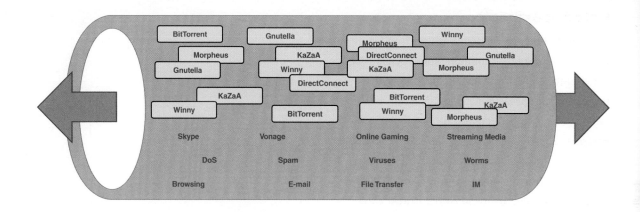

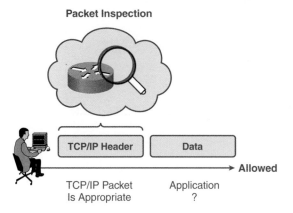

Packet Inspection

Deep packet inspection allows network devices to look beyond the packet header into the data portion of the packet (Layers 4 through 7 of the OSI model) and make decisions based on this additional information.

In doing so, the network can become application-aware and can distinguish one application from another.

Any packet inspection method is only as good as the way it specifies what to look for. Incomplete specifications may result in false positives, miscategorizing, and dropping the wrong traffic.

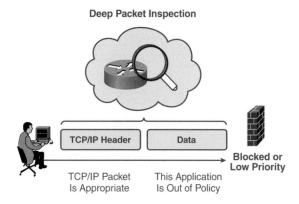

Deep Packet Inspection

At-a-Glance: Deep Packet Inspection

Catalyst Example

Using a sample deployment with a Cisco Catalyst 6500 running a Programmable Intelligence Services Accelerator (PISA), the benefits of deep packet inspection can be demonstrated. Mission-critical applications can be recognized on the network and prioritized, providing a higher level of service and guarantees for network resources. Undesirable applications, such as peer-to-peer file-sharing programs, can be deprioritized to the lowest class of service or dropped altogether. Worms can be identified using Flexible Packet Matching (FPM). Then they can be dropped before they propagate across the network and consume valuable network resources.

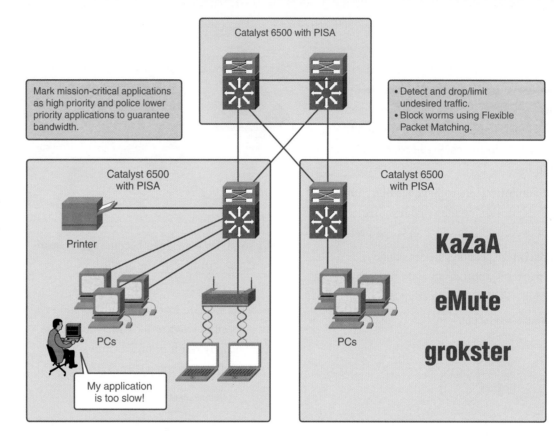

Packet Inspection

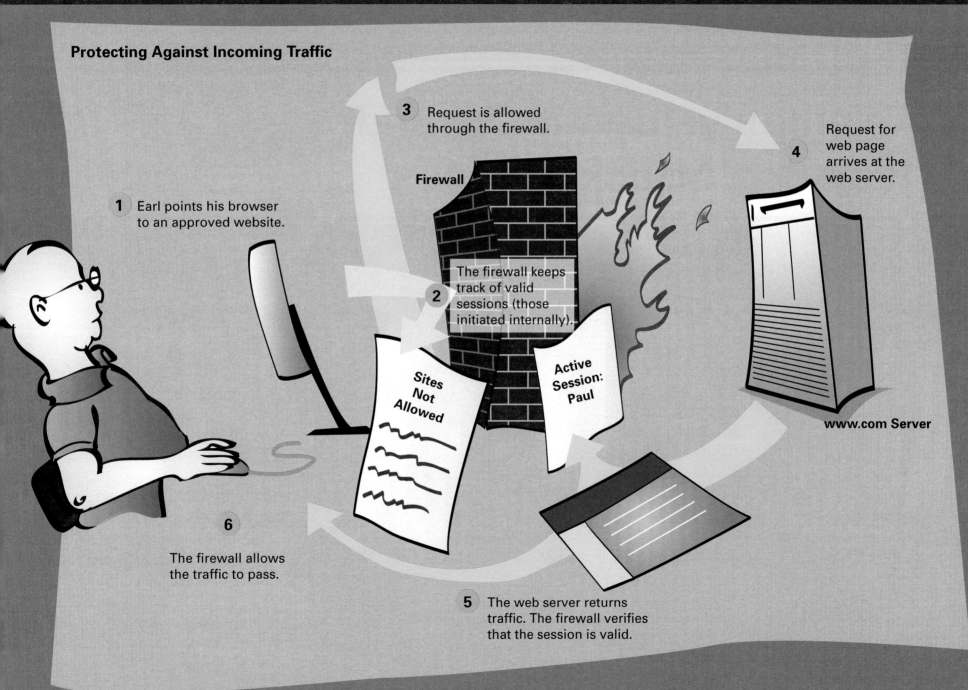

Protecting Against Incoming Traffic

1 Earl points his browser to an approved website.

2 The firewall keeps track of valid sessions (those initiated internally).

Sites Not Allowed

Active Session: Paul

Firewall

3 Request is allowed through the firewall.

4 Request for web page arrives at the web server.

www.com Server

5 The web server returns traffic. The firewall verifies that the session is valid.

6 The firewall allows the traffic to pass.

Telemetry: Identifying and Isolating Attack Sources

Normal or Abnormal

Although it is critical to deploy the best security tools and systems available, including IBNS, firewalls, IPS, and NAC, it is possible to overlook one of the most useful security tools—"hiding in plain sight."

Using common network traffic monitoring and analysis tools (such as Cisco NetFlow) that are available on many core Cisco network products (including routers and switches), you can gain a deep understanding of what a network looks like during normal operations and when an anomaly is present in the network.

If you understand and study the normal, the abnormal can become apparent. What comprises abnormal may vary from network to network and from attack to attack. It could include large traffic spikes from a single source in the network, higher-than-typical traffic "bursts" from several or many devices in the network, or traffic types detected that are not normally sent from a known device type.

Detection is half the battle, and understanding what is normal can give network administrators the visibility needed to more easily notice anomalies.

Telemetry is a way to provide a statistics-based analysis and management of network anomalies. This is different from packet inspections, because the telemetry system doesn't look at the actual data in the packet. It simply looks at traffic patterns. Over time it can differentiate between normal traffic levels, acceptable anomalies, and anomalous behaviors that look like attacks.

Using Telemetry to Combat Attacks

After an anomaly or anomalies are identified, the sources must be found and eliminated. Again, understanding the normal behavior of hosts and different device types on the network, including applications that are normally present in a business, is critical to isolating attack sources.

Using a suite of tools available on the network, hosts originating the attack vector (whether knowingly or unknowingly) can be isolated, and appropriate actions can be taken on the network to halt traffic as close to the sources as possible.

Finally, network administrators can schedule remediation for the affected hosts to remove the malicious software enabling the compromise, and being used for coordinated attack vectors, such as a DDoS attack from within the business itself, using the business's own computer assets.

At-a-Glance: Telemetry

Why Should I Care About Telemetry?

Security "battles" have traditionally been waged at the perimeter of the network, where the objective was to keep attacks originating on the Internet from penetrating the edge of the network. However, with the proliferation of sophisticated worms, viruses, and highly organized botnets, perimeter security measures are insufficient for most businesses.

In addition, many attack vectors that were once originated or orchestrated from the Internet now often enlist the internal business network to carry out attacks from sources within the business.

Such attacks are costly to businesses in terms of productivity losses, unnecessary network upgrades, and intervention costs. Internal attacks are also aimed at theft of information, theft of services, phishing, and other types of direct attacks. Telemetry addresses this issue and allows network administrators to take corrective actions.

What Problems Need to Be Solved?

One of the biggest hurdles to overcome is determining that an attack is under way on the network, which often means differentiating false positives from actual attacks.

Rapidly identifying sources of an attack, determining whether it is a direct or indirect attack, and then taking appropriate actions to drop the traffic

from compromised hosts or servers being used for the attack incident must all be done in a matter of minutes.

Network administrators must also be able to isolate and quarantine compromised hosts for intervention and remediation.

What Does Telemetry Do?

Telemetry lets you determine the source of malicious traffic events in the network and shut them

down. To take advantage of telemetry, tools and procedures must be put in place along with good network operations practices, far in advance of attacks taking place.

Critical actions during an attack involve identifying an event or attack through anomaly detection, classifying the type of event, tracing back to the sources, and mitigating or reacting to halt the attack.

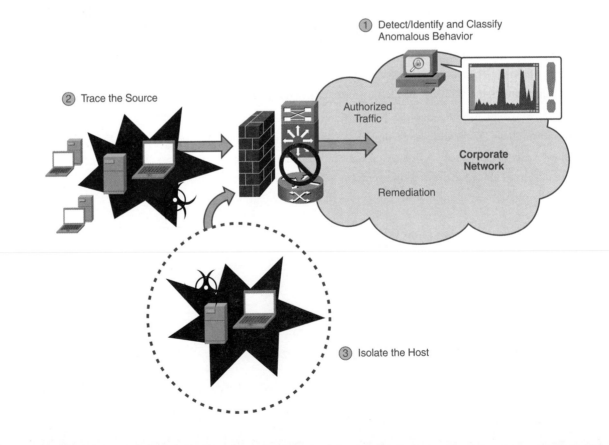

1. Detect/Identify and Classify Anomalous Behavior
2. Trace the Source
3. Isolate the Host

Authorized Traffic

Corporate Network

Remediation

At-a-Glance: Telemetry

Anomaly Detection

The key to telemetry is baselining network behavior under normal operating conditions, using tools such as Cisco NetFlow. This baseline test should be performed over several days (or even weeks) at different times of day and under different traffic loads. When you understand what normal network behavior looks like, anomalies will be apparent. Baselining uses several types of information:

- Average/peak network utilization
- Percent distribution of packet types and application devices joining or leaving the network

The telemetry system investigates all traffic anomalies and classifies them as an attack symptom or a false positive. The system can learn from the false positives, which improves system efficiency and accuracy over time.

Source Location Using Traceback

After a traffic anomaly is detected, and it is determined that an attack is under way, the telemetry system locates the sources of the anomaly using network tools and techniques such as Cisco NetFlow, ICMP Backscatter, packet accounting, traceroute, CAM lookups, and IP Source Tracker.

These tools help identify and locate the host IP, MAC, access switch, and access switch port information.

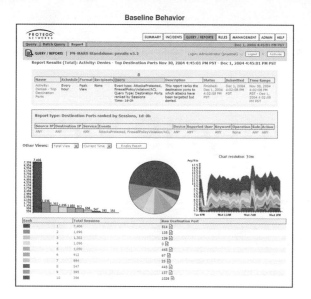

Baseline Behavior

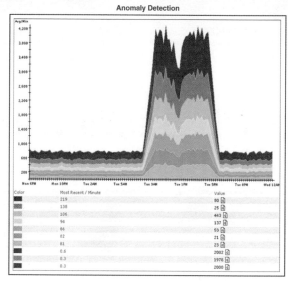

Anomaly Detection

Mitigation/Reaction

As soon as the sources of the attack are known, the telemetry system allows a network administrator to isolate the host(s) and halt the effects on the network. Tools for host isolation include unicast MAC address filtering, access control lists, and Source-Based Remote-Triggered Black Hole (SRTBH) filtering.

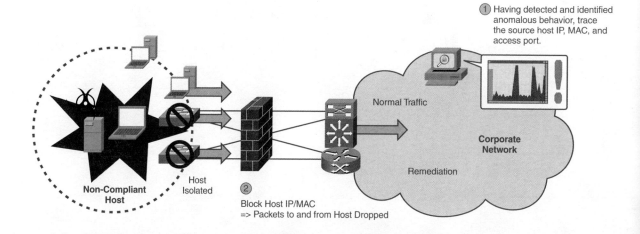

① Having detected and identified anomalous behavior, trace the source host IP, MAC, and access port.

Normal Traffic

Corporate Network

Remediation

Non-Compliant Host

Host Isolated

② Block Host IP/MAC => Packets to and from Host Dropped

Physical Security: IP Video Surveillance

Locks on the Doors

The first step to securing a network is to restrict physical access to the network devices, network access ports, and other points of entry. Network devices need to be kept in locked communications rooms with access tightly controlled.

Physical security can also include the use of motion detectors (sometimes wired to lights or alarms), cameras (or decoy camera), and other measures and deterrents.

As discussed earlier, employees need to be educated about security threats, such as tailgating, so that they are not threat enablers themselves.

But despite the best intentions, we cannot always rely on these measures to keep out bad guys who may be trying to steal assets, plug into a network port to gain access, or other malicious acts.

Video Surveillance

Visibility is a prerequisite to action. If we cannot see or detect a threat when it is occurring, we cannot take action. We have discussed a number of security tools and systems that provide visibility into the network to detect attacks. Video surveillance is yet another important form of visibility. It provides a view into potential threats that are physical in nature, such as an intruder trying to gain access to a communications closet or the corporate business location.

One of the most vulnerable areas of a business is the branch office. Although headquarters locations may be heavily secured, including security staff, vigilant employees, and high-tech corporate badge readers and door locks, branch offices may have a much more relaxed security stance. Especially in small offices, where everyone knows everyone, security measures may not seem as necessary. Another factor is cost. It may be cost-prohibitive to employ the same security measures in small offices as in corporate locations.

Whether at the corporate headquarters or branch offices, physical security measures such as badge readers and video surveillance are critical. Closed-circuit TV (CCTV) video surveillance systems can be cost-prohibitive, especially for branch office locations. However, IP-based video surveillance, which can plug into the corporate network (which must be there anyway), can enable security staff to easily deploy video surveillance at virtually any location in the business where network access is available (even wireless). Such an integrated approach can be done at low cost and can be centrally managed, making it practical to extend headquarters security practices wherever necessary.

At-a-Glance: Physical Security

Why Should I Care About Physical Security?

As modern threats have evolved, physical security measures, such as real-time video surveillance, have found many applications beyond traditional uses, including school systems, ATMs, and many workplaces. Video surveillance also offers the ability to perform passive monitoring, recording and reviewing events and providing critical pieces of evidence for locating and prosecuting criminals.

Video surveillance technology is not new and has been a critical component of security for businesses, but traditionally, it has employed analog camera technology and recording equipment. With the advent of digital camera technology, IP-enabled video surveillance systems offer distinct advantages over traditional systems:

• Lower deployment costs

• Lower operational costs

• A higher degree of flexibility and accessibility

• Integration with other IP applications

What Problems Need to Be Solved?

With the large installed base of analog cameras, any solution should be able to integrate with traditional systems.

New (traditional) camera deployments require expensive cabling for power and video signals. If you want to record something, you have to route video signals to monitors (for viewing purposes) and store the records, both of which traditionally require a system of dedicated cabling.

Just providing the storage that is required to store large volumes of digital video feeds can be a daunting task.

Converging video surveillance onto an IP network must be done in such a way that the cameras, signals, monitors, and recorders are accessible by the right staff (security and facilities employees) and are protected from intrusion by others (general employees and nonemployees).

For every camera feed requiring recording, a DVR (or VCR with analog systems) is required.

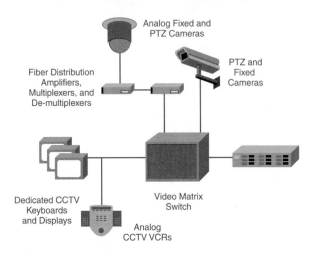

Digital Systems Overview

Digital IP-enabled video surveillance systems use digital cameras and monitors. They can use the

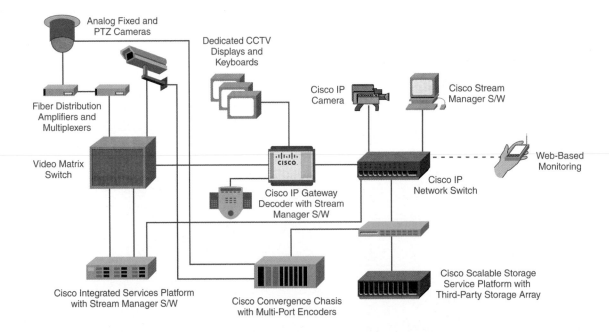

At-a-Glance: Physical Security

same digital storage systems used for other corporate data. Another advantage of digital systems is that video signals are carried over the same corporate network used for employee computer systems and applications. Traditional analog system investments can also be leveraged through the use of integration tools.

IP-Enabled Video Systems

One of the biggest advantages of digital IP-enabled video systems is the relatively low deployment cost. If you leverage the existing data network resources, the total cost of a digital system can be less than a comparable analog system.

IP-enabled digital cameras can also take advantage of Power over Ethernet (PoE) and can use the wireless network to significantly lower cabling requirements.

Real-time and recorded video streams are accessible by any device on the network, including fixed computers or mobile laptops and PDAs. This provides tremendous flexibility for deploying, operating, and accessing video surveillance.

It's worth mentioning that when first introduced, IP cameras tended to have low-quality recordings. This was due in part to lenses (low lighting, zooming, and so on) and poor compression technology.

Both of these issues have gotten better in recent years. These systems should also have their own security (encrypted video streams, for example), especially when they are shared across corporate networks.

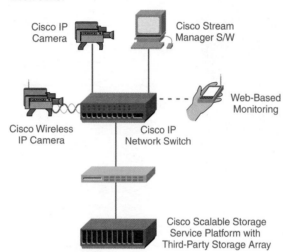

Cisco IP Camera
Cisco Stream Manager S/W
Cisco Wireless IP Camera
Cisco IP Network Switch
Web-Based Monitoring
Cisco Scalable Storage Service Platform with Third-Party Storage Array

Video Rule Manager
CISCO
Video Alarms
Objects/Humans/etc. Detected, Identified, Tracked, and Tagged

Bells and Whistles

In addition to providing cost-effective surveillance, digital IP-enabled video systems can provide advanced services such as motion detection and analytics.

When integrated with other applications, digital video signals can automatically trip alarms, notify security staff, and even provide streaming video feeds to mobile devices.

Physical and Logical Security

Physical Security

Keep gear and wiring closets locked and restrict access.

If possible, keep the main and backup power separate from each other and from the other gear.

Power House

Front Entrance

Make sure entries are locked or have badge readers.

Loading Dock

Look for *"piggy backers" or suspicious service people.

*Illegally Entering Behind Someone Who Has Badged In

Software Security
Encourage Strong Passwords

Good

Username: **LEONARD**

Password: **TZg3B47**

Time to Crack: Six Months
(Password Changed Every Four Months)

Strong Passwords = Mixed Upper-/Lowercase with Numbers

This kind of password gives 9.54×10^{22} possible combinations.

Not Good

Username: **LEONARD**

Password: **MRSPOCK**

Time to Crack: 37 Seconds

Hacker PC with Password Cracker

Looks for weaknesses such as common words, themes, and dates.

MRSPOCK

Part VI

Data Centers and Application Networking

Moving Data Efficiently

Companies move massive amounts of data around the network through the course of a typical day. As companies move toward a more global approach to business, "normal" business hours have become 24-hour operations with activities and data following the sun. With all this data flying around, it is important for companies to effectively manage their data to keep costs down and productivity up.

This part begins with a look at data centers. Data centers are just what you might think they are—massive banks of data storage devices connected in a single location. Data centers are anything but simple, though, especially considering companies' dependence on data. This chapter looks at how data centers work and how they interface with the rest of the network.

Before the emergence of large off-site data centers, data typically was stored at headquarters and branch offices in smaller file servers. In some cases the data was pulled at the time it was needed. In other cases, the data was "pushed" closer to the users before it was asked for to increase productivity. This method of prestaging data is called *caching*. This chapter also looks at Storage Area Networks (SAN). SANs are still common for smaller enterprises and are in wide use today across many networks.

Within the past several years there has been a shift in the corporate model. At one time most employees worked at a headquarters facility, and few worked remotely or in small branch offices. Today almost every enterprise within the Fortune 5000 has several large regional sites throughout the world that are often considered to be headquarters facilities within their geographic region. With so many employees outside the main headquarters, it is critical from a productivity standpoint that these employees have fast access to the data and applications required for them to complete their missions. It is usually cost-prohibitive for companies to duplicate data centers or SANs at every location, so companies must find a way to get the most data to geographically dispersed users as fast and as efficiently as possible.

It turns out that through the use of two methods, remote users get access to information and applications so fast, that for all they know, the data and applications reside on their local network. The section "Wide Area File Services" looks at how large amounts of data can be moved from the data center out to remote locations. The section "Wide Area Application Services" discusses how remote users can get local performance from remote application servers.

Data Centers

Store Once, Use Often

Data centers are centralized locations where companies house their business-critical network and server resources. Data centers provide secure centralization of corporate computing resources. Mainframes, application and web servers, Unified Communications services clusters, data storage, secure printers, Internet connectivity, and network core switches are examples of devices that are commonly located in the data center.

IT functions, such as network and server operations and support, generally sit near the data center. Satellite data centers provide regional services as well as disaster recovery for the primary data center. Having these resources centrally located provides administrative benefits but also presents network-design challenges.

Whether accessing a server in the data center, exchanging files with a remote office worker, or accessing the Internet, most network activity passes through the data center at some point. Additionally, the data center houses much of the company's critical data and computing resources. High-bandwidth networking and business-resiliency measures become critical design factors in providing smooth and reliable services.

Located in the data center are applications that support business-critical functions as well as network operations and network-based applications, such as IP telephony, video streaming, and IP videoconferencing.

n-Tier Model

Mainframes, server farms, and blade servers represent the heart of corporate computing resources. Today's data-center server-farm design incorporates what's called an *n*-tier model. This model describes a method of separating application services into manageable and secure tiers. The *n* indicates that there can be any number of distinct tiers in the data center, though typically three. The purpose of separating these functions into separate tiers is to break the dependence of all functions residing on a single server. Separating the customer-facing applications from the back-end servers increases the scalability of the services and eases the management of large-scale server farms.

The first or front tier is the actual application a user might run, such as customer resource management (CRM), enterprise resource planning (ERP), email, or order processing. The application might or might not be web-based, although most modern applications use web services to some extent. This tier provides the client-facing services.

The next tier, the middle tier, provides the glue between the client-facing application and the back-end database and storage servers. Typically, these middleware applications provide the business logic that maps corporate data to how a company operates.

The final tier, the back end, contains all the databases, storage, and raw data to be shared with the various applications.

Functions and Requirements

These server farms must have a supporting network infrastructure. Although the growth and design of data centers tend to happen gradually over time, what evolves is a layered approach in which the data center network is divided into distinct functions. These layered functions include the following:

- **Aggregation:** Connects the data center to the corporate backbone network.

- **Front end:** The servers that users interact with.

- **Application:** The servers running code that glues the front-end applications to the back-end data and reflects the business processes in how the data is used. Also called middleware or business-logic software.

- **Back end:** Where data is stored, typically in relational database systems, such as Oracle.

- **Storage:** The actual storage devices in which data is stored.

- **Backup:** Data is stored and retrieved for either transactional or backup purposes.

- **Data center network transport:** High-speed optical networking that facilitates the sharing of data between distributed data centers. Larger companies implement distributed data centers to provide redundancy in case a server farm or entire data center goes offline.

In each case, the network must provide the infrastructure, security, and management to accommodate the requirements for each layer, including the following:

- **High availability**: Access to data center applications, data, and networking services must continue in the event of a device or network failure.

- **Scalability**: Because servers are centralized in the data center, the network must be able to handle the sheer amount of traffic from corporate users to the central location, as well as server-to-server traffic. Additionally, data center services must be able to scale to multiple locations when distributed data centers are needed.

- **Security**: Data center devices must be physically secure, and the data and applications must be protected from internal and external threats.

- **Management**: The IT staff monitors, configures, and troubleshoots network and server resources.

- **Virtualization** (covered in Part IX): Instead of building redundant data centers for every division of a company, you can leverage the same data centers across multiple entities using virtualization technologies.

At-a-Glance: Data Centers

Why Should I Care About Data Centers?

Data centers house computing resources used to support business-critical applications and accompanying computing resources such as mainframes, servers, and server farms. The applications housed in business centers vary from business to business, but they typically include those related to financial, human resources, e-commerce, and business-to-business. Server farms within the data center also support many network operation applications, such as e-mail, Unified Communications, Media on Demand (MoD), and Telepresence.

By consolidating critical computing resources under a controlled, centralized management, data centers enable enterprises to operate around the clock or according to their business needs. With fully redundant backup data centers, enterprises can reduce the risk of massive data loss in the event of natural disaster or malicious attacks.

What Problems Need to Be Solved?

Building a data center requires extensive planning. You can think of it as building a network within a network. The specifics of each data center are highly personalized to the company deploying it, but some issues must be solved:

- **Facility planning:** The location and supporting equipment.

- **Storage methods:** Format and technologies.

- **Distribution:** Retrieval, and fast/reliable transport of data.

- **Backing up:** Connection methods and frequency.

- **Management:** Making the whole thing work.

- **Security:** Protecting from inside misuse and external theft.

- **Automation:** Data centers are huge, so automating some IT tasks is important for efficiency and cost.

Types of Data Centers

Data centers are defined by what type of network they support. The three basic classes are Internet, intranet, and extranet. Each type of data center has specific infrastructure, security, and management requirements for its supporting server farms:

- Internet server farms are accessed from the Internet and typically are available to a large community. Web interfaces and web browsers are widely available, which makes them pervasive.

- Intranet server farms should have the same ease of access as Internet server farms, but they should be available only to internal Enterprise users.

- Extranet server farms fall somewhere between Internet and intranet server farms. Extranet server farms use web-based applications. But unlike Internet or intranet, they are accessed by only a selected group of users (business partners, customers, or trusted external users) who are neither Internet- nor intranet-based.

Data Center Layers

Data centers can be logically divided into six logical layers. These layers do not correlate to the OSI layers. This list represents one of a number of ways to look at data centers. These layers are based on logical functions:

- **Aggregation:** Consists of network infrastructure components that connect all data center service devices, such as firewalls, content switches, Call Managers, and Content Distribution Managers.

- **Front-end:** Contains FTP, Telnet, e-mail, web servers, and other business application servers.

- **Application:** Performs translations between user requests and the back-end database systems.

- **Back-end:** Houses security infrastructure, management infrastructure, and the database systems that interface directly with the business data.

- **Storage:** Consists of the infrastructure, such as fiber-channel switches as well as storage devices. There should always be a secondary (backup) storage facility that is updated regularly. In cases where data is backed up synchronously (in real time), the two storage layers can load-balance for increased efficiency.

At-a-Glance: Data Centers

• **High-speed interconnect:** Consists of the optical devices used to communicate between distributed server farms across multiple data centers.

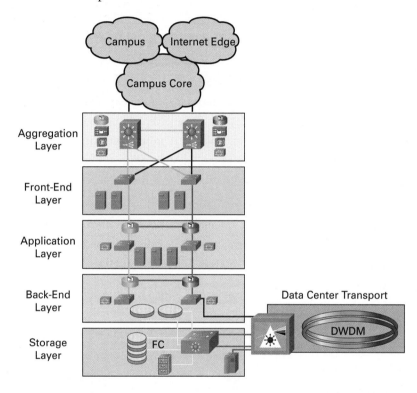

Distribution (*n*-Tier Model)

As the importance and size of server farms have increased, the limitations of a traditional client/server model of data storage and retrieval have become more evident. The *n*-tier model separates the server farm functions into distinct tiers, which improves both efficiency and ease of management. The model typically has three tiers. The first tier typically runs the user-facing applications,

the second tier maps user requests to the data, and the third tier is where the data is actually stored.

Traditional Client/Server Versus *n*-Tier

Like all design considerations, both the traditional client/server model and the *n*-tier model have pros and cons. For example, the client/server model is easier to set than the *n*-tier model, but it does not

scale well because of the heavy demands it puts on the server. When making these design considerations, is it very important to design for (or at least understand) the demands that will occur one or two years from the date of installation. If your company doubles year over year, you may end up redesigning the data center if you build it to serve the current demand.

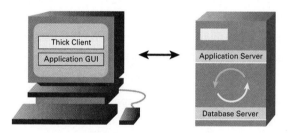

Traditional Client/Server

Requires heavy management. Processes info, and then presents it. Exchanges mostly data.

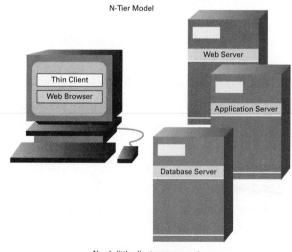

N-Tier Model

Needs little client management. Only presents information. Exchanges data and format.

At-a-Glance: Data Centers

Data Center Facilities

The housing of critical computing resources such as those found in a data center typically requires specialized facilities and trained personnel to run a 24/7 operation. The efficient, protected, and secure operations of these business-critical systems require consideration of and planning for the following items:

- Power capacity
- Cooling capacity
- Cabling (raised flooring or overhead tracks)
- Temperature and humidity controls
- Fire and smoke detection systems
- Restricted access and surveillance systems
- Space planning for future scaling

Although some of these items may seem like overkill, loss of data can actually cause a business to fail, so protecting the data and the equipment that store and transport it must never be shortchanged.

Storage Methods

Storage services include both the consolidation of information and the methods of connectivity. The basics of storage services are explained here.

Storage methods include Network Attached Storage (NAS), which uses specialized file servers to connect storage devices to a network, and Storage Area Networks (SAN), which are independent networks designed to connect storage devices.

NAS is optimized for file-based access to shared storage over an IP network. SANs are optimized for the efficient collection, storage, and retrieval of raw data in the form of bits or blocks.

The primary connection method is Small Computer Systems Interface (SCSI, pronounced "scuzzy"), which uses a parallel bus interface to connect to storage devices. SCSI commands can be transported over fiber (optical) or IP (referred to as ISCSI).

A newer connection method called Serial Advanced Technology Attachment (SATA) is now making inroads because of its high connection speed (3 Gbps). As a side note, the older methods have been retroactively classified as Parallel ATA (PATA).

Data Center Management

Management services typically are overlaid on top of all other services. Every layer of the data center model requires its own set of management considerations but must be supported by different organizational entities or even by distinct functional groups within the enterprise.

Specific management categories include configuration management, fault management, performance management, security management, and accounting management. Each of these categories must be included in the planning of the management services.

Security Services

Given the importance of the data center, security plans should encompass all services and all devices supporting those services. The security features include access control lists (ACL), firewalls, Intrusion Detection Systems (IDS), and Authentication, Authorization, and Accounting (AAA).

Putting a security plan in place for all services and devices ensures that there are no "back doors" into the data center.

Data Center Application: Corporate Expense System

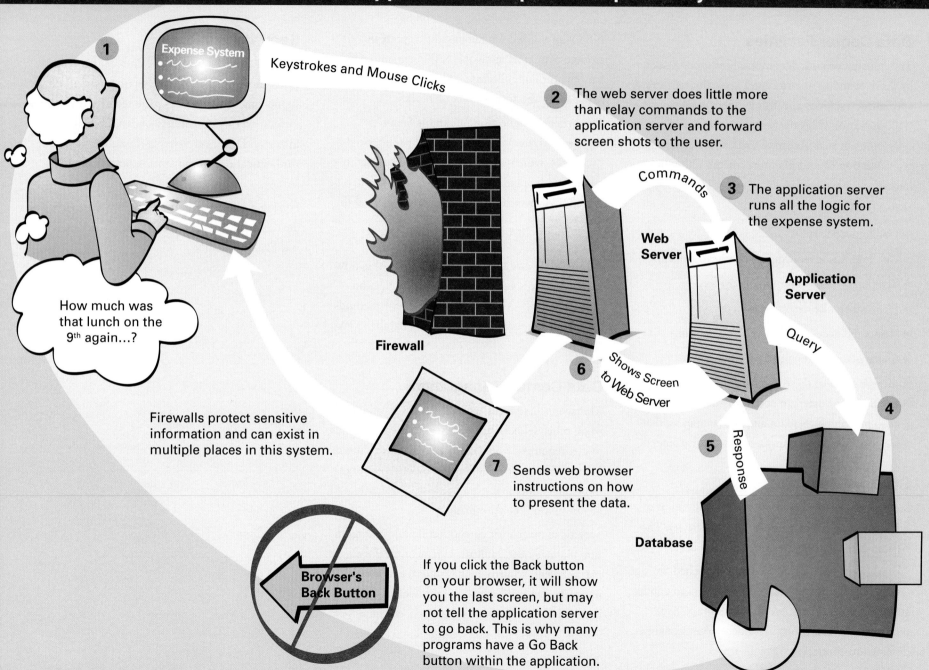

1

Expense System

Keystrokes and Mouse Clicks

How much was that lunch on the 9th again...?

2 The web server does little more than relay commands to the application server and forward screen shots to the user.

Commands

3 The application server runs all the logic for the expense system.

Web Server

Application Server

Query

Firewall

Firewalls protect sensitive information and can exist in multiple places in this system.

6 Shows Screen to Web Server

4

5 Response

7 Sends web browser instructions on how to present the data.

Database

Browser's Back Button

If you click the Back button on your browser, it will show you the last screen, but may not tell the application server to go back. This is why many programs have a Go Back button within the application.

Storage Area Networks

Efficient Deployment of Critical Data

In an effort to improve business productivity, corporations are implementing web and Internet applications such as customer relationship management (CRM), enterprise resource planning (ERP), and e-mail. This move has resulted in the accumulation of large amounts of corporate data, and these voluminous stores of data are critical to a company's operation. Large amounts of data require large amounts of storage. SANs have emerged as the premiere technology for advanced storage requirements. SANs address an IT manager's needs by providing a scalable, manageable, and efficient deployment of mission-critical data.

Traditional JBOD (just a bunch of disks—and no, we did not make that up) directly attached storage (DAS) networks are file system- and platform-dependent. The disks are associated with a single set of servers, and only the attached host can access them. Examples include SCSI, SATA, fiber channel, and enterprise system connection (ESCON).

Redundant Array of Inexpensive Disks (RAID) addresses fault tolerance. Because SAN removes the device, operating system, and location dependencies of traditional DAS, new capabilities emerge. Storage expansion no longer has an impact on servers, and vice versa. Bandwidth is available on demand, and load-balancing can occur across multiple active paths.

Aside from offering advanced technology for storage needs, SANs also reduce costs when deploying highly scalable storage versus traditional DAS. Hence, SAN reduces cost and offers new levels of performance and scalability previously unavailable.

SAN addresses the following issues currently experienced with DAS:

- Difficulty of managing large, distributed islands of storage from multiple locations
- Complexity of scheduled backups for multiple systems
- Difficulty of preparing for unscheduled outages
- Inability to share storage among multiple systems
- The high cost of distributed disk farms

SAN addresses these issues by doing the following:

- Reducing management costs through centralized control for monitoring, backup, replication, and provisioning.
- Reducing subsystem costs through any-to-any connectivity between storage and servers. This setup allows networks to match servers with underutilized storage subsystems.
- Reducing backup costs through the centralization and consolidation of backup functionality.
- Offering highly available disk services by providing redundant multiple paths between servers and storage devices. This provision allows for automated failover across all storage in an easily scalable manner.
- Offering highly scalable and location-independent disaster recovery. You can replicate entire data centers to multiple locations, allowing quick and efficient switchover if the primary data center becomes unavailable. DAS networks are unable to provide this level of disaster recovery.

Fiber Channel and IP

The two access methods available for SANs are fiber channel (the official name is Fibre Channel) and Internet Protocol (IP). Dedicated fiber-channel networks attach servers to storage devices. The fiber-channel network passes around data blocks (blocks are used by disk access), which the servers access through host-bus adapters. The servers then attach to LANs to provide the information to the rest of the network. SAN components include host-bus adapters, storage systems (RAID, JBOD, tape, and optical disk), hubs, switches, and SAN-management software.

Fiber channel is an American National Standards Institute (ANSI) standard that combines both channel and network technologies. SCSI and IP are the primary upper-layer protocols available on fiber channel. Fiber channel usually operates at 1 to 4 Gbps, but some 8-Gbps and 10-Gbps solutions have been developed.

You can use several topologies for fiber-channel deployment:

- **Point-to-point:** Dedicated connections between a server and storage device. This method is suitable when storage devices are dedicated to a single file server.

- **Arbitrated loop:** Storage and file servers connect to each other in a closed loop with up to 126 nodes. Maximum bandwidth is 100 MB shared between all the nodes. Therefore, the number of attached nodes directly affects the loop's performance.

- **Switch fabric:** As with Ethernet, performance and reliability vastly improve when moving from shared media (such as an arbitrated loop) to switched fabrics. A fiber-channel switch offers up to 100 Mbps to each switched port. You can trunk switches together to attach up to a theoretical 16 million nodes.

The other access method to fiber channel is IP. Because SANs connect to IP networks, the storage can be accessed across LANs, WANs, metropolitan-area networks (MAN), and the Internet. You can manage the devices using Simple Network Management Protocol (SNMP) and operate in a secure mode with the use of Internet Protocol Security (IPsec), firewalls, and virtual local-area networks (VLAN). Storage devices can connect to Ethernet devices. 10-Gbps Ethernet is an increasingly popular SNA option.

Whereas fiber channel separates disk-block-based traffic from the rest of the network, IP-based SAN tunnels block traffic through the IP network using the ISCSI protocol. ISCSI uses Transmission Control Protocol (TCP) as its transport. Fiber Channel over IP (FCIP) is another technology that allows fiber-channel networks to connect to each other over LANs, MANs, and WANs. FCIP uses TCP to tunnel fiber-channel block traffic across the IP network.

Infiniband

Some specialized data center applications require extremely low-latency connections between application servers and storage devices. Examples include high-performance computing arrays used for geological exploratory modeling, and high-performance trading environments, in which delays in financial or stock trades of even a few milliseconds can cost thousands or millions of dollars.

Infiniband is one data center technology targeted at such high-performance, low-latency applications. In addition to low latency, Infiniband links support bandwidth of 2 to 8 Gbps. Data center technology is evolving every day, and more technologies in this area will undoubtedly appear on the market in the coming years.

At-a-Glance: Storage Networking

Why Should I Care About Storage Networking?

Most companies use online storage to house business-related information. As more information from business functions such as sales, inventory, payroll, engineering, marketing, and human resources is stored online, the efficient acceptance, management, and retrieval of this information become more critical to the success of the business. By storing data in common devices, companies can also leverage economies of scale, reducing the total cost of data storage.

What Problems Need to Be Solved?

For many years, information was stored in server-centric architectures. As businesses grew and had greater storage needs, additional servers were added when and where they were needed.

However, this DAS approach is limited in its ability to scale because it is expensive to manage and uses resources inefficiently. This is because servers are added where needed (in each department, for example), and each is associated with a specific CPU. Additionally, standard activities such as backing up data or adding capacity are difficult and inefficient.

What Is Storage Networking?

To overcome the drawbacks of server-centric storage, a network-centric model called *storage networking* has been developed. Storage networking is the software and hardware that enable storage to be consolidated, shared, accessed, replicated, and managed over a shared network infrastructure. To understand how storage networking works, you must understand the different storage methods and technologies.

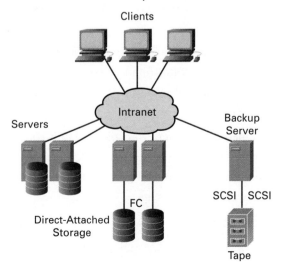

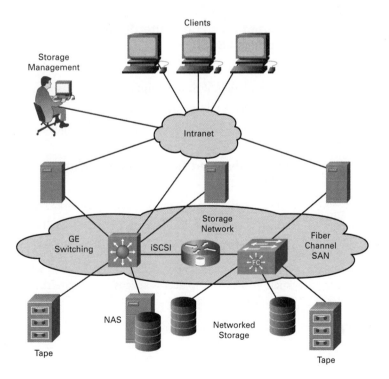

Traditional Server-Centric Storage Methods

- **Redundant Array of Inexpensive Disks (RAID):** RAID is a fault-tolerant grouping of two or more disks that a server views as a single disk volume. It is a self-contained, manageable unit of storage.

- **Just a Bunch Of Disks (JBOD):** Aside from being one of our favorite acronyms, JBOD is a simple and efficient method for raw storage. Each drive is independently attached to an I/O channel.

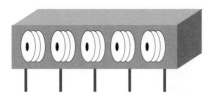

This method has limited scalability because it requires separate servers to manage multiple volumes of disks. Drives share common power supplies and physical chassis.

Storage Networking Technologies

This section briefly summarizes some common storage technologies.

Small Computer Systems Interface (SCSI)

SCSI (pronounced "scuzzy") is a parallel bus interface port used to connect peripheral devices such as RAID, tape devices, and servers. SCSI is a low-cost method of directly connecting devices but is limited with regard to scalability and distance.

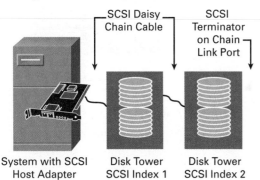

System with SCSI Host Adapter   Disk Tower SCSI Index 1   Disk Tower SCSI Index 2

SCSI Daisy Chain Cable   SCSI Terminator on Chain Link Port

Fiber Channel

A fiber channel is both a physical connection and a Layer 2 protocol used by SANs. Fiber channel is the most common method of transporting SCSI commands and data between servers.

Fiber channel capabilities have kept up well with companies' ever-increasing need for bandwidth. Using fiber channel, application servers can access data on a SAN without impacting the company IP network.

Internet Small Computer Systems Interface (iSCSI)

iSCSI (pronounced "i-scuzzy") is a method of encapsulating SCSI data and command frames into IP packets, enabling universal access to storage devices and SANs over standard TCP/IP networks.

Serial Advanced Technology Attachment (SATA)

As file sizes and disk storage space grow ever larger, access speed must also increase. Users typically want to retrieve a 10-gigabit file just as fast as they would get a 500-kb document. Technologies such as SATA keep access speeds up despite the huge growth in file sizes.

Retrieval Methods

The two main methods of retrieving stored data are block retrieval and file retrieval.

A block is the largest amount of data that can be accessed in a single operation. Blocks are the most elemental units of storage. SANs access blocks directly.

A file is composed of several blocks. In NAS systems, the server organizes blocks into files.

Network Attached Storage (NAS)

NAS uses a specialized file server to connect storage devices to a network. NAS is well suited for collecting, storing, retrieving, and sharing data over IP networks. NAS also supports multiple operating systems and file system protocols:

- Network File System (NFS) supports sharing of files and other resources across a network infrastructure.

- Common Internet File System (CIFS) and Small Message Block (SMB) are alternatives to NFS used to share files and other resources across a network.

- Hypertext Transfer Protocol (HTTP) is commonly used for Internet browsers, which essentially aids in transferring files from web servers to web browser clients.

At-a-Glance: Storage Networking

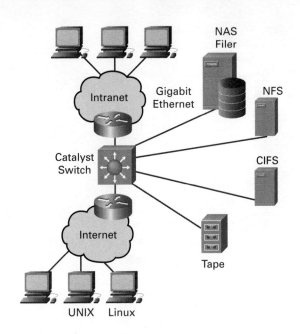

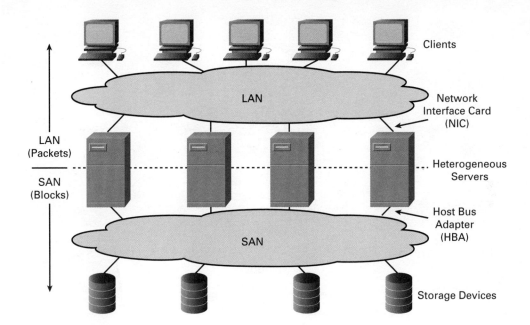

NAS is optimized for file-based access to shared storage over an IP network.

Storage Area Network (SAN)

A SAN is an independent network specifically designed to connect storage devices. SANs are optimized for the efficient collection, storage, and retrieval of raw block data. Most SANs use fiberchannel interconnections and require a media converter to connect to an IP network.

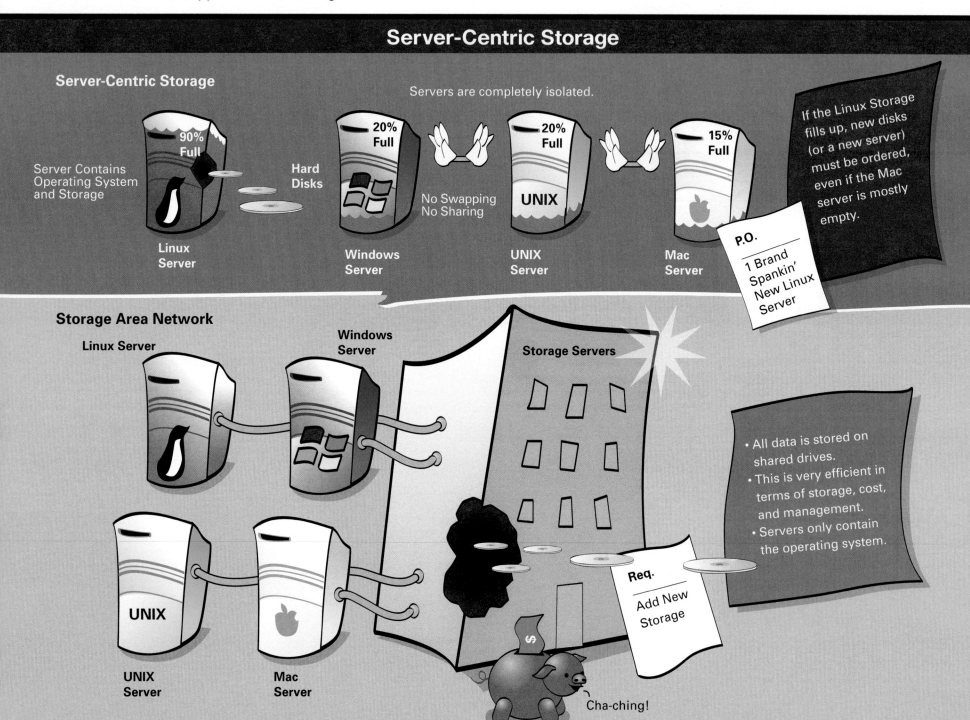

Caching

Moving Content Close to the User

Since the 1990s, the World Wide Web has taken off as fast as air conditioning. The Internet boom has created challenges for network engineers, including congestion, inconsistent quality and reliability, and cost-efficient scalability.

Examples of these problems include the following:

- Not being able to access a news website during a huge news event because the web servers are unable to handle the enormous number of simultaneous users

- Trying to view web pages located in another country

- A company with international presence trying to localize its web pages for each country

Network caching provides a means to localize network content closer to the requester. Caching addresses the preceding problems by accelerating content delivery and optimizing WAN link utilization. In other words, it moves the content closer to the user. Examples of cacheable content include web pages, audio files, and streaming video.

How Caching Works

Caching works in cooperation with specific choke points in a network. You can localize traffic by strategically placing caching devices in a network. Network caches transparently store frequently accessed content on hard drives, intercept requests for that stored content, and present the page to the user. Thus, the request never makes it to the intended destination, saving bandwidth and server resources. Caching is also often implemented on proxy servers of a corporate network. A proxy server is a web server that is a mirror or copy of the main server, located closer to a user or community than the main server.

An example of caching follows:

1. A user enters a URL in her browser.

2. A network device (such as a switch) analyzes the request. If the request meets certain criteria, the network transparently redirects it to a local network caching device.

3. Upon receipt of the request, the caching device determines whether it has the requested content stored locally. If it doesn't, the caching device makes its own request to the original web server.

4. After the original web server returns the content, the cache server stores the content on its hard disk and returns the content to the original requester. The material is now cached locally.

5. Later, if another user requests the same web page, the cache intercepts the request and responds by returning the locally stored copy, never communicating with the original web server.

6. Because the request was fulfilled locally, the user perceives a fast response time (which is good). Also, the request never leaves the local network, thereby saving WAN and Internet costs and reducing the load on the destination web server.

A cache server can provide its effectiveness to multiple locations. One place is at a company's main access point to the Internet. You can reroute all outbound requests to the local cache, thereby saving Internet access fees and providing quicker responses for frequently requested pages. Another location is at branch sites, such as at a chain store, remote sales office, or bank branch. By caching content locally, the network can conserve WAN bandwidth for more mission-critical applications.

Caching More Than Web Pages

The initial benefits of caching were realized with static web content. However, video and audio files are also appropriate candidates for caching. One example is a CEO's address to the company. You can broadcast the address live and then store it as video on demand for people to watch when they have time. You can push the broadcast to local caching servers so that an employee in another country can watch the video without having it stream from the location of the original video. To the overseas employee, the performance is fast, because the content is local. Additionally, as other employees overseas watch the video, the WAN link back to the origin is unaffected.

Storage Caching: From Disk to Memory

Another method of caching uses storage caching appliances that bring data "closer" to the user and improve performance via large memory caches for database data.

Issues Affecting Caching

During a sudden surge of web traffic, a caching device can become overloaded, no longer able to handle additional web requests. To solve this problem, cache engines determine when they reach a particular load limit. At the point of overload, the cache device refuses additional requests and forwards subsequent requests directly to the destination web server to handle directly.

After the cache device can process the backlog of requests, it intercepts requests again. Another issue is keeping the cached content current. The cache device becomes less effective if it can't show the same content as if the user visited the web server directly. An example might be a stock-tracking page: What good is the caching device if the stock price is an hour or day old compared to the actual website?

You have three different ways to indicate whether content can be cached and how long it can be cached. The first method is in the actual HTTP document. HTTP can specify whether a document is cacheable. Additionally, with HTTP 1.1, the web page author can specify the expiration time for a particular page. HTTP 1.1 also allows a caching device to send small requests to the source web server so that it can determine whether content has changed.

The second method of ensuring content freshness is by configuring the caching device. You can configure the cache device to "expire" pages at a certain rate, at which the cache device makes requests to the source web servers for updates to the pages.

The final method to ensure content freshness is through the user's configuration of his browser. A user can ensure fresh content by clicking the Reload/ Refresh button. Browsers by default cache web content locally, and you can configure them to do no caching either explicitly or using the Shift-Reload/ Shift-Refresh method. Newer methods of intelligent caching store the rendering of the page and fetch only the updated content from the server. This method balances the advantages of caching with the need to have current data.

Caching

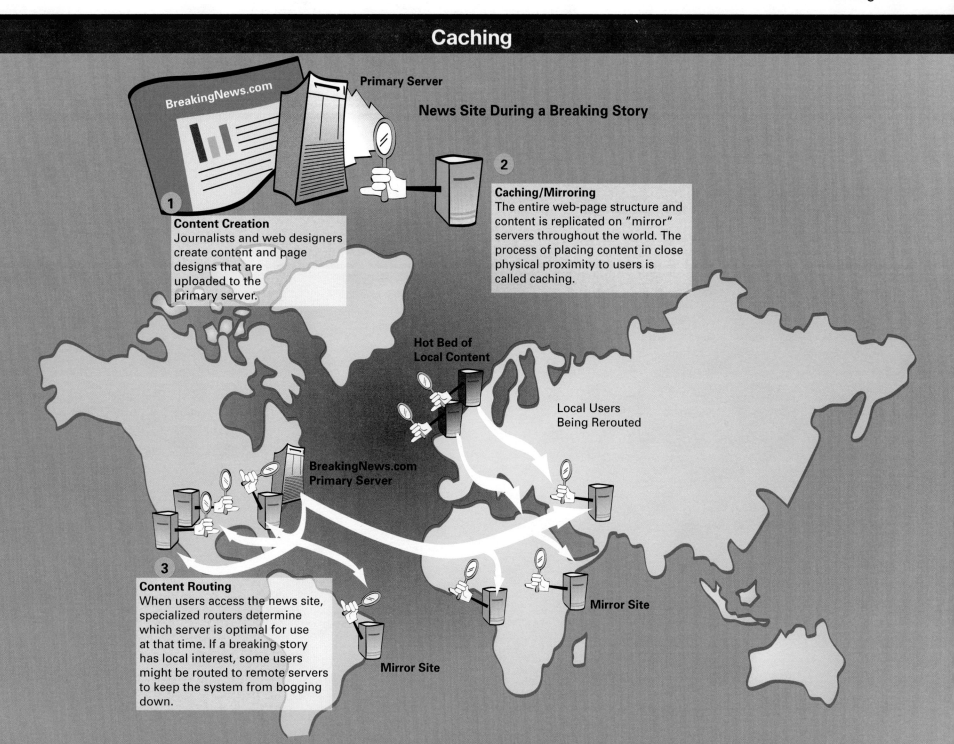

News Site During a Breaking Story

Primary Server

BreakingNews.com

1 Content Creation
Journalists and web designers create content and page designs that are uploaded to the primary server.

2 Caching/Mirroring
The entire web-page structure and content is replicated on "mirror" servers throughout the world. The process of placing content in close physical proximity to users is called caching.

Hot Bed of Local Content

Local Users Being Rerouted

BreakingNews.com Primary Server

3 Content Routing
When users access the news site, specialized routers determine which server is optimal for use at that time. If a breaking story has local interest, some users might be routed to remote servers to keep the system from bogging down.

Mirror Site

Mirror Site

Wide Area File Services

Branch Offices Rule

Once upon a time, the corporate headquarters was king, with the majority of employees who worked for the company going to work at the headquarters. In the service economy, companies needed geographic coverage and local offices near their customers, which fueled an explosion of branch offices.

A branch office can be anything from a gas station or convenience store, to a retail store in a shopping mall, to a stock-trading location, to your local bank branch.

Branch offices are everywhere. Just like in the headquarters location, applications that run in the data center have file storage requirements are also required in branch offices. So there has also been an explosion in local file servers in branch office locations.

The difficulty is that branch offices rarely have the IT staff to manage file servers, leading to either additional costs or poorly managed servers.

Centralizing Storage

Centralizing storage in the headquarters data center is strongly preferred, instead of having a myriad of distributed file servers in far-flung branch offices. This greatly simplifies operations, including backups and disaster recovery planning, as well as regulatory compliance issues. Companies only need a team of central IT staff administering the file servers in the central data center.

The trick is how to have central file servers being used by employees in branch offices over a WAN without impacting application performance. The WAN, because of its limited bandwidth and relatively longer latencies than a LAN, inherently slows down file access (to a grinding halt if we are not careful).

Enter Wide Area File Services (WAFS)

The answer is to introduce a technology that can make the WAN seem like a LAN from a file services point of view—and this is the essence of Wide Area File Services (WAFS). With WAFS, branch office employees can use applications that rely on file servers that reside in a distant location—back in the corporate headquarters data center—and not notice any degradation of file access speeds.

At-a-Glance: Wide Area File Services

Why Should I Care About Wide Area File Services?

The traditional model of heavily centralized businesses has quickly evolved into a more distributed model, giving businesses geographic coverage and agility.

Estimates are that 40 to 60 percent of employees work at non-headquarters sites, making it increasingly critical for workers at branch offices to have access to the same services, applications, and information as those working at the central headquarters.

One of the more significant costs of providing applications and services at branch locations are the file systems. Distributed file servers at each branch location create a number of operational issues:

• Remote management of the file servers

• Data replication and disaster recovery

• Avoiding productivity losses in the event of a file server failure

• Consuming critical WAN bandwidth and resources by moving files back and forth and to and from the corporate headquarters

WAFS provides the means to give branch employees the tools they need without creating the operational issues just noted.

What Problems Need to Be Solved?

The object of a WAFS is to provide a virtualized file server system, in which applications run in the

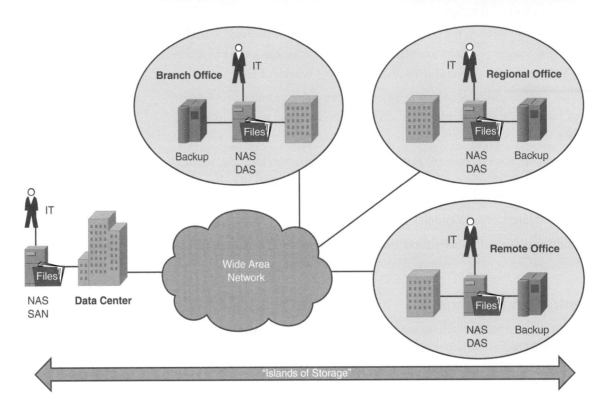

branch office as if the file servers were local. After this is accomplished, these files must be transported across the WAN intelligently to conserve critical bandwidth resources. There must also be a means to centralize file systems at the corporate headquarters without compromising application performance. In addition to the optimization challenges, government and industry regulations—including Sarbanes-Oxley, HIPAA, PCI, and other similar data management and security mandates—must be adhered to.

How Cisco WAFS Works

The Cisco WAFS solution consolidates file servers in the data center at the corporate headquarters site. Branch office applications communicate with an edge file engine (FE), which provides transparent access to file servers in the data center as if they were local to the branch office LAN. The WAFS FE normally is a dedicated hardware appliance installed at headquarters and the branch office(s). The FE also optimizes file service accesses, reducing "chatty" protocols to the essential communication across the WAN to conserve bandwidth utilization and preserve application performance.

At-a-Glance: Wide Area File Services

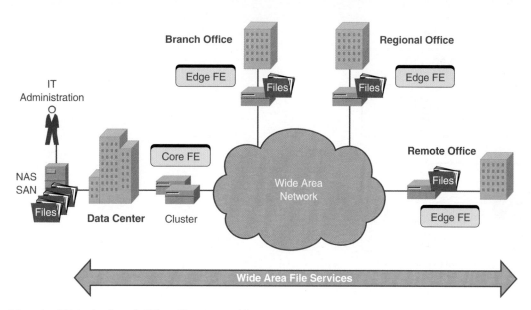

Wide Area File Services

After the FE is deployed, IT staff can provide appropriate management, backups, and disaster recovery for all file servers centrally in the headquarters data center, reducing risk exposure. The FE does not change the application. It operates at the transport protocol layer (Layer 4) rather than at the application layer (Layer 7).

Ensuring Transparency

WAFS transparency is important, because it ensures that applications run without disruption. In the data center, the Core FE provides a transparent interface (Server FE) so that file services "believe" they are communicating directly with clients. Similarly, in the branch office, the Edge FE provides a transparent interface (Client FE) so that

clients believe they are communicating directly with file services. The Core FE and Edge FE use a proprietary transport protocol, which is optimized to provide high application-to-server performance while being transparent in the implementation.

Caching

Caching is the process of preloading information that is likely to be used, in close proximity to where it will be used. Intelligent caching is critical to achieving the performance required by today's high-end business applications. Cisco WAFS provides caching locally for files being used or modified by the branch office. With *data read caching*, when a user opens a file, a copy is stored on the local appliance. From then on, with each request, the Cisco FE checks to see if the data has changed.

File System Transparency

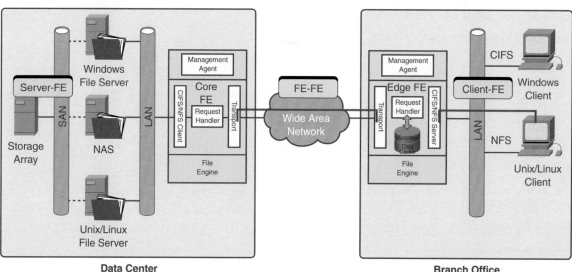

Data Center   Branch Office

At-a-Glance: Wide Area File Services

File Caching

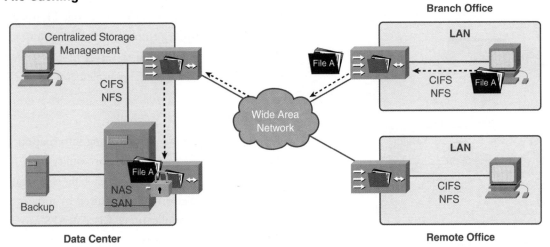

If it has not, the data is served as a local request with LAN-like performance.

This setup not only helps minimize the amount of bandwidth consumed when files are accessed, but it also helps ensure that a stale file is never served.

Wide Area Application Services

Centralizing Applications

For all the reasons we want to centralize storage, it is also highly desirable to centralize application servers.

Again, the trick is how to have central application servers being used by employees in branch offices over a WAN without impacting application performance. The WAN, because of its limited bandwidth and relatively longer latencies than a LAN, inherently slows down applications (to a grinding halt if we are not careful).

Because most employees at a typical company now work in branch offices, it is highly preferable that those employees be as productive as those working at the corporate headquarters. To do so, they must have access to the same applications and have near-LAN performance with those applications as well.

Enter Wide Area Application Services (WAAS)

The answer is to introduce a technology that can make the WAN seem like a LAN from an application point of view. This is the essence of Wide Area Application Services (WAAS). With WAAS, branch office employees can use application servers that reside in a distant location—back in the corporate headquarters data center—and not notice any degradation of application performance.

At-a-Glance: Wide Area Application Services

Why Should I Care About Wide Area Application Services?

Like WAFS and the other services described earlier, network performance for employees at nonheadquarters sites is critical in today's geographically dispersed businesses.

What Problems Need to Be Solved?

Application performance requirements at branch locations create a number of challenges, including the following:

- Additional WAN bandwidth requirements

- Latency requirements between the employee workstation at a branch across the WAN to the application servers to ensure adequate application response time

By optimizing WAN performance, applications run in the branch office transparently as if the application servers are local, saving on capital and operational expenses. One key consideration is compliance with government and industry regulations, including Sarbanes-Oxley, HIPAA, PCI, and other similar data management and security mandates.

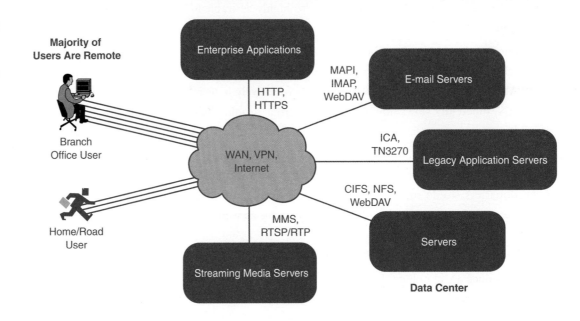

How Wide Area Application Services Works

The Cisco WAAS solution provides a suite of functionalities that increase application performance in branch offices, including the following:

- Protocol optimizations to minimize the frequency of WAN traversal

- Compression of traffic that must traverse the WAN

- Caching of information locally to reduce WAN bandwidth consumption

Cisco WAAS also provides WAFS, offering an integrated approach to branch office application performance as well as file systems services.

Transparency

Transparency is important in the implementation so as not to disrupt existing applications. In the data center, the Core Wide Area Engine (WAE) provides a transparent interface (Server-WAE) so that application servers and file services believe they are communicating directly with clients. Similarly, in the branch office, the Edge WAE provides a transparent interface (Client-WAE) so that clients believe they are communicating directly with application servers and file services. The Core WAE and Edge WAEs use a set of protocols to communicate between them. The protocols are optimized to provide high application-to-server performance while being transparent in the implementation.

At-a-Glance: Wide Area Application Services

WAFS Uses Mapped TCP Flows

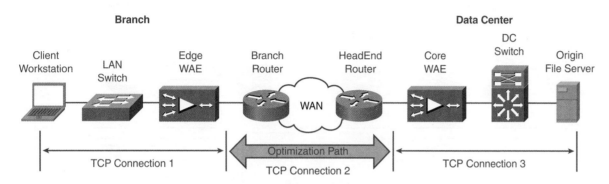

In addition to optimizing the communications protocols themselves, additional optimizations, such as payload compression, provide additional performance improvements and WAN bandwidth savings.

The benefits of this may not be clear to the average user, but all of these methods work in concert to reduce the bandwidth requirements. This in turn decreases both the cost of the infrastructure (routers) and the service (the connection fees you pay to the service provider based on the size of the "pipe"). For a large global enterprise with dozens or even hundreds of sites, this could easily translate into a per-year savings of tens or even hundreds of millions of dollars.

TCP Compatibility

Normal TCP flows are a two-way protocol, containing a series of messages that must be acknowledged by the recipient.

Each message and acknowledgment that traverse the WAN add incremental delay to an application's response time.

TCP Flow Optimization (TFO) minimizes the number and frequency of messages and acknowledgments that traverse the WAN. On the client side (in the branch office), TCP messages are acknowledged locally by the Edge WAE, eliminating the need to traverse the WAN for most TCP ACKs.

Similarly, on the server side (in the data center), the Core WAE provides local TCP acknowledgments.

At-a-Glance: Wide Area Application Services

By reducing the number of WAN traversal cycles required for application servers to carry out responses to clients, application response times for branch office employees are dramatically improved.

DRE

Data Redundancy Elimination (DRE) compresses traffic that traverses the WAN, minimizing the WAN bandwidth required to provide high-performance applications to branch office employees. DRE works by caching frequently transmitted data segments and transmitting a label representing the information (a much smaller piece of information to transmit than the original information).

At the destination, Cisco WAAS reverses the DRE encoding process using the DRE cache, restoring the data payloads to their original information. Use of DRE is between the Core WAE and Edge WAE and is completely transparent to the client workstation and application servers.

TCP Flow Optimization (TFO)

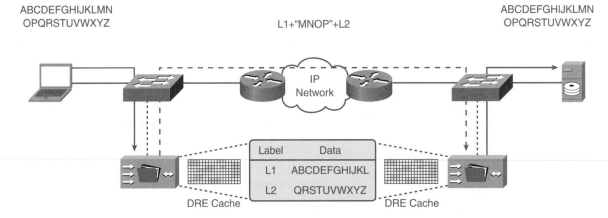

Data Redundancy Elimination (DRE)

Part VII

Unified Communications

Communication on the Data Network

Not too long ago there was a single "network" called the public switched telephone network (PSTN). Of course, this is the worldwide phone system, and for a very long time it was the world's biggest network. Somewhere along the line, some smart people figured out that by using different frequencies to represent 1s and 0s, computers could communicate. As soon as this technology became popular, the speeds were too slow for big data transfers, so a "data-only" network was created. Then some smart people came along and figured out how to turn the human voice into 1s and 0s, and voilà—we have voice on the data network.

It turns out that is it much easier to put voice on a data network than the other way around. While we are at it, why not throw live video streams on it, too? Over the past several years, not only has there been a big migration to put voice, video, and data on a single digital network (called convergence), but also to use some of the "intelligence" of the network and applications to improve the reach and effectiveness of voice and video. This section focuses on how these communication tools work on the network.

We start with a focus on the basics of using the data network to make phone calls. This section looks at how voice over Internet Protocol (IP) or Unified Communications works. "Voice over IP" goes a bit deeper, explaining how the human voice (or any sound, really) is converted to a digital signal so that it can be transported over a network that can communicate with only 1s and 0s.

One of the main issues with putting voice on a data network is that phone conversations happen in real time. This means when two people speak, they typically want to hear the words as they are being spoken rather than having delays. The section "Quality of Service" looks at one of the key features that makes voice calls work on the network.

Later in this part we look at another issue that people have today in dealing with too many devices, between their mobile phone, desk phone, e-mail, and other tools. "Unified Personal Communications" looks at a tool that helps workers consolidate all these tools into a single device. Along with that, "Meeting Collaboration Spaces" looks at some tools that use network intelligence to ensure that the best communication method is used for a given situation. We look at traditional and IP-based videoconferencing and telepresence

Sometimes people can communicate with only certain tools, whether that's voice, instant messaging (IM), or e-mail, depending on where they are and what they are doing. Sometimes you may want all your incoming calls to go directly to voice mail unless a customer or your spouse calls. "Presence and Location-Aware Services" looks at some tools that make this possible.

One of the key applications of voice on the data network is IP call centers. These systems provide one of the best examples of how the voice and data capabilities of a single network can be used in a business solution.

We end this part with a technology that makes mass communication such as video broadcasting, media streaming, and collaboration solutions possible. The part ends with a discussion of IP multicast, which conserves network bandwidth by avoiding the unnecessary duplication of data streams destined for multiple users. Without this technology, networks would be prone to delays or even crashes due to excessive traffic.

Voice over IP

Making Calls over the Web

Traditionally, voice traffic traveled across circuit-switched connections of the PSTN. Corporate customers often had so many phone lines that they often deployed their own telephone exchanges using private branch exchange (PBX) networks or networks of private lines and time-division multiplexers (TDM). Although they had trunks into the PSTN (trunks are PSTN connections that can carry dozens of calls), these traditional networks tended to be proprietary, closed systems that were expensive to maintain, upgrade, and scale.

Voice over IP (VoIP) provides voice services such as phones, call routing, and voice mail using the data network. Thus, both the data and voice networks can converge into a single IP network, facilitating the ability to integrate computer-based applications with phones and videoconferencing. Migrating to a VoIP-based telephony network reduces the total cost of ownership for voice services in the following ways:

- **Toll charges:** VoIP carries traffic through a corporation's private IP network, thereby bypassing the dedicated leased voice lines used to connect remote offices. Eliminating the use of dedicated leased voice lines lets a company avoid toll charges and monthly fees for these dedicated circuits and converge its voice traffic onto the data network it is already paying for.

- **Administration costs:** Because VoIP shares the same network as data applications, you have only one network to manage. Traditionally, separate duplicate teams managed the voice network and the data network. There is also large savings in not having to run new cables for new lines or other changes.

- **Employee mobility:** Working from home or remote locations is a trend that has demonstrated increased employee productivity. Imagine conducting business over your work phone from home. With technologies such as virtual private networks (VPN) and broadband services, employees can work from home or an airport using the tools (computer and phone) they use at work as if they were sitting at their office desks.

- **Productivity:** Integrating VoIP with other corporate systems, such as employee directories, collaboration tools, e-mail, and calendaring systems, provides new levels of productivity that were not possible with traditional PSTN telephony.

- **Application integration:** IP phones are incorporating extensible markup language (XML) browsers into their video interfaces. Therefore, a company can extend enterprise applications to employees who do not need a computer. For example, retail store employees can use a web application on an IP phone to enter their timecard.

Additionally, mobile employees can make VoIP calls using their notebook computers and software-based phones. They can also retrieve their voice mail by simply downloading their e-mail. Ultimately, the convergence of enterprise applications with VoIP will increase productivity and efficiency in ways not possible with traditional PBX networks.

Unifying Communications

Unified Communications refers to a suite of converged communications services, including voice, voice mail, audioconferencing, videoconferencing, web conferencing, instant messaging, contact centers, and others. Convergence has two dimensions:

- Communications services operate over the IP network using technologies including VoIP and video over IP.

- Communications services are integrated seamlessly so that the user experience is as productive as possible.

For example, because VoIP calls are digital, voice mail can be captured as an audio file and listened to using a computer, or even e-mailed to a recipient's e-mail system. An audioconference can be launched by joining digital VoIP streams on the network and using the contact directory within the office e-mail and calendaring software to select meeting participants.

A Unified Communications network consists of four distinct layers:

- **Client layer:** Actual devices a person interacts with: IP phones, IP videoconferencing equipment, software-based phones, laptop computers, handheld computers, and PDAs

- **Infrastructure layer:** Traditional devices associated with data networks: routers, switches, and gateways
- **Call-processing layer:** Call control and subscriber directories
- **Application layer:** Voice mail, unified messaging (imagine receiving voice mail in your e-mail box or listening to your e-mail over the phone), personal and business productivity applications

Client Layer

The client layer consists of phones, video equipment, and software-based phones. These are the devices people interact with. One issue that implementers face when trying to convert their traditional PBX systems to IP networks is how to provide power to the phones. Traditional phones simply plug a single cable into the wall for both power and voice services. Because IP phones plug into IP networks (usually via Ethernet), traditional data networks are unable to provide power. At first glance, an IP phone must have two cables: a network cable and a power cable. However, the network switches that the IP phones are connected to can supply inline power over the same Ethernet cable (called Power over Ethernet [PoE]) as the data connectivity.

Devices at the client layer are responsible for translating the audio stream into digital data. IP phones use digital signal processing (DSP) to "sample" the audio received from the headset and convert it into digital data. This process is similar to taking a photo with a digital camera.

Infrastructure Layer

From the perspective of delivering the reliable voice services people expect on the PSTN, the infrastructure layer is the most critical. It is the job of the infrastructure to ensure that a call (in the form of VoIP packets) is carried from source to destination in a reliable and timely manner.

Traditional data networks tolerate delay or some degree of packet loss because of the nature of the applications that they were designed for, such as access to relatively low-speed mainframe applications. However, because calls happen in real time, calls with delayed or lost packets deliver frustrating audio to the receiver, in which a call either becomes choppy or gets dropped. Implementing QoS and properly provisioning a network ensures that the data network handles calls in the manner traditionally associated with the PSTN.

Telephony gateways are also a critical part of the infrastructure layer. Telephony gateways bridge the worlds of traditional TDM telephony networks to Unified Communications networks. Gateways have several purposes:

- Bridging the PSTN to an IP network
- Connecting legacy PBXs to an IP network
- Tunneling legacy PBXs and phones to other legacy PBXs

Call-Processing Layer

CallManager is the center of the call-processing layer. CallManager fills the role of the digital switch in the PSTN or a PBX in a corporate telephone network. It provides the connectivity, signaling, and device control and intelligence for IP phones and gateways. In addition, CallManager performs operations, administration, maintenance, and provisioning (OAM&P).

Cisco CallManager is responsible for establishing a call between two phones, but after the call is established, CallManager removes itself, and the phones talk to each other directly. The call control (ringing the phone, directing the call, providing dial tone) is handled separately from the call's actual content.

When someone dials a number, CallManager looks up the number, rings the phone on the other end, and provides the ringing sound to the person who dialed the number. When the person at the other end picks up the phone, CallManager leaves the picture, because the two phones communicate directly.

Dial plans define the accessibility of all entities in a voice network. Dial plans also provide alternative path routing and policy restrictions. In Unified

Communications, CallManager also provides Call Admission Control (CAC) functionality. When a user places a call over an IP wide-area network (WAN) (to or from a branch office), CallManager must determine whether enough bandwidth is available across the slower-speed WAN. If the capacity exists, CallManager passes the call through. If not, CallManager may attempt to pass the call through the PSTN. The CAC and the dial plan must be tightly coupled to ensure that calls are passed efficiently and appropriately through the network. For example, a worker in one state might dial the internal five-digit extension of a coworker in another state. If the IP WAN is filled to call capacity, the call is redirected across the PSTN.

Application Layer

With the convergence of Unified Communications and IP data networks, it is easy to create new applications that merge the worlds of phones, video, and computers. Examples of these applications include the following:

- **The ability to use speech recognition in combination with call-handling rules:** Users can set up personalized rules that provide call forwarding and screening on-the-fly. They can forward calls to other user-defined locations such as their homes or cellular phones. Additionally, users can use voice commands to receive, reply to, record, skip, and delete messages.

- **The merging of voice, e-mail, and fax messaging into a single "inbox":** Users can access their voice, e-mail, and fax messages from their IP phones, cellular phones, or PCs (via e-mail).

- **The mobility of a phone number:** A user can log into any phone and have it assume his phone number. Thus, an employee based in Greenville, South Carolina, can travel to the company's Wheaton, Illinois, office and use the phone (with her Greenville phone number) as if she were home. This mobility presents issues that haven't existed before, such as how to handle a 911 call. If you make a call to 911 from a phone in Illinois using a phone number that is based in South Carolina, how is the 911 call properly directed to the local emergency services?

- **Contact-center processing:** See the later discussion on IP call centers.

- **Integration of existing customer applications,** such as ERP, CRM, and inventory management. Users can log customer orders and enter (or even scan) inventory or shipments directly into their VoIP phone for immediate processing into the back-end database.

Deployment Models

Unified Communications has four deployment models:

- **Single site:** Unified Communications is implemented in a single location.

- **Multisite independent call processing:** Unified Communications is implemented in multiple remote sites, but calls between the sites travel across the PSTN.

- **Multisite with distributed call processing:** Unified Communications is implemented across multiple remote sites with call-processing and voice-messaging equipment present at each location. Calls travel across the IP WAN as the primary path, with the PSTN as a secondary path.

- **Multisite with centralized call processing:** Unified Communications is implemented across multiple sites, with call processing and voice messaging centralized in a single location.

For large corporations, true independence from traditional PBX occurs when they implement either a distributed or centralized call-processing model. In both cases, the IP network is the primary path for all corporate calls, with the PSTN serving as backup when either the IP WAN is down or it has insufficient resources to handle calls.

The distributed model places call-processing and voice-messaging equipment at multiple corporate locations. CallManager, voice-messaging equipment, and other resources at each location act as a tightly coupled system with the other locations. The distributed model works well in cases where a merger or acquisition has taken place or in cases where a legacy PBX is being migrated to VoIP over time on a branch-by-branch basis.

The centralized model places call-processing and voice-messaging equipment in a central location. Remote locations contain only the basic infrastructure, such as switches, routers, gateways, and endpoints such as IP phones. The centralized model may be easier to administer and troubleshoot because of a single point to set up and manage the dial plan and endpoint provisioning, and it may require less overall equipment.

Whether a distributed or centralized model is used depends on the company business model and requirements. Centralized offers the lowest overhead to manage, but it does have limitations. Distributed may require more administration at more than one location, but it can offer some flexibility from location to location that may be required.

For example, if a business has a large headquarters and many very small branch offices, such as a gasoline retailer, a centralized model is advantageous. But in the case of a very large department store retailer, a distributed model may offer faster and easier administration.

At-a-Glance: Voice over IP

Why Should I Care About Voice over IP?

Before VoIP, separate networks were required to carry voice and data traffic: circuit-switched voice traffic and packet-switched data traffic. The two networks actually operated on the same types of wires, but the physical network infrastructure was optimized for the circuit-switched voice traffic, because voice traffic existed first and accounted for the vast majority of the traffic.

Over the past 20 years, however, the volume of data traffic has increased exponentially. Several studies suggest that data traffic will exceed voice traffic sometime in the next several years. This figure has been greatly accelerated given the emergence of VoIP to the home and applications such as Vonage. In fact, the switch may have already happened.

Because bandwidth is a limited, and therefore expensive, resource, there is continuous pressure to use it efficiently. One of the best ways to do so is to converge the voice and data networks. Convergence also reduces training and operational costs because there is only one network to maintain and pay for.

Because the primary network is now packet- (data) based, it makes more sense to modify voice signals to traverse IP networks than vice versa.

What Problems Need to Be Solved?

Converting Analog Voice Signals to Digital Packets

All sounds (including speech) are analog waves composed of one or more frequencies.

A Pure Tone

Someone Making an "Ahhh" Sound

For VoIP networks, these analog signals must be converted into digital packets before they are transported over the IP network. After being transported, the signals are re-created into sound waves for your listening pleasure. All this signal processing must occur in real time, however, which normally requires compression technology of some kind.

Finally, to accurately replicate the experience of an analog call, some additional noise must be injected into the signal. An early finding of digital phone calls was that people were so comfortable with the background noise of analog calls on the PSTN, digital calls were unnerving because they had no such noise. Digital phone systems such as VoIP inject what is called "comfort noise" into every call. It's a bit of an odd concept if you think about it: having to degrade a call's quality to make people comfortable with the technology.

Transporting Packets in Real Time

Because of the nearly worldwide existence of circuit-switched telephony, VoIP will always be compared to its circuit-switched predecessor.

The sound quality of VoIP is based on the network's ability to deliver packets with a very high success rate (more than 99 percent) and minimal delay (less than 250 milliseconds end to end). Voice call quality has well-established standards. Although some people using VoIP may be willing to tolerate lower-quality sound in exchange for free long distance, for business applications, VoIP quality must match that of circuit-switched telephony.

Analog Voice-to-Digital Conversion

With traditional telephony systems, the sound waves produced by the human voice are converted into analog electrical signals that are easily transmitted down a wire. On the receiving end of the connection, the electric signals are used to excite a diaphragm (speaker), which produces a very good representation (or analogy) of the original signal.

Analog signals are composed of continuously variable waveforms having an infinite number of states. Therefore, theoretically they can be exactly replicated. For digital telephony (including VoIP), the original signal must be converted into a digital stream (or series of packets) on the transmitting end and then re-created on the receiving end.

Analog-to-digital conversion is accomplished by sampling. Sampling is the process of taking

At-a-Glance: Voice over IP

instantaneous measurements of an analog signal and converting them into a digital representation. If enough samples are taken, the original analog signal can be replicated by "connecting the dots" of the instantaneous measurements.

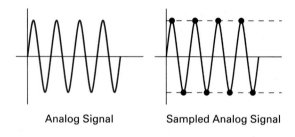

Analog Signal   Sampled Analog Signal

To correctly replicate the original signal, the proper ratio of samples must be taken. If too few samples are taken, more than one signal (frequency) will be able to connect the dots. This is called aliasing. Taking too many samples, however, is not always better. Oversampling, as it is called, can improve the accuracy of the replicated signal, but at some point it will consume too many resources (CPU, bandwidth) without yielding additional benefits.

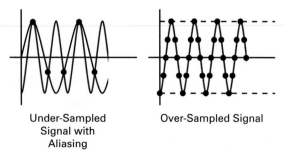

Under-Sampled
Signal with
Aliasing

Over-Sampled Signal

It turns out that the ideal sampling rate for any signal is twice that of the sound's highest frequency. In other words, a sound with a frequency of two cycles per second can be accurately re-created by digitally sampling it at four samples per second. This rate is called the Nyquist Rate, named after the AT&T engineer who discovered it. The Nyquist theorem states that any analog signal can be digitally re-created by sampling it at twice the highest frequency contained in the original signal. Typically analog signals are sampled at just over the Nyquist Rate for digital conversion.

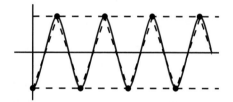

Correctly Sampled Signal with
Approximated Recreation

Compressing Voice

One of key issues with VoIP is the conservation of bandwidth. Because the routing information contained in VoIP packets can more than double the packet's size, it is important to compress the voice data as much as possible. There are three levels, or orders, of compression. The first order is to simply not transmit what cannot be heard. A typical conversation is mostly silent (hard to believe, but

true). It is possible to optimize the VoIP bandwidth by not transmitting unless there are sounds to actually carry.

The second order of compression is to get the most out of the digital conversion of the analog signal. Remember that the analog signal has an infinite number of states, but the digital representation must be a series of 1s and 0s and is limited by the number of bits used. More bits means more sound levels (a good thing) and more bandwidth required (a bad thing). For example, an 8-bit digital signal could represent 256 sound levels. Any instantaneous measurement taken in the analog-to-digital (A/D) process is represented by one of these levels. This is called quantization. It turns out that by stacking more levels at low amplitudes (rather than having them evenly spaced out), you can use fewer bits to get the same quality you would by using more levels (without consuming additional bandwidth). This works because the majority of voice signals fall into relatively low frequencies.

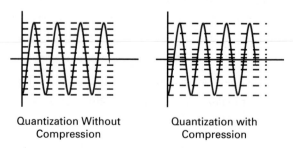

Quantization Without
Compression

Quantization with
Compression

The third order of compression is to not send the actual voice data. Speech signals can be modeled using pitch and tone. There are wide variations in tone and pitch data, but these can be stored in lookup tables. Modern computing techniques and impressive statistical modeling enable the table location (or vectors) of the pitch and tone information to be sent across the network. On the receiving end, the vectors are applied to the tables, and the sound is re-created.

Typically compression techniques sacrifice some level of sound quality for bandwidth savings. Different combinations of sampling and compression techniques are standardized into VoIP coder/decoder (codec) standards. Codec standards are each evaluated against a baseline for voice quality and are given a score according to how well they convey voice calls.

A number of standards exist (too many to list here), but here are two common codecs:

- G.711 specifies an 8-kHz sampling rate and 8 bits per sample, with no compression.

- G.729a specifies an 8-kHz sampling rate and 16 bits per sample, uses compression known as Algebraic Code-Excited Linear Prediction (ACELP), and may optionally suppress silence.

A common way to deploy codecs is to use a very high-quality codec such as G.711 for the majority of business VoIP calls and possibly use a bandwidth-saving codec such as G.729a for calls across low-bandwidth remote connections, such as teleworker connections.

Comfort Noise

The digital signals used in VoIP are usually much "cleaner" than the analog signals used in circuit-switched telephony. This is because in analog systems, any amplification of the signal also amplifies noise, resulting in the static heard in the background during calls. With digital signals, noise can be cleaned out, and a much more pure sound can be achieved. This may seem like a good thing, but it actually causes problems.

It turns out that on analog calls the slight background noise indicates an active connection. Because most of the world's phone users have been "trained" to hear this noise, the absence of the static on digital calls really bothers people and makes them wonder if they are still connected ("Hello?"). To mitigate this "problem," digital systems inject static on the receiving end to let users know the connection is still working. This injected static is called "comfort noise."

Voice over IP

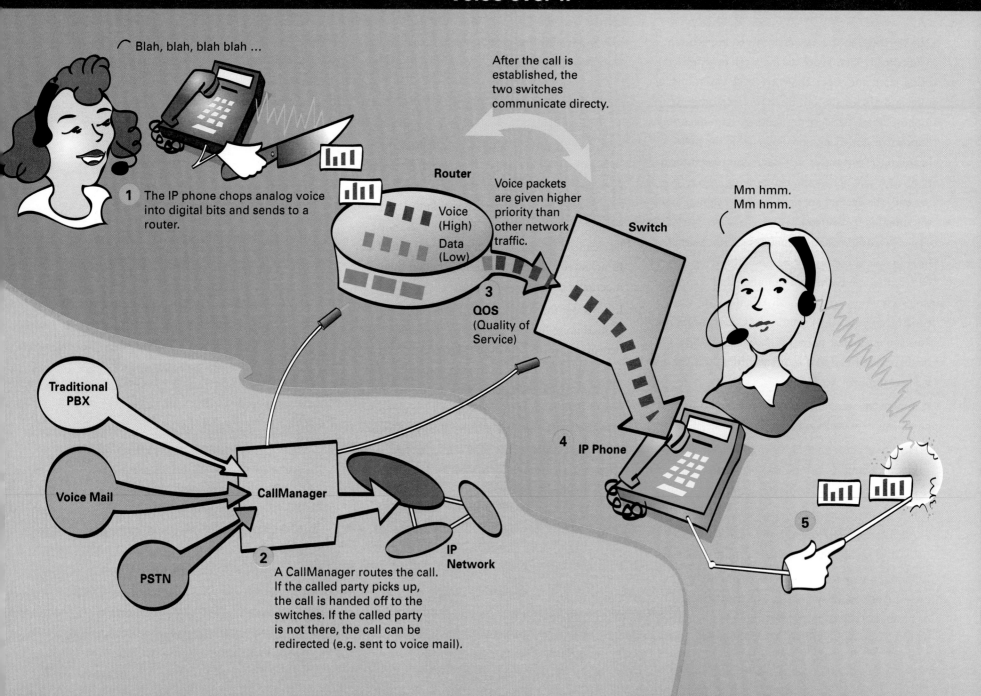

Blah, blah, blah blah ...

After the call is established, the two switches communicate directly.

1 The IP phone chops analog voice into digital bits and sends to a router.

Router

Voice (High)

Data (Low)

Voice packets are given higher priority than other network traffic.

Switch

Mm hmm. Mm hmm.

3 QOS (Quality of Service)

4 IP Phone

Traditional PBX

Voice Mail

CallManager

PSTN

IP Network

2 A CallManager routes the call. If the called party picks up, the call is handed off to the switches. If the called party is not there, the call can be redirected (e.g. sent to voice mail).

5

At-a-Glance: Unified Communications

Why Should I Care About Unified Communications?

Traditionally, voice traffic (telephony) has been transported using the circuit-switched PSTN. Many large businesses and organizations also employed their own internal telephone system using a PBX. Unfortunately, this meant that businesses not only had to deploy a separate network for data traffic (such as e-mail and Internet), but also had to pay long-distance charges for calls to remote branches or partners.

IP telephony is a method of operating a telephony service over a data (IP) network. This has several advantages:

- Reduced cost and complexity, because there is only a single network to manage (the IP network)

- Reduced long-distance charges (toll bypass)

- Ease of adding people or moving them around, because phone numbers are all provisioned in software rather than hard switch connections

- Additional services such directory lookup, videoconferencing, and several call center applications

What Problems Need to Be Solved?

Customers who move away from circuit-switched voice technology can consolidate their separate networks into one network, reducing the number of circuits brought into a facility. This is because integrating IP technologies with existing technologies allows some services to be carried over the data network, decreasing the need for separate PSTN circuits.

Explaining Toll Bypass

Toll bypass is the ability of IP telephony users to avoid (or bypass) long-distance (toll) charges.

The following figure illustrates where the fees are levied.

- **Traditional telephony:** Charges accrue for access to local phone carriers. In addition, a long-distance provider also collects a fee for transport over its system. If this company maintains a data network, it must also pay a different local provider for access to the data (IP) network.

- **Unified Communications:** With this method, a local service provider also charges for access, but in this case there is no charge for the long-distance transport of the packets or a charge for time spent using the network.

Making a Call on an IP Phone

The figure shows the steps involved in making a call from one IP phone to another. In this case

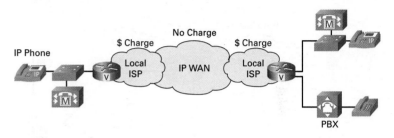

CallManager is in a centralized location. The steps would be slightly different in cases where the phones were co-located or where there were

At-a-Glance: Unified Communications

CallManagers at each location. In addition, if a call were made from an IP phone to a non-IP phone, the call would be routed through a gateway to the PSTN. All of this is transparent to users.

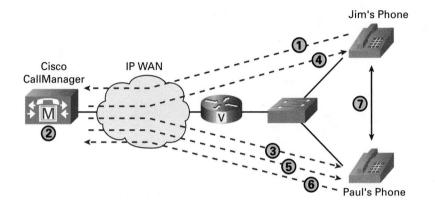

1. Jim dials Paul's number.

2. The CallManager looks up the dialed number and matches it to the IP address of Paul's phone.

3. A connection is set up between the two phones.

4. Jim hears a ring tone.

5. Paul's phone rings.

6. Paul picks up the phone. The two phones are connected via the IP switched network.

7. Jim asks Paul what he's going to wear to work tomorrow.

The Big Picture

The figure shows a basic end-to-end picture of a VoIP system. An important ability of any VoIP system is to be able to still reach phone numbers that are "off-net." This means still on the PSTN or even on another VoIP system that is reachable only through the PSTN as a gateway between VoIP systems. Note that VoIP systems also can use the PSTN when the IP network experiences a failure.

Client Layer

This layer includes the IP-based phones. Analog-to-digital conversion (and the reverse process) and compression take place here.

Call Processing Layer

An IP version of a PBX is required to perform call setups and teardowns. This layer also performs CAC and conference management.

Application Layer

Voice mail, faxing, call forwarding, and directory services are all performed at this layer. Although these are add-on services, they are business-critical. This layer offers features common in traditional telephony, such as call forwarding.

Infrastructure Layer

This layer is responsible for delivering the voice packets. For IP telephony to be a suitable replacement for traditional telephony, it must be just as reliable. Quality of service (QoS), high availability, and overall network design play significant roles at this layer.

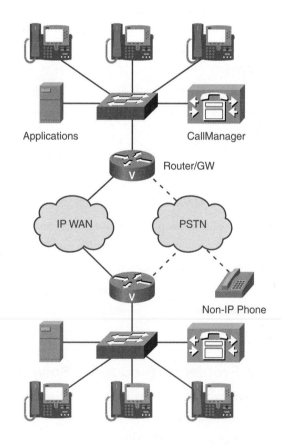

Voice over IP: Toll Bypass

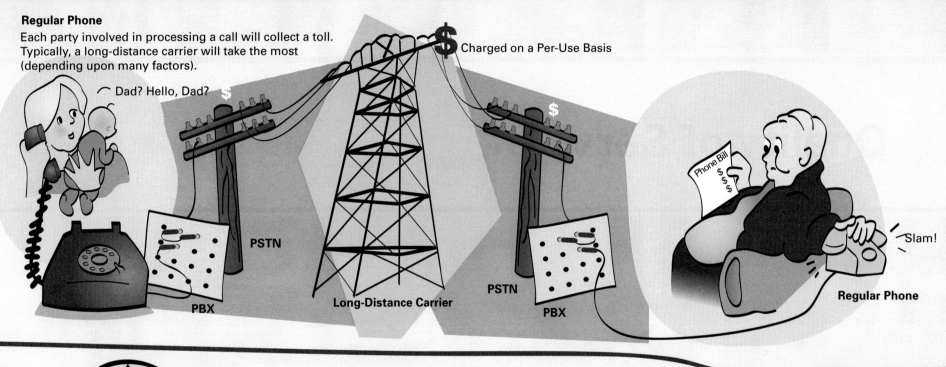

Regular Phone

Each party involved in processing a call will collect a toll. Typically, a long-distance carrier will take the most (depending upon many factors).

Dad? Hello, Dad?

$ Charged on a Per-Use Basis

PSTN

PBX

Long-Distance Carrier

PSTN

PBX

Phone Bill

Slam!

Regular Phone

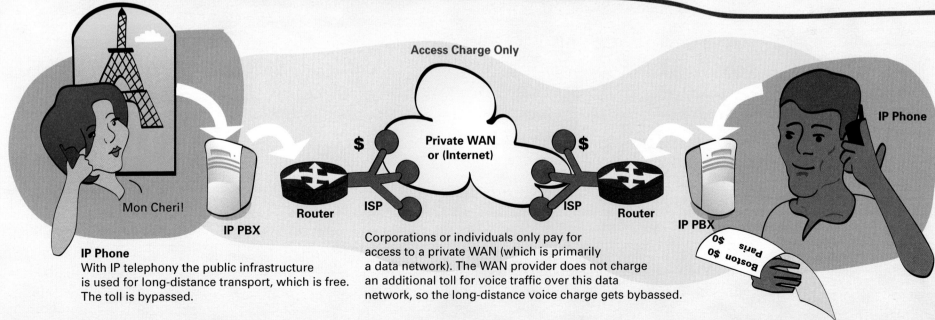

Access Charge Only

Private WAN or (Internet)

Mon Cheri!

IP PBX

Router

ISP

ISP

Router

IP PBX

IP Phone

Boston $0
Paris $0

IP Phone

With IP telephony the public infrastructure is used for long-distance transport, which is free. The toll is bypassed.

Corporations or individuals only pay for access to a private WAN (which is primarily a data network). The WAN provider does not charge an additional toll for voice traffic over this data network, so the long-distance voice charge gets bybassed.

Quality of Service

Converged Networks and QoS

Traditionally, computer networks transported data applications and provided file storage services. The modern business network is also the communications backbone, supporting many applications, including delay-sensitive data, but also voice, high-quality video, and web-based conferencing and collaboration. Because the network is now a communications backbone, it must provide predictable, measurable, and sometimes guaranteed services.

But the network has finite resources in terms of bandwidth, how many packets can be switched and routed through it, and how quickly packets can be passed to their destinations. To provide a communications backbone, the network must manage its resources to provide the service levels needed for many applications to coexist on the network.

Different applications have different requirements. Some applications may have fairly tolerant requirements. For example, with web page browsing, it typically does not matter if the response time is delayed a second or two. Other real-time communications applications, such as VoIP and video over IP, have much stricter tolerances, in which delay is measured in milliseconds, not seconds. Without proper intelligence in the network, some applications could get in the way of real-time applications, causing poor voice quality or other undesirable levels of service.

As mentioned, in many cases an application such as a web browser is not impacted by waiting a second or two. It's the network's job to figure out which applications can wait and which need to be transported immediately.

What Is QoS?

QoS is a collection of features designed to ensure reliable, timely delivery of voice and other "real-time" packets across an IP network. Unlike data files, which can be broken up, sent in random order, and reassembled at the receiving end, it is critical for voice packets to arrive in order with minimal delay. QoS does just that. Think of it as VIP treatment for packets.

QoS allows different types of applications to contend for network resources. Voice, video, and critical data applications may be granted priority or preferential services from network devices so that they do not degrade to the point of being unusable.

The QoS toolset includes mechanisms for managing network bandwidth, marking and prioritizing packets, and intelligent queuing algorithms that engage when the network is congested. Each type of application can be assigned a relative priority on the network. For example, VoIP may be assigned relatively high, and web browsing may be assigned relatively low.

When network resources are not in contention—that is, plenty are available—QoS generally lets the network switch packets in a first-in-first-out (FIFO) queuing strategy. When there is contention for network resources—that is, when the network experiences congestion—QoS engages to provide a more intelligent queuing strategy to protect the service level of the highest-priority applications, while asking applications with lower priority to wait.

QoS is not only useful in protecting high-priority traffic. It also protects the network from undesirable traffic such as the exponential propagation of worms (as discussed in Part IV, "Network Availability"). It's worth noting that QoS can't fix everything. For example, QoS is not designed to compensate or make up for an underprovisioned network or a real-time application's inability to communicate efficiently.

QoS and Unified Communications

The majority of applications in the Unified Communications suite are high-priority real-time applications, with relatively strict demands on the network. VoIP and video over IP, for example, need to stay within strict tolerances to have sufficient voice quality and video display quality to be usable. Other types of applications in the Unified Communications suite may be more tolerant. For example, with application sharing and instant messaging, it is not noticeable if response time increases to a second or two.

So, what factors matter for Unified Communications?

- **Loss** is the difference between the number of packets sent and received. Loss typically is a function of availability. If the network is designed to be highly available, loss during periods of noncongestion should be near zero. During periods of persistent network congestion, however, the engaging of QoS can determine which packets are more suitable to be selectively dropped to alleviate the congestion.

• **Delay (latency)** is the amount of time it takes a packet from the sending point to reach the receiving endpoint. In the case of voice, this is the amount of time it takes for sound to travel from the speaker's mouth to the listener's ear. For video over IP, the time that is discussed is "camera to glass," meaning the amount of time from when an image is captured by the video camera to when it is displayed on the screen at the other end.

• **Delay variation (jitter)** is the difference in delay between two packets. For example, if a packet requires 100 ms to traverse the network from the source to the destination, and the subsequent packet requires 125 ms to make the same trip, the delay variation is 25 ms.

Each application has its own characteristics that determine its particular tolerance for latency, jitter, and loss. For example, for a high-quality VoIP call, tolerances should be less than 150 ms end-to-end one-way delay, less than 20 ms jitter, and less than 1 percent packet loss. Video over IP has similar constraints. These strict tolerances are required because these are real-time applications, and their users notice excessive delays in audio or video. (Recall what it used to be like to talk on an international phone line.)

For real-time applications, standards have emerged to translate degradation of voice or video quality into a number for objective measurement and comparison. One such standard, called the Mean Opinion Score (MOS), assigns a score to the quality of a communication:

1. Bad quality: Very annoying

2. Poor quality: Somewhat annoying

3. Fair quality: Slightly annoying

4. Good quality: Perceptible issues, but not annoying

5. Excellent quality: No perceptible issues

The higher the MOS rating, the better the quality for a phone call or video session. Typically, any score of 4 or greater (such as 4.2, 4.7, and so on) is the target aimed for in network design.

You may be wondering why 5.0 is not the goal. The reason is twofold. First (and most important), this would significantly increase the cost of VoIP in terms of CPU and bandwidth requirements. Second, except for a few musicians out there, most people would never notice the difference.

Other applications such as web browsing typically have much higher tolerances, perhaps 5 seconds or more end-to-end delay, many seconds of jitter, and several percent for loss. Quality issues with these applications are not as perceptible to users. Therefore, the most common quality "score" used is application delay: the response time of a given application from the time when a user presses the Enter key until she sees the content change on her computer screen, for example.

At-a-Glance: QoS

Why Should I Care About QoS?

QoS refers to a network's perceived and measured performance, typically thought of in terms of the sound quality of a voice call or the availability of critical data. Without implementing a QoS strategy, applications such as Unified Communications, videoconferencing, and mission-critical data applications are subject to "best-effort" (nonguaranteed) transmission. This can result in choppy voice or video during times of network congestion or loss of critical data.

The figure illustrates the differences between VoIP and (noncritical) data.

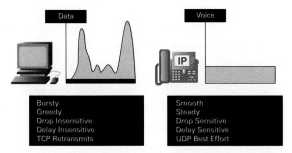

Data	Voice
Bursty	Smooth
Greedy	Steady
Drop Insensitive	Drop Sensitive
Delay Insensitive	Delay Sensitive
TCP Retransmits	UDP Best Effort

What Problems Need to Be Solved?

The Three Evils

The three parameters that define QoS are loss, delay, and delay variance (jitter). Controlling these three interdependent factors allows you to control an application's QoS.

- **Loss** refers to the percentage of packets dropped. In a highly available network, this should be less than 1 percent. For Unified Communications and Telepresence, loss should approach 0 percent.

- **Delay** refers to how long it takes a packet to reach the target destination. Delay is composed of fixed delay (serialization, quantization, and so on) and variable delay (network congestion). The total end-to-end delay should be less than 150 ms.

- **Delay variation or jitter:** Jitter is the difference in the delay times of consecutive packets. A jitter buffer is used to smooth out arrival times, but there are instantaneous and total limits on the buffer's ability to smooth out arrival times. Unified Communications typically targets jitter of 20 ms or less.

Three Steps to Quality

To mitigate the effects of the three evils, you must ensure that the network can properly handle packets on time and won't drop sensitive packets. To achieve QoS, you must first leave room (bandwidth) for certain packets, and then you must identify which packets require special treatment. Finally, you must have rules for how these packets should be treated. These three steps are called provisioning, classification, and scheduling:

- **Provisioning** is the process of ensuring that the required bandwidth is available for all applications, as well as for network overhead traffic, such as routing protocols. Provisioning should consider not only today's requirements but also future capacity and growth.

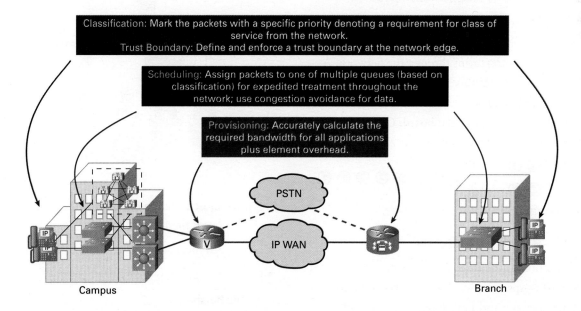

Classification: Mark the packets with a specific priority denoting a requirement for class of service from the network.
Trust Boundary: Define and enforce a trust boundary at the network edge.

Scheduling: Assign packets to one of multiple queues (based on classification) for expedited treatment throughout the network; use congestion avoidance for data.

Provisioning: Accurately calculate the required bandwidth for all applications plus element overhead.

Campus   PSTN   IP WAN   Branch

At-a-Glance: QoS

• **Classification** refers to marking packets with a specific priority denoting a requirement for special service from the network. This can be done at different places in the network by Layer 2 or Layer 3 devices, or by endpoints themselves. Typical classification schemes identify priorities of Critical (voice and mission-critical data), High (video), Normal (e-mail, Internet access), and Low (fax, FTP).

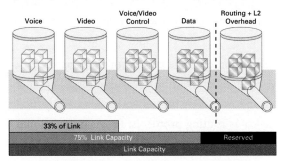

The above percentages are just starting guidelines; each network and application might require different allocations of bandwidth.

• **Scheduling** is the process of assigning packets to one of multiple queues (based on classification) for priority treatment through the network. A good example of this is commercial airline boarding schemes. First-class passengers board first. All frequent flyers may then board. Group 1 may board next, followed by Group 2, and so on.

Low-Bandwidth Tools

In addition to the three main steps to ensure QoS, some link-specific tools are also needed, such as traffic shaping and Link Fragmentation and Interleaving (LFI), especially when routing traffic over low-bandwidth (768-kbps or slower) links. Traffic shaping is a method of throttling back packet transmission rates. If line-speed mismatches exist between remote offices, the service provider connecting the offices may be forced to drop arbitrary packets going to the slower link.

To keep high-priority packets from being dropped, an enterprise can engineer its traffic by provisioning its traffic on the slower link. Traffic engineering also allows the enterprise to decide which packets can be, or should be, dropped (low-priority packets) when instantaneous congestion occurs.

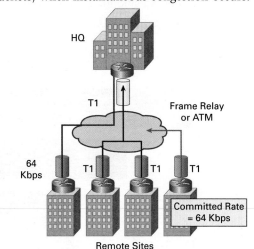

The three most common cases of traffic engineering occur when there are

• Line-speed mismatches

• Oversubscription, planned or unplanned

• Traffic bursts

In addition to network congestion, one of the primary contributors to both delay and jitter is serialization delay. This is often caused by a time-sensitive packet getting "stuck in traffic" behind a large data packet (such as FTP). Link fragmentation is the process of breaking up large packets to allow smaller, more time-sensitive packets to proceed through the network in a timely manner. Interleaving is the processes of "weaving" the time-sensitive packets into the train of fragmented data packets.

Traffic shaping is a technique to deal with instantaneous or sustained bursts of traffic above a desired rate. For example, if a connection can handle 10 Mbps, but a burst occurs that is 12 Mbps, followed by a period of 8 Mbps, traffic shaping smoothes out the traffic to stay within the 10-Mbps overall line limit. Traffic shaping works by delaying part of the traffic burst until the traffic rate falls below the line rate, and the delayed traffic can then be transmitted. As a result, instead of the traffic being peaks and valleys, it is "smoother" and more linear and is shaped flatter—hence the term traffic shaping.

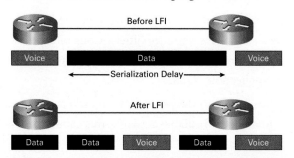

How Packets Are Prioritized

Unified Personal Communications

Too Many Communications, Too Little Time

The telephone was the primary form of communication for many years. But today we have many choices for how we communicate. We can telephone (and there are about a dozen ways we can do that), we can call people on their mobile phones, leave a voice mail, send e-mail, join an audioconference, call on a video phone, join a web conference and share applications, instant message, and so on.

If we needed a different device for every type of communication, we would also need about a dozen arms to carry them. Fortunately, we have the concept of unifying personal communications.

Unify Me

Unifying communications means different things to different people, but most people agree on a couple of key elements. Different communications systems are converging, making it hard to tell where one stops and the other begins. For example, with VoIP-based systems, you usually can listen to your voice mail from a computer by clicking the message's audio file. Often meeting conference bridges have a facility to share applications between the participants' computers.

The second element of unifying communications is device convergence. Mobile phones are also still cameras, video cameras, MP3 players, and handheld computers in the case of a PDA. Laptop computers can act as a VoIP telephone endpoint (called a "softphone," a merger of the terms "software" and "phone"). Laptop computers equipped with small video cameras can also act as a video phone. The laptop and handheld computer, or PDA in particular, are both heading toward being a unified communications device, supporting a whole suite of possible communications.

Unified Communications is also the Cisco term for unification of business communications, including voice, video, instant messaging, e-mail, application sharing, conferencing, and call centers.

Cisco Unified Personal Communicator (CUPC)

The Cisco Unified Personal Communicator (CUPC) refers to an integrated Unified Communications client that runs on a laptop or handheld computer, bringing together many forms of communications on a single device. Types of communications include voice, video, instant messaging, voice mail, e-mail, application sharing, and web conferencing and collaboration.

The CUPC endpoint is integrated into the business Unified Communications system. Therefore, it has a phone number in the corporate dial plan and is integrated into all other communications systems in the business, making it a very productive tool for employees.

At-a-Glance: Unified Communications

Why Should I Care About Unifying Communications?

To operate and grow a successful business, employees must be able to communicate with other employees, suppliers, customers, and other businesses through a diverse set of communications media, including

- Voice
- Mobile voice
- Voice mail
- Audioconferencing
- E-mail
- Instant messaging
- Videoconferencing
- Web conferencing

Communications must be accessible wherever employees are: at a corporate headquarters desk, at branch offices, on the road, and from home. When not integrated, diverse communications methods can lead to inefficiencies and difficulties in trying to bridge different types of communications. Missed or inefficient communications lead to loss of productivity, more costly business transactions, and missed opportunities.

What Problems Need to Be Solved?

Providing a single application that integrates multiple communications paths and media types requires coordination among many teams and technologies.

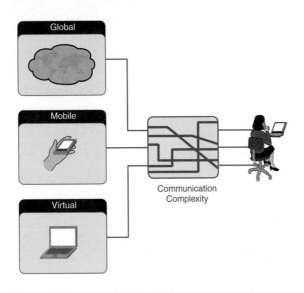

The solution must bridge different communications systems and media and provide real-time access to people on the right systems when they are needed.

How Unifying Communications Works

The Cisco Unified Communications solution provides a suite of communications services that, when integrated, provide seamless connections between types of communications. The system gives employees the ability to access these tools from a desk, laptop, home, or while traveling.

Visual interfaces let employees easily manage their communications, no matter which form they are in, such as e-mail, voice mail, IM, or web conference.

Reach out and Touch Someone

Time and productivity are lost when people try to reach each other and try to figure out which communication method they can use. Unified

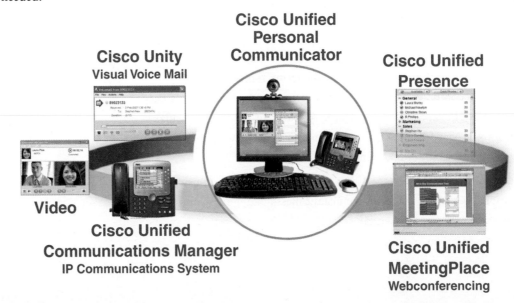

Cisco Unity
Visual Voice Mail

Cisco Unified Personal Communicator

Cisco Unified Presence

Video

Cisco Unified Communications Manager
IP Communications System

Cisco Unified MeetingPlace
Webconferencing

At-a-Glance: Unified Communications

Communications allows people to see how to best reach the people they need to communicate with, whether through instant messaging, phone, or videoconferencing. Unified Communications greatly speeds up the communication process, which often means closing a deal faster or responding to a customer issue faster.

This system improves the chances of reaching people, reducing missed communications and having to retry with other forms of communication. For example, you can find out via Presence and Instant Messaging whether someone is available, see what her preferred or current communications medium is, and click to call.

Increased Productivity

Productivity can also be enhanced through the use of a single "in box" for communications. This allows users to easily see a history of their communications or listen to voice mail through the same visual interface. They can respond with one of several communication types, such as e-mail, voice mail, or click to call back.

With this tool, employees can sort and manage communications as they would with e-mail, no matter where they are or what device they currently have access to.

Management Capabilities

Employees can improve their productivity by taking advantage of powerful call management capabilities. Users can make a call from a desk phone using a visual directory or use a softphone on a laptop to click-to-dial from an instant-messaging contacts list. Users can easily add capabilities to the communication, such as adding a voice call to an instant messaging session or converting to a multiperson web conference to share documents.

Visual screen "pops" can alert people to incoming calls and, by integrating with the corporate directory, display their standard directory information.

Meeting Collaboration Spaces

Meetings, Meetings, Meetings

Did you ever participate in Take Your Child to Work Day, only to have your kids sum up your years of education, long hours, hard work, and hard-learned experience like this: "It's boring. They sit in meeting rooms with people all day."? Anyone who has ever worked for a company knows that the one place we all seem to spend the majority of our time is in meetings.

Traditionally, the business meeting was a place you went. You packed up your notebook (the paper kind, not the computer) and pen and headed to a drably decorated conference room to get the day's status report, or to argue with the other participants, who were just as excited as you to be there.

If you were "lucky," the meeting also had visuals, and you got the pleasure of listening to a presenter drone on and on and on (we call this "death by PowerPoint").

Without wireless network access, laptops were not that useful. Typically participants stood in line for only a single wired network port, far in advance of the meeting (much like an opening of *Star Wars*). The standard meeting communications systems were old-fashioned face-to-face, and an audio bridge for those lucky enough—err, unlucky enough—not to be physically in the meeting room.

Meetings Are an Activity, Not a Place

Business meetings are (thankfully) quickly evolving into a collaborative activity that can occur regardless of the participants' location. Meetings happen anywhere, at any time, planned or unplanned. An unplanned meeting may start with two people instant messaging about an idea. Audio and a few more participants can be added on-the-fly. The meeting can even grow into a full-fledged web conference, with computer screens being shared with others electronically so that everyone can see what is being discussed.

To be most productive, meetings have many different forms of possible communications, and participants can move from one type to another in an integrated way. For example, to attend a meeting, participants may click the calendar item in their calendaring system to launch a meeting client. They can do so in a meeting room, or more often at their desks, or wherever they happen to be at the meeting time. The client automatically places a call to the participants' chosen number and device for joining the audio (and possibly video) conference.

Participants can see who is attending and who is speaking, because Presence (discussed in the next topic) is integrated. As the meeting progresses, participants can discuss ideas with audio, share slides that are displayed on everyone's laptop screen, send e-mail, and even discuss an idea offline with someone using instant messaging. Participants can also see and review meeting minutes as they are being typed. (This is helpful for colleagues who never manage to show up on time.)

What makes all this possible is the tight integration of various communications under a Unified Communications system.

At-a-Glance: Meeting Collaboration

Why Should I Care About Meeting Collaboration?

Communications and how people collaborate are rapidly changing:

Point-to-point	→	Multipoint
Voice-only	→	Rich-media
PSTN phone	→	Multiple devices
Wired	→	Wireless
Non-real-time	→	Real-time
Scheduled	→	Ad hoc

In addition to the changing nature of communications technologies, employees are increasingly geographically separated. Businesses need to acquire skill sets in different locations, as well as provide increased geographic coverage for their business.

Traditional audioconferencing rarely covers the types of communications needed for today's meetings, which increasingly rely on sharing slide presentations remotely, or real-time editing and exchange of documents. All employees need easy access to a common collaboration system that supports not only voice but also rich media. Not having such a system can harm productivity and can create a significant gap for employees lacking equivalent access.

What Problems Need to Be Solved?

To unify communications, a single collaboration application that integrates multiple communications media types is required. This application must support rich media communications such as document and desktop application sharing and video, allowing all participants to share and collaborate. Unified Communications must also support many devices with different levels of capabilities, from a phone or cell phone for audio up through a laptop or desktop computer with complete audio, video, and web conference application capability. The system must also integrate the collaboration scheduling and joining processes with current standard calendaring systems, such as Microsoft Outlook.

How Does It Work?

The Cisco Unified MeetingPlace solution provides easy collaboration for employees. This solution is highly integrated with other Cisco Unified Communications systems, including Unified VoIP Communications, Unified Video Conferencing, Presence, and others. This solution also supports scheduled or ad hoc conferencing and allows sharing of presentation slides and documents and easy transfer of sharing control among participants.

Working with What You Have

Unified Communications is most useful when it integrates with the scheduling applications that

At-a-Glance: Meeting Collaboration

employees already use. By integrating with Microsoft Outlook for easy scheduling, there is no need to provide separate web conferencing information adjunct to the Outlook meeting notice. This makes it easy to join the web conference meeting space by using click-to-join within Outlook, which provides one-click access to join an audio bridge and collaboration space for meetings.

Videoconferencing

Cisco Unified MeetingPlace integrated with Cisco Unified Video Conferencing can add video capability to the meeting space. With ubiquitous access from many devices, employees have the flexibility to participate in the rich media forms that each device can support.

For example, laptops with a softphone can join and participate in audio, document, and desktop application sharing, launched from Outlook. Cell phones may join with audio only. Video phones may join audio and video. Users can also share any application running on one of the participant's desktops, including slides, documents, live applications user interfaces, and even streaming media.

Presence and Instant Messaging

Unified Communications also integrate with Presence and instant-messaging applications. With this feature, multiperson IM sessions can turn into ad hoc web conferencing meetings, adding voice and video capabilities on-the-fly.

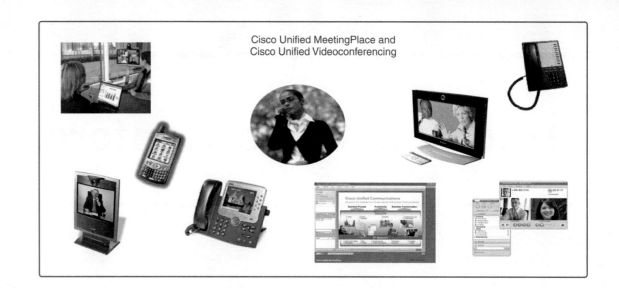

Cisco Unified MeetingPlace and Cisco Unified Videoconferencing

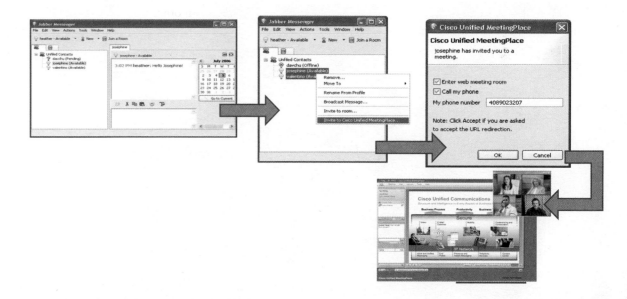

Traditional Videoconferencing

I See You

Videoconferencing is similar to an audioconference call in that multiple people connect to a central site to communicate with each other. Videoconference networks are converging onto IP networks, allowing greater flexibility and lower cost.

Traditional videoconferencing systems used a protocol called H.320, which allowed the transmission of video across public telephone lines using ISDN. Typically, companies built expensive videoconference rooms that were shared, requiring reservations. During the videoconference, people wanted to share presentations and images and view notes or whiteboard scribbles. The cost of videoconferences was high in both the investment in equipment and the monthly cost of ISDN, especially because these systems were not IP-based and used non-IP telecom protocols (which means they were completely separate from the corporate network).

Although the cost of creating these videoconference nodes is high, the expense is still less than flying a group of people to a common location, putting them up in hotels, and so on, especially for international meetings. Typical uses of videoconferences include the following:

- Executive broadcasts and communications
- High-impact meetings
- Training

With the convergence of video and voice-over-IP networks, videoconferencing was a natural technology to transfer to converged IP networks.

Video over IP Networks

The introduction of videoconferencing over IP networks had to resolve two issues:

- Providing videoconferencing equipment that could operate on traditional data networks (using TCP/IP over Ethernet networks, for instance)
- Connecting existing H.320 videoconference locations to the IP-based systems

The International Telecommunications Union (ITU) H.323 protocol is the standard for real-time multimedia communications and conferencing over IP networks. For videoconferencing, H.323 breaks the dependence on expensive conferencing equipment, costly monthly network fees, and dedicated facilities. H.323 lets you connect videoconferencing equipment anywhere a traditional IP network connection exists. Individuals and teams can plug inexpensive video cameras into the corporate network, or across the Internet, and conduct videoconferencing essentially anywhere without dedicated facilities.

Although H.323 addresses the real-time transmission of video and audio, users still want to write and view whiteboard notes, exchange files, or share an application. The ITU T.120 protocol addresses these tasks. The standard identifies how to reliably and efficiently distribute files and graphical information in real time during a videoconference.

As with any real-time or multimedia application, the IP network design must accommodate the requirements of these protocols. For videoconferencing, the network must ensure that the video and data transmissions reach their destinations in a timely manner, with minimal loss and delay. To accomplish this task, the networks use quality of service (QoS) prioritization and queuing mechanisms.

Traditional application traffic is tolerant of network delays or drops because networks can always retransmit the data. Videoconferencing traffic has a different traffic profile from that of data but is similar to voice traffic. There is no need to retransmit video frames if some are lost, because the video and audio continue to move forward. However, network delay or loss can cause the videoconference to look choppy or, worse, appear to lock up. Participants in a videoconference can find the delay frustrating and even unproductive.

Aside from QoS, the network must also handle the sheer capacity of videoconferencing traffic. Video and multimedia generate a large amount of network traffic. Therefore, videoconferencing might not be possible on slow WAN links or congested network connections.

At-a-Glance: IP Videoconferencing

Why Should I Care About Videoconferencing?

Traditional videoconferencing consisted of room-based systems that connected to other room-based systems via satellite or ISDN connection. These fixed systems were expensive and proprietary and provided little flexibility or data sharing capability. Even with these limitations, videoconferencing provides a good alternative to traveling to remote sites for meetings and is a good vehicle for executive communication.

Alternatively, IP videoconferencing can be conducted from any PC or connected location, providing application sharing and whiteboard capabilities cheaply and effectively over corporate and public IP networks.

With IP videoconferencing, all parties can see each other at the same time. With conference management, all parties can also view and manipulate applications. This is different from traditional videoconferencing, which was all point-to-point and offered little or nothing in the way of collaboration.

What Problems Need to Be Solved?

- **Bandwidth:** Videoconferencing requires a great deal of bandwidth. A local-area network (LAN) typically has sufficient bandwidth to accommodate videoconferencing, making the WAN (and the physical connection to the WAN) the critical constraint, potentially a bottleneck.

- **QoS:** Regardless of the amount of bandwidth available, it is always preferable to employ quality of service (QoS) design practices. Most networks are intentionally overprovisioned, but even those that are are prone to instantaneous congestion. A good QoS design is one of the best ways to use the available bandwidth most efficiently.

- **Legacy systems:** Many legacy videoconferencing systems are still in use today. The migration strategy for converting to an IP videoconferencing system must take legacy systems into account.

Videoconferencing Equipment

Endpoints are the cameras, microphones, and application-sharing tools that people use to participate in a videoconference. It could be as simple as a cheap camera and microphone connected to a PC.

H.323

The H.323 protocol was developed specifically for multimedia communications over a packet-switched network. Multimedia in this case refers to audio, video, and general data communication.

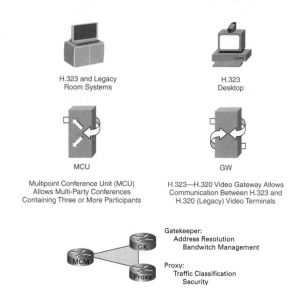

H.323 and Legacy Room Systems

H.323 Desktop

MCU
Multipoint Conference Unit (MCU) Allows Multi-Party Conferences Containing Three or More Participants

GW
H.323—H.320 Video Gateway Allows Communication Between H.323 and H.320 (Legacy) Video Terminals

Gatekeeper:
Address Resolution
Bandwitch Management

Proxy:
Traffic Classification
Security

H.323 has many benefits:

- Standardized compression of audio and video, allowing multivendor equipment and support
- Hardware or operating system independence
- Efficient use of bandwidth with multipoint conferencing (multicast)
- Bandwidth management features

T.120

The T.120 protocols define the methods of document conferencing and application sharing (also known as data conferencing) within a multimedia conference. The standards specify how to efficiently and reliably distribute files and graphical information in real time during a multipoint multimedia meeting. T.120 ensures interoperability between

At-a-Glance: IP Videoconferencing

end terminals in the absence of prior knowledge of the other terminals. T.120 is a complementary protocol technology that can be integrated and used with H.323 calls. The standard also allows data-sharing applications such as whiteboards, graphic displays, and image exchanges.

Zones

If the network has no gatekeepers, endpoints may directly call each other if the network addresses are known. This approach requires a full-mesh design, though, and is suitable for only very small networks.

Single Zones

When gatekeepers are present in the network, all video endpoints and equipment must register with the closest gatekeeper, which controls traffic on the network. Each cluster of terminals and equipment controlled by a single gatekeeper comprises a zone. After it is defined, the gatekeeper acts as the central point for all calls within its zone, providing address resolution, CAC, and call control services to registered endpoints.

A single zone is suitable for small to medium-sized campuses, or for several small locations connected via a WAN.

Multiple Zones

For large campuses or several campuses connected via a WAN, and with multiple endpoints, a multi-zone solution is required. This type of architecture

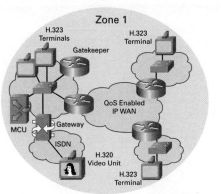
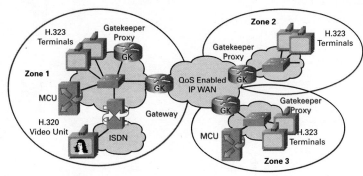

typically is deployed for the scalability it provides; single-zone configurations cannot handle high-bandwidth demand. This architecture also provides improved latency performance and eliminates single points of failure for videoconference services.

Intrazone communication follows the same procedure as a single-zone solution. However, for communication across different zones, the gatekeepers of each zone must establish a communication link.

More complex networks require a hierarchical gatekeeper scheme to provide end-to-end connectivity for all gateways and terminals. The higher-level gatekeeper is called a directory gatekeeper. The following figures illustrate the importance of the directory gatekeeper with regards to network efficiency and simplicity.

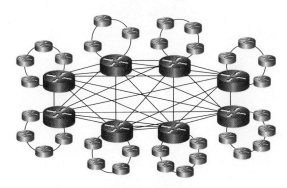
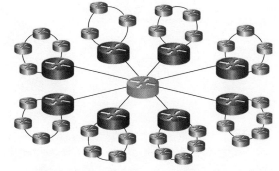

Multiple Gatekeepers Result in an Overly Complex Network

Gateway Gatekeeper Directory Gatekeeper

Multiple Gatekeepers with a Directory Gatekeeper Result in a Simpler Network

Videoconferencing

Everyone's screen
has the same view:
- All Participants
- Access to Multimedia
  - Slides
  - Whiteboards
  - Document Collaboration

**Board Room
Briefing
in Tokyo**

**Conference
Manager**
Everyone logs in here.

The conference manager
receives multiple video stream
feeds and re-packages them as
one picture in a video stream.

**Engineer on
East Coast**

**Meeting Hall
in L.A.**

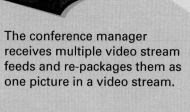

Videoconferencing Application E-Learning

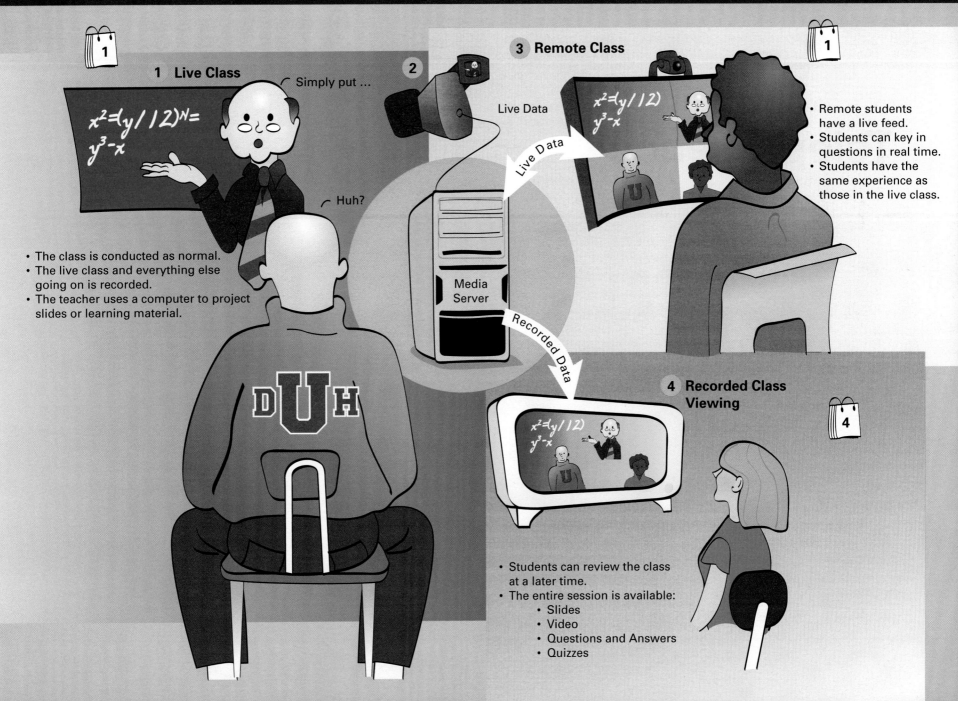

Telepresence

Conferencing Gets Simple

Audioconferencing revolutionized standard meeting practice, but when it was first established, it required a conference operator to admit participants and manage the conference. Conferencing evolved to being easy enough that employees could quickly and easily organize their own conference bridges. (However, we have been in plenty of meetings where the "ease" of today's conference bridge technology continues to elude some of the brightest engineers.)

VoIP makes conferencing more flexible and cost-effective. Because the VoIP packets are already digital encodings of audio, they can "simply" be routed to a conferencing server, a really fast computer, that can take the digital audio streams, combine them, and replay them back out to all the participants. Mix in a dash of being able to point and click on a laptop to schedule and host a conference, and voilà—conferencing can be used by everyone.

Video Killed the Radio Star

Videoconferencing has been around for a while, starting with (as previously discussed) specialized videoconferencing rooms that were connected by high-speed connections through the PSTN. Seeing people added another dimension to meetings.

Video over IP again made conferencing more flexible and cost-effective. The data network hosting videoconferences, although bandwidth-consuming, was yet another proof point for converging applications and media onto the network.

But something was still missing. Videoconferencing did not really take off to the extent that audioconferencing did.

The Next-Best Thing to Being There

What if someone told you that you could attend meetings in person halfway around the world without ever boarding a plane? You would probably think you were in a sci-fi movie. But it is not that far-fetched. It is possible. Well, almost.

Telepresence is a new category of communications and collaboration designed to make meeting participants feel like they are in the same room, even though they may be thousands of miles apart. Based on high-definition video, Telepresence pushes the envelope of what can be done with networks and stretches the imagination of what is possible.

Simply put, Telepresence is based on two or more mirror-image rooms connected by high-definition video displayed life-size on plasma HDTV screens. The rooms and screens are positioned in such a way that the participants in the room feel like their remote participants are in the room with them. The meeting experience is so realistic that people turn to make eye contact, often forgetting whether the person they are talking to is physically in the room or distant. The system typically is designed to accommodate 10 to 12 people per room (as opposed to a large conference hall).

All that's missing is a way to shake hands. Cisco has not figured out that part yet, but they are working on it.

At-a-Glance: Telepresence

Why Should I Care About Telepresence?

To be competitive, businesses must be able to cover expansive geographies and leverage global resources. This leads to an increase in the need for face-to-face meetings between people in many locations. However, travel costs are growing, and security concerns sometimes make travel more difficult. Therefore, there is a strong need to have virtual meetings where participants can remain in their respective locations but participate as if they are all at the same location. Traditional videoconferencing provides one means for people to have face-to-face virtual meetings, but the technology has significant limitations. Telepresense provides a means to overcome these issues.

What Problems Need to Be Solved?

To be effective, a Telepresence solution must make people feel as if they are in the same meeting room, when in reality they are in different locations, attending the meeting virtually.

The solution must provide a high-quality virtual meeting experience that is consistent and repeatable. The solution must also keep operational costs down; if dedicated high-cost connections and circuits are required, the solution will be cost-prohibitive.

For an IP-based solution, the corporate network must be capable of transporting the traffic required for a virtual meeting, with specialized requirements. Scheduling and connecting virtual meetings must be easy and straightforward so that participants can focus on the meeting, not on the technology.

What Does Telepresence Do?

The Cisco Telepresence solution provides a high-quality virtual meeting experience, making participants feel like they are in the same meeting room. Telepresence uses high-definition (HD) video and audio to connect two or more locations in a realistic but virtual meeting room. Integrated with Cisco Unified Communications for ease of use, the system literally requires a single press of a button to create the virtual meeting and connect the participants.

IT Furniture

Because of the need for a consistent, high-quality experience, the Cisco Telepresence solution includes not only Cisco networking hardware and software, but also furniture and lighting engineered to exact specifications. Telepresence meeting rooms are designed to be mirror images of each other and are engineered so that the Telepresence display screens look and feel like an extension of the meeting room and table.

Participants are displayed in life-size images on high-definition plasma video screens with true 1080p resolution. (For the uninitiated, 1080p means that the display resolution is 1920 pixels wide by 1080 pixels tall.)

High-definition audio speakers and microphones provide directional sound, adding to the experience. When a participant on the right speaks, sound is projected from her direction, leading participants to turn in her direction and even make eye contact. Because of the life-size images, directional sound, and mirrored rooms, participants have the feeling that virtual participants are in the same room, leading to a much more natural meeting behavior and experience.

Telepresence over IP

Alternative solutions require dedicated high-definition video circuits, which add significant startup and operational costs.

The Cisco Telepresence solution uses video over IP, allowing businesses to leverage their existing corporate networks.

Each Telepresence screen is driven by a high-definition H.264 codec, with HD plasma display, HD video camera, and HD audio speaker and microphone.

At-a-Glance: Telepresence

The Telepresence solution is also compatible with legacy H.323 technologies, so it is possible to conference in legacy videoconferencing endpoints. However, they will not experience the same meeting experience as someone using a Telepresence endpoint.

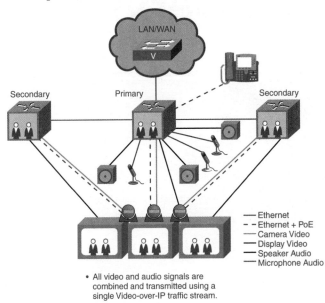

— Ethernet
- - Ethernet + PoE
— Camera Video
— Display Video
— Speaker Audio
— Microphone Audio

• All video and audio signals are combined and transmitted using a single Video-over-IP traffic stream.

• This requires only a single Ethernet port to connect to the corporate network

Three Telepresence screens are connected for a large meeting room. A single screen can be used for a smaller room with fewer participants. In the figure, all video and audio signals are combined and transmitted using a single video-over-IP traffic stream. The system requires only a single Ethernet port to connect to the corporate network.

A Telepresence call (with three full screens) requires approximately 8 to 12 Mbps of bandwidth, with possibly higher bursts when there is a lot of movement on the video screens. Therefore, Telepresence endpoints are connected to the IP network via FastEthernet (100 Mbps) or Gigabit Ethernet (1000 Mbps) access ports.

QoS Required

Because of the tight tolerances required to transmit high-definition video, Telepresence is a demanding application for the network. As such, Telepresence requires QoS in the campus, WAN, and branch locations where Telepresence endpoints are deployed. Service provider selection for

WAN/MAN services is also critical, to make sure that Telepresence sessions can be properly transported between corporate locations.

Multipoint Connections

Often you need to connect more than two locations into a virtual meeting. This requires a Multipoint Conferencing Unit (MCU) to connect multiple Telepresence endpoints. Each Telepresence endpoint transmits its HD video and audio signals to the MCU, which combines signals from all Telepresence endpoints and returns the signals to be displayed. When there are more participants than can be simultaneously displayed, the MCU manages switching of the screens based on algorithms that determine who is speaking.

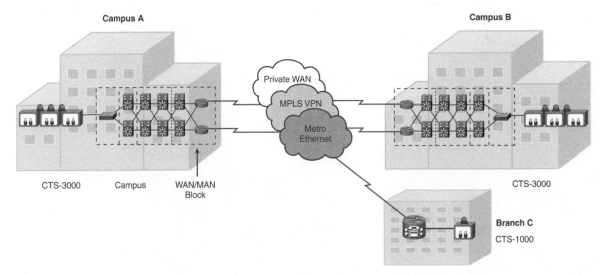

Presence and Location-Aware Services

I Sense a Presence

One of the challenges with having so many communications options is that it is sometimes difficult to know which forms of communication are available to the person you want to call, at what times, and at what contact numbers. And if multiple types are available, which do they prefer to be reached with?

Presence is about providing an integrated way for people to manage their different forms of communication. Using such information as which forms of communication can be handled by the endpoint device currently being used, what network resources the person has at his current location, and what the recipient's communication preferences are, presence helps connect people in the most productive ways.

With personal settings, people can establish preferences for how they want to be contacted. For example, when I am in a meeting, I can accept only instant messages and e-mail, and when I am traveling I prefer to be contacted via voice mail on my mobile phone.

The Importance of Location

Location and presence are related. Location can help define what communications options are available to a person, and even which are appropriate. For example, when a person is at her desk with access to high-speed wired network services, she can accept almost any type of communication as long as the device she is using supports it.

However, if the same person is traveling and using a handheld computer or PDA/mobile phone, most likely she can't accept video calls, and she may or may not be able to participate in web conferencing for application sharing.

Location intelligence provided by the network can augment presence-based applications. Location can also be used for other purposes, such as being able to pinpoint the origination of a 911 call.

This technology is still in its early stages. It will continue to evolve and improve through the next several years.

At-a-Glance: Presence and Location-Aware Services

Why Should I Care About Presence and Location-Aware Services?

Employees can reach each other, and customers can reach a business, using various types of communication, including live voice, voice mail, video, e-mail, instant messaging, and web conferencing. Various devices are used for communication, including wired telephones, cell phones, smartphones/PDAs, laptops, and desktop computers.

Although all these communication methods allow people to reach each other at nearly all times, not all devices support every type of communication. For example, telephones typically do not support e-mail, and some computers are not equipped to support voice and video. The combination of types of communication and types of devices can lead to inefficient communications in which the originator cannot reach the recipient on the right form of communication at the right time.

This relatively low success rate in reaching people leads to productivity losses if the communication is between employees, or potentially lost revenue and opportunities if the communication is between customers and a business. Location-based services allow people to communicate efficiently using tools that are best suited to the availability and locations of the users.

What Problems Need to Be Solved?

The biggest hurdle to overcome is finding a way to connect people with the right communications at the right times. The first step is to allow people to set preferences for their preferred forms of communication. This includes different preferences depending on where they are and what device they are using. Then those preferences must be integrated into the network.

After the preferences are set, the right forms of communication must be enabled based on the capabilities of each device. Intelligently restricting or avoiding forms of communication that devices do not support or restricting or avoiding where those devices are used allows the system to work without a lot of manual intervention. If the form of communication is hard to use, it will never get adopted. Therefore, it's important to provide a single application to manage different forms of communication, enabling people to easily select the best option to reach a recipient.

How It Works

The Cisco Unified Presence solution provides association of communications devices to the communications services they use, providing real-time indications of a person's willingness and ability to accept different forms of communication. The Presence server receives information about devices people are using and the capabilities of those devices. The Presence server also stores information

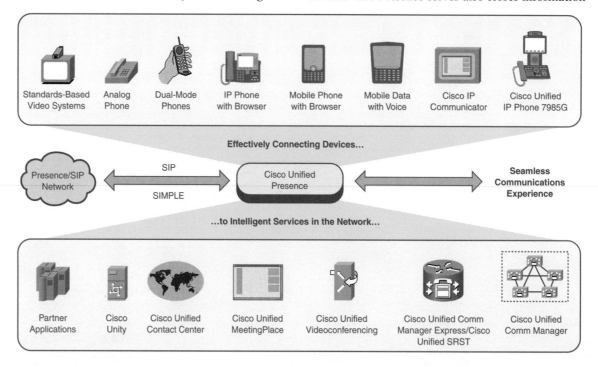

Standards-Based Video Systems · Analog Phone · Dual-Mode Phones · IP Phone with Browser · Mobile Phone with Browser · Mobile Data with Voice · Cisco IP Communicator · Cisco Unified IP Phone 7985G

Effectively Connecting Devices...

Presence/SIP Network — SIP / SIMPLE — Cisco Unified Presence — Seamless Communications Experience

...to Intelligent Services in the Network...

Partner Applications · Cisco Unity · Cisco Unified Contact Center · Cisco Unified MeetingPlace · Cisco Unified Videoconferencing · Cisco Unified Comm Manager Express/Cisco Unified SRST · Cisco Unified Comm Manager

At-a-Glance: Presence and Location-Aware Services

about the types of communication methods people prefer and what communication types people currently have available to them.

Session Initiation Protocol (SIP) and a new protocol, SIP for Instant Messaging and Presence Learning Extensions (SIMPLE), are the two primary communications mechanisms for how devices communicate with the Presence Server. XML capability is also possible for custom extensions that want to use the Presence database information.

Present and Accounted For

A user's Presence includes his or her status:

- Online
- Offline
- Working remotely
- Available
- In a meeting
- Not available

As shown in the figure, the solution allows a user to see who is available and by what means they can communicate. This helps reduce communication delays and enhance productivity.

Presence also includes awareness of the type(s) of device(s) a person is currently using and the device's capabilities, such as

- Using a laptop that can support e-mail and instant messaging
- Using a cell phone that can support voice but not video or e-mail

Another important component is the ability to incorporate a user's preferences for communication tools that are often situation-dependent on work location:

- When in a meeting, prefers instant messaging
- When working remotely, prefers voice and then e-mail
- When offline, prefers voice mail
- When online in the office, prefers video calls, and then voice, and then e-mail, and then instant messaging

Let's Go Live

Communications may start out in one form but then transition to other forms as a conversation proceeds. The Cisco Unified Presence solution optimizes productivity by monitoring the various communication options and helping people use the tools that are best suited to the situation.

For example, a session could start with Instant Messaging and turn into an impromptu web conference to have voice, video, and application sharing. Communications options that are not available between two parties are also known. This helps avoid failed attempts using a communication medium that is unavailable because of either device incompatibility or the recipient's current context or location. For example, when a recipient is in a meeting, voice and video communications can be unusable, but instant messaging may still be a viable option for communication.

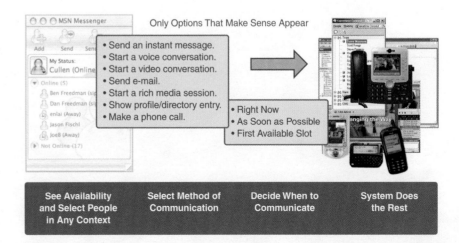

IP Call Center

Why Can't I Talk to a Real Person?

"Press 1 to use our automated attendant. Press 2 to speak with a representative."

Customer service, support, and sales are sophisticated in how they handle and direct calls to the appropriate representative. From an automated attendant answering the phone, to the automated redirection of a call, to the interaction of phone and computer applications, call-center applications allow a company to efficiently and effectively manage customer calls. Although this setup is possible in traditional voice networks, the convergence of voice with IP networks opens new possibilities and an ease of administration not previously available.

Anatomy of a Contact Center

Whether you call a computer company for support, an insurance company to make a claim, or an airline to check the status of a flight, you interact with a call center in some fashion. Likewise, when you receive a call during dinner asking whether you want to subscribe to a newspaper, a call center is interacting with you. The goal of a call center is to efficiently route a call to the appropriate person or call service while managing call queues when there are more calls than available call-center employees.

Here are the primary components of a contact center:

- **Private branch exchange (PBX):** Provides traditional call-handling functionality.

- **Interactive voice response (IVR):** Affectionately known as "Silicon Sally," IVR is computer software that provides a series of audible menus for the caller to interact with. The IVR interprets key presses and, more recently, uses voice recognition to walk the caller through a series of menus. Based on the caller's selections, the IVR can return information to the user, ending the call, or direct the call to an agent as appropriate.

- **Automatic call distribution (ACD):** Depending on the vendor, ACD provides any of the following functionality:
  - Call distribution based on customizable rules
  - The ability to hold callers in a queue

  - Music On Hold, customizable messages and advertisements that play while the caller waits in a queue

- **Computer telephony integration (CTI):** Allows computer applications to interface with the telephone equipment. For call centers, the caller's phone number, account number, or any piece of information the caller provides can serve as the key for an application. For example, when a customer calls her insurance company with questions, the call agent application can intercept the calling phone number and automatically display the customer's personal account information to the insurance agent.

You can put all these components together in endless combinations; no two call centers operate the same. Vendors provide the functionality described here in different packaging and levels of functionality.

From the Caller to the Agent, and Back Again

Contact centers can exist in many forms, but in general, a caller interacts with one of two models: inbound or outbound. The goal is to redirect the call to the appropriate live person or audible application that serves the caller. With an *inbound* contact center, the customer initiates the call to the company. Examples of inbound calls include contacting the following:

- An insurance company to make a claim
- An airline to check a flight schedule
- A bank for account information
- A computer company for technical support
- A mail-order company to make a purchase
- The power company to report an outage

A traditional ACD determines where to route the call. With an IP-based call center, the IVR, intelligent contact management (ICM), and PBX are like a virtual ACD. Generally, the caller interacts with an IVR first. The IVR replaces the traditional switchboard operator or receptionist by giving the caller a list of options. Based on the caller's responses, the IVR either returns a code to the ACD or runs an application that addresses the caller's need. With the application, the caller either receives the information he needs and hangs up or interacts further. When the IVR returns a code, the ACD then determines where to route the call, which might eventually be a group of call agents.

When managing calls destined for a group of agents, the ACD typically provides a series of functions that help manage a queue of callers. The caller remains on hold, and he or she might hear music, status messages, or advertisements while waiting in the queue. When an agent becomes available, the ACD transfers the call to the PBX, finally linking the customer to a person.

With an IP call center, the IVR might serve as the queue point rather than the traditional ACD. The other model, *outbound*, lets a system dial many numbers and then transfer the call to a live agent after it finds a number to ring or a person to answer. It appears that the agent called the caller directly. Examples of this method include the following:

- Subscription solicitations from a local newspaper
- Special offers from insurance companies
- A public-opinion poll conducted by a political party
- A loan company pursuing delinquent customers

With this model, an outbound dialer device parses through lists of phone numbers and dials each one. Based on defined rules, the dialer device hands the call to the ACD after it finds a live person, an answering machine, or simply a ring. The ACD transfers the call to either an automated recording or a live agent. The call then proceeds.

Generally, for both methods, time is of the essence. Callers become frustrated and angry when forced to talk to recordings or sit in queues for any period of time. So the various systems that make up the call center must be tightly integrated and fast.

Managing Caller and Contact Agent Efficiency

As companies conduct business across multiple time zones and countries, they need to provide contact center services that do the following:

- Balance loads across multiple contact centers.
- Provide support wherever the sun is shining (around the globe).
- Allow contact agents to seamlessly work in remote locations. (You never know where your call is actually directed, except perhaps from the accent of the agent you interact with.)

New Methods for Customer Interaction

The Internet created new methods for customers and companies to interact. Aside from the telephone, customers need to be able to contact a company through the web and e-mail. Interactive web-based "chat"-type support is popular. As various industries adopt these additional contact methods, customers begin to expect all other industry competitors to do so as well. To the customer, it should not matter whether she uses e-mail, interactive chat, web submission, or the telephone: A company should respond with the same quality and priority regardless of the method. For the company with a traditional phone-based call center, migrating to this multiple-method model can be difficult.

Today's IP-based contact-center software manages e-mail, phone calls, and other contact methods all from the same set of tools.

At-a-Glance: IP Contact Center

Why Should I Care About IP Contact Center?

If you have ever called an 800 number for customer service, you probably have been routed through a call center. Call centers have been around for many years. But with the advent of IP-based call centers, they have become incredibly powerful and flexible tools used for customer service, ordering, and technical support.

What Problems Need to Be Solved?

All call centers face the task of receiving calls, collecting caller information, queuing callers, and finally routing callers to the agents on duty. In addition, IP-based call centers often provide an additional layer of sophistication in the form of integrated computer applications that display caller information to the agent at the moment the agent is are connected to the user.

IP call centers must also be capable of receiving and processing calls from traditional telephony systems. These centers also have critical availability needs. A great deal of revenue and customer satisfaction results are derived directly from the call center. The lights have to stay on at all times.

IPCC Equipment

The section details the primary components of an IP-based call center (IPCC). In many cases several of these functions reside in a single box but are shown separately for clarity:

- **Intelligent Call Management (ICM)** distributes voice and data information to the CM and IVR systems and agent desktops.

- **CallManager (CM)** provides telephony features such as basic call processing, signaling, and connection services.

- **Peripheral gateway (PG)** provides a connection between IPCC components such as the CM and IVR to the ICM. The PG directs traffic between the devices.

- **Computer-Telephony Integration (CTI) server** provides the connection to the agent's desktop. The CTI server provides incoming call information and an agent and receives agent activity reports (log in, available, wrap up, and so on) as well as call control functions (answer, hold, transfer, release).

- **IVR** prompts users for information, collects caller-entered digits, and generates announcements such as queuing information ("Your call will be answered in approximately 5 minutes.").

- **VoIP gateway** provides a traditional telephony connection to the IP-based call center.

Two Simple Call Flow Examples

In this first example, a customer dials a toll-free telephone number over a traditional PSTN line:

1. The call is routed through a voice gateway. Information such as the dialed number (DN), the calling line ID (CLID), and any caller-entered digits (CED) is sent to the ICM.

2. The ICM starts a user-defined routing script to choose the most appropriate IVR (there could be several across a region or country). The call is then queued on the IVR.

3. The caller chooses a transaction that can be completed with only the IVR, so she is not routed to a live agent.

In the next example, a second customer dials the call center from an IP phone:

1. The ICM routes the call to the most appropriate IVR and queues the call. The IVR can collect additional information (account number, order information, SSN, and so on) or simply inform the customer of the approximate wait time.

2. CallManager reserves the agent for the incoming call.

3. When the ICM detects that an agent has become available, it sends a message (which includes the call context information) to CallManager. CallManager instructs the CTI server to notify the agent desktop of the incoming call.

At-a-Glance: IP Contact Center

4. The agent is notified that the call is coming in. It also receives the user information collected, which appears on the agent's computer screen.

5. CallManager connects the call to the agent. Because the caller is online, the agent can also share computer applications with that person.

Other Cool Stuff

IPCC offers a lot of opportunities for contact centers over the traditional ones. These improvements include better administration capabilities, the ability to go from online chat with a representative directly into a call, and other high functionality and money-saving features:

- **Routing to specialized agents:** In some cases VIP customers need to be routed directly to specialized agents (such as a $1 million investor calling a brokerage house). The IPCC allows this to happen quickly and easily. With the CTI server, the agent has all the user's information on his or her computer screen before the call is even connected.

- **Following the sun:** Using an IP-based call center, a company can avoid expensive third-shift costs by migrating its call-center operations from east to west as the day goes on. At first, calls are routed to remote agents until a new local shift staffs up, at which time the local call center begins handling all the operations and call distribution.

- **Remote workers:** IPCC presents a powerful solution for companies that experience seasonal spikes in call-center activity (such as a catalog company during the holidays). With the widespread availability of high-speed Internet access, temporary workers can work from home with the same effectiveness as those working out of a call center.

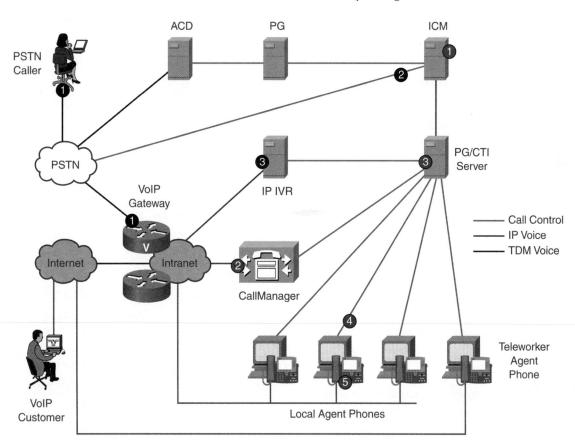

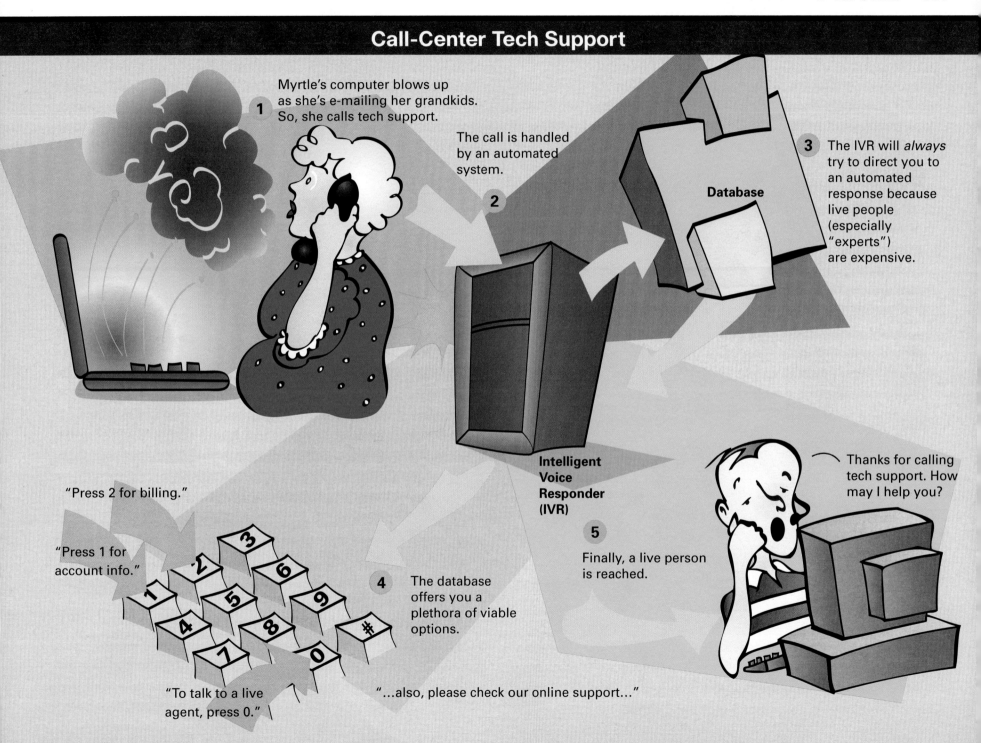

Call-Center Tech Support

1 Myrtle's computer blows up as she's e-mailing her grandkids. So, she calls tech support.

The call is handled by an automated system.

2

Database

3 The IVR will *always* try to direct you to an automated response because live people (especially "experts") are expensive.

Intelligent Voice Responder (IVR)

"Press 2 for billing."

"Press 1 for account info."

4 The database offers you a plethora of viable options.

5 Finally, a live person is reached.

Thanks for calling tech support. How may I help you?

"To talk to a live agent, press 0."

"...also, please check our online support..."

Call-Center Telemarketing

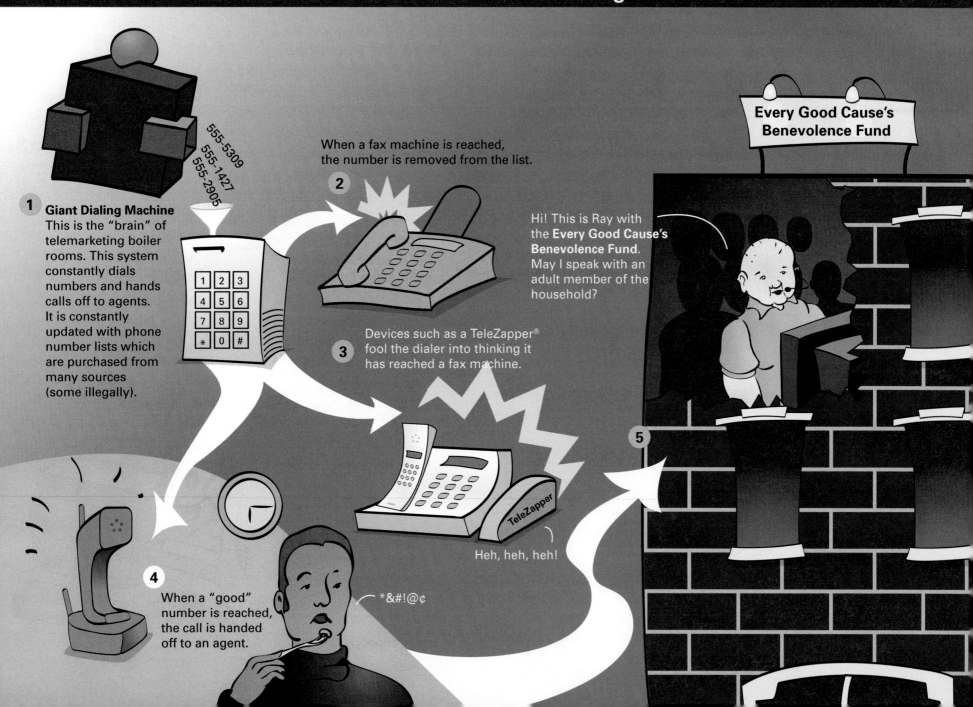

555-5309
555-1427
555-2905

1 **Giant Dialing Machine**
This is the "brain" of telemarketing boiler rooms. This system constantly dials numbers and hands calls off to agents. It is constantly updated with phone number lists which are purchased from many sources (some illegally).

When a fax machine is reached, the number is removed from the list.

2

3 Devices such as a TeleZapper® fool the dialer into thinking it has reached a fax machine.

Hi! This is Ray with the **Every Good Cause's Benevolence Fund**. May I speak with an adult member of the household?

5

Every Good Cause's Benevolence Fund

4 When a "good" number is reached, the call is handed off to an agent.

Heh, heh, heh!

*&#!@¢

TeleZapper

Multicast and IPTV Broadcasts

Watching Movies Without Flooding the World

IP multicast is a bandwidth-conserving technology based on IP in which data intended for multiple receivers is efficiently transmitted with a single stream. IP multicast best serves streaming audio, video, and data applications such as software distribution or stock-quote broadcasts.

Consider this example: A corporate officer needs to deliver a live video broadcast to the company's employees. Doing so across an IP network using traditional IP protocols would require that the video feed be replicated once for every user. For a branch office across a WAN link, 20 employees watching the video on their computers would result in the video stream being replicated 20 times across the WAN. Not only is this highly inefficient, but the typical WAN link could not handle the amount of traffic being transmitted. IP multicast protocols allow users to request a particular multicast service (which can be audio, video, or data). The network then determines the source of the multicast transmission and routes the multicast stream to its destination.

Multicast protocols ensure that only one copy of the stream is transmitted across any given link. Therefore, in the preceding branch-office example, only one copy of the video broadcast would be transmitted over the WAN and then would be replicated to each user at the LAN level. Multicasts relate to the concept of a group. The receivers who express an interest in receiving a particular data stream define the group. A receiver must join the group by using Internet Group Management Protocol (IGMP), which requires that routers and switches must support IGMP to communicate with the receiver (application). Not until the receiver joins the group can she receive the data stream.

A multicast IP address identifies a group. The Internet Assigned Numbers Authority (IANA) assigns multicast IP addresses using the IP Class D address space of 224.0.0.0 to 239.255.255.255. The routers in a network are responsible for identifying the shortest, most efficient path from the multicast transmitter to its group of receivers. The Layer 2 LAN switches are responsible for receiving the singular transmission and replicating it to each of the registered receivers. Of the multicast-related routing protocols, the primary protocol is Protocol-Independent Multicast (PIM). The routers use PIM to make forwarding decisions. PIM determines the shortest path for each multicast group based on the IP routing protocol running on the router (such as Enhanced Interior Gateway Routing Protocol [EIGRP] or Open Shortest Path First [OSPF]).

Using Reverse Path Forwarding (RPF), routers use the existing unicast routing table to determine upstream and downstream neighbors and eliminate any loops. PIM operates in three different modes: sparse, dense, and sparse-dense. The mode determines when the routers start forwarding packets to the group. Sparse mode employs a "pull" model, and dense mode uses a "push" model. In sparse mode, packets are not transmitted through the network until a receiver specifically asks to join the group.

In dense mode, packets are transmitted throughout the network without regard for registered users, and the network prunes transmission to parts of the network where no receivers are registered. Sparse mode is more efficient in that traffic goes only where requested, whereas dense mode blasts everywhere initially.

The third mode is sparse-dense mode (developed by Cisco), in which the network intelligently determines which mode to use as opposed to just configuring one or the other. Sparse mode generally is implemented for standard video and audio transmission in corporate networks.

A core component of a sparse implementation is the *rendezvous point (RP)*. The RP is the central clearinghouse for multicast transmitters and group receivers. Multicast transmitters register themselves with the RP, and the network forwards requests from group receivers to the RP. The RP then facilitates the transmission of the data stream to the receivers. If the RP fails or disappears from the network, receivers cannot register with senders. Therefore, a network needs multiple RPs. Anycast-RP is a protocol based on Multicast Source Discovery Protocol (MSDP) that facilitates the fault-tolerant implementation of multiple RPs.

Dense mode floods traffic to every corner of the network. This brute-force method makes sense only when there are receivers on every subnet in a network. After traffic begins flowing, routers stop the flow of (or prune) traffic to subnets that have no receivers. Companies generally do not implement dense mode except for special circumstances because of its fire-hose approach to data-stream replication.

Although PIM makes sense in a corporate network, it requires that a network be planned and configured to handle the particular implementation of PIM properly. This setup is impractical across the Internet and shared IP networks for which there is no guarantee that multicast is configured consistently or properly. Multiprotocol Border Gateway Protocol (MBGP) allows the scalable advertising and transmission of MBGP routes through the Internet.

At-a-Glance: IP Multicast

Why Should I Care About IP Multicast?

Many applications used in modern networks require information (voice, video, or data) to be sent to multiple end stations. When only a few end stations are targeted, sending multiple copies of the same information through the network (unicast) causes no ill effects.

However, as the number of targeted end stations increases, the harmful effects of duplicate packets become dramatic. Deploying applications such as streaming video, financial market data, and IP telephony-based Music On Hold without enabling network devices for multicast support can cause severe degradation to a network's performance.

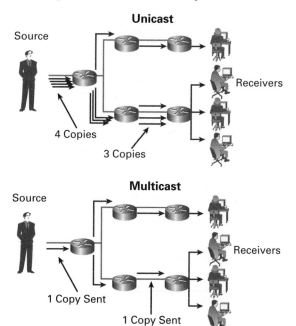

What Problems Need to Be Solved?

Multicasting requires methods to efficiently deploy and scale distributed group applications across the network. This is accomplished by using protocols that reduce the network load associated with sending the same data to multiple receivers and that alleviate the high host/router processing requirements for serving individual connections.

Internet Group Management Protocol (IGMP)

IGMP is a protocol that allows end stations to join what is known as a multicast group. Joining a multicast group can be thought of as like subscribing to a session or service where multicast is used. IGMP relies on Class D IP addresses to create multicast groups.

When a multicast session begins, the host sends an IGMP message throughout the network to discover which end stations have joined the group. The host then sends traffic to all members of that multicast group. Routers "listen" to IGMP traffic and periodically send out queries to discover which groups are active or inactive on particular LANs. Routers communicate with each other using one or more protocols to build multicast routes for each group.

Multicast Distribution Trees

Multicast-capable routers create distribution trees that control the path that IP multicast traffic takes through the network to deliver traffic to all receivers. The two basic types of multicast distribution trees are source trees and shared trees.

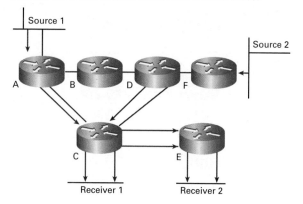

With source trees (also known as shortest-path trees), each source sends its data to each receiver using the most efficient path, as shown in the preceding figure. Source trees are optimized for latency but have higher memory requirements, because routers must keep track of all sources.

With shared trees, shown in the following figure, the multicast data is sent to a common point in the network (known as the rendezvous point) before being sent to each receiver. In the figure, Router D serves as the rendezvous point, and all multicast data is routed through it. Shared trees require less memory in routers than source trees but may not always use the optimal path, which can result in packet delivery latency.

At-a-Glance: IP Multicast

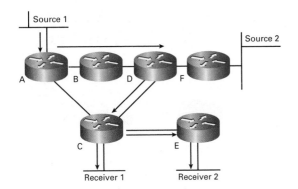

Layer 2 Multicast

A Layer 2 switch forwards all multicast traffic, which reduces network efficiency. Two methods, Cisco Group Management Protocol (CGMP) and IGMP snooping, were developed to mitigate this inefficient switch behavior.

Cisco Group Management Protocol (CGMP)

CGMP allows Cisco Catalyst switches to make Layer 2 forwarding decisions based on IGMP information. When configured on switches and routers, CGMP ensures that IP multicast traffic is delivered only to ports that are attached to interested receivers, or multicast routers. With CGMP running, any router receiving a multicast join message via a switch replies to the switch with a CGMP join message. This message allows Layer 2 forwarding decisions to be made.

IGMP Snooping

IGMP snooping improves efficiency by enabling a Layer 2 switch to view Layer 3 information (IGMP

join/leave messages) sent between hosts and routers. When an IGMP host report is sent through a switch, the switch adds the host's port number to the associated multicast table entry. When the switch hears the IGMP leave group message from a host, the switch removes the host's table entry. IGMP requires a switch to examine all multicast packets and therefore should be implemented only on high-end switches.

Multicast Forwarding

In unicast routing, traffic is routed from the source to the destination host. The router scans its routing table for the destination address and then forwards a single copy of the unicast packet out the correct interface.

In multicast forwarding, the source sends traffic to several hosts, represented by a multicast group address. The multicast router must determine which direction is the upstream direction (toward the source) and which one is the downstream direction (toward the hosts). When more than one downstream path exists, the best ones (toward the group address) are chosen. These paths may or may not be the same path that would be chosen for a unicast packet. This is called Reverse Path Forwarding (RPF). RPF is used to create loop-free distribution trees.

Protocol-Independent Multicast (PIM)

PIM is IP routing protocol-independent and can leverage whichever unicast routing protocols are

used to populate the unicast routing table. PIM uses this unicast routing information to perform the multicast forwarding function. Although PIM is called a multicast routing protocol, it actually uses the unicast routing table to perform the RPF check function instead of building a completely independent multicast routing table. It includes two different modes of behavior for dense and sparse traffic environments—dense mode and sparse mode:

- In **PIM dense mode**, the multicast router floods traffic messages out all ports (referred to as a "push" model). If a router has no hosts or downstream neighbors that are members of the group, a prune message is sent, telling the router not to flood message on a particular interface. Dense mode only uses source trees. Because of the flood and prune behavior, dense mode is not recommended.

- **PIM sparse mode** uses what is known as an "explicit join" model. In this model, traffic is only sent to hosts that explicitly ask to receive it. This is accomplished by sending a join message to the rendezvous point.

An **Anycast Rendezvous Point (RP)** provides load balancing, redundancy, and fault tolerance by assigning the same IP address to multiple RPs within a PIM sparse mode network multicast domain.

Multicast

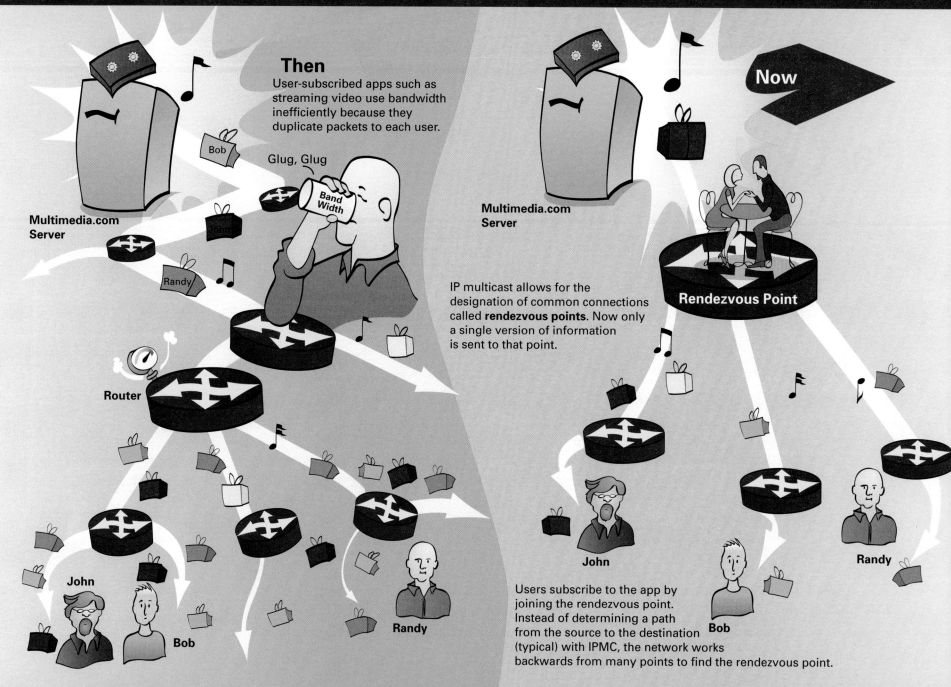

Then
User-subscribed apps such as streaming video use bandwidth inefficiently because they duplicate packets to each user.

Glug, Glug

Multimedia.com Server

Router

Bob

John

Randy

Now

Multimedia.com Server

IP multicast allows for the designation of common connections called **rendezvous points**. Now only a single version of information is sent to that point.

Rendezvous Point

John

Bob

Randy

Users subscribe to the app by joining the rendezvous point. Instead of determining a path from the source to the destination (typical) with IPMC, the network works backwards from many points to find the rendezvous point.

Part VIII

Mobility

Wireless World

At this point, you should have enough information to understand how networking works. For the most part, smart IT people can wire together all the networks and connect all the devices to the switches and the routers and the data centers and light it all up and make it go. There's only one slight problem. We have decided (after most of this connecting stuff took place) that we really don't like those wires. Hmmm. Back to square one.

This section focuses on wireless networking, which adds a whole new dimension and, as you will see, a whole new set of design considerations and challenges. Because we are back to basics, we will go back to the LAN or, in this case, wireless LAN [WLAN]. "Selecting and Building Wireless Networks" takes a look at basic wireless design from the perspective of the IT staff. As you will see, there is a lot more to it than just plugging in a couple of wireless routers.

One of the biggest considerations and concerns with wireless networking is security. In fact, wireless security was and is such a concern that it still has a big impact on companies choosing whether to adopt or allow wireless networking. The next section looks at why wireless security is such a concern and how these issues are resolved.

The first three topics in this section cover just the basics, but it turns out that users want and sometimes demand more. The fourth topic in this section looks at one extension of basic wireless networking—having city-wide wireless access. Also called municipal or muni wireless, more and more cities are deploying this type of service.

We follow with another new adaptation of wireless, voice over IP (VoIP) over wireless networks. This technology presents quite a few challenges that must be overcome, but after they are solved, significant productivity gains can be enjoyed. Of all the technologies discussed in this book so far, wireless VoIP is potentially one of the more challenging technologies for IT staffers. A much simpler but no less important wireless technology is guest access. It gives visitors Internet access in a way that does not compromise internal network security.

This section closes with an interesting operational use of wireless: using the wireless system to locate and track company assets. More and more companies, especially those with a lot of physical assets, are finding that Radio Frequency Identification (RFID) and location-based services are a great way to keep an eye on their stuff.

Mobility and Wireless Networks

Throwing Away the Ties That Bind

The evolution of the telephone reveals one consistent evolving design principle: People do not want to be tied to a particular location when using the phone. The first phones were attached to the wall, and people leaned down or stood on their toes to speak into the horn and listen to the response. Then the mouthpiece and listening device were combined into a single handset and connected to the phone by a cord. The phone still hung on the wall, but you could rest the handset against your head and talk to the other person comfortably. Finally, the phone was liberated from the wall. A cable attached to the phone itself allowed the caller to comfortably move the phone around the room. The caller was still restricted by the length of the phone cable, but at least she could lie on the couch while talking to a friend.

Then came cordless phones. The caller could be anywhere in the house, or even in the garden, and still comfortably speak with friends and family. This change was revolutionary in the independence it provided.

This same principle of independence applies to WLANs. Notebook computers and personal digital assistants (PDA) are commonplace in corporations. People take their computers with them to meetings, customer sites, airports, and hotels.

Until recently, this mobility meant dragging a cable and being restricted to sitting somewhere near the wall where the cable plugged into the network. With wireless networking, the computer user can easily access the network wherever he is as long as a wireless access point (AP) is nearby. Breaking the dependence on a cable and a wall jack is quite liberating.

Some benefits realized with the introduction of wireless networking include the following:

• Computer users can access the corporate network and Internet anywhere on campus. This offers unprecedented convenience, flexibility, and productivity.

• Temporary networks are easier to set up when making moves, additions, and changes or when setting up war rooms or temporary work spaces.

• It is easier to collaborate on the spot. Users can exchange files or handle requests for information when in meetings, for example.

• Users can exchange data with servers directly rather than wait to download it from a wired connection. Users can also continue to exchange data with servers while they move across the campus or warehouse. This flexibility is important in warehouses and manufacturing, for example.

WLANs are meant to complement existing wired networks. Wireless access points (similar to traditional Ethernet hubs) provide access to devices that have wireless network interface cards. The access points connect to an Ethernet switch and typically are configured on their own VLAN. Wireless bridges can provide wireless connectivity as well. This setup allows for longer-distance connectivity between buildings, for example. The current WLAN (Wi-Fi) standards include 802.11a, 802.11b, 802.11g, and the newly arrived 802.11n, which offers unprecedented range and speed.

In general, WLANs cannot achieve speeds quite as fast as wired networks (although they are getting pretty close). The size and orientation of the antenna, the transmission power setting, and the existence of obstructions (such as walls or trees) determine the distance, speed, and coverage area between the transmitter and receiver. If you must achieve connectivity at greater distances, you can reduce the data rate or jack up the power. With Wi-Fi, trade-offs occur between greater distance and faster transmission speeds.

Home wireless networks are based on the same Wi-Fi standards as corporate wireless networks. For a more thorough discussion of wireless networks in the home, pick up a copy of *Wireless Home Networking Simplified* (Cisco Press, 2006).

At-a-Glance: Wireless LANs

Why Should I Care About Wireless LANs?

A WLAN is a local-area network of computers or terminals connected by radio frequencies. Unlike traditional LANs, WLAN users are free to move about while staying connected to the network.

Because of this mobility, WLANs offer businesses great flexibility when implementing a new network or when looking for new office space. A WLAN can be implemented in a building not set up for traditional networking, saving companies the time and expense of making a new space business-ready.

WLANs typically are used to connect users to a corporate network, but they also can be used to connect physically separated buildings. This implementation is called building-to-building (or point-to-point) bridge systems. The figure lists the advantages of WLANs over traditional LANs.

It's worth noting that although this technology has some obvious similarities to the wireless technology you are using in your home, there are some significant differences when it is deployed in a corporate setting:

- Wired networks:
  — PCs must plug into Ethernet jacks.
  — Temporary networks are difficult to set up.
  — Data files typically are shared after work sessions because of a lack of connections.
  — Faster speeds and better security.

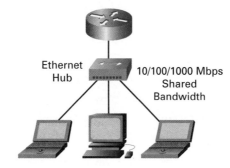

Ethernet Hub

10/100/1000 Mbps Shared Bandwidth

- Wireless networks:
  — PCs can access the network from anywhere on the campus.
  — Temporary networks are easy to set up.
  — Data and files are easily shared during work sessions.
  — Slower speeds; less secure than wired systems.

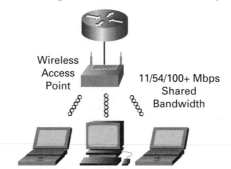

Wireless Access Point

11/54/100+ Mbps Shared Bandwidth

What Problems Need to Be Solved?

WLANs present network administrators with some new issues:

- Unlike wired Ethernet, WLANs must trade off between power, throughput, and power consumption of mobile devices on battery power.

- One of the advantages of WLANs is mobility. Therefore, WLANs must employ schemes that allow users to remain connected as they move about a building or campus.

- Signal interference from other WLANs or from other transmission sources or obstacles such as walls or buildings can degrade WLAN performance.

WLANs present new security issues such as access control and data privacy.

In Building Systems

In buildings, WLANs give employees the flexibility to move about freely while staying connected to the network. The number of access points required depends on the size of the building and the desired throughput. Trade-offs must be made between power, battery life, and transmission throughput. Remember that in addition to receiving a signal, the PC must transmit a signal to the nearest AP. In general, the range of a wireless access point (indoor models, anyway) is 100 to 200 feet or so.

Wireless transmission causes a significant power drain on a laptop battery.

The following figure shows the trade-off between coverage and throughput for an 802.11b signal. The actual distance/throughput numbers will be different for different wireless standards, but the drop-off ratios tend to be similar. DSS stands for Direct Sequence Spread Spectrum. DSS is a wireless

At-a-Glance: Wireless LANs

multiplexing scheme used to combine multiple signals into the same block of frequencies.

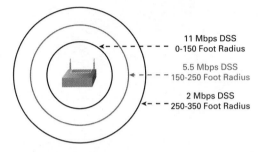

11 Mbps DSS
0-150 Foot Radius

5.5 Mbps DSS
150-250 Foot Radius

2 Mbps DSS
250-350 Foot Radius

WLAN Roaming

Because wireless APs are relatively inexpensive, and the desire for bandwidth is high, most companies choose to deploy multiple APs with a reduced transmission radius and increased throughput. This solution, however, introduces the need to implement a WLAN roaming scheme. Roaming is a term used to describe switching from the control of one AP to another.

APs should be positioned so that there are no "dead spots." As a user moves away from one AP, the power and signal quality decrease. A good roaming plan ensures that as this happens, another AP signal will be sufficiently strong to take control of the wireless connection. This handoff is executed through a combination of the network and wireless client working together, transparently to the user (much like cellular phones). Wireless handoff can occur only on the same VLAN. If a user moves between two VLANs, connectivity will be lost until the device authenticates on the new VLAN.

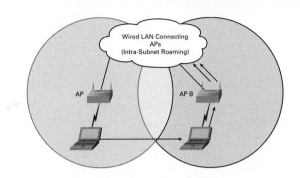

Wired LAN Connecting
APs
(Intra-Subnet Roaming)

AP   AP B

Building-to-Building Bridge Systems

Wireless bridges create a single LAN by linking remote networks. For simple networks, the bridge connects to a hub or switch on the LAN. If the network contains multiple subnetworks, the bridge is connected to a router. Wireless bridges are a convenient and cost-effective solution for rapidly growing companies and for those located in areas where a fixed connection is either expensive or impractical.

In some cases building-to-building Wi-Fi wireless bridges offer superior price and performance over competing technologies such as the following:

- Direct cable connections:
  - High installation costs
  - Difficulty overcoming physical barriers such as lakes, highways, and other buildings
  - Often require approval from local governments

  - Inflexible after deployment
- Telephone line connections:
  - High monthly service fees
  - High installation and equipment costs
- Microwave connections:
  - Expensive
  - Require licensing
  - Difficult to install

Security Issues and Options

Security is a major concern for WLANs. There are two main security issues with WLANs:

- **Access control:** Because WLANs use radio waves for access, any WLAN client in the area can access the network. There are known cases of hackers accessing networks while sitting in a car outside a building. Businesses should protect their networks by using centralized user authentication schemes to protect against unauthorized access to the network. This prevents people from getting free Internet access or using your access to launch illegal network attacks on other networks.

- **Privacy:** Privacy is also an issue with WLANs. Unlike fixed connections, which send information from point to point, WLANs broadcast information everywhere. This information can be "scooped" out of the air by those with the desire and know-how to get it. Therefore, it is essential to encrypt the data packets that are transmitted through the air.

Wired LANs

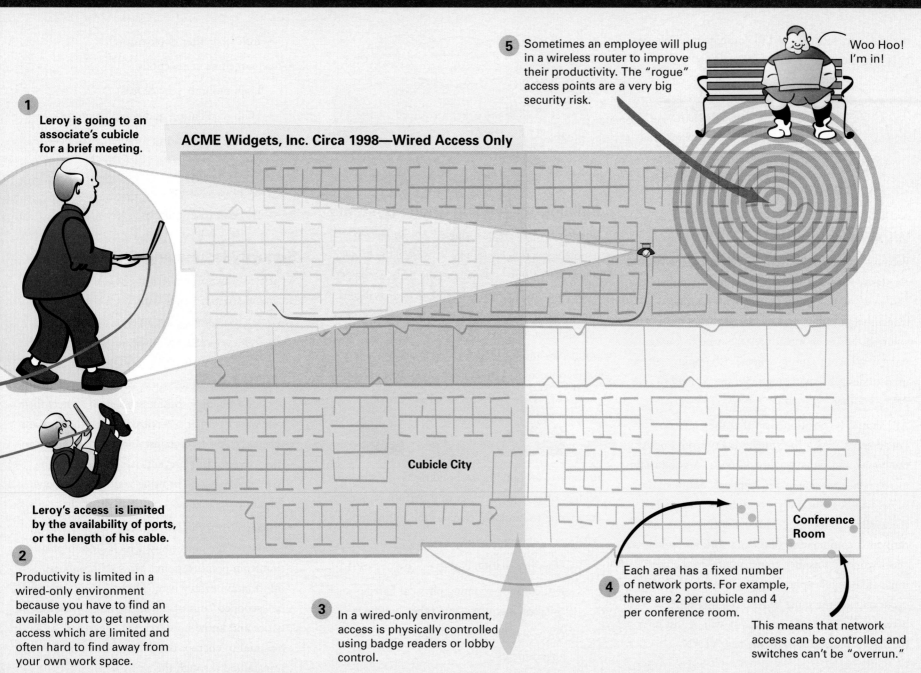

5 Sometimes an employee will plug in a wireless router to improve their productivity. The "rogue" access points are a very big security risk.

Woo Hoo! I'm in!

1 Leroy is going to an associate's cubicle for a brief meeting.

ACME Widgets, Inc. Circa 1998—Wired Access Only

Cubicle City

Conference Room

Leroy's access is limited by the availability of ports, or the length of his cable.

2 Productivity is limited in a wired-only environment because you have to find an available port to get network access which are limited and often hard to find away from your own work space.

3 In a wired-only environment, access is physically controlled using badge readers or lobby control.

4 Each area has a fixed number of network ports. For example, there are 2 per cubicle and 4 per conference room.

This means that network access can be controlled and switches can't be "overrun."

Wireless LANs

1 Productivity can be improved because employees can connect from anywhere, allowing improved collaboration and saving people from really boring meetings.

2 In a wireless system, a single switch can be overrun because a large group of employees can gather in a single area.

Even though Lewis must enter a 14-digit access code he can never remember...

SB0217J5624X82

Corp. Cafeteria

ACME Widgets, Inc. Circa 2001—Wireless Access

...he's able to work almost anywhere in the building.

3 In a wireless system, access is more of an issue because now access can be gained from outside the building.

Cubicle City

Conference Room

Selecting and Building Wireless Networks

Designing a Wireless Network

Although it may seem a bit trivial to the casual user whose idea of assembling a wireless network is connecting his Linksys router to his cable modem, designing a wireless network on a corporate scale takes real engineering skill and effort.

Some key considerations must be addressed; they are quite different from what is involved in implementing a wired network. The first of these is which wireless standard is to be used. There are several, each of which has pros and cons. Another consideration is where signal coverage will be (and not be, for that matter). For example, a company may want to allow access to reach to an outdoor eating area, but not reach across a street or into another building for security or interference reasons. Site planning must also be done to ensure that no interference occurs between APs within the same system, requiring the same type of planning required for cellular networks.

Another key consideration, and one that was never a problem for wired networks, is spontaneous system overloading. To see why this is a problem, remember that the network was designed with a fixed number of ports assigned to each switch. Let's say, for example, that one switch typically covers 50 cubicles and offices, each with two ports, and ten meeting rooms, each with ten switch ports. That's 200 ports per switch and a maximum of 200 devices that can access the network from that switch. Because cubicles typically do not appear out of thin air, it's not likely that any one switch will be overrun with users.

Wireless, however, does not have this built-in safeguard. Imagine an "all hands" corporate presentation in a large conference hall, which is covered by a single access point. What happens during the break, when 250 employees all decide to open their laptops and check their e-mail? Without some situational planning, the IT department could be in for some long days.

The good news is that over the years, and through trial and error, some best practices have been developed. They make the design process much easier on both the IT department and the users.

At-a-Glance: Designing Wi-Fi Networks

Why Should I Care About Wireless Design?

As employees rely more on mobility in the workplace to increase productivity, wireless access is a critical part of any network. Productivity gains due to wireless access are estimated to be 30 percent or more, as employees use wireless access in meeting rooms, hotspots, and other areas lacking wired access.

Wireless access to e-mail, corporate applications, and collaboration applications is now a minimum expectation by employees. Without it, they feel at a disadvantage. Companies that do not provide wireless access for their employees (and even their guests) will find themselves under pressure from competitors that do leverage the technology.

They may also have a higher instance of employees connecting their own wireless access points into live Ethernet ports, which creates a security risk. This is called the "rogue" access point problem.

What Problems Need to Be Solved?

Selecting a wireless network model that serves the needs of both the company and its employees is a critical part of any deployment. Performance is also key, because wireless users expect to have the same level of service, and access to the same applications, as wired clients.

From an IT perspective, the deployment must provide a balance of adequate coverage and service levels with deployment and operational costs. Finally, a unified wireless solution must meet the needs of different wireless and mobility services, now and in the future.

Cisco Unified Wireless Architecture

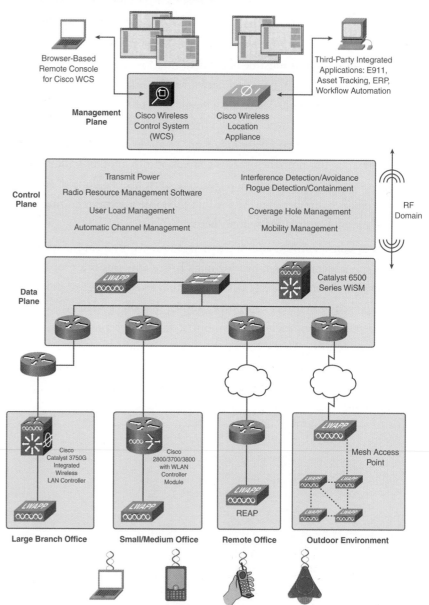

At-a-Glance: Designing Wi-Fi Networks

Cisco Unified Wireless Solution

The Cisco Unified Wireless solution with Wireless Control System (WCS) provides an integrated approach for wireless and mobility services deployment and operations, including the following:

- Wireless client access
- Roaming
- Security
- Location-based services
- RF management

The data plane includes wireless APs at the headquarters campus and also at the branch offices, providing unified wireless access to many types of clients. The control plane includes management of APs and radio frequency (RF) coverage, as well as detection of rogue APs and interference. The management plane includes integrated third-party applications, such as those relying on location-based services.

Wireless Standards

There are different wireless network standards to choose from, including a, b, g, and n. These letters refer to the 802.11 technical standard extensions, such as 802.11a. We will focus on the a, b, and g standards, because they account for the majority of the deployments at the time of publication.

802.11b, 802.11g, and 802.11n are compatible standards, using up to 14 overlapping channels in the 2.4-GHz band. In the U.S. (and several other countries), only 11 channels are used.

Only three channels—1, 6, and 11—are nonoverlapping. These are primarily the channels assigned to access points.

802.11a is incompatible with 802.11b/g/n. It uses 12 (different in some countries) nonoverlapping channels for indoor use in the 5-GHz band. 802.11a also has additional channels designed for outdoor use.

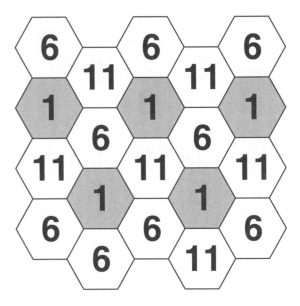

Typical Channel Plan for 802.11b/g

Eight channels are primarily assigned to access points. Unlike other standards that use 1, 2, 3 type number schemes, 802.11a uses channel allocations of 36, 40, 44, and so on.

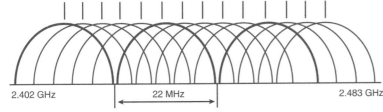

Channels

1 2 3 4 5 6 7 8 9 10 11 12 13 14

2.402 GHz   22 MHz   2.483 GHz

802.11b/g Channels at 2.4 GHz

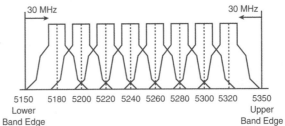

30 MHz   30 MHz

5150   5180 5200 5220 5240 5260 5280 5300 5320   5350
Lower   Upper
Band Edge   Band Edge

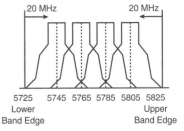

802.11a Channels at 5 GHz

20 MHz   20 MHz

5725   5745 5765 5785 5805 5825
Lower   Upper
Band Edge   Band Edge

At-a-Glance: Designing Wi-Fi Networks

Typical Channel Plan for 802.11a

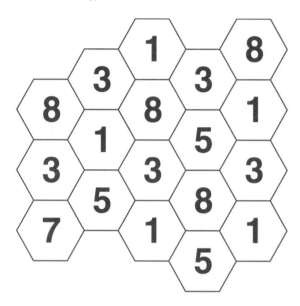

WLAN RF Coverage Site Survey

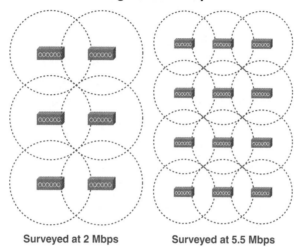

Surveyed at 2 Mbps Surveyed at 5.5 Mbps

Effects of Lowering WLAN AP RF Power

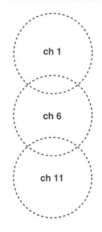

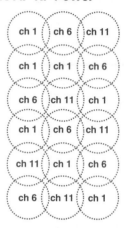

180 Users Per Floor
30 mW Transmitter Power
3 Access Points
60 Users Per AP
11 Mbps Data Rate

180 Users Per Floor
5 mW Transmitter Power
18 Access Points
10 Users Per AP
11 Mbps Data Rate

Wireless Network Designs

Many factors need to be considered in the design of the wireless network:

• RF environment within the buildings

• Data rates desired

• Number of clients

• Transmit power

• Applications and their requirements

RF surveys should be conducted before a deployment so that you understand which environment may dictate the best design. Higher data rates may require a higher density of APs to ensure proper bandwidth. Applications with special demands, such as voice over wireless, may also increase AP density requirements.

The two figures show two examples of wireless surveys and channel plans for an 802.11b deployment.

At-a-Glance: Designing Wi-Fi Networks

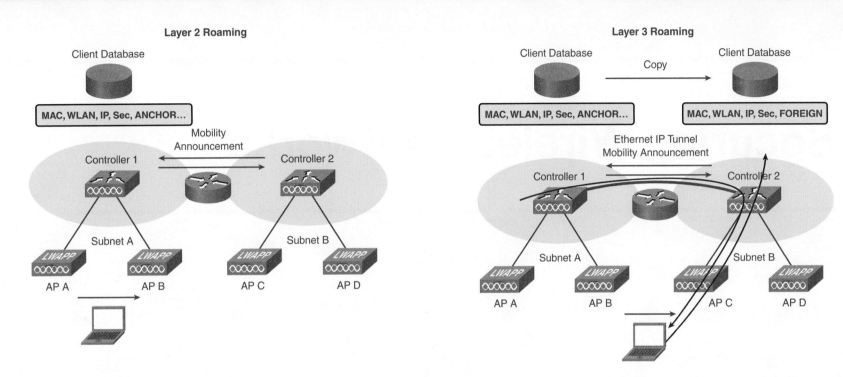

Portability Versus Mobility

Wireless access with laptops typically is "nomadic." This means that users use a laptop in one location and then move to a new one. Therefore, roaming is not much of an issue. However, with increased use of PDAs and voice-over-Wi-Fi-capable devices, roaming capability is essential.

The Cisco Unified Wireless solution provides both Layer 2 and Layer 3 roaming. With Layer 2 roaming, the client stays within the domain of a single Wireless LAN Controller (WLC) for the entire

session. In a Layer 3 roaming environment, the client roams between two different WLC domains, requiring the exchange of client information. Roaming is handled automatically by the Cisco Unified Wireless solution, transparent to the client endpoint.

Securing Wireless Networks

Locking Down Wireless

For every networking innovation, there is a hacker looking to exploit it. The advent of wireless networking was no different; in fact, the hackers had a field day with this one early on. The reason is that before wireless, hackers had only two ways to get into a network: They could either penetrate it from the Internet or could get physical access to a live switch port inside the network.

Despite all the news about hacking, breaching a corporate network from the Internet is extremely difficult. This method provides a lot of anonymity (always a plus when breaking the law). If someone can get access to the switch port, the technical stuff is easy. There is, of course, the matter of being caught and detained, though.

When wireless came about, it was a dream for hackers, because they could sit in a car in the parking lot, or even on a bench outside, protecting their anonymity while taking advantage of what was a live port on the network.

You may be wondering why those clever IT guys didn't see this coming. The truth is, they did. In fact, wireless was viewed as such a problem that many companies refused to implement it because of the security risks. However, wireless became accessible and affordable on the consumer side. Corporate employees instantly understood the productivity gains of being able to remain connected while away from their desks. As soon as the prices of wireless routers began to drop, they did what made sense to them. They plugged their own wireless access points—literally, their own personal hotspots—into the ports in their offices so that they could roam around and check e-mail.

Now IT had a huge problem. Not only was wireless a known security risk, but they had open wireless APs that they did not control all over their networks. This was the birth of the "rogue" AP, and it made their security look like Swiss cheese. This is when something really interesting happened. IT realized that the wireless cat could not be stuffed back in the bag. Wireless was here to stay. The people had mandated that they have wireless access, and IT departments realized it was better to "own" wireless so that they could properly secure it.

Balancing Security and Access

Most people in networking believe that balancing security and access is a zero-sum game: give to one, and you must take from the other. Wireless security was no different in the beginning, because users were forced to enter 26-digit hexadecimal codes to gain secure wireless access. It was a pain, but that was the price you paid for checking your e-mail when meetings started to get boring.

Wireless security has come a long way from the "easily" breached Wired Equivalent Privacy (WEP) security keys to the more secure Wi-Fi Protected Access (WPA) and WPA2 security standards. Ease of use has also been improved. Laptops are usually preconfigured by IT so that users can securely connect without a lot of additional steps.

At-a-Glance: Securing Wi-Fi

Why Should I Care About Wireless Security?

With wired networks, intruders need to gain physical access to a building to gain access to the network via a port. With wireless networks, security is a concern because intruders only need to be in the proximity of the building to "see" the wireless signal. In addition, with wired networks intruders need access to your wire to eavesdrop, but for wireless networks they only need to be in the proximity of your client to potentially conduct eavesdropping.

Additional security measures need to be employed on wireless networks to give them the same security confidence level as with wired networks.

An additional security threat presented by wireless networks is someone plugging in a "rogue" access point, essentially an unauthorized wireless network that can put a huge hole in a business's network security policies.

What Problems Need to Be Solved?

For WLANs to be secure, the first challenge is how to secure the process of associating a client to the wireless network to prevent unauthorized wireless access.

Next, there needs to be a way to secure the communications between a client and the wireless network to prevent eavesdropping, balancing security measures with the ease of use still required for clients to access the network.

As mentioned earlier, a secure WLAN implementation needs to be able to mitigate the threat of "rogue" or unauthorized wireless access points.

Wireless security is not a trivial thing. Early attempts at so-called "wired equivalence" (WEP, for example) gave/give a false sense of security in this regard. That is, WEP made people think that they were secure when it was actually a pretty easy thing to crack.

Securing Wireless Networks

The Cisco Secure Wireless solution provides an integrated approach for deploying secure wireless and mobility services.

Clients are secured via a device "health check" and admission control with Cisco Clean Access (CCA).

Host intrusion prevention is assured with Cisco Secure Agent (CSA).

The wireless access interface is secured via 802.1x/EAP-FAST sign-on authentication, WPA and WPA2 Wi-Fi encryption, and best-practices wireless network.

Finally, the wireless network is secured via an integrated Intrusion Detection System (IDS) and "rogue" (unauthorized) wireless AP detection and mitigation. This is a unified approach to wired and wireless security because many of the features just discussed are also deployed in the wired network.

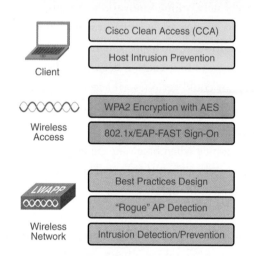

Wireless Encryption

The first important step in securing wireless is to follow best practices for client authentication and encryption. By using Extensible Authentication Protocol (EAP) and Flexible Authentication via Secure Tunnel (FAST) to authenticate wireless clients, only authorized clients are given access to the network. After they are connected, WPA or WPA2 (preferred) is used for encryption key establishment. After EAP-FAST is successful, a pairwise master key (PMK) is created.

WPA and WPA2 use a four-way handshake process to generate a pairwise temporal key (PTK) that is kept secret. WPA2 uses the Advanced Encryption Standard (AES) algorithm, adding security above WPA.

At-a-Glance: Securing Wi-Fi

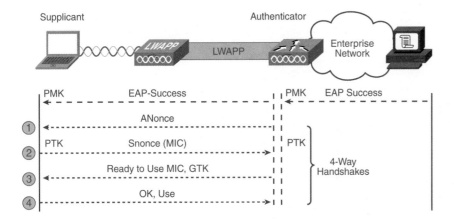

EAP-FAST Authentication

802.1x — RADIUS

EAP-Identity-Request
EAP-Identity-Response — Forward Identity to ACS Server
EAP-Request EAP Type — EAP-Request EAP Type
EAP-Response – EAP Type — EAP-Response – EAP Type
Authentication Conversation Is Between Client and Authentication Server
EAP-Success — EAP-Sucess

WPA Encryption Key Establishment

Supplicant — Authenticator — Enterprise Network

PMK EAP-Success — PMK EAP Success
① ANonce
PTK ② Snonce (MIC) PTK
③ Ready to Use MIC, GTK — 4-Way Handshakes
④ OK, Use

Health Checks

By their nature, laptops and other mobile devices inherently get exposed to more opportunities for infections by viruses, malware, spyware, and so on. Given that, it is a good wireless security practice to add a "posture check" to the authentication process to ensure that the client is healthy before gaining access. Cisco Network Admission Control (NAC) using Cisco Clean Access (CCA) performs an additional challenge to client devices to "prove their health" before being allowed to access the wireless network. The definition of a "healthy" device is determined by the IT staff. It can include the following:

• Free of viruses and other malware

• Correct antivirus software and signature files are loaded

• Operating system updates are current

• Custom policy checks added by IT staff

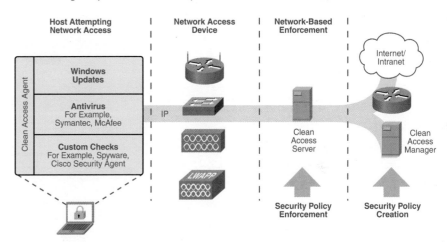

Unhealthy devices are placed in a "quarantine" wired or wireless network for remediation and are not permitted to access the rest of the production network. See Part V, "Securing the Network," for a more in-depth discussion of NAC and CCA.

Rogue Access Points

"Rogue" or unauthorized wireless access points provide a serious security threat to a network. Locating and shutting down such unauthorized APs can be difficult without automated detection and location systems. The Cisco

At-a-Glance: Securing Wi-Fi

Unified Wireless solution uses authorized wireless access points to scan the environment for "rogue" access points. Detection information is provided to the WLCs, which can then assist in correlation and isolation and provide the information to the WCS. Wireless topology information can be married with building layout diagrams to provide visual indications of "rogue" AP locations so that IT staff can take appropriate actions to shut them down.

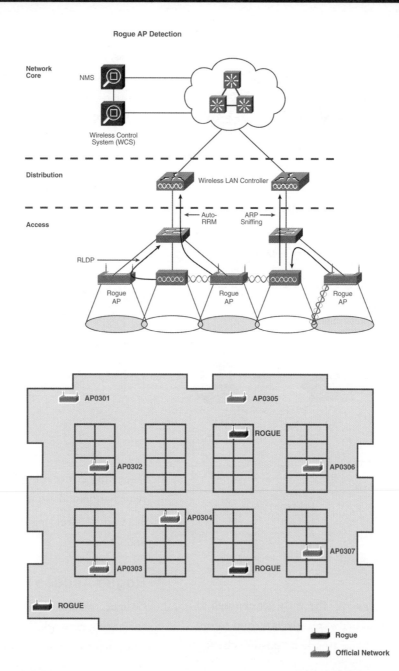

Outdoor and Municipal Wireless Networks

It's Just Like a Building, Only Way Bigger

Maybe we're all just being greedy. Fifteen years ago most people didn't even have an e-mail account. Few had ever connected to the Internet. Five years ago everyone you know probably had an e-mail account; in some cases it was the only way you communicated with them. Then came wireless networking, because those e-mails couldn't wait until the end of the meeting, so we had wireless throughout our workplace and home.

Now, not even this is good enough. We want to connect at the park, or while waiting in line at the DMV, or while on a city bus, or while camped out on a curb waiting for a parade to start. In other words, we want to be connected now, now, *now*, and everywhere. So much for work-life balance.

All kidding aside, the need for connectivity is seemingly insatiable. Many towns and cities are catching on and are looking to install citywide (also called municipal or muni) wireless for a number of reasons. One of the primary reasons is that just as it does for corporate workers in an office, wireless connectivity can increase the productivity of city workers and officials. In addition, the availability of muni wireless makes for a happy populace, especially when it is offered for free.

Of course, citywide wireless access involves some unique considerations. There is the obvious issue with scale, but designers must also deal with the elements, because access points are likely to be outside.

There is also the issue of connecting the access points back to the physical network, because cities don't come with handy drop ceilings to run cables through. As with any wireless system, security is also a concern, especially when secure channels (such as police traffic) must be maintained on the same network used for public access.

One major issue with muni Wi-Fi is funding and return on investment (ROI). Some free and even subscription muni Wi-Fi systems have failed because of a nonsustainable business model to fund and maintain the systems. It's also worth noting, though, that some cities fund these systems through public works (tax-supported) projects.

At-a-Glance: Municipal Wi-Fi

Why Should I Care About Municipal Wireless?

The rapid growth of wireless users is driving widespread adoption and deployment of wireless networks. Unlike cell phone usage, in which users must remain connected while in motion, wireless laptops typically require "nomadic" usage. Users connect and use the wireless network in one location, and then they stop and disconnect, and then they connect again in another location.

Two trends are driving the adoption of municipal Wi-Fi (citywide outdoor wireless):

- Portable wireless devices with built-in 802.11 Wi-Fi are fast appearing, including PDAs, smartphones, and portable handheld computers.

- Legacy wide-area wireless data networks, such as Cellular Digital Packet Data (CDPD), are aging and are unable to provide the bandwidth required for today's applications.

- As a counterpoint, a few 3G/4G (broadband cellular) solutions in development also have some potential for muni Internet. These systems are not as broadly available and have other issues relative to Wi-Fi, but they will likely see some measure of success.

Many cities and municipalities are considering deploying wide-area Wi-Fi networks. These networks will provide wireless connectivity services to city agencies, such as Emergency Services, and at the same time will provide wireless services to citizens. Muni Wi-Fi is in its early stages, but it is real and is being deployed by major cities.

What Problems Need to Be Solved?

Indoor 802.11 Wi-Fi networks are limited in their coverage area, allow easy access to APs, and have limited power requirements given their small footprint. In addition to having much larger coverage areas, outdoor Wi-Fi systems include equipment that must endure much different environmental conditions than indoor systems.

The deployment of significant numbers of outdoor wireless APs must be rolled out without incurring prohibitive logistics and costs for cabling each AP to a central network.

Finally, a single physical wireless network that can be securely shared to provide wireless services to multiple agencies and citizens must be planned for current and future usage.

High-Level Diagram

The Cisco Outdoor Wireless Mesh solution provides an 802.11 wireless network that can be deployed over a wide area, such as a university campus, city, or municipality. Government or public buildings can be used as the anchor points for the Root Access Points (RAP). A network of Mesh Access Points (MAP) can then be deployed in significant numbers across the area of coverage.

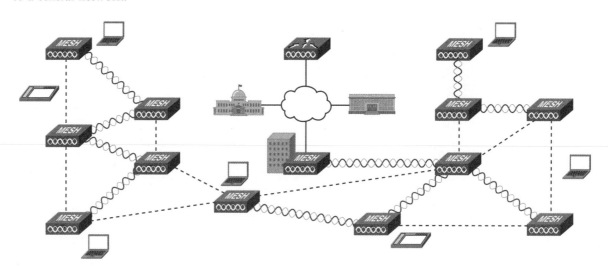

At-a-Glance: Municipal Wi-Fi

Wireless Mesh Deployment

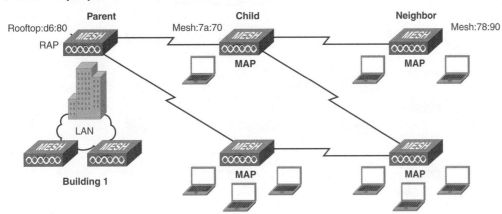

The mesh provides a wireless backhaul to the wired network and also provides multiple paths for traffic to be routed through. Mesh networks provide a practical way to deploy wireless 802.11 networks over a wide area.

Wireless Backhaul

One feature that makes outdoor Wi-Fi practical and cost-effective to deploy is the concept of a wireless backhaul. Indoor wireless networks typically use wired cabling to connect APs to network infrastructure. For outdoor wireless networks over a wide area, cabling to every AP would be cost- and logistics-prohibitive. Cisco Outdoor Wireless Mesh AP products incorporate one radio (2.4 GHz) for wireless clients to access the network, and a separate radio (5.8 GHz) to connect the AP back to the rest of the wireless network. Without a completely wireless AP, muni Wi-Fi systems would be too expensive to install and maintain.

Muni Access Points

RAPs provide the primary connection points into the rest of the network. MAPs provide access for clients. MAPs typically are installed on light/power poles, and RAPs typically are deployed on building rooftops.

MAPs can be connected to each other and to RAPs to form a *mesh*.

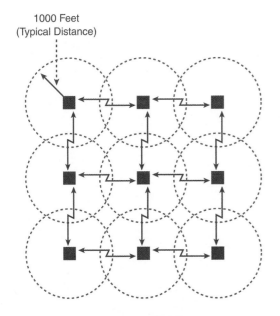

Wireless Backhaul

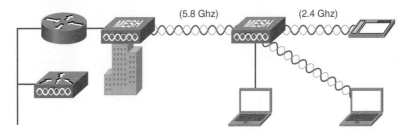

At-a-Glance: Municipal Wi-Fi

Security

To make a municipal Wi-Fi network deployment cost-effective, the wireless services are often shared by a number of agencies and citizens. Security is achieved by proving secure connectivity to the right network for each client while blocking clients from networks they are not authorized to use.

Cisco Unified Wireless and Outdoor Wireless Mesh networks using 802.1x/EAP-FAST authentication can dynamically assign clients to the appropriate wireless network partition based on their login credentials. For example, a client device that logs in with credentials of an employee of Agency 1 is mapped to the wireless network that permits access to only the back-end network services for Agency 1. This allows city employees to access services not needed by the general public.

Citizens are treated as "guests" on the network and are mapped to the wireless network providing Internet access only.

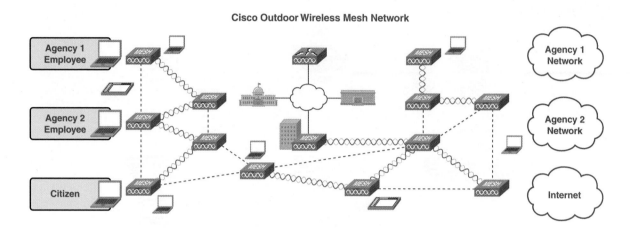

Cisco Outdoor Wireless Mesh Network

VoIP over Wireless Networks

Wireless VoIP

For more than 100 years, phones were attached to a wall and connected to a switched network using copper wires. Then, in seemingly rapid-fire succession, the system went digital. Then cordless technology let us break away from the wall. Then cellular technology let us break away from homes. Then the phone system was ported to the data IP network. And now we want to move around the office with our phone the same way we do with our laptop. And we don't just want to move around with our cell phone. We want to move around with our desk phone—the one associates and customers call us on. We wanted it, and we got it. Man, are we spoiled!

Wireless VoIP might seem like a natural extension of VoIP technology, because the wireless system is already in place, right? Well, not quite. Moving VoIP to the wireless network actually presents some huge challenges for IT staffs. First is the issue of the phones moving around. Unlike network access for a laptop, there are issues with call processing, voice quality, and bandwidth requirements. (Nothing can wreck an IT guy's day like a conference room full of people reaching for their VoIP phones on break.)

Another big issue for wireless VoIP is that people use phones in places where they would not use their laptop. It sounds strange, but when the IT folks were installing the WLAN, they probably didn't worry about having coverage in stairwells because nobody would stop there, open his laptop, and check his e-mail. He would, however, want to make, take, or continue a call while walking up the stairs.

Finally, there is the issue of mobility. Unlike wireless laptop users, wireless VoIP users expect to use the system while moving. This requires a lot of power and puts a big strain on the battery life of VoIP devices, among other issues. This also has some serious design implications well beyond those for data-only wireless networks.

Although this may seem like a bunch of big problems, they are worth overcoming because of the productivity gains that wireless yields. Besides, the IT guys don't have much on their plates. Just connect the phone to the wireless thingy.

At-a-Glance: Wireless VoIP

Why Should I Care About Wireless VoIP?

Wireless access to data applications increases productivity by enabling employees to access applications regardless of their location. Another way to increase productivity is to enable the same flexible access to voice communications.

Cellular phones can provide mobile voice access, but they are not integrated with the corporate voice system and can raise costs. In addition, multiple phone numbers, voice mail boxes, contact lists, and directories can be a drain on productivity. Integrating VoIP communication systems into the wireless network increases both productivity and reachability.

What Problems Need to Be Solved?

The design of the wireless network that can support VoIP-enabled clients is different from one intended for data only. You must consider things such as maintaining connectivity while clients travel between AP zones and maintaining coverage in places such as stairwells (where employees would likely use a phone but not check e-mail). Ensuring voice quality on WLAN systems shared with data clients is also a primary consideration, as is integrating wireless and wired communications systems, including single-number reachability and voice mail. As with any wireless technology, security is also a concern.

Integrating Cisco Wireless Networks with Unified Communications

The Cisco Unified Wireless solution provides integration with Cisco Unified Communications, enabling a single wireless network to support both data and VoIP clients. Packet prioritization is enabled within the wired and wireless network to ensure voice quality.

Coverage and Quality

For proper coverage and call quality, the density of wireless AP placement needs to be sufficient. With wireless laptops, access tends to be nomadic. With this usage model, losing connectivity while in motion and then reestablishing a session in a second location is not a significant issue.

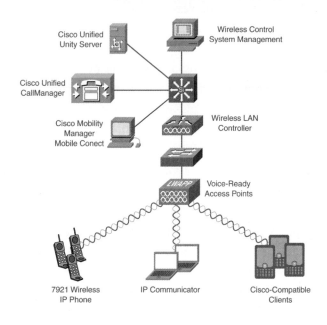

VoIP Over Wireless Site Survey

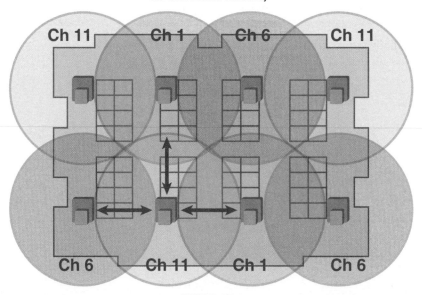

15 20% Overlap

At-a-Glance: Wireless VoIP

With wireless VoIP, clients inherently move between access points. It's critical to maintain a session during a voice call. Overlapping access point coverage of 15 to 20 percent is one element of maintaining call quality.

Packet Loss

The voice quality of VoIP over wireless calls is affected by packet loss just as it is with standard VoIP. Unacceptable packet loss can occur if a single wireless AP is handling too many simultaneous calls, resulting in degraded voice quality and eventually dropped calls. Call capacity per AP therefore must be managed to preserve voice quality. When the design limit is reached, Call Admission Control (CAC) prevents additional calls from connecting through that AP.

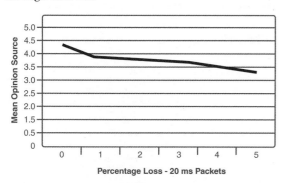

QoS for Wireless VoIP

Just like wired networks, for wireless networks to carry voice calls with good voice quality, quality of service (QoS) techniques are required. Network

Managing Call Capacity per AP

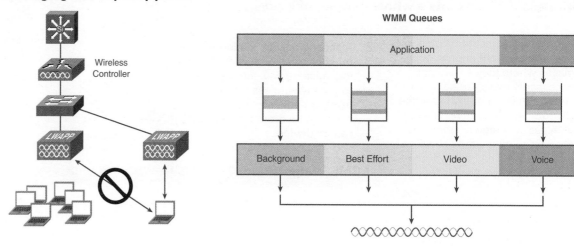

administrators must consider both upstream (client-to-network) and downstream (network-to-client) traffic flows. QoS service policies should be mapped between wired network and radio interface.

Wireless multimedia (WMM) is a form of wireless QoS being standardized within the Wi-Fi Alliance based on 802.11e and 802.1p standards.

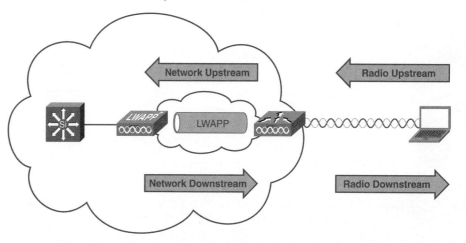

Wireless VoIP

Wireless VoIP presents a whole new set of issues.

1 People will expect to be able to use wireless VoIP phones in places where they would not necessarily expect to be able to check e-mails. For example, the IT group may not have designed wireless coverage in stairwells because workers don't check e-mail there. They will want to talk there, however.

2 A second design challenge that must be overcome is maintaining voice quality. If there are too many wireless VoIP callers using a single access point, calls can be dropped or access can be denied.

Hello? Hello?

Dropped Call

3 Another issue: Unlike PC-based wireless in which a worker will connect and use the computer, then move and reconnect, wireless VoIP users want to maintain a connection while moving between access points. This "roaming" ability must be designed in.

Leroy has been promoted to department manager and finds he's always on the phone.

Charlene talks to her mom every day.

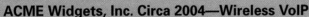

ACME Widgets, Inc. Circa 2004—Wireless VoIP

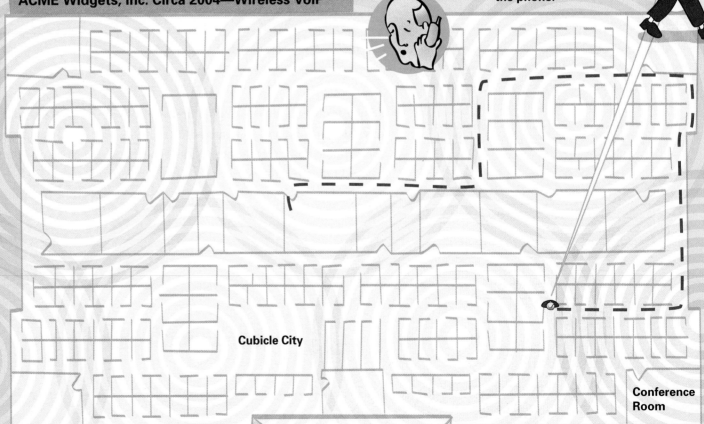

Cubicle City

Conference Room

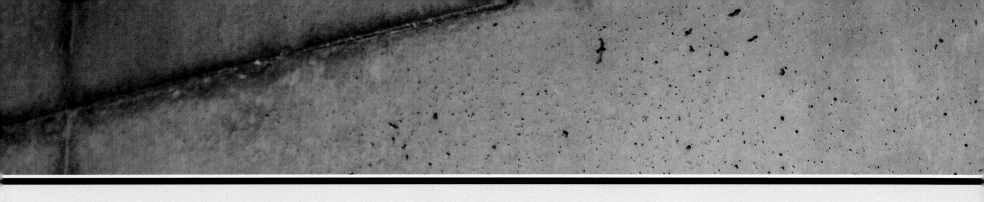

Wireless Guest Access

Mi Casa Es Su Casa

It's amusing to think how little time it has taken us to go from being excited that wireless was available in some places to demanding that it be everywhere in our work environment. Now, even when you visit another company, you pretty much expect to obtain guest access to that person's network so that you can connect back to your office, e-mail, and other communication tools and information.

Guest access is pretty easy to figure out. The tricky part is making it simple enough that any visitor can connect without help from your IT staff. Trust us—the day one of your IT staffers is caught hanging out in the lobby helping the salesmen who are waiting around to get connected, the deal is off.

Guest access has to be simple and secure. By secure, we don't mean encrypted. We mean that guest traffic does not mingle with our traffic, and guests get punted straight to the Internet. For the most part, the security of their data is entirely up to them. This group must also be prevented from impacting the performance or bandwidth of our own corporate users (in other words, "best effort").

At-a-Glance: Wireless Guest Access

Why Should I Care About Wireless Guest Access?

Wireless access has become pervasive. Employees rely on it to maintain their productivity. Many enterprises have incorporated partners, suppliers, and services vendors into their business processes, some effectively acting (at least for a certain amount of time) like employees of the business. A common requirement is for these trusted business vendors and partners to have access to the Internet on location so that they can connect to their host company to fulfill their job requirements.

Even visiting customers have come to expect to be able to access the Internet to maintain their connectivity and productivity while visiting. As businesses become more heavily integrated with suppliers and other businesses, the need to provide some form of network access on your premises for nonemployees will increase, eventually becoming a standard practice.

What Problems Need to Be Solved?

To accommodate visitors (some of whom may not have technical backgrounds), the network must automatically recognize and identify "guest" devices seeking access to the network. After they are detected, the system must provide access control and credentials (one time or otherwise) to manage access by "guest" users. Typically the user is then given "guest" access through the hosting corporate network, securely mapping "guest" network

sessions to the Internet gateway and restricting access to other parts of the hosting network. Most enterprises will want to leverage the investment in the existing wireless network to provide "guest" access, instead of deploying a parallel network.

Providing Wi-Fi Guest Access

The Cisco Unified Wireless solution provides an integrated "guest" access service. This solution leverages the same wireless network infrastructure as corporate wireless access for employees. "Guest" traffic is securely mapped to the Internet gateway, and access to the corporate network is restricted to employees who provide the proper login credentials.

Wireless Guest Access Design

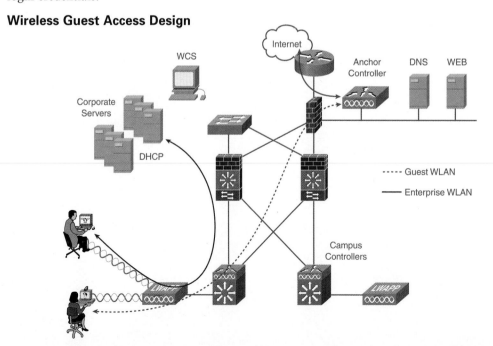

Guest SSID

Cisco wireless APs allow multiple Service Set IDs (SSID) to be configured in each AP, providing what appears to be separate connection points for employees and guests. In addition to SSIDs, all "guest" SSID traffic is securely tunneled to a "guest" wireless controller in the corporate DMZ, safely separating guest traffic from internal traffic. Typically the guest SSID allows for open access, and the corporate system has secure authentication (such as WPA) turned on.

Differentiated levels of service can be applied to ensure that employee traffic receives higher priority than "guest" traffic.

At-a-Glance: Wireless Guest Access

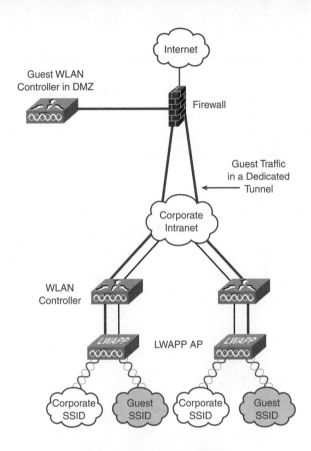

Guest WLAN Controller in DMZ

Guest Traffic in a Dedicated Tunnel

3. When the guest arrives, he or she connects to open SSID.

4. After the guest is connected, a web-authentication portal intercepts traffic and prompts the guest for his or her login information.

5. Guest traffic traverses an Ethernet-over-IP tunnel to the WLAN controller in the DMZ (external web access).

6. The guest can manually log out, disconnect, or time out based on automatic scheduling.

Guest Access: Step by Step

The following sequence provides a step-by-step flow of how a guest is given Internet access over the corporate wireless network:

1. A guest login is created (usually by an administrative assistant or other employee).

2. Credentials can be e-mailed or printed for guests or visitors.

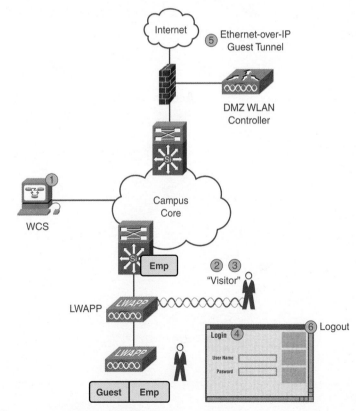

RFID and Location-Based Services

Finding Your Stuff

One of the biggest problems that large companies face is finding their stuff. This might sound a little silly at first, but consider how much equipment it takes to run a hospital, or a manufacturing plant, or an engineering test facility. Those types of businesses have tens or even hundreds of millions of dollars of equipment located all over a building or plant or campus, and a lot of it is portable. Now add to that typical employee churn and people's tendency to hoard or hide equipment that they use often.

So what happens when a company needs to locate the "machine that goes bing!" for a procedure or find a piece of equipment for maintenance, or when it needs to prevent an expensive piece of equipment from being walked out the door? Unless the company has some sort of location technology in place, the unfortunate answer is that it must go looking for the item. This is often time-consuming, frustrating, and fruitless. The good news is that most companies already have a technology in place to help them find their stuff. It's their WLAN.

Wireless LANS: They're Not Just for Checking E-Mail on the Toilet Anymore!

Okay, that was uncalled for. But the point is, the same technology that allows you to check your e-mail from anywhere in the building can also help you find your stuff. With the addition of a Wi-Fi asset tag that can communicate with the in-building wireless access points, and some software that allows you to use several Wi-Fi APs to locate the device, you can find any piece of equipment in a matter of seconds. This process is called *triangularization*, a term sometimes used interchangeably with *triangulation*.

A technology called Radio Frequency Identification (RFID) not only allows for asset tracking but also provides instant inventory capability for thousands of devices per second. With an RFID solution, a company can instantly process an entire pallet of goods as it comes through the door, and track the location of the forklift as it places the goods in the warehouse. RFID is something of an umbrella technology. It can be used as a standalone deployment or can be integrated with Wi-Fi or other wireless solutions.

At-a-Glance: Location-Based Services

Why Should I Care About Wireless Location Services?

Wireless network technology has applications outside of providing wireless access. One such application is location-based services, which is the process of determining and monitoring the location of business-owned assets.

Assets can be anything of value to the business in which knowing the item's location is important:

- Laptop computers
- Specialized medical equipment in hospitals
- Shipments of products or supplies
- Sensors and alarming
- People (scary but true)

In addition to tracking known assets, location-based services allow a company to track undesirable or unauthorized assets, such as the following:

- "Rogue" wireless access points
- "Rogue" laptops

Location-based services can increase productivity, lower operational costs, and enhance business process control, all of which are important to companies.

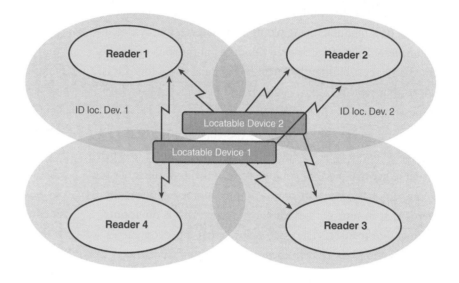

What Problems Need to Be Solved?

Location-based services require two basic components:

- **Locatable devices:** Whatever is to be tracked must have an electronic wireless asset tag or wireless client.
- **Readers:** A sensor (or several sensors) must pick up the signal of locatable devices and provide information on them.

Different types of electronic wireless (RFID) tags exist. They use different radio frequencies, including LF, HF, and UHF tags for short distances (less than 6 feet), Wi-Fi clients and tags for distances up to 300 feet, and cellular telemetry for distances up to 20 miles. Many different combinations of readers, tags, and technologies exist, each of which works better in some deployments and worse in others. Up-front planning is critical to ensure that readers can identify asset locations with the desired accuracy.

At-a-Glance: Location-Based Services

Radio Frequency Identification (RFID) Technologies

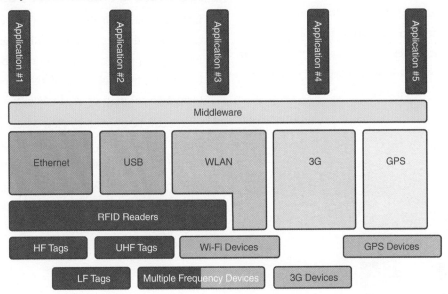

Unified Wireless and Location Services Architecture

The Cisco Unified Wireless solution provides an integrated infrastructure for location-based services. This solution leverages the same wireless network infrastructure as corporate wireless access for employees. It can locate and track 802.11 Wi-Fi clients and 802.11 Wi-Fi tags.

Because many types of RFID tags are not Wi-Fi-enabled, meaning that they do not use 802.11 wireless, a bridging device is needed. Such devices are called RFID *chokepoints*. Chokepoints can read the RFID tags and then transmit their information over the IP network. By integrating chokepoints, other types of RFID tags (those not transmitting on Wi-Fi frequencies) can also be read. This system is compatible with integrated third-party solutions (such as PanGo and AeroScout).

At-a-Glance: Location-Based Services

Planning

Planning and placement of wireless APs are critical to achieve the tracking accuracy necessary to locate assets. To determine the location of a device using Wi-Fi devices and tags, at least three APs need to be within about 70 feet of a device. This allows for tracking accuracy of about 1 foot.

For a building-wide deployment, planning tools can assist in positioning the right number of APs at the right locations. Location services leverage the same wireless network infrastructure used for corporate wireless access, but typically a higher density of APs is required.

Monitoring Asset Location

Information about the signals received from Wi-Fi clients and devices is collected by the Cisco Location Appliance. The data can then be combined with building floor plans or local maps to form a visual map of Wi-Fi devices using WCS.

Filters can be applied to view assets with desired characteristics. Determining the presence and location of "rogue" devices, such as unauthorized wireless APs, is also possible. Third-party applications can be integrated to provide tracking of other types of short-proximity RFID tags via chokepoints.

Cisco Unified Wireless Architecture Including Location Services

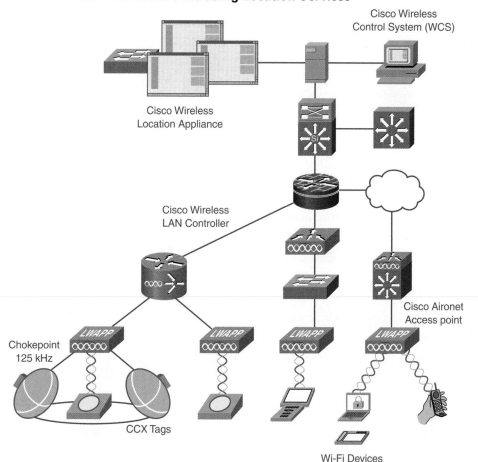

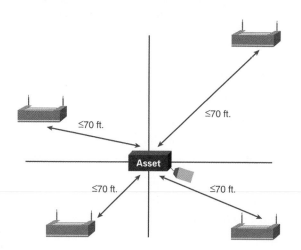

Wireless Location Services

2 Using the same locationing technology, IT and Management are able to locate equipment (so long as it has been properly "tagged").

It's time to do maintenance on the data projector, but no one remembers who used it last, or where they put it. Using the locationing system, what used to be a three-day search, now takes two minutes.

Data Projector

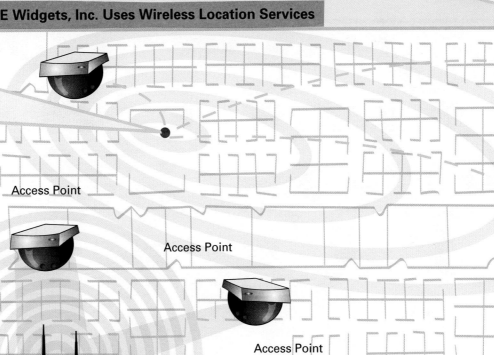

ACME Widgets, Inc. Uses Wireless Location Services

Access Point

Access Point

Access Point

1 Despite the fact that the company has wireless, some enterprising soul plugs a wireless router into a network port. This is a **huge** security risk. Fortunately, the IT-owned system is able to locate this "rogue access point" and appropriate action can be taken.

Rogue Access Point

Part IX

Virtualized Networks

Now that you know how everything in a network goes together, it's time to break it all apart again. It sounds a bit crazy, but the truth is that little is simple about today's networks. They are complex, and they are a big investment. New resources are added or required on almost a weekly or even daily basis. To better handle this never-ending stream of network additions, many IT groups have begun to virtualize parts of the network, including data centers, infrastructure, and even applications. The idea behind virtualization is to pool network resources to reduce costs, size, and expense while making it appear as if all these services are standalone and purpose-built.

Think about virtualization as being like living in an apartment with three roommates. The four of you could each rent a separate apartment, pay your own rent, pay for your own utilities, have to furnish your unit, and have to clean it or hire a cleaning service. This is nice if you can afford it, but what if you can't? Chances are you may be sleeping on an air mattress, building shelves with cinder blocks and milk crates, eating mac-n-cheese a lot, and probably skimping where you can on utilities. The advantage is that it's extremely private, and you can do whatever you want to in your unit. You can be a slob if you choose.

Another option is for the four of you to share an apartment. You split the rent and utilities, you each provide part of the furnishings, and you all chip in for a single cleaning service. Overall, your apartment furnishings and quality of living probably will improve. Privacy may be an issue. There would have to be some level of coordination between roommates about what resources and spaces are to be shared and which ones are personal and private. You probably also would need some agreements about what is acceptable and what is not. For example, hanging your socks to dry in the living room probably is out.

Virtualization of networks is very similar. Each department or work group could set up its own network, its own voice services, its own file servers, and its own WAN to connect to members of the department at another location. Doing so would be fairly cost- and resource-prohibitive. A better option is to share the same network and resources such as file servers. Each work group unit would have access to a set of shared resources and some allocation of private resources, splitting the overall IT costs with other work groups.

This section starts by looking at virtualizing data centers and network storage. Here users get access to file storage or applications that appear to be purpose-built (standalone) data centers or servers but that are actually single data centers with logical partitions.

Next we look at virtualizing the network itself. This is important when a company wants to leverage its investment in a single physical network but wants to share it among several agencies or departments with some level of privacy. For example, a police department may need a private network for dispatch services without building a network that is physically separate from the local municipal network. In other words, the department needs a shared network to look like a network that only it has access to. This gives some guarantee of security and bandwidth availability.

We end this section, and the book, with a brief look at what you can do using virtual network solutions. It turns out that utilization can be increased while decreasing costs and overall complexity. This is covered in the section "Applications of Virtualized Networks." It is not exactly a simple concept, but it does help simplify what would otherwise be a complex system.

Virtualizing Data Centers

Growth of the Data Center

As the Internet, e-commerce, and application usage grow, the corporate data center is experiencing an explosion of growth. A number of factors are involved:

- Every new application, website, or collaboration approach requires more storage and more servers—the powerful computers where applications run.

- Past data from transactions can be just as valuable as new data, so it is hard to get rid of. It just keeps accumulating, so storage tends to need exponential additions to keep up with demand.

- Regulatory and industry compliance adds mandates for keeping more and more data for longer and longer. Again, this leads to the need for more storage.

- For disaster preparedness, many companies are investing in secondary and backup data centers in different geographic locations than their primary center.

- Remote applications that take advantage of all this new and stored data end up driving the need for more servers and more network tools.

All the growth in the data center leads to a number of issues that directly impact a company's expense budget, including space, power, and operational complexity.

Data Center Virtualization

The main idea with data center virtualization is to abstract the physical equipment in the data center—storage devices, servers, load balancers, and so on—from the applications that run on them.

By doing so, resources can be purchased and deployed in a pool and allocated logically to applications, lowering overall equipment requirements and costs. New applications can more quickly be brought online by provisioning from the already deployed resource pool. As applications age out, their resources can be harvested back into the pool for efficient redeployment.

Going back to our apartment example, four people living separately need to stock up on food and supplies. So they head to the store and each purchase paper towels, milk, and eggs. The paper towels only come in packs of eight, so even though they each need maybe two rolls for the month, they are each stuck buying and storing eight rolls. Similarly, they each may need just a splash of milk each morning for coffee and one egg, but they are stuck buying a half gallon of milk and a dozen eggs, much of which probably has to be tossed out on garbage day.

Meanwhile, the four people sharing an apartment go shopping together. Together they buy eight rolls of paper towels, a half gallon of milk, and a dozen eggs. Their pooled expenses result in 75 percent savings. They may consume these and need to go back to the grocery store, but they probably waste much less.

Virtualized data centers are similar in that multiple work groups, departments, agencies, or whatever the logical groupings are within the business can save the company money by pooling their resources and using only what they need.

Another main advantage of the virtualized data center is ease of operations. Provisioning services at an application level and across the suite of resources in a virtual environment reduces complexity because each resource doesn't have to be provisioned separately.

At-a-Glance: Virtual Data Centers

Why Should I Care About Virtual Data Centers?

The growth in business applications has led to exponential growth requirements for data centers in terms of computing servers and storage. In addition, the proliferation of hundreds of different server platforms has become an operational nightmare for IT groups. Space and power requirements also add costs to business operational expenses. As a bit of trivia, cooling systems (and the associated power requirements) are one of the largest expenses (if not *the* largest).

The addition to expenses, several government and industry regulatory requirements also make disaster recovery planning very difficult for companies with ad hoc file and application servers.

Virtual data centers allow IT groups to meet the growing need for new applications without unmanageable increases in complexity or cost. The net result is an increase in business agility and a reduction in the length of time needed to bring new applications and services online.

What Problems Need to Be Solved?

The first step in virtualizing data centers is centralizing and consolidating disparate computing and storage environments. During the virtualization process, physical computer and storage equipment are decoupled from the applications that execute on them.

Operational efficiencies can also be gained (a key driver in this process) by reducing the overall server and storage equipment requirements. To be effective, the system must provide an easy way to quickly provision and manage new application services.

Data Center Virtualization

The Cisco data center virtualization solution provides decoupling of physical computer and storage equipment from the application services they provide. This solution provides flexibility in the allocation of computing servers to applications, eliminating the need for dedicated servers for each application. This solution also supports the clustering of computer servers for high-performance computing applications.

A management tool allows for quick and easy provisioning of new applications with VFrame. VFrame allows IT staff to quickly set up and manage application and storage environments for a work group or new application needed by the business. They do this by allocating a virtual set of resources (storage and servers) using existing physical equipment. The IT administrator defines the services needed to VFrame, such as 100 GB of storage and 1 megaflop (roughly a million computational cycles per second) of computing power. VFrame takes care of configuring the underlying disk arrays and computers to create the application environment.

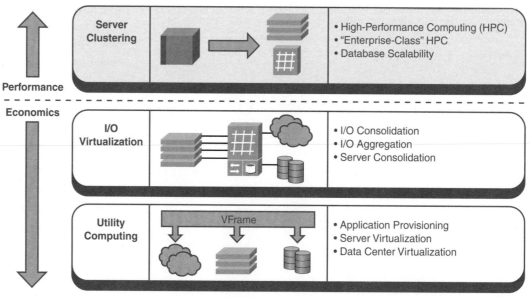

At-a-Glance: Virtual Data Centers

Fixed Versus Virtual

In a fixed data center, applications are physically tied to servers and storage resources. New applications require new resources.

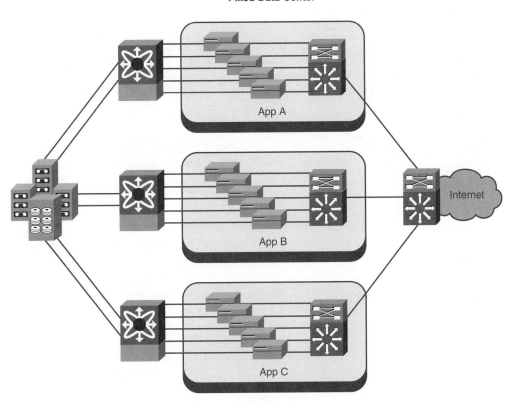

Fixed Data Center

App A

App B

App C

Internet

At-a-Glance: Virtual Data Centers

In a virtualized data center, physical resources are "pooled," and applications are allocated a virtual set of resources. This reduces overall server requirements by raising equipment utilization.

This system also makes it faster and easier to bring new applications online by allocating existing server and storage infrastructure to the applications using VFrame. Previously it may have been necessary to purchase new storage disks, purchase new application servers, install them, test them, and then finally provision them for the new application. This process could take weeks or months.

Data Center Migration

Data center virtualization can take several migration steps, starting with consolidation of the server and storage servers.

To virtualize the server and I/O services in the data center, it is necessary to implement a unified interconnect fabric to enable shared pools of computer and storage servers. In "plain English," this means that fiber-channel or ATM links are replaced with Ethernet.

Finally, virtualization of applications environments can occur, in which applications are mapped to resources dynamically, instead of being tied to specific server equipment.

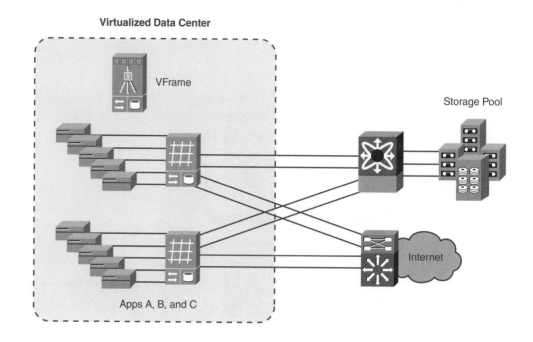

Virtualizing Network Infrastructure

Leveraging Network Investment

Although businesses have become increasingly reliant on applications for productivity, they have also become reliant on their network infrastructure. The network enables their business models and has become engrained in everything they do.

When a business model needs to change, often so does the network that supports it. For example, if a large bank with several hundred branches acquires another bank, also with a few hundred branches, their applications need to merge, and their network infrastructures need to be connected and merged.

As another example, suppose the Site Services and Security department decides it needs to cut costs by migrating security and video surveillance systems onto the network, instead of maintaining a separate network infrastructure.

Going back to our apartment example yet again, suppose one roommate has a weekend visitor, so an extra place to sleep is needed. Or suppose one of the roommates decides to start working from home. Either case means something is likely to change inside the apartment, either temporarily or permanently. We would like to be able to simply absorb the changes and keep the living arrangements going.

A Network Is a Network

On the surface, it would seem there is not necessarily a problem. Why not just put the new bank branches and applications on the network? Why not just add the video camera and badge reader endpoints to the network?

One major concern is security. We may not want any random employee to be able to access specialized applications and devices such as ATMs and security endpoints. There also could be regulations or laws requiring proper separation of networks during an acquisition, for example.

Another concern could be service levels. We would want to ensure that adding more bank branches to the network is done in such a way that our existing bank branches are not negatively impacted.

Virtualizing Network Infrastructure

One solution is to implement a Cisco network virtualization solution. Virtualizing the network has some similarities to virtualizing the data center. Essentially it involves decoupling the physical network equipment from the networking services being provided.

Through network virtualization, multiple virtual networks can coexist on the same physical network infrastructure, managed by a single IT support staff, but with nearly complete separation of traffic and security policies.

Virtualization avoids the costs of implementing discrete network infrastructures by permitting a number of entities to securely share a single network investment.

You may be wondering why all the people who need to use the network can't just plug in and use it. After all, IP networks already can accept more and more clients.

The answers have to do with security, regulations, and service levels. Think about our apartment example again. The four roommates can share an apartment, but rules must be made about how long one person can tie up the bathroom, who has access to the living room and when, who does the dishes, and whether it's all right to "borrow" each other's food. Most likely there will also be strict rules about not sharing toothbrushes and coffee cups, as well as showing respect for other people's belongings.

Network virtualization has similar challenges. Some resources, such as DHCP services, may be fine to share. Others, such as a database of sensitive customer information, may need to be kept private for only the department or agency responsible for it.

At-a-Glance: Virtual Network Infrastructure

Why Should I Care About Virtual Networks?

Businesses make major investments in their networking infrastructure, sometimes to the tune of hundreds of millions of dollars for a single large enterprise. Events such as mergers and acquisitions, the addition of specialized devices and applications, guest access, and the need for functional or department-level domains necessitate an approach with separate secure network partitions. Having dedicated physical networks is cost-prohibitive. Therefore, securely sharing a single physical networking infrastructure is necessary.

What Problems Need to Be Solved?

The coexistence of multiple network partitions on a single physical networking infrastructure must be planned in advance to avoid future design and performance issues.

One key requirement is to plan the identification and classification of devices connecting to the network and determine how they will be assigned to the appropriate network partition.

Within secure network partitions, traffic must be isolated from traffic in other partitions. The enforcement of policies must also be mapped to network partitions such that the services and devices within them can operate securely.

The system must also be flexible enough to handle devices that are unmanaged, such as "guest"

devices, which must be categorized and treated accordingly. Unmanaged means that the IT staff do not control the asset, such as a laptop that a guest brings onsite. It's unreasonable to assume that the guest will hand over his laptop to the IT staff to comply with company policy. This likely would be upsetting to the IT staff.

High-Level Diagram

The Cisco network virtualization solution provides an end-to-end architecture that offers secure partitioning of the physical networking infrastructure into multiple virtual networks. These virtual networks can support mergers and acquisitions, segregation of specialized agencies, guest networks, hosted network services, and other applications.

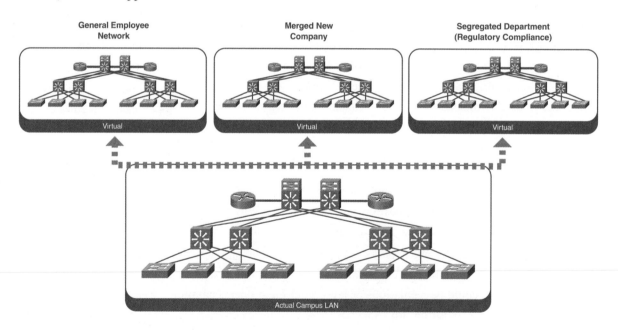

The solution covers endpoint devices, through the network infrastructure, and into the data center where services reside.

With this solution a single physical networking infrastructure investment can be leveraged for multiple uses, raising utilization and avoiding the costs of building multiple dedicated networks.

At-a-Glance: Virtual Network Infrastructure

Three-Part Framework

Cisco network virtualization is implemented as a three-part architectural framework that includes the following components:

- **Access control** authenticates clients and devices attempting to gain network access and authorizes clients into the appropriate network partition.

- **Path isolation** securely isolates traffic within assigned network partitions across the networking infrastructure.

- **Services edge** maps network partitions to the appropriate services that each partition has access to, based on a set of policies.

A number of technologies are available within each part of the framework, so you can choose the best one for the customer's requirements.

Think of this framework like your bank's ATM system. Access control is like having a unique ATM card with a security PIN with which only you can identify yourself to an ATM. Path isolation is like the ATM network keeping banking transactions separated from each other so that your withdrawal request does not get mixed up with someone else's deposit request. Finally, services edge is mapping your withdrawal request to your bank account back in the bank's data center. You have access to only your bank account, not other people's accounts.

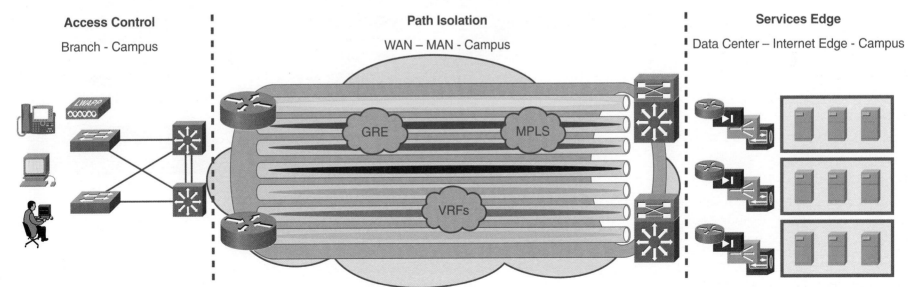

At-a-Glance: Virtual Network Infrastructure

Authentication and Isolation

In the campus, 802.1x Identity-Based Networking Services (IBNS) (discussed in Part V, "Securing the Network") can be used at the network edge to authenticate, authorize, and admit devices to the appropriate network partition. In the access layer, VLANs represent the first level of path isolation. Across the campus backbone, traffic isolation technologies such as GRE, .1Q VLAN trunking, VRF-Lite, and MPLS are used to provide secure network partitions. At the handoff between the campus network and data center, policies can be enforced that map partitions to allowed services.

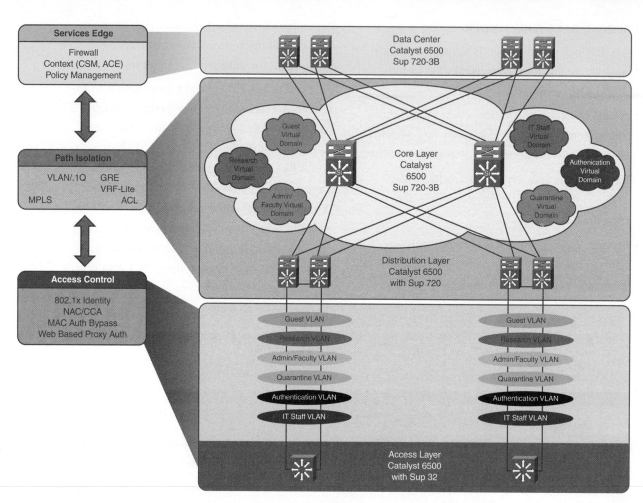

At-a-Glance: Virtual Network Infrastructure

Partitions Across the WAN

Between corporate locations (campuses, branch offices, and data centers), the WAN and MAN networking infrastructure must also preserve network partitions. Similar to the campus access layer, the branch office LAN can employ access control technologies such as 802.1x IBNS to authenticate, authorize, and assign devices to the appropriate network partition. Across the WAN and MAN backbone, traffic isolation technologies such as GRE, MPLS VPNs, and DMVPNs (all discussed earlier in this book) are used to provide secure network partitions.

At the handoff between the campus network and the WAN/MAN, network partitions are mapped to their respective partitions in the campus, allowing flexible use of different technologies within different parts of the network. For example, we can use a multi-VRF approach in the campus and map partitions to a DMVPN approach across the WAN. At the transition point between the campus and the WAN, we can map the two approaches together to preserve partition isolation across the entire end-to-end network path.

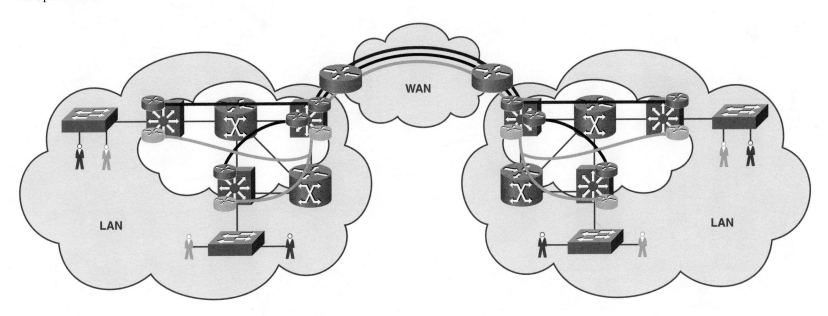

Applications of Virtualized Networks

What Can You Do with Virtualized Networks?

A number of applications exist for virtualized networks. What they have in common is the need to have multiple entities securely share a single physical network infrastructure. This topic discusses just a few of the use cases.

Corporate Employee "Clean" and "Dirty" Networks

With the implementation of intelligent endpoint authentication and admission onto the network, using solutions such as 802.1x IBNS and Network Admission Control (NAC), there is a need to separate the "clean" endpoints, network, and services from the "dirty."

With virtualized networks, we can implement a "clean" network partition. As soon as employees authenticate and ensure that their laptop or computer is "healthy," it is admitted to the "clean" network and has access to normal applications. Endpoints found to be "dirty" (with a virus or other noncompliance issue) are admitted only to the "dirty" network, with access only to remediation services. In this type of system, each endpoint is scanned to ensure that all virus prevention signatures (or other criteria or credentials) are up to date.

Guest and Partner Networks

Businesses have an increasing need to support network access for guests, whether they be customer visitors, vendors, or otherwise, and partners who are trusted vendors or contractors critical to the business operation.

By applying network virtualization, we can identify guest and partner devices and securely assign them to restricted network partitions. Here they may access the Internet and perhaps a subset of appropriate applications.

Isolating Specialized Devices and Applications

Many devices traditionally have been connected in separate closed networks, such as ATMs and IP video surveillance cameras on closed-circuit TV (CCTV) networks. Many of these devices are migrating to IP networks. But it is still desirable to keep such devices accessible to only authorized personnel.

Using network virtualization, specialized devices can be placed in private network partitions, accessible only by authorized users who can authenticate and join the same network partition as the devices.

Load Balancing

Using network virtualization, administrators can plan for changes in the network. These changes could accommodate longer-term changes in traffic utilization, such as the offshoring of a particular function. They also could accommodate short-term changes, such as preparing for a conference in which a large number of users will cause spikes on local servers.

Providing Hosted Networks to Entities Within Entities

A retail model growing in popularity is the "all service" store, in which a large retailer hosts several other retailers inside the store property. For example, a large grocery store may host a bank, a cell phone kiosk, a film processor, and so on. Each of these entities needs connectivity back to its company. One option is to have each company provide its own WAN connectivity into the store. This could lead to a dozen or more connections into each store. Multiply that times several hundred or thousands of stores, and costs really add up.

What if the same large retailer could host these entity-within-a-store networks, providing the hosted companies network services using the same network infrastructure that the hosting retailer has to have anyway for its own connectivity? Furthermore, what if the large retailer could offset its own WAN connection costs by charging for the hosted network services?

Using network virtualization, it is entirely possible to provide a number of private hosted networks, with each entity having its own private partition. The collection of partitions is mapped back over the WAN to the retailer headquarters, where each aggregated connection can be mapped to a corresponding extranet gateway and back to the hosted company's network.

Now, whenever the retailer opens a new store location, there is no need for a dozen entities to pursue connections of their own. The new store and its network can quickly provide hosted network partitions for each of the smaller retailers.

Departmental Virtual Networks

Increasingly, companies are struggling to comply with a myriad of industry and government regulations stipulating how financial and customer data is handled and protected. Regulations including the Health Insurance Portability and Accountability Act (HIPAA), Sarbanes-Oxley, Payment Card Industry (PCI), and Basel II (in Europe) contain specific provisions governing the handling of information. They also specify precautions that companies must take.

Network virtualization can help achieve compliance with such regulations by restricting employee populations to application services that are appropriate by departmental function. For example, Human Resources, Engineering, Finance, and Manufacturing could all be assigned to respective virtual network partitions. Data flowing between Finance and outside departments could then be regulated—even protected with firewalls if desired.

Challenges with Virtual Networks

Many applications and collaboration systems rely on open networks—unrestricted communication between endpoints. Placing endpoints within virtual network partitions by definition restricts the flow of traffic to appropriate other endpoints and applications. The two aims (open and closed) can be diametrically opposed at times, creating challenges for virtualized networks.

One of the keys in implementing virtual networks is to understand the necessary traffic flows between virtual partitions and to make sure that designs allow such communication.

At-a-Glance: Virtualized Network Applications

Why Should I Care About Virtualized Network Applications?

Several business problems have similar requirements for secure access to logical network partitions.

Cisco network virtualization provides an end-to-end solution to address this problem. This powerful architectural approach enables many new applications and potential business models. In many cases the solution is a matter of turning on the right features in existing network infrastructure devices, such as access switches, WAN routers, and so on.

What Problems Need to Be Solved?

Virtual networks address several business-level problems:

- Allowing employees with "clean" devices to access the corporate network and services, while restricting "dirty" devices to only remediation services

- Isolating specialized devices, such as ATMs, IP video surveillance systems, and manufacturing robots into private network partitions, inaccessible by general employee devices

- Providing "guest" and partner access to the corporate network, restricting these user populations to a small appropriate subset of applications and services

- Hosting network services of other enterprise entities within another business entity—for example, hosting kiosks of other retail businesses within a larger retail business location

High-Level Diagram

Cisco network virtualization supports many different use cases and applications of virtualized networks. The system uses the three framework elements of network virtualization: access control, path isolation, and services edge. Users select the technologies within each Place in the Network (PIN) and within each network virtualization framework element that are best suited to the applications being used.

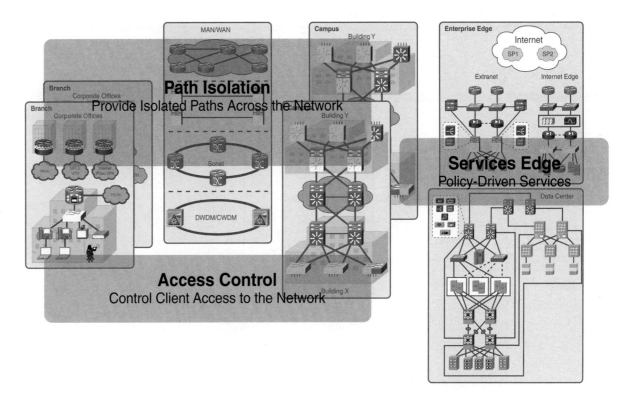

At-a-Glance: Virtualized Network Applications

Network Admission Control

The Cisco network virtualization framework can be used for employee access and to enforce NAC as follows:

- **Access control** uses 802.1x IBNS to authenticate clients and devices attempting to gain network access, authorizing "clean" employee devices to the "Healthy" network and "dirty" devices to the "Quarantine" network.

- **Path isolation** securely isolates traffic in the "Healthy" network partition from traffic in the "Quarantine" network partition.

- **Services edge** maps the "Healthy" network partition to the full suite of appropriate employee application services, while restricting access by the "Quarantine" network partition to remediation services only.

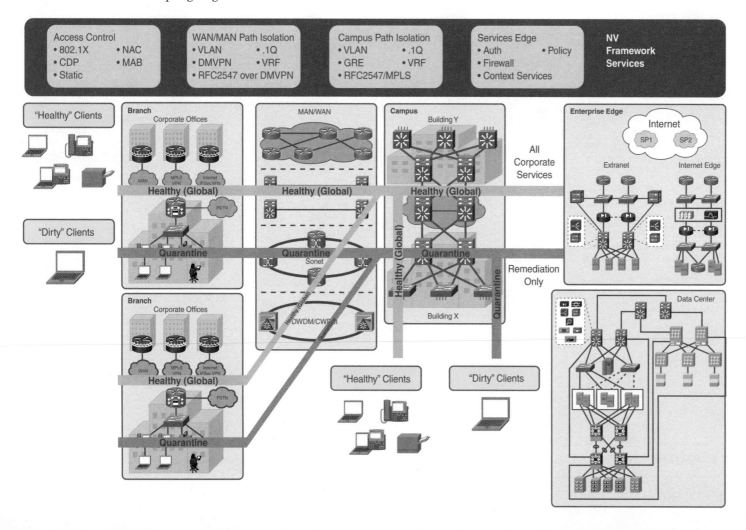

At-a-Glance: Virtualized Network Applications

Guest and Partner Access

The network virtualization framework can also be used to provide guest and partner access domains:

- **Access control** uses 802.1x IBNS to authenticate clients and devices attempting to gain network access, authorizing "guest" and "partner" devices to appropriate virtual networks.

- **Path isolation** securely isolates traffic in the "Guest" and "Partner" networks from traffic in the general employee network.

- **Services edge** maps the "Guest" network to the Internet gateway service and maps the "Partner" network to a set of appropriate partner application servers.

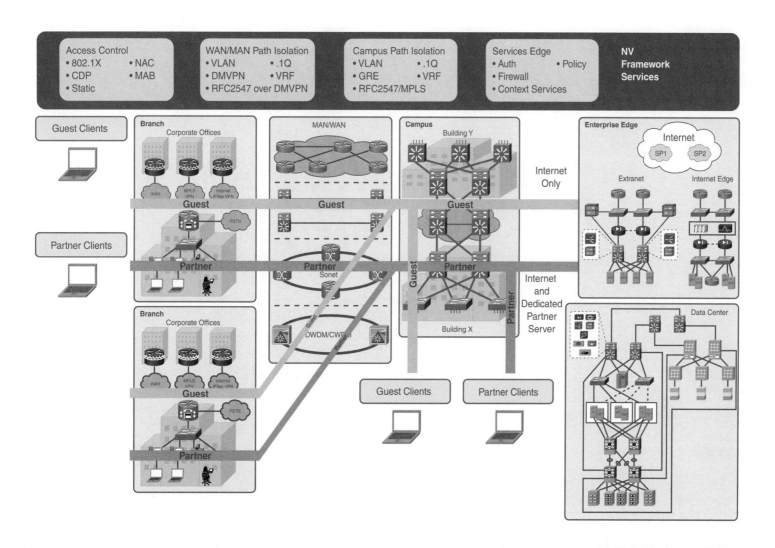

At-a-Glance: Virtualized Network Applications

Device Isolation

The Cisco network virtualization framework can be used to isolate specialized devices, such as ATMs and manufacturing robots, as well as to provide hosted network services for in-store kiosks:

- **Access control** uses MAC Auth Bypass (MAB) and static port assignment to map specialized devices (ATMs, IP video surveillance cameras, building HVAC systems, manufacturing robots, hosted entity kiosks, and so on) to private virtual network partitions.

- **Path isolation** securely isolates specialized device traffic and hosted entity traffic in their corresponding virtual network partitions.

- **Services edge** maps the virtual networks to the appropriate applications services—for example, mapping hosted entity networks to the extranet gateway connecting back to the entity headquarters location.

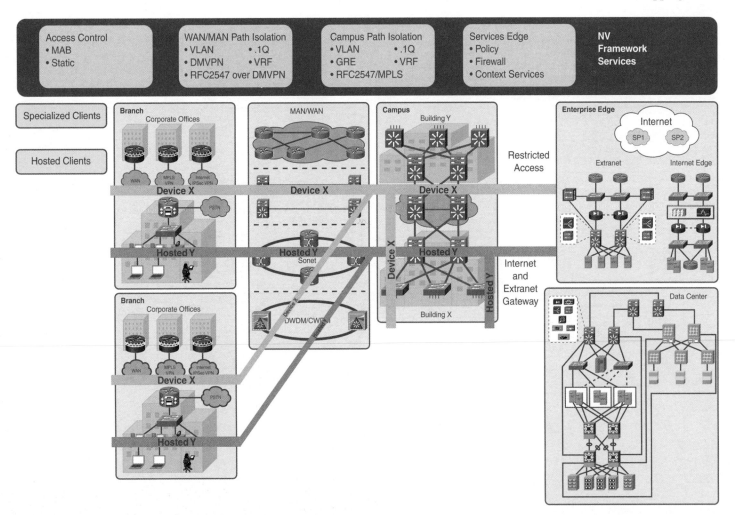

Evolution of Virtual Networks

1 In the beginning, the sales and marketing employee worked at a terminal that simply registered commands and prompts. These were issued from a mainframe computer somewhere in the building. There was no interfacing between terminals and little to no intelligence in the terminals.

Sales/Marketing

Name:
Phone:
Date of sale:

2 Then, dedicated PCs were installed that ran their own bootable operating systems and software and had their own memory. Still, there was no collaboration between stations.

Sales/Marketing

Accounting

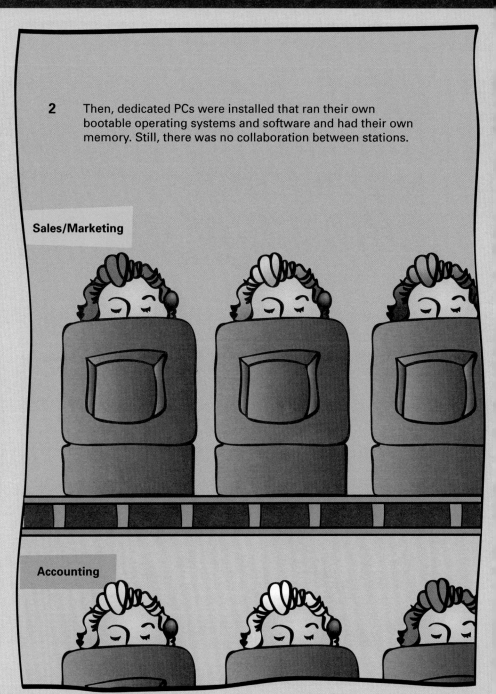

Evolution of Virtual Networks

3 Once computers were networked together, interdepartment collaboration became much easier.

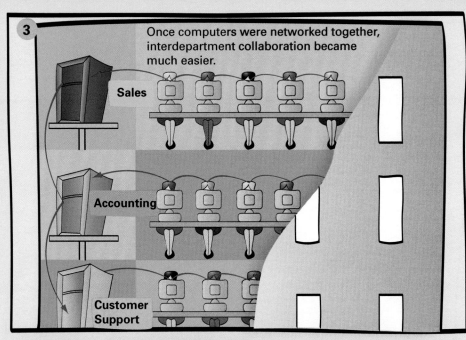

5 Companies responded by creating dedicated servers that could be accessed globally. In most cases, servers were dedicated to applications or departments (such as finance).

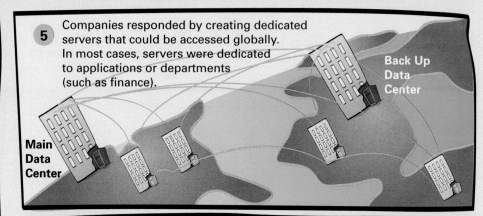

4 When companies began to expand globally, collaboration (between regions) became a problem once again.

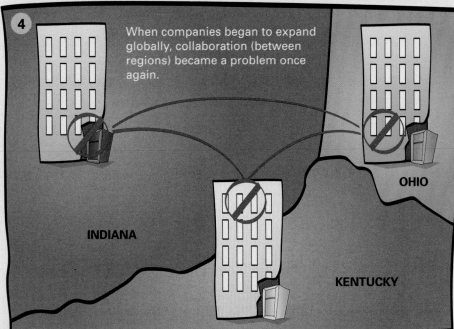

6 Eventually, companies decided to consolidate all servers into a single data center (backed up, of course) that was segmented logically. In these new servers, much of the intelligence is located in the data center and the terminal provides screens much like the client server systems from 20 years ago. How's that for progress?

Index

About the Authors

Jim Doherty is the Chief Marketing Officer at CipherOptics. Before joining the CipherOptics team, he held leadership positions with Symbol Technologies and Cisco Systems. He has more than 16 years of technical marketing and engineering experience and has led various marketing campaigns for IP telephony, routing and switching solutions, and network security solutions. He is the coauthor of the *Networking Simplified* series, published by Cisco Press. He is a former Marine Corps sergeant. He holds a B.S. in electrical engineering from North Carolina State University and an MBA from Duke University.

Neil Anderson is the Senior Manager of Technology Systems Engineering with Cisco Systems. He has more than 20 years of broad engineering experience, including public telephone systems, mobile phone systems, Internet, and home networking. At Cisco, his focus is on business networks in the areas of network architecture, wireless, security, unified communications, and emerging technologies. He is the coauthor of the *Networking Simplified* series, published by Cisco Press. He holds a B.S. in computer science.